Orphans of Versailles

Orphans of Versailles

The Germans in Western Poland 1918-1939

RICHARD BLANKE

THE UNIVERSITY PRESS OF KENTUCKY

Copyright © 1993 by The University Press of Kentucky

Scholarly publisher for the Commonwealth,
serving Bellarmine College, Berea College, Centre
College of Kentucky, Eastern Kentucky University,
The Filson Club, Georgetown College, Kentucky
Historical Society, Kentucky State University,
Morehead State University, Murray State University,
Northern Kentucky University, Transylvania University,
University of Kentucky, University of Louisville,
and Western Kentucky University.

Editorial and Sales Offices: Lexington, Kentucky 40508-4008

Library of Congress Cataloging-in-Publication Data

Blanke, Richard.
    Orphans of Versailles : the Germans in Western Poland, 1918-1939 /
Richard Blanke.
        p.   cm.
    Includes bibliographical references and index.
    ISBN 0-8131-1803-4 (recycled acid-free paper) :
    1. Germans—Poland—Western and Northern Territories—History.
2. Western and Northern Territories (Poland)—History.   3. Western
and Northern Territories (Poland)—Ethnic relations.   I. Title.
DK4600.O3342B53   1993
943.8'100431—dc20   92-19216

This book is printed on recycled acid-free paper meeting
the requirements of the American National Standard
for Permanence of Paper for Printed Library Materials. ∞

To Fred, Roman, Marie, and Claire

Contents

Acknowledgments   ix

Abbreviations   xi

Introduction   1

1. Establishment of the German Minority, 1918-1922   9

2. The Great Exodus   32

3. Coming to Terms   54

4. The Piłsudski Era and the Economic Struggle   90

5. The Minority in the International Arena   121

6. The Impact of National Socialism   163

7. The Minority in 1939   207

Conclusion   238

Appendix A. Western Polish Place Names: Official Polish and German Equivalents   242

Appendix B. Population of Western Poland and German Proportion, 1910-1931   243

Bibliography   246

Notes   269

Index   307

Maps

1. Prussian Poland/Western Poland, 1919-1939   2

2. Ethnographic Composition of the German-Polish Borderlands, 1910   22

Acknowledgments

This study has benefited from the assistance of numerous individuals and institutions, and it is a pleasure to express thanks to some of them here. The Research Funds Committee at the University of Maine provided the original "seed money" in the form of a faculty summer research grant. Subsequently, the project received generous support from the Fulbright Commission and the American Council of Learned Societies, which allowed me to spend a sabbatical year in proximity to European archives and libraries. A grant from the International Research and Exchanges Board financed a summer visit to Poland for the same purpose. Special thanks go also to the Herder Institute in Marburg/Lahn, which has the single best collection of published sources on German-Polish problems; in the course of the year I spent there, Frau Eisinger and her colleagues patiently produced a significant proportion of this collection for my perusal. Thanks also to the Volkswagen-Stiftung, which provided affordable accommodations in Germany; to the Russian and East European Center at the University of Illinois, Champaign-Urbana, for the summertime use of its fine library; to Harvard University for providing "outsiders" generous access to its vast holdings, and to Libby Soifer and Barbara Jones of the inter-library loan office at the University of Maine Library for essential services when I was unable to be at these other places.

The list of individuals to whom I am indebted is headed by my wife, Ann, without whose support and competence in other matters this project would not have been possible (and without whom it would not have been worth undertaking in the first place). Thanks also to Hans Lemberg for varied help and kindness during a sabbatical in his country; to Tomaš Olejniczak, who made research during a chaotic time in his country somewhat easier; to Bill TeBrake and Kim Pelletier, who made my belated entry into the world of the word processor less traumatic; to Baycka Voronietsky for help with Polish officialdom; to David Smith, Stew Doty, and other colleagues at Maine who were always willing to discuss this project with me; to John Kulczycki, Mieczyslaw Biskupski,

Anne Young, and others who wrote in behalf of it on more than one occasion. Finally, sincere thanks to those who will point out the shortcomings and inevitable errors of the work that follows, and so help advance the project itself.

Abbreviations

AO	Auslands-Organisation (Foreign Organisation) (NSDAP)
BBWR	Bezpartyjny Blok Współpracy z Rządem (Non-partisan Block for Cooperation with the Government)
BdA	Bund der Auslanddeutschen (League of Germans from Foreign Lands)
DAI	Deutsches Auslands-Institut (German Overseas Institute)
DB	Deutschtumsbund zur Wahrung der Minderheitenrechte (German League for the Protection of Minority Rights)
DCVP	Deutsch-Christliche Volkspartei (German-Christian Peoples Party)
DDP	Deutsche Demokratische Partei (German Democratic Party)
DJiP	Deutscher Jungblock in Polen (German Youth League in Poland)
DKVP	Deutsch-Katholische Volkspartei (German-Catholic Peoples Party)
DKWB	Deutscher Kultur- und Wirtschaftsbund (German Cultural and Economic League)
DNVP	Deutsch-Nationale Volkspartei (German-National Peoples Party)
DOV	Deutscher Ostmarkenverein (German Eastern Marches Association)
DP	Deutsche Partei (German Party) (Silesia)
DS	Deutsche Stiftung (German Foundation)
DSAP	Deutsche Sozialdemokratische Arbeits-Partei (German Social-Democratic Labor Party)
DSb	Deutscher Schutzbund (German Protective League)
DSP	Deutsche Sozialdemokratische Partei (German Social-Democratic Party)
DSV	Deutscher Schulverein (German School Association)
DV	Deutsche Vereinigung (German Union)
DViSus	Deutsche Vereinigung in Sejm und Senat (German Union in Sejm and Senate)

DVP   Deutsche Volkspartei (German Peoples Party)
HBB   Hollandse Buitenland Bank (Dutch Overseas Bank)
JDP   Jungdeutsche Partei (Young German Party)
KPD   Kommunistische Partei Deutschlands (Communist Party of Germany)
KNP   Komitet Narodowy Polski (Polish National Committee)
KVP   Katholische Volkspartei (Catholic Peoples Party)
NRL   Naczelna Rada Ludowa (Supreme National Council)
NS   National-Sozialistisch (National-Socialist)
NSDAP   National-Sozialistische Deutsche Arbeiter Partei (National-Socialist German Workers Party)
ONR   Obóz Narodowo-Radykalny (National-Radical Camp)
OZN   Obóz Zjednoczenia Narodowego (Camp of National Unity)
PCiJ   Permanent Court of International Justice
POW   Polska Organizacja Wojskowa (Polish Military Organization)
PPS   Polska Partia Socjalistyczna (Polish Socialist Party)
PZZ   Polski Związek Zachodni (Polish Western Association)
SPD   Sozialdemokratische Partei Deutschlands (Social-Democratic Party of Germany)
VA   Volksdeutscher Arbeitskreis (Ethnic-German Collective)
VDA   Verein für das Deutschtum im Ausland (Association for Germans in Foreign Lands)
VDB   Verein Deutscher Bauern (Association of German Farmers)
VDK   Verein Deutscher Katholiken (Association of German Catholics) (in Poland)
VoMi   Volksdeutsche Mittelstelle (Ethnic-German Center)
VR   Volksdeutscher Rat (Ethnic-German Council)
ZOKZ   Związek Obrony Kresów Zachodnich (Union for the Defense of the Western Borderlands)
ZPS   Związek Powstańców Śląskich (Union of Silesian Insurgents)

Introduction

The Paris peace settlement of 1919 spawned a host of new national minority problems in many parts of Europe. Whether or not there were more such problems than before can be debated, but certainly the newly created minority problems were a chief destabilizing element during the interwar period. They were a major source of domestic discord in many states, contributed significantly to international tensions, threatened at times to monopolize the attention of the League of Nations, and figured prominently in the return to war in 1939. This was especially true of the million or so Germans consigned to the resurrected Polish state. No other European minority problem attracted more attention, showed up more often on the League's agenda, or was more immediately associated with the outbreak of World War II. The sudden reversal of roles for the two peoples involved made this particular problem all the more volatile. A Polish government now confronted a German minority in a region where power relationships had been the other way around for more than a century. Those Germans who were left in Poland by the peace settlement had to deal not only with their own loss of dominance; in the eyes of their Polish neighbors they remained associates of the repressive prewar Prussian regime and agents of German revanchism. The result was a national confrontation with few parallels in recent history.

This book seeks to describe and analyze the dilemma of the German minority in western Poland in all its considerable complexity. It is not meant to be "victimological"; nor is it a brief for one side against another. It seeks simply to understand the difficult situation of those Germans who lived in the lands ceded to Poland after World War I. It is aimed primarily at historians of Germany who may have wondered just what became of all those Germans before they resurfaced as a pretext for war in 1939. Though much of this story takes place in a Polish political context, historians of Poland will probably find references to that context rather elementary. The recent literature on the minority itself is not large—neither German nor Polish scholars seem to consider it entirely within their province— and this account is based on primary sources wherever possible. It is

MAP 1. Prussian Poland/Western Poland, 1919-1939

written by an "outsider" who considers himself equally close to the two peoples involved. Of course, freedom from national partisanship does not mean "objectivity" on other counts; this study doubtless reflects its author's sympathies for individuals over states, economically and culturally vigorous minorities over inert and envious majorities, and reason over nationalist passion. Similarly, the scant attention this study pays to today's "politically correct" trinity of race, class, and gender results not from oversight but from conviction. It reflects the author's view that what matter most in history are those things that transcend such classifications: ideas, political power, economics, and the decisions and character traits of key individuals.

Another qualification needs to be explained in greater detail. This work focuses on those who were politically as well as ethnically German: that is, citizens of Germany until 1918. True, there was a German population of some significance in many parts of interwar Poland that had *not* belonged previously to Germany; a German minority of some size was inevitable, therefore, however the frontier was drawn. In formerly Russian Poland, the main center of German life was Łódź, whose 60,000 Germans constituted 11 percent of that city's population. Most of the Łódź Germans were engaged in industry, mainly in the textile industry for which the city was famous and which had been established in the nineteenth century mainly by German entrepreneurs looking for a way into the high-tariff Russian market. Another 100,000 Germans lived in formerly Austrian Poland; the largest single concentration here was Bielitz/Bielsko, a majority-German town in Austrian Silesia. Even in distant Volhynia in eastern Poland/western Ukraine there were about 250 majority-German farming villages. Using the last prewar census figures compiled by the several partitioning regimes, German publicists claimed as many as 2.2 million Germans—more than 7 percent of the total population—in what had become Poland by 1921.[1] While the German population of formerly Prussian Poland was quickly depleted by a major exodus (see Chapter 2), the number of Germans in the rest of Poland increased during the interwar period. Indeed, there were more Germans living in formerly Russian and Austrian Poland in 1939 than in the formerly Prussian part; by then, Łódź was home to the largest remaining concentration of Germans, and Bielitz was proportionately the most heavily German town in Poland.

For this reason, one cannot ignore the German population of formerly Russian and Austrian Poland or deny its importance. Many postwar German scholars, perhaps because most of them have roots in central rather than Prussian Poland, prefer to treat the German minority (or *Volksgruppe*) throughout Poland. They comment on the distinction between the ex-Reich areas and the rest but do not make it a primary consideration. This

may be a reflection still of interwar efforts to transcend partition boundaries, downplay regional differences, and establish a single, Poland-wide
organization of Germans; especially in the 1930s, traditional regional
distinctions and mentalities were criticized as anachronistic and an obstacle to the minority's more effective organization.[2] Whether most Polish
Germans ever internalized this new perspective remains debatable, however.

In any case, this book is concerned primarily with how Germans reacted to a radical change in their political situation and in their "dominant-
subordinate" relationships. From this perspective, the dilemma facing
Reich Germans after 1918 was fundamentally different from that faced by
Germans elsewhere in Poland. Most Germans in the formerly Russian
and Austrian partitions had never known anything but minority status;
because they were used to life in the diaspora, the onset of Polish rule did
not constitute so significant a change. Indeed, after decades of Russifica-
tion, some even looked forward to a marked improvement in their situation. Moreover, one has to assume that most Germans who emigrated to
places that had never been part of a German state (and were not likely to
become so in the future) understood that they would always constitute a
minority. Alternatively, they would be assimilated by their non-German
surroundings; indeed, assimilation seemed almost inevitable in the longer run, the result less of purposeful state efforts than of natural and
essentially voluntary processes. Though the dominant *Grenz- und Auslanddeutschtum* perspective of the interwar period could not accept it, the
ancestors of these Germans may well have reckoned with eventual assimilation and were not overly concerned about it. In this respect, Germans in
central and eastern Poland were not very different from the millions of
Germans (including my own forebears) who came to the New World and
discarded most traces of German nationality within a generation or two.

Germans in Prussian Poland, by contrast, did not see themselves as
an immigrant population; most of them had lived their entire lives in
places that were, and presumably always would be, politically German,
whatever the local mix of nationalities. Even in Poznania, the most heavily
Polish province in Germany and the center of the Prussian Polish national
movement, Germans owned two-thirds of the land, made up more than
two-thirds of those engaged in business, and paid close to three-quarters
of the income taxes.[3] Though they constituted only a minority of the
population, they did not view themselves as colonists or temporary
occupiers about to be dislodged. Few had given any thought to how they
might get along in a predominantly Polish political environment; they
were certainly not prepared for such an outcome. Until the closing days of
World War I they had little cause to imagine themselves as anything but
citizens and residents of Germany. The change of sovereignty was there-

fore both abrupt and unexpected; almost overnight, they went from being part of the dominant group in a powerful and economically developed nation-state to being a vulnerable and mistrusted minority in a state whose economy and political culture were quite different. Because of this fundamental psychological difference between the Germans of Prussian Poland and those living elsewhere in the new state, I focus primarily on the former.

To some extent, this book can also be viewed as a study in nationalism—but of a kind that does not figure much in general or theoretical works on this subject, which tend to be most interested in "emerging" peoples or in nationalism as a rationale for aggressive state action. They often have little to say about "fallen" peoples, previously dominant nationalities who were used to being in charge until the tables were turned. This is a serious omission, for the twentieth century has witnessed, and continues to witness, numerous such inversions around the world; the behavior of these dispossessed minorities has been historically significant and needs to be better understood. This work deals with one such case but does not test theoretical hypotheses or comment explicitly on nationalist theory. In short, it is a historical account of a national minority, not a theoretical study of nationalism.

Despite its prominence in the politics of interwar Europe, the problem of the German minority in Poland has not attracted a great deal of scholarly attention, especially from non–central Europeans. True, there is a voluminous literature dating from the interwar period, often containing useful factual information, but most of it is tendentious or journalistic. The German minority in interwar Poland belongs among those historical problems that once attracted a great deal of politically motivated attention, only to slip into obscurity once the political circumstances changed. There exists, for example, no comprehensive book-length treatment of this problem in English (which is the gap which this study seeks to fill). The topic has been given surprisingly little attention even in postwar Germany; most German work has been done by scholars with personal roots in the minority. Though these are not necessarily apologetic, they are often uncritical of the many errors of perception and judgment by Polish Germans and their leaders, including their general lack of flexibility, continued orientation toward the Reich, dependence on Reich financial support, and ready embrace in the 1930s of one of this century's least savory (and least intelligent) political doctrines. The political constraints that governed historical writing in former East Germany, by contrast, made the problem of German minorities in eastern Europe either taboo or the province of the most obdurate of party ideologues.

Most of the research on this topic in the past several decades has been done by Polish historians. If many German historians have been reluctant to criticize the minority's behavior, Polish scholarship has displayed an equally uncritical attitude toward this minority's treatment by the Polish government and people. Even those historians who are more than critical of other aspects of interwar Poland have been reluctant to break with traditional nationalist perspectives on the German minority. To cite just a few representative opinions (most of them difficult to reconcile with the material presented in the following chapters): Stanisław Potocki denies that Germans in Poland had much to complain about; they were treated tolerantly and even enjoyed a "privileged" existence.[4] Marian Drozdowski also refers to the "relatively privileged position of the German minority."[5] Przemysław Hauser argues that anti-German measures had an essentially "defensive character"; they were a necessary response to German expansionism, of which the German minority served as an important tool. Hauser defends even the periodic outbreaks of popular violence against the minority as "directly proportional to the German threat." Polish officialdom, he writes, "far from adopting a consistently anti-German attitude, showed great liberalism in some questions."[6] Marian Mroczko, though critical of the "bourgeois" ideology of Polish integral nationalism between the wars, has little but praise for the most aggressive of the anti-German nationalist organizations.[7]

Some historians do concede that the German minority was not treated very well; Jerzy Krasuski, for example, remarks that "it would obviously be insincere to try to deny that Poland conducted such a [de-Germanization] policy; . . . Polish policy aimed at getting rid of the greatest possible number of Germans in Poland and the liquidation of their property to the maximum extent." He denies, however, that this policy was the "brutal" thing described by Germans, and others contend that such treatment was justified by prevalent German attitudes or behavior.[8]

The frequent references to the "privileged" minority pertain to its relatively strong economic position and imply that this position was not entirely legitimate, that it was due to favoritism under the Prussian regime or economic aid furnished by the Reich after 1918. Drozdowski argues that Poles, despite their new political dominance, continued to suffer "exploitation and oppression" at the hands of "German capital" even after 1918. The continuing economic disparity between the two peoples had a negative impact on Polish national consciousness; no Polish government, therefore, could ignore it. Poland, in other words, was justified, indeed obliged, to attack the socioeconomic position of the German minority (and thus the minority itself). Drozdowski questions whether Poland's very cohesion as a nation was possible without "restraining the economic and cultural influence of Germans in western Poland." He laments only the fact that the government could not do more, that the Polonization of economic life in western Poland was "effectively hampered" by the Germans' ability to appeal discriminatory policies to international agencies (see Chapter 5).[9]

Jerzy Tomaszewski, author of one of the most liberal-minded (and critical) accounts of Polish nationality policy between the wars, asks the question that most others skirt, "whether Poland in the interwar years really took advantage of the chances for positive coexistence with the minorities [or] whether some fatal complex of objective factors made it impossible to find an understanding." But he too believes that officials "had to try to weaken the economic position of the Germans," a "privileged" position that they enjoyed primarily as a result of discriminatory policies under the Prussian regime; "the guarantee of formal legal equality [by the Polish Constitution and the Minorities Protection Treaty] created the danger that the domination of the formerly dominant people, achieved in the course of centuries, would endure."[10]

Many of these same historians do criticize Poland's treatment of other minorities, especially the Ukrainians and Byelorussians. Andrzej Chojnowski points out the "strange paradox that the Polish state, rebuilt as the result of efforts of the Polish people over more than one hundred years, became at once the instrument of national suppression of the non-Polish ethnic groups which inhabited its territory." But these sympathetic remarks refer to the eastern Slavic minorities, who were struggling for "liberation," not to the Germans, who just wanted to hold on to their favored position.[11] Tomaszewski classifies eastern Slavic national movements as "leftist," thus positive and aimed at legitimate liberation, whereas the German national movement in Poland was of the "right" and interested basically in maintaining its ability to oppress others.[12] Roman Wapiński argues that important Polish national interests suffered because the government treated all minorities alike: that is, the same as the Germans, who presumably deserved such treatment.[13]

Only a few Polish historians have seriously questioned interwar Poland's treatment of its German minority. Alfred Kucner contended several decades ago that "the possibility of winning over the German minority . . . for the Polish state idea was not exploited. . . . The German people might have been won over to cooperation in the context of the Polish state under the condition of being assured a normal life."[14] Tadeusz Kowalak does not share this view in general, but he agrees that there was a missed opportunity to attract at least some Polish Germans away from National Socialist influence in the 1930s; nationalistic officials "sometimes even made the struggle against National Socialism [among Polish Germans] more difficult."[15] Others have noted official Poland's tendency to treat all Germans alike, to prejudge them all as enemies of Poland, which strengthened the hand of their nationalist leaders, forced them to turn to the Reich for support, and hurt primarily the economically weaker members of the minority. Tomaszewski explains this tendency with reference to the psychologically difficult situation after 1918, where "those who had often been looked down upon or even despised found themselves in the role of the ruling people. . . . All forms of political activity among the minorities were viewed with deep dislike and exaggerated as an irredentist threat, even where it was really only [a manifestation of] the desire for legal equality."[16] On the whole, critical reevaluations of the treatment of the German minority remain rare, even in the most recent Polish accounts. Indeed, the most frequently expressed criticism alleges that official policy was insufficiently vigilant and consistent rather than excessively harsh; a government that really understood the mortal danger posed by the German minority in Poland would have pursued de-Germanization with much greater vigor.

This book takes issue with many of the views outlined above, in part because they are factually incorrect but also because they pose the wrong questions from a one-sided perspective. It appears, of course, in the wake of fundamental political change in Poland itself and in that country's relationship with Germany. One result has been a greater freedom of Polish historians to make up their own minds about such sensitive historical issues. To date, however, even the more sophisticated and liberal-minded Polish historians seem reluctant, even after fifty years, to view things from the minority's own perspective or to "understand" the minority's difficult situation. Indeed, merely posing the problem in these terms may strike some who are emotionally close to this area's national conflicts as naive or raise suspicions of apologetic intent. But the political situation in central Europe has changed fundamentally; no one can any longer suppose that an account of the dilemma of the German minority in interwar Poland is related to frontier issues or to Poland's right to the area itself. Precisely because the political context in which this problem was viewed for so many years has disappeared, to some extent *only* because it has disappeared, one can and should confront the question itself: What was it like to be a German in the territories ceded to Poland after World War I? How did the new minority, the Polish government and society, and official Germany respond to the new situation?

1

Establishment of the German Minority, 1918-1922

Poland acquired its large population of formerly German citizens in several installments between late 1918 and mid-1922. Most of the province of Poznania (Posen) came under Polish rule as the result of an armed insurrection in December 1918, before the peace conference in Paris began its formal deliberations. Another large area, comprising most of West Prussia and parts of three other provinces, came under Polish rule in January 1920 as a result of the Versailles Treaty. A third significant group of Germans came under Polish rule as a result of the 1921 plebiscite in Upper Silesia and the division of that province according to the Geneva Convention of May 1922.

Poznania

Poznania was the chief stronghold of the Polish national movement in Prussia, which exploited the collapse of German authority at war's end to make its bid for independence. On the day of the armistice, November 11, 1918, Polish nationalists, led by Reichstag deputy Wojciech Korfanty, organized a "National Council," soon redesignated the "Supreme National Council" (Naczelna Rada Ludowa, or NRL). The NRL proclaimed itself the new provisional government of Poznania and called for elections to a Prussian-Polish parliament, or *sejm*. A "provincial nutrition bureau" was also set up to give the NRL control over the movement of food out of this key food-producing region, and thus some leverage with the government in Berlin. Armed support for the NRL was provided by Polish patriotic societies, including Sokół ("Falcon") societies (with about 14,000 members throughout the Reich), "Scouts" (*Hacerzy*), and above all a "Polish Military Organization" (Polska Organizacja Wojskowa, or POW). The POW was founded as an underground of just a few hundred members in early 1918 but grew rapidly as German power collapsed. Its arms were provided by deserters from the German army or confiscated from smaller German units and armories. A separate militia (Straż Ludowa) with about 5,800 members at year's end and a "security force" (Wach- und Sicherheits-dienst) with another 1,800 armed members comple- mented the POW.[1]

At the same time, however, the "councils" (*Räte*) movement, which was spreading rapidly throughout Germany, also manifested itself in Poznania. A largely German "Soldiers Council" was organized on No- vember 10; August Twachtmann, a sergeant from Hamburg, was its chairman. A "Workers Council," with six Polish and five German so- cialists on its ruling board, appeared at about the same time; the two councils were soon joined to form the Poznań (Posen) "Workers and Soldiers Council." Though its majority was German, this organization was sympathetic to Polish national aspirations. When a crowd of Polish nationalists gathered in the Poznań marketplace and fired weapons to back demands for parity between Poles and Social Democrats (SPD) on the council, the latter quickly complied. Since several of the Social Demo- crats were Polish, this meant a Polish majority on the council which soon established its authority over the fifty or so similar bodies in the province. But while the Poznań Workers and Soldiers Council claimed political authority throughout much of Poznania, it also recognized the NRL as the legitimate representative of the province's Polish population. It cooper- ated with the NRL in Polonizing local and provincial administration; many county executives (*Landräte*), mayors, and other officials were re- moved or obliged to accept Polish supervisors.[2]

In short, most of Poznania witnessed a de facto Polish takeover, gradual and largely nonviolent, during the several weeks after the armi- stice. German members of the Poznań Workers and Soldiers Council, aside from being in the minority, were mostly unsophisticated workers or soldiers drawn from other parts of Germany who were most interested in an early return home. Twachtmann's reaction to the reported approach of Polish armed units was symptomatic; "We won't let ourselves be beat up here. . . . Let them come; we'll gladly surrender the city to them."[3] Socialism had always been weak in Poznania, among Germans and Poles alike; the lack of support for the SPD among local Germans inclined its leaders toward a policy of cooperation with the Poles. German Social Democrats stressed the primacy of class consciousness over nationalism and thought they could interest Poles in the idea of revolutionary soli- darity across national lines. They seemed content to let the Poles have their way locally, pending the outcome of the peace conference. The new government in Berlin encouraged them in this attitude by dismissing or transferring to the West any German officials who obstructed the pro- Polish course or questioned the Poles' real intentions.[4] Polish members of the workers and soldiers councils, on the other hand, were usually members of the "intelligentsia"; in class terms, most of them qualified as "bourgeois." Few of them were socialists; indeed, most of them sympathized with the rightist National Democrats. Many of them served simultaneously on Polish national councils and kept their eyes firmly on the nationalist agenda. Thus the new regime in Poznania was a rather awkward combination of provincial German socialists and the principal leaders of the Polish national movement in Germany.[5]

In the northern part of Poznania, in the *Regierungsbezirk* ("regency") of Bromberg/Bydgoszcz, events took a different course. Following brief skirmishes with representatives of the old order, German socialists removed the local military commander and took control of the city of Bromberg. The population of Bromberg was about 85 percent German at the time, so this revolutionary takeover was essentially a German affair. Local Poles organized national councils and were given token seats on the Workers and Soldiers Council, but they did not bid seriously for power. Like the German socialists in Poznań, they urged their outnumbered supporters to be patient and await the outcome of the Paris peace conference.[6]

The new government in Berlin was preoccupied with more pressing matters, and its response to developments in Poznania, including its own loss of effective authority in much of the province, was passive or confused. Its first priority was to secure the steady supply of food from this province. Otherwise, it just wanted to avoid trouble and wanted revolutionary Germans and Poles to get along together. The widespread breakdown of German military discipline in the wake of the armistice demoralized many officials and undermined their ability to defend German interests in Poznania. The desertion rate was high, and army commanders had few troops they could rely on. Polish formations, by contrast, grew steadily, thanks in part to these same deserters.[7] On November 15, the German government did authorize a special *Heimatschutz-Ost* (Homeland Defense-East) to forestall an actual seizure of power by Polish military forces. The Poznań Workers and Soldiers Council protested, however, that such a force was unnecessary and would be viewed by Poznanian Poles as a provocation. Undersecretary for Defense Paul Goehre tried unsuccessfully to reassure the NRL that "we could not wage a war if we wanted to. . . . That is not the former army but a sand dune; it wants peace."[8] The government then dispatched State Secretary of the Interior Helmut von Gerlach to Poznań on November 19 to evaluate the situation.

Gerlach was an Independent Socialist (USDP) and pacifist who was primarily concerned to avoid Polish-German conflict. He declared his government's support for majority rule, for national self-determination, and for the use of the Polish language in provincial administration. He ordered local officials to begin using that language, though virtually none of them were able to do so. He agreed with the NRL that the *Heimatschutz* was "unnecessary" and would be "unfortunate." In his view, most Germans and Poles were getting along sufficiently well; the introduction of new armed units into the province would only upset things. "Actual power in Poznania is in the hands of the Polish National Council," he wrote. "The Polish population is united, the German divided. . . . To assume that the whole province could be held by German armed force is to misread the situation. . . . Force is of no use against the Poles, for our soldiers do not want to fight any more. Sending troops to the East only means delivering arms to the Poles." Gerlach expressed confidence that Polish nationalists did not intend to preempt the peace conference and that the NRL was able to maintain order. The "old Junker East" was finished, he concluded; peace, democracy, and good relations with the Poles were now the top priorities.[9]

In this spirit, the German government did not interfere with Polish-run elections to the new *sejm*, which met December 3-6, 1918, at Poznań. Members of this assembly expressed their confidence that Poznania would soon be part of Poland; there was much nationalist celebrating and pictures of Wilson and other Entente leaders were on display. The National Democrats were in control and proposed one of their own, Wojciech Trąmpczyński, as the new provincial governor. Resolutions were passed calling for the expulsion of anti-Polish officials, recognition of the Polish "government-in-exile" in Paris, reversal of the eighteenth-century partitions, and the establishment of a Polish militia in each town, to be funded by a "national tax" on Prussian Poles. But there were also some conciliatory gestures, including the promise of full equality for Germans in the new Poland and continued food deliveries to the Reich.[10]

Despite the efforts of Polish leaders to avoid direct conflict with Germans, there were some isolated clashes between Polish and German formations. This prompted the dispatch of another delegation of officials from Berlin in mid-December: Prussian Minister-President Paul Hirsch, Interior Minister Eugen Ernst, Major Friedrich Willisen of the *Heimatschutz*, and Gerlach. They determined that tighter control over the border with Russia was necessary, so the *Heimatschutz-Ost* was rechristened *Grenzschutz-Ost* (Border Defense-East) to reflect this new mission. The NRL, however, continued to oppose the introduction of additional German troops into Poznania even after the government promised to recruit exclusively from locals and to let the NRL have a say in Grenzschutz operations.[11]

Meanwhile, German nationalists in Prussian Poland, sensing a lack of support from Berlin, also turned to national councils *(Volksräte)* to defend their interests. They appealed both to their own government and to U.S. President Woodrow Wilson for protection in the face of alleged Polish aggressiveness. In Poznań, the head of the German national council was Alfred Herrmann, a democrat and outspoken opponent of previous Prussian Polish policies. Elsewhere, however, German national councils tended to reflect the conservative, nationalist views of most Poznanian Germans. They polemicized vigorously against both Herrmann and the new government in Berlin, whose very legitimacy they were loath to acknowledge and which they now blamed for letting Polish nationalists get the upper hand in much of the province.[12] In an effort to unite these national councils and suppress ideological differences, a group of German nationalists in Bromberg organized a *Deutsche Vereinigung* ("German association") on December 1, 1918, which launched a campaign to keep Prussian Poland part of Germany. Its leader was Georg Cleinow, member of the chauvinistic Deutscher Ostmarkenverein (German Eastern Marches Association, or DOV), former editor of the nationalistic *Grenzboten*, and chief of public information in occupied Poland during the war (until his opposition to Germany's decision to grant nominal independence to Russian Poland in 1916 led to his dismissal). Others active in this organization, and prominent subsequently in the minority's affairs, were Kurt Graebe, Friedrich Heidelck, Max Hildebert Boehm, and Carl Georg Bruns.[13]

The new government in Berlin, of course, wanted only to distance itself from Prussian Polish policies in general and DOV attitudes in particular. So long as German national councils in Poznania seemed to reflect such attitudes, they found little favor in Berlin. Cleinow and his associates railed as much against the SPD, which they accused of incompetence and blindness to the Polish danger, as they did against the Poles. Reich officials had previously ordered Cleinow out of Poznań because of his feud with Herrmann and other local democrats; not without justification, they saw his efforts as counterrevolutionary as well as counterproductive with respect to the Poles. The DOV itself, so prominent in the political life of prewar Prussian Poland, largely dropped from sight after the armistice. Most Poznanian Germans now considered it politic to distance themselves from that organization; its members, fearing reprisals under a future Polish regime, were often among the first Germans to head west.[14]

While these changes were taking place inside Prussian Poland, other centers of Polish political authority demanded to be taken into account. The first of these was that quasi-independent Polish state established in November 1916 in consequence of Germany's halfhearted effort to attract Polish support against Russia. Polish nationalists had every reason to be anti-Russian, if not pro-German, and some were willing to go along with this strategy, at least at first. Józef Piłsudski, for example, after aligning himself with Austria-Hungary as the partitioning power least opposed to the restoration of Poland, agreed to join this new regime's ruling council and put his Polish Legion under its authority.[15]

But then came the Russian revolution (March 1917) and the new Russian government's apparent recognition of Poland's right to independence, which also freed the Entente powers to come out in support of Polish independence. The German strategy, on the other hand, was fatally undermined by General Erich Ludendorff's insistence that Germany retain not only Prussian Poland but also an additional "border strip" (Grenzstreifen) to be carved out of the Russian partition. German support for the national aspirations of Lithuanians and Ukrainians, some of whose lands Polish nationalists wanted for themselves, also undermined German-Polish cooperation. Lured by the prospect of greater real independence for a territorially greater Poland than Germany was willing to concede, Piłsudski broke with the Central Powers and quit the Warsaw regime in July 1917. He was imprisoned in Germany and his Polish Legion disbanded, though the Warsaw regime itself maintained a shadow existence. The Bolshevik coup d'état (November 1917) destroyed any thought of Polish cooperation with a democratic Russia, so reliance on the western powers became the only remaining Polish strategy, the simultaneous (or successive) defeat of both Russia and Germany the ideal outcome of the war. As this outcome loomed, the Warsaw regime became more assertive; it declared its full sovereignty on October 7, 1918, and staked its claim to Prussian as well as Russian and Austrian Poland. After the abdication of German Emperor William II on November 9, Piłsudski was released and returned home a national hero. The Warsaw government recognized him as supreme commander of Polish military forces and then as head of the government itself. Rival regimes in Cracow and Lublin also recognized his leadership after he agreed to a mostly socialist and "populist" cabinet.[16]

Meanwhile, however, the western powers had recognized another organization as representative of Polish interests: a "Polish National Council" (KNP) dominated by National Democrats whose vision of Poland's future differed significantly from Piłsudski's. Piłsudski was always more concerned about Poland's one-time eastern possessions; his plans for a large federal state extending eastward presupposed an anti-Russian posture. National Democrats such as Roman Dmowski, on the other hand, had in mind a smaller (perhaps) but ethnically more homogeneous Poland; their greater concern to gather in the economically developed western Polish lands controlled by Germany presupposed an anti-German posture. The latter position was clearly more compatible with Entente interests; National Democrats also enjoyed much more support in Prussian Poland than did Piłsudski. The problem was that one of these regimes controlled most of Poland itself, while the other one spoke for the country in Paris. To bridge the gap, the KNP dispatched Ignacy Paderewski to

Warsaw in December. Under the agreement reached by Piłsudski and Paderewski, the latter was recognized as premier of a unified government, pending national elections. (The National Democrats were later victorious in these elections, and Paderewski formed the first parliamentary government, Piłsudski continuing as "chief of state.")

Whatever Paderewski achieved in Warsaw, the most important result of his trip was the Poznanian Insurrection of December 1918. He proceeded from Danzig (Gdańsk) to Warsaw by way of Poznań, where the NRL assembled a large crowd to hear him speak. Since he was accompanied by a couple of allied officers, Entente as well as Polish flags were on display at this rally. After he had moved on the next day, local Germans staged a counterdemonstration and tore down the Entente flags. This led to an exchange of gunfire between Polish militia and either German soldiers or armed German civilians, depending on the account.[17] The following day (December 28, 1918) Polish militia occupied Poznań and imposed martial law. The German garrison surrendered and was disarmed and dispersed; top officials, including Oberpräsident Johann von Eisenhart-Rothe and the commander of the V Army Corps, General Friedrich von Bock und Polach, were arrested. Many other Germans were disarmed; their homes were searched, and some were interned.[18]

This insurrection has been much celebrated in Polish nationalist historiography, perhaps because it stands out from the long history of unsuccessful Polish uprisings. Most Polish accounts explain it as a spontaneous popular response to German provocations, including the arrival of the first *Grenzschutz* units and the growing assertiveness of German nationalists. German accounts are more inclined to see it as a well-planned coup, one that claimed few lives on either side primarily because Germans were too demoralized and disorganized to mount much resistance.[19] Some believe that this military takeover was an attempt to create "established facts" to help the Polish cause in Paris: Poland's territorial claims might be looked on more favorably if it were already in possession of them. Others argue that it was largely superfluous: Poles were already in effective control of the province, and the insurrection achieved little that they were not virtually certain to get out of the peace conference in any case.[20] Still others attribute the uprising to intra-Polish rivalries, particularly National Democratic desires to establish a counterweight in Poland itself to the "leftist" government in Warsaw.[21]

The insurrection spread quickly from Poznań to most of the rest of the province. Most places were surrendered after little or no resistance by officials wanting only to avoid bloodshed. As in Poznań, German weapons were confiscated, homes searched, a curfew imposed, and German signs and monuments removed. Where German forces counterattacked, as in Inowrocław/Hohensalza, the local German population was either expelled or imprisoned.[22] In most cases, however, the regular German army was nowhere to be seen; it was in "process of dissolution, . . . incapable of resistance or action . . . due to lack of leadership and discipline."[23] German efforts at mediation were without effect; Bromberg Regierungspräsident Fritz von Bülow invited Korfanty to Berlin for talks, but these foundered on Korfanty's demand that Bülow surrender his own position to a Pole. When Prussian Interior Minister Ernst came to Poznań to talk with leaders of the insurrection, Twachtmann (of the Workers and Soldiers Council) warned him that he was wasting his time; most Poles, he had concluded, were motivated by an "indescribable hatred" of Germans.[24] In short, the government was unable to provide the kind of protection Poznanian Germans had come to expect and they were left essentially to fend for themselves.

A few days after the outbreak of the Poznanian Insurrection, the Independent Socialists, who were most willing to seek an understanding with the Poles at almost any price, pulled out of the German government. The *Grenzschutz* was then strengthened, and an official call went out for volunteers to help halt the Polish advance in Poznania. Instead of mobilizing a major force outside the province and then moving to retake it, however, the government continued to send smaller reinforcements to existing units. About 1,000 such troops arrived at the Poznań railroad station in early January only to be disarmed and sent home.[25] When the "Council of Ten" in Paris learned of the Poznanian Insurrection, it reiterated its own intention to determine the Polish-German frontier and warned that "possession gained by force will seriously prejudice the claims of those who use such means."[26] The allied officers who accompanied Paderewski to Poland also warned Piłsudski against any military intervention in Prussian Poland. But no steps were taken to compel the Poles to give up their gains, which left it up to Germany and the Germans in Poznania to try to do so themselves.

Aside from the *Grenzschutz*, the German cause was supported by improvised armed units (for example, of railroad workers) and Free Corps (including the notorious Rossbach Corps, which retook Kulmsee/ Chełmża from Polish insurgents in late January). These forces managed to limit the Polish insurrection to its Poznanian nucleus and in some places even to push it back. Fighting was fiercest on the "northern front"—that is, in the Netze/Noteć region—where hundreds died on each side.[27] By early February a stable front had developed, though the Germans continued to build up their forces with the evident intent to retake Poznania. Before they could act, however, the Entente powers imposed a cease-fire, the "Trier armistice" of February 7, 1919. Despite occasional skirmishes, the truce held until the terms of the peace settlement were unveiled.

In consequence of the Poznanian Insurrection of December 1918, the

German population in Poznania was introduced rather inauspiciously to Polish rule, by means of a violent seizure of power. The fighting that followed was bloody enough; it claimed about 1,200 members of German units and an estimated 1,700 on the Polish side. The Polish-occupied parts of Poznania were cut off economically as well as politically from the rest of Germany. As many as 8,000 Germans were interned for several months in a former prisoner-of-war camp at Szczypiorno near Kalisz.[28] Among those interned was the head of the United Evangelical Church in Poznania, Superintendent Paul Blau, and thirty-nine pastors. Even after his release, Blau was not permitted "for political reasons" to travel to Berlin— not if he wished to return. In July 1919 the NRL announced that his church now belonged to the Polish Lutheran Church; any communications with his erstwhile superiors in Berlin should go by way of Warsaw. Other Germans complained of curfews, unequal access to rationed food, opened mail, looting, and a general deterioration of law and order under the insurgents' regime in Poznania. The German government charged that much of this disorder was purposeful, that the German population of Polish-occupied Poznania was being "forced by terrorization to flee."[29]

On the other hand, Polish authorities did permit Poznanian Germans to participate in elections for the German National Assembly on January 19, 1919. With most Poles not voting, 51 percent of the vote in Poznania went to anti-republican parties (DNVP and DVP) at a time when they attracted only 14 percent in Germany as a whole. The parties of the "Weimar Coalition," which garnered 75 percent of the vote throughout Germany, were supported by only 48 percent of Poznanian Germans.[31] This contrast may reflect in part the traditional conservatism of the Germans in this province; it doubtless also reflects their unhappiness with the weak response of the Weimar regime to Polish advances.

In any case, several hundred thousand Germans found themselves under Polish rule as a result of the Poznanian Insurrection. The circumstances of this takeover, by force and before the peace conference (which was to make this situation permanent) got under way, did not constitute a happy beginning for this new minority.

West Prussia/Pomorze

Another large population of Germans, living primarily in the province of West Prussia, came under Polish rule as a result of the Versailles Treaty. Germans who were resigned to the loss of most of Poznania claimed to be surprised when most of West Prussia was also awarded to Poland. They were aware of KNP demands for the return of whatever had belonged to Poland before 1772 (Poznania, West Prussia, and Ermland) as well as some lands that had not (such as Upper Silesia and the remainder of East Prussia), and there was also a reference in Wilson's thirteenth "point" to Poland's right to "access to the sea." But Germans thought they had sufficient arguments to retain West Prussia: the province as a whole was 65 percent German by population (1910). Poles constituted a majority in only twelve of twenty-nine counties, and Germans owned most of the land in all but one of these. Thus Germans in West Prussia tried to convince themselves at first that the redrawing of frontiers would not affect them, that some nonterritorial way would be found to provide Poland with the promised access to the Baltic.[32]

Of course, a different reading of the demographic data produced arguments for giving at least some of West Prussia to Poland. Even absent such arguments, France—one of the powers devising the new frontiers—wanted a larger, stronger Poland and a smaller, weaker Germany. Endowing Poland with plenty of formerly German territory would not only enable that country to stand up to Germany but provide added incentive to do so. In the words of a French memorandum of December 24, 1918, "the more we enlarge Poland at the expense of Germany, the more certain we shall be that she will remain her enemy."[33] Another of the Big Three powers, the United States, established an "inquiry" under Colonel Edward House to determine its position on frontier issues. Its East European section was headed by a pro-Polish Harvard professor, Robert Lord. U.S. Secretary of State Robert Lansing also seemed receptive to most Polish territorial demands, including Danzig.

But neither the KNP, the French, nor pro-Polish American officials were able to persuade Wilson to embrace the more far-reaching Polish territorial demands, such as Danzig and East Prussia. KNP leaders Dmowski and Paderewski enjoyed only mixed success in their efforts to win over American opinion on this issue. Paderewski's flamboyance raised questions about his level-headedness; Dmowski's unabashed anti-Semitism clearly hurt the Polish cause. Dmowski did not believe that Jews could be truly Polish; he did not think that Jews and other minorities should even enjoy voting rights in the new Poland. He accused Polish Jews of collaborating with the German occupiers and of working against Poland's interests in the West. Paderewski and others denied that Dmowski spoke for Polish nationalism in general and appointed a token Jew to the KNP. But they could not persuade Dmowski to soften his position (or limit the damage, at least, by not communicating directly to American audiences).[34] KNP efforts to shake charges of anti-Semitism were also undermined by continued reports of anti-Jewish incidents filtering out of Poland. Moreover, a decisive role in the British delegation belonged to Lewis Namier, who was quite hostile to Poland, apparently as a result of having grown up there as a Jew. He denounced the Franco-

Polish proposals as a gratuitous effort to humiliate Germany and warned that "the Germans will accept humiliation from their real conquerors, but not from the Poles."[35] Prime Minister David Lloyd George and other British leaders were also beginning to think more about future relations with Germany and less about satisfying Polish territorial aspirations.

To resolve these continuing differences among the allies, a "Polish Frontier Commission" was set up in February 1919. At first, its American members tended toward the Polish-French position and seemed ready to let both Danzig and West Prussia east of the Vistula go to Poland, despite heavy German majorities in both places. Against British opposition, the commission's March recommendations reflected this position. But when the Council of Ten took up these recommendations, Lloyd George was adamant: "The proposals of the Polish Frontier Commission that we should place 2.1 million Germans under the control of a people which is of a different religion and which has never proved its capacity for stable self-government throughout its history must, in my judgment, lead sooner or later to a new war in the east of Europe."[36] He succeeded in getting the recommendations returned to committee for revision.

Wilson then moved still closer to the British position, persuaded by suggestions that the Polish appetite for Danzig was comparable to the French appetite for the Saarland or the Italian appetite for Rijeka/Fiume, both of which he opposed. He expressed a belated realization that "the only real interest of France in Poland is in weakening Germany by giving Poland territory to which she has no right."[37] He was also unhappy with Piłsudski's armed incursion into eastern Galicia and threatened at one point to terminate aid to Poland if this did not stop. On the subject of Danzig, he became more adamant even than Lloyd George and insisted that that city, if separated from Germany, should become a "free city" under League of Nations protection. By the time the draft treaty was presented to the Germans in May 1919, the two Anglo-Saxon leaders had also secured plebiscites for two other areas that France wanted Poland to get outright: the Marienwerder District (West Prussia east of the Vistula) and Masuria (in southern East Prussia).[38] Paderewski was unable to persuade them to change their position on the Danzig, Marienwerder, and Masurian questions. Indeed, while the draft treaty was being considered by Germany, Wilson and Lloyd George began to equivocate about yet another item on Poland's list of territorial demands: Upper Silesia.[39]

When German leaders were presented with the draft treaty, nothing seemed to upset them more than the proposed cession of Upper Silesia. This seemed to be the one stipulation that might even tempt them to reject the treaty altogether, however suicidal such defiance would surely be. Lloyd George proposed, therefore, that the disposition of Upper Silesia also be decided by plebiscite. Wilson balked: "We know the ethnographic facts, and there is no need to add a plebiscite which was not imposed by the 14 Points." [40] Even when he later gave in on this issue, he continued to insist that the result was a foregone conclusion in view of the province's solid Polish-speaking majority. Paderewski, more familiar with the ambivalent national orientation of many Upper Silesians, was less sure of the outcome; he feared that Germany would carry the western, agricultural part of the province and might well emerge with an overall majority. For this reason, he demanded that the plebiscite vote be counted by commune, not just in the aggregate; anticipating some kind of partition as the likely outcome, he wanted grounds for having at least the eastern, industrial areas awarded to Poland. [41]

Allied insistence that Poland agree to a "Minorities Protection Treaty" in return for such lands as it did receive was viewed by Polish leaders as yet another setback. The idea was first proposed, and pushed hardest, by western Jewish leaders concerned about reports of anti-Jewish violence in newly independent Poland. Reports of pogroms accompanied the entry of Polish troops into Vilnius and Pinsk in 1919; even the Haller Army, recruited in France during the war and still containing many French officers, was linked to anti-Semitic actions in several towns of central Poland. [42] Both the United States and Great Britain dispatched commissions to investigate these reports. Essentially, they verified the anti-Semitic acts themselves but stopped short of alleging official Polish involvement in them. [43] Even before they filed their reports, however, the treaty-makers had decided that minority protection treaties were necessary. Not only Poland but Czechoslovakia, Romania, Yugoslavia, Greece, and (later) the three Baltic states and Turkey were also obliged to sign agreements promising fair treatment of newly created national and religious minorities. They could not be revoked unilaterally, were to take precedence over conflicting clauses in these countries' own laws or constitutions, and were to be enforced by the League of Nations. [44]

The Polish minorities treaty, for example, stipulated that minorities would enjoy equal protection of life and liberty and the free practice of religion (Article 2); those who chose to retain their previous citizenship could take their movable possessions out of the country duty-free (Article 3); non-Poles were promised the same civil and political rights as ethnic Poles, equal access to public employment and the professions, use of their language in the courts (Article 7), their own educational, religious, and social institutions (Article 8), and elementary schools supported by public funds and conducted in their own language wherever a "considerable proportion" of one minority resided (Article 9). Any member of the League Council could bring alleged violations of this treaty before the League or to the Permanent Court of International Justice at The Hague (Article 12). [45]

Though Polish leaders were frankly forced to sign this treaty, some tried to put the best face on it. Jan Ciechanowski, *chargé* in London, conceded that "after all, pogroms and anti-Jewish excesses have taken place in Poland"; accepting this treaty would improve Poland's image in world opinion; make eastern Slavs and Lithuanians more amenable to federation with Poland, and allow the country to make similar demands of Germany in the future.[46] But most Poles who commented on the Minorities Protection Treaty expressed resentment that such treaties were imposed only on states "newly created, enlarged, or defeated," and that even some of those were exempted—most significantly, Germany. Others were reminded of the legal pretexts for foreign intervention in Polish internal affairs in the eighteenth century. But when Paderewski took these complaints to French Premier Georges Clemenceau, he was told that the treaty was the price Poland had to pay for the lands it wanted. As Paderewski reported back to the Sejm on June 30: "These guarantees constitute one of the main conditions of our independence. . . . The Polish delegates have signed the [Minorities Protection] Treaty because they had to do it."[47]

The Sejm approved the treaty by a vote of 286 to 41, but the majority was motivated more by *Realpolitik* than by the conviction that approval was justified or necessary. In subsequent years, Polish leaders displayed only a grudging acceptance of their obligations under this treaty. The idea that some Polish citizens could appeal over the head of a supposedly sovereign government to international bodies was especially irksome. Poland, complaining that such regulations relegated certain countries to second-class status, periodically demanded that other states accept similar obligations. They did not do so, of course, and so Poland soon began to contemplate unilateral renunciation of the Minorities Protection Treaty.[48]

Under the Versailles Treaty as amended, Poland received about 90 percent of the Prussian province of Poznania, about 66 percent of West Prussia, and smaller bits of East Prussia and Silesia. Germany retained most of the predominantly German counties (*Kreise*), though several that were both majority German and contiguous to Germany (such as Zempelburg/Sępólno, Lissa/Leszno, and Birnbaum/Międzychód) were included in the grant to Poland. Drawing a frontier through the German-Polish borderlands was of course impossible to do without leaving large minorities on either side. (See the ethnographic map.) For example, in 40 of the 72 counties into which Poznania and West Prussia were divided, the *minority* nationality constituted at least 25 percent of the population. In fact, although the German territory transferred to Poland under the Versailles Treaty was majority Polish overall, a sizable German minority was present almost everywhere: of the approximately three million in-

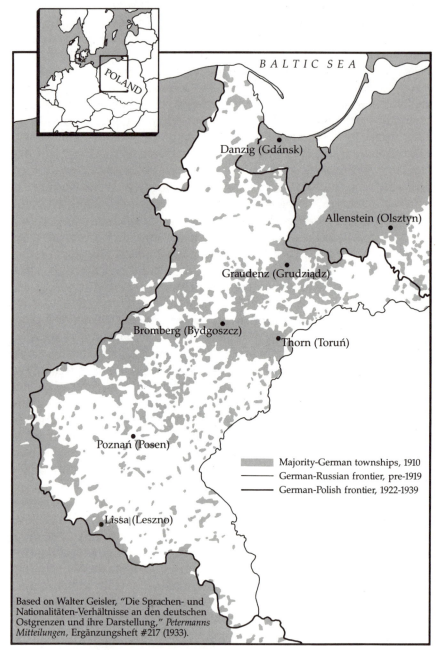

MAP 2. Ethnographic Composition of the
German-Polish Borderlands, 1910

habitants of these ceded lands, about 1.1 million were German, according to the 1910 census.[49]

Article 91 of the Versailles Treaty provided that "German nationals residing habitually in [these areas] will acquire Polish nationality *ipso facto*," except that "German nationals or their descendants who became resident in these territories after January 1, 1908, will not acquire Polish nationality without a special authorization from the Polish state." The choice of the year 1908 was not entirely arbitrary; it marked the passage of Prussia's forced-sale "Expropriation Law" under which Polish estates could be taken by the state for subdivision into farms for German settlers. The law was rarely invoked, and had had no impact on the national balance in Prussian Poland, but it possessed great symbolic importance in Polish eyes. The Versailles Treaty also made provision for Germans and Poles alike to choose citizenship in either country (husbands and fathers would speak for their entire families) within two years from the implementation of the treaty: that is, until January 1922. If their choice did not coincide with their country of residence, they were free (but not, apparently, required) to emigrate and take their movable property with them. They were not required to sell their immovable property, but Article 297 authorized Poland to "liquidate" (with compensation) the property of German citizens. Poland also came into immediate possession of any property of the German empire, the Prussian state, and the Hohenzollern dynasty lying within its new lands.[50]

The reaction to the Versailles Treaty by most Germans in the areas to be ceded is not difficult to imagine. When its terms were first announced, German national councils, especially in majority-German places, denounced them in often drastic terms. Cleinow charged that the government in Berlin, or "those men who have usurped this name, have concluded a peace which leads us into servitude." The Bromberg German National Council, of which he was chairman, launched a "formal protest before the whole world against the planned violation of the right of self-determination, against the intention to turn over two million members of the German cultural nation to the revenge and hatred of the fanatical Polish nation."[51] Three thousand Danzigers passed a resolution promising "never to bow to the Polish yoke and rather to fight to the last drop of blood."[52] Of course, talk of armed resistance to the peace terms was irrational. But as Erich Koch-Weser observed at the time, although "there can be no other resistance than passive resistance, tell that to someone who is to become Polish!"[53] Nor were such sentiments limited to the nationalist right; democrats and leftists were just as "chauvinistic" (in the words of a Polish historian), just as upset to learn that their communities were to go to Poland.[54]

This first reaction of defiance, including even calls for senseless resistance, culminated in discussion of a fantastic *Oststaat* idea: at a meeting of German national councils in Bromberg, May 28, 1919, Cleinow urged the creation of an independent "eastern state"; before the Versailles Treaty took effect, Prussia's eastern provinces were to secede from Germany in armed defiance of Berlin, Poland, and the western powers as well. Others who were more or less seriously involved in this plot included August Winnig, the Social Democratic "Reich Commissioner for the East"; the West Prussian *Oberpräsident*, Adolf von Batocki; and the local army chief, General Otto von Below. When word of the conspiracy reached the National Assembly at Weimar, there were calls for Cleinow's arrest. This proved unnecesary, however, for most of those involved in the plot soon acknowledged that it was futile. After a first planning session on June 25, 1919, the plan was vetoed by military leaders whose participation was indispensable, including Armee-Oberkommando-Nord chief of staff General Hans von Seeckt.[55] Overall, Cleinow and other exemplars of prewar Prussian-German *Polenpolitik* did not cut a very impressive figure during the turbulent postwar period. Following the collapse of his *Oststaat* scheme, Cleinow briefly took up the task of persuading Germans to remain in the ceded territories; he had harsh words for those ("even trained officers") who sold out and left for the Reich. After a couple of house searches by Polish police, however, he too pulled out, just a few months after the Versailles Treaty went into effect.[56]

Spokesmen for the German cause in the ceded areas urged all those who were entitled to become Polish citizens to do so. They expressed confidence that Polish authorities would be tolerant and not seek reprisals for the way Prussian Poles had been treated in the past.[57] Most Germans remained nervous, however, especially because of the perceived lack of support from the Berlin government, which seemed slow to demonstrate its concern for those slated for transfer to Poland. Official assurances that Poland would restrain itself, or be restrained by the language of the treaties, sounded hollow and did not seem to be supported by developments in insurgent-occupied Poznania. Even those who were free of paranoia or responsibility for past Prussian Polish policies had reason to fear the loss of privileges and status based on nationality, as well as diminished personal security, property rights, and such other benefits as had derived from Germany's relatively efficient administration. They could also anticipate a decline in economic conditions and probably an influx of poorer Poles from the formerly Russian and Austrian partitions. One can scarcely exaggerate the reorientation of thought and behavior that the new situation demanded of both peoples, but especially of the Germans. The number of changes attending the formal transfer of sovereignty to Poland tests the imagination, and most of them were viewed negatively by local Germans.

Polish leaders, hoping to forestall either desperate acts of resistance by Germans or their rapid, destabilizing flight westward, tried to reassure them. In proclamations issued both before and after the terms of the Versailles Treaty were revealed, the NRL promised that "peacefully inclined citizens of German nationality who resign themselves to the new conditions and want to become loyal citizens of the Republic of Poland have nothing to fear for their future. . . . Fellow citizens of German nationality will neither now nor in the future suffer any injustice. . . . In keeping with its liberal traditions, the Republic of Poland will grant its citizens of German nationality full equality of rights, full freedom of religion and conscience, access to state offices, freedom to cultivate their native language and national character, as well as full preservation of property." Prussian state officials were even urged to stay at their posts and assured that they would be "taken into the Polish civil service where possible."[58]

Formal Polish takeover of the territory granted by the Versailles Treaty took place without incident on January 20, 1920. The changeover was orderly and peaceful, especially in contrast with the events of the previous year in Poznania. Most Germans stayed away from the ceremonies, as their national councils suggested, but others commented favorably on the good behavior of Polish troops and even found some comfort in their "Prussian" discipline and bearing. Some Germans reassured one another that Poland would need their experience, skills, and economic clout. Even former DOV members such as Ludwig Raschdau expressed confidence that "we can live [in Poland] with the Minority Protection Treaty."[59] Germans themselves had already removed the more provocative symbols of the Prussian regime, including statues of Prussian kings, before Polish authorities arrived, and in Bromberg and elsewhere Polish representatives had been added to formerly all-German city councils. Some Germans tried even harder to get on the good side of the new rulers by flying Polish colors or learning a few bits of the Polish language.[60] Still others became suddenly ambivalent about their national identity; even some members of the DOV now concluded that they were Polish after all. Most Germans, however, remained sullen and shunned those countrymen who seemed too ready to welcome Polish rule. Much of the optimism quickly dissipated, and German leaders submitted their first grievance to Piłsudski—complaining of economic and cultural discrimination—before Polish rule was even two months old.

It was most difficult for Germans to resign themselves to Polish rule if they were in the majority locally and so saw no reason for having been assigned to Poland in the first place. This attitude was common throughout the ceded districts of West Prussia, now the Polish province of Pomorze. Especially after the one-sided Marienwerder and Masuria plebiscites, many Germans believed that most people in the majority-Polish "Corridor" would also have preferred to stay with Germany. According to prewar census figures, Pomorze was 43 percent German; Upper Silesia, which voted 60 to 40 percent to remain with Germany, was only 40 percent German. And in the Marienwerder district, the one part of West Prussia that was permitted to vote on its future, much the same pattern emerged as in Upper Silesia: about two-thirds of the Poles did choose Poland, but the remaining one-third voted for Germany. In other words, though there was never a serious prospect of a plebiscite in the rest of West Prussia, there were reasons for Germans to think that they would have done well in such a poll, and this doubtless contributed to their resentment.[61]

Upper Silesia

A third sizable population of Germans was transferred to Poland as a result of the division of Upper Silesia following the 1921 plebiscite there. As in Poznania, Polish nationalists tried first to seize this area by force (August 1919). German forces managed to suppress this uprising but were compelled by Entente pressure to grant amnesty to the insurgents and let them return to their jobs. Local elections held in November 1919 were won by Poles in many communities, which meant that they took over local administration. In February 1920, German rule of the plebiscite district was replaced by an "Inter-Allied Commission," including representatives of France, Britain, and Italy. The French were clearly dominant, however: they provided the military commander (General Henri le Rond), most of the civilian administrators, and 13,000 of the 15,000 occupation troops. The British were assigned to oversee the northern agricultural counties, and the Italians several counties in the southwest, but the French retained charge of both the capital, Oppeln (Opole), and the key industrial region around Kattowitz/Katowice.

The French left no doubt of their preference that this highly indus-trialized province not remain with Germany. French officials were openly pro-Polish and did what they could to aid the Polish cause in the plebiscite campaign. Germans complained of French intervention in the (still of-ficial) Prussian courts to overturn verdicts they did not like, the disarming of Germans while a blind eye was turned to Polish armed formations, the intimidation of German sympathizers in smaller towns and villages under Polish control, and other indications of French partisanship. The plebi-scite area was largely cut off from normal contact with Germany. Upper Silesia was not represented in the German Reichstag; German citizens needed a visa from allied authorities to enter the area; German officials, including the Archbishop of Breslau (Wrocław) (in whose diocese this overwhelmingly Catholic region lay), could not enter even as visitors. Tax revenues had to remain inside the plebiscite area, and much of the region's principal product, coal, was diverted from its traditional German markets. There was also a separate railroad administration, and the plebiscite district printed its own postage stamps.[62]

This was all part of a systematic allied effort to reduce the powerful German advantage of incumbency and so ensure a fairer vote. The same thinking guided the decision to hold the plebiscite only after fourteen months of allied rule (and two years, four months after the armistice). Unfortunately, the allied occupation force was unable to keep German and Polish nationalists apart or prevent them from exploiting local advantages to suppress the other side. The resulting decline of law and order was especially unsettling for Germans, whose superior socioeconomic status was best exploited in an ordered environment. Instead, Polish nationalists, complaining of repression by Prussian police, turned again to armed revolt in August 1920. This second uprising was also suppressed, this time by allied forces, but not before it had won important concessions, including replacement of the mostly German provincial police force by a new "plebiscite police" composed of equal numbers of Poles and Germans.[63]

The French bias in favor of the Polish cause, which surfaced again during this uprising, led to serious differences within the allied regime. British representatives blamed the French for the ease with which the uprising had spread through the industrial region and charged that French partiality made "the chances for the conduct of a really impartial plebiscite small."[64] Poland, on the other hand, was increasingly concerned that the plebiscite would turn out badly; it was especially worried about the provision that all adults born in Upper Silesia, regardless of how long they had been away, were entitled to vote in the plebiscite. This had apparently been a Polish idea originally, based on the fact that most emigrants from Upper Silesia were Polish-speaking. But because most of them had subsequently undergone quite thorough Germanization, their participation now threatened to be a big boost for the German cause. Wojciech Korfanty, who returned to his native province from Poznania to preside over the Polish plebiscite campaign, urged Poles to treat such "out-voters" as intruders and with appropriate harshness. An almost hysterical article in the quasi-official *Kuryer Poranny* referred to a "wild invasion of an alien horde of Prussians; . . . 200,000 armed crusaders are to storm into this ancient Polish land. . . A whole army of paid mercenaries of Germandom, who have come from a foreign land, the sons of the German bureaucracy who have broken into this land in masses at the request of the Prussian government, are to contest the rights of the Polish people to their own land; all these fictitious 'emigrants' who are author-ized to vote by the thousands in Silesia because there were well-known delivery hospitals in Beuthen (Bytom) and other Silesian cities to which German women from the whole Reich came to give birth to their German offspring." The article warned of a "fire storm" on election day, including "armed struggle, . . . streams of blood," and another St. Batholomew's Day massacre as Silesian Poles encountered the "fat, bearded faces of the German vassals."[65]

The out-voter provision was partially offset by another which enfran-chised only those who had lived in the province since 1908 (the Expro-priation Law again); most recent immigrants were German. But Polish misgivings about the outcome of the plebiscite proved well founded: nearly 60 percent of those voting chose continued union with Germany. This was not primarily a result of the out-voters; decisive was the fact that about 40 percent of Polish-speaking Upper Silesians cast their vote for Germany, providing the German side with its majority. The Polish cause did best in those places where Poles were already in charge of local administration, especially if these were also in the area of French occupa-tion; Germany did notably better in the British and Italian sections.[66]

The German cause was doubtless aided by several factors that the Polish national movement was helpless to offset: for example, Germany's economic strength, good educational system, and extensive network of social protection. Moreover, "upwardly mobile" Upper Silesians, includ-ing the more prosperous farmers and the workers in better-paying jobs, had long associated enhanced socioeconomic status with a shift to Ger-man nationality. Some became German altogether (that is, "objectively"), but most continued to speak Polish while identifying politically with Germany (that is, they became "subjectively" German). In one presum-ably typical Upper Silesian village analyzed in detail by the pioneering sociologist Józef Chałasiński, fewer than 10 percent of the inhabitants were German by native language, yet 33 percent of the newspapers sold there were German, and 34 percent of the village's vote in the 1921 plebiscite went to Germany. When Chałasiński conducted this study in the early 1930s, after this community had been part of Poland for ten years, many local "Poles" continued to exhibit signs of a subjective Ger-man national consciousness.[67]

Of course, Germany also faced a number of handicaps in its effort to attract the votes of Upper Silesian Poles. Chief among these was the long history of official discrimination against Poles in Prussia. Fortunately for the German cause, the new, democratic government in Berlin claimed to have turned over a new leaf, and the Catholic Center Party—which Polish Upper Silesians had traditionally supported—had a major role in this government. The new Polish government, on the other hand, was dominated by National Democrats, who enjoyed little support among Silesian Poles. Moreover, the Polish economy was already in bad shape, plagued by inflation, shortages, and currency problems. There was also the war with Russia in 1920-21; it was successfully concluded just before the voting took place in Upper Silesia, but by forcing a return to conscription, exacerbating the economic problems, and temporarily raising questions about Poland's very survivability, the war too doubtless hurt the Polish cause.

The outcome of this plebiscite, above all the role of Polish-speaking Silesians in the German victory, remained a source of anguish for Polish nationalists in the following years. This was reflected in the especially aggressive de-Germanization policies applied to the part of this province subsequently awarded to Poland (and discussed below). In the short term, Polish nationalists reacted defiantly to the plebiscite result and denied that it was an accurate reflection of the national feelings of most Upper Silesians. Prompted by rumors that the western powers might leave the entire province with Germany, Polish nationalists resorted again to "direct action," launching their third major uprising in conjunction with "Kościuszko Day" festivities, May 3, 1921. Once again, the French did little to interfere with this insurrection and allowed it to gain quick control of the central industrial region. The other powers were less willing to let the insurgents have their way; Italian forces lost twenty lives in one clash with insurgents.[68] While the Polish government did not intervene openly in its behalf, neither did it condemn the insurrection. Lloyd George did condemn it as an act of "unlawful and predatory violence" and implicitly invited the Germans to respond in kind. The German government organized a *Selbstschutz* (Self-defense) and also invited some *Freikorps* (Free Corps) units to lend their assistance. The momentum of the Polish uprising was halted finally by the *Selbstschutz* at the battle for the Annaberg (Góra Sw. Anny), May 21, 1921, followed by the imposition of a cease-fire and the gradual reassertion of allied control over the plebiscite district.[69]

Unable to agree among themselves, the allied powers turned the final disposition of the Upper Silesian problem over to a League of Nations panel comprising a Chinese chairman and delegates from Belgium, Spain, and Brazil. Its charge was to divide the province in such a way that the two nations would get approximately the same percentage of inhabitants as had voted for it in the plebiscite, while leaving the smallest possible minorities on each side. Poland had the greater reason to be satisfied with the result, it received 46 percent of the people and the bulk of Upper Silesia's industry, including the major cities of Kattowitz and Königshütte/Królewska Huta (which had voted 65 percent and 75 percent respectively for Germany). Britain's Lord Curzon tried to console the

Germans, assuring them that they were bound to continue to dominate both parts of the province economically because of the different "national characteristics" of the two peoples. But most Germans felt that they now had yet another territorial grievance; the lost areas of Upper Silesia soon placed second only to the Corridor on the list of German revisonist demands.[70]

To ease the trauma of partition somewhat, the powers did stipulate that Upper Silesia continue as a single economic entity, at least in some respects, for the next fifteen years. The German and Polish governments were charged with working out an agreement to implement this idea, which took the form of the Geneva Convention of May 15, 1922. The Geneva Convention also contained provisions similar to those of the Minorities Protection Treaty, and it too was subject to League of Nations enforcement. One difference, however, was that the Upper Silesian guarantees applied equally to the German and Polish parts of that province. On each side of the new frontier, minorities were promised freedom from discrimination in public employment and the professions (Article 67), the rght to publicly supported education in their own language (Articles 68-69), and the right to use their language in dealing with state officials (Article 134). A most important clause, given the ambivalent national orientation of many Upper Silesians, was contained in Article 74: "nationality" was to be a matter of individual choice, not something automatically deduced from native language, and not subject to review or correction by officials. Poland also agreed to forgo the right (under the Versailles Treaty) to liquidate German property in eastern Upper Silesia for the fifteen-year duration of the Geneva Convention.

A "Mixed Commission" (consisting of a neutral president and two representatives each from Germany and Poland), and an "arbitral tribunal" or *Schiedsgericht,* (consisting of a neutral judge and one judge each from Germany and Poland), were created to supervise this agreement. The president of the Mixed Commission throughout the life of the Geneva Convention was Felix Calonder, former president of Switzerland and representative of that country's small Romansh-speaking minority. Georges Kaeckenbeeck of Belgium, author of an important account of this experiment in the international mediation of national disputes, served as head of the *Schiedsgericht.*[71]

The Geneva Convention went into effect July 15, 1922; Poland took over its share of Upper Silesia and acquired an additional German minority population. It is difficult to determine exactly how large this minority was. According to the 1910 census, fewer than 30 percent of the inhabitants of what was now Polish Upper Silesia declared themselves to be German by language. In the 1921 plebiscite, however, about 44 percent of the voters in this same area were "subjectively" German in the sense that they voted to remain in a German state. If the out-voters are subtracted from the German vote and the number of children and other nonvoters is estimated, the number of "subjective Germans" in Polish Upper Silesia in 1922 may have approached 330,000.[72]

The territory granted to Poland outright, without plebiscite, contained about 1.1 million Germans at the time of the 1910 census. Without trying to determine post-1910 natural growth or net migration, one can estimate that the number of Germans who came under Polish rule after World War I probably approached 1.4 million with the inclusion of eastern Upper Silesia. A minority of this size, and with its distinguishing characteristics, would have constituted a major problem for the most enlightened Polish leadership. As it was, enlightened leadership—on nationality questions, at any rate—was in short supply in interwar Poland. As a result, an unpromising demographic situation soon developed into a chronic political impasse that eventually proved fatal for Poland and for the German minority alike. Responsibility for what followed cannot be assigned exclusively to the Polish government or to Polish nationalism, of course; most members of this new German minority deeply resented and could not bring themselves to accept the changes that had come over them. Many did not even wait to see what life would be like under a Polish regime; they departed for the Reich, either before the onset of Polish rule or shortly thereafter. Thus, the opening chapter in the history of the German minority in interwar Poland as such concerns the "great exodus," the migration of much of the affected population to the Reich.

2

The Great Exodus

The extensive postwar exodus of Germans from the territories ceded to Poland was not only unique among the Reich's lost lands; it was altogether unprecedented in European history. By the end of 1921, roughly half the German population of Poznania and Pomorze—592,000 people, according to official German figures—had left.[1] Poland conducted its first national census in 1921 (minus Upper Silesia, which had not yet been partitioned.) According to this tabulation, only 1,059,194 Germans remained in all of Poland; they constituted 3.9 percent of the total population. In Pomorze, 175,771 Germans remained, constituting 18.8 percent of that province's population; 327,846 lived in the ceded parts of Poznania, where they made up 16.7 percent of the population. There are no reliable figures for net migration or natural growth in this area for the period 1910-21; reliable figures for legal emigration to Germany exist only for the period after mid-1919, and one can only guess at the considerable number who left illegally. One must rely, therefore, on the census figures compiled by the two successive regimes: the German census of 1910 and the Polish of 1921. A simple comparison between these indicates that the German population of Pomorze and Poznania in 1921 (503,617) was less than half (46 percent) of the 1910 figure.[2]

To be sure, both governments have been accused of undercounting their minorities. The 1921 Polish census in particular was challenged by Poland's minorities on grounds that it underestimated the number of non-Poles. Officially, Poland's population was only 14.3 percent Ukrainian, 7.8 percent Jewish, 3.9 percent Byelorussian, and 3.9 percent German. But others calculated that national minorities approached 40 percent of the total: 18 percent Ukrainian, 10 percent Jewish, 6 percent Byelorussian, and 5 percent German. Contemporary figures showing Poland to be only 64 percent Catholic but 22 percent Orthodox or Uniate lend some support to arguments that the census figures were low, especially for the eastern Slavic minorities, for there was general correlation between nationality and religion in Poland. Orthodox and Uniates (Greek Catholics) were normally Ukrainian or Byelorussian while Roman Catholics were over-whelmingly Polish and Lutherans were primarily German. (With Upper Silesia excluded, there were only 56,931 German Catholics in Poland, just about the same as the number of Polish Protestants: 67,775.[3])

However imprecise the 1921 tally of Germans in Poland, however, there is no doubt about the exodus itself and its approximate scope. It is equally clear that no one involved in drawing up the peace settlement or in planning for the postwar period, whether German, Polish, or "allied/associated," anticipated the departure of so many people in such a short time. The exodus from Poznania began soon after the armistice; most Germans quickly recognized that this province was almost certain to go to Poland. The number of departures rose most dramatically in the wake of the Polish insurrection at the end of 1918. Emigration fever then spread to West Prussia during the spring of 1919, with the awareness that much of that province would also go to Poland, and to Polish Upper Silesia follow-ing that province's partition, despite the more substantial protection of minority rights promised by the Geneva Convention. The German ex-odus from Polish Upper Silesia was somewhat less precipitous than elsewhere—about 30,000 Germans left during the first year after parti-tion—but the percentage who eventually left (69 percent as of 1931) exceeded even the figure for Poznania and Pomorze.

The exodus from Poznania and Pomorze peaked during the first months of Polish rule—more than 23,000 left in April 1920, the peak month—and continued at gradually diminishing but still significant lev-els for several years after the 1921 census. Hermann Rauschning, whose controversial study of this exodus is still the most extensive, reckons that about 800,000 Germans were more or less compelled to leave western Poland between late 1918 and 1926. He derives this figure basically from the difference between the number of Germans in this area according to the 1910 census and the number remaining in 1926 (759,000), supple-mented by an estimate of natural-growth rates after 1910.[4] (In the rest of Poland, those regions which had not belonged to the Reich, where Germans were used to living as a minority, there was no such exodus. Indeed, their numbers actually increased, from about 320,000 in 1921 to 364,000 in the late 1930s.)[5]

Rauschning provides a wealth of material; unfortunately, he does not always identify his sources, and some have challenged his findings. Gotthold Rhode, for example, notes that Reich agencies registered only about 470,000 Germans as immigrants from the ceded territories as of 1925. He can only estimate the ability of such agencies to take note of those arriving from Poland; the number who made the move illegally, often avoiding official detection, was apparently considerable, and others died or moved to third countries. But Rhode believes that only about 575,000

Germans left Poznania and Pomorza after the war. He attributes much of the difference between his estimate and Rauschning's to people of ambivalent national identity who identified themselves as German in 1910 but as Polish in 1921. Alfons Krysiński, writing during the interwar period, claimed to have identified at least 39,000 Poles—34,000 of them Protestant—who had been "German" in 1910. Even with this adjustment, however, Krysiński estimates the size of the 1918-26 German exodus from Pomorze and Poznania at more than 800,000; he adds another 100,000 from Polish Upper Silesia. Other Polish scholars have put the total figure as high as one million.[6]

The German urge to leave was most pronounced in the cities and towns of western Poland. Civil servants, including teachers and pastors, were usually among the first to depart, followed by German professionals for whom the state and its employees historically had provided much of the clientele. Lawyers trained to practice under Prussian law were virtually forced to relocate. German merchants, often without proficiency in Polish and already under pressure from a rapidly developing and (thanks to Prussian school policy) bilingual Polish merchant class, also left in large numbers. Next came their employees when their enterprises came under Polish ownership, as was normally the case. Industrial workers, especially the less skilled among them, anticipating diminished social protection, weaker labor unions, and low-wage eastern Polish competition, also frequently left without much hesitation. Skilled German artisans and merchants with something unique to offer, on the other hand, often stayed and prospered, even with a mainly Polish clientele. But the bulk of the German urban population of Pomorze and Poznania moved to Germany; by 1926 it had declined by a stunning 85 percent.[7]

The exodus of Germans also included the Jews of western Poland, in part because they identified with German nationality but also because of persistent reports of mistreatment of Jews elsewhere in Poland. As a result of the steady emigration of Jews from this region during the nineteen-century, the Jewish population of Poznania, Pomorze, and Upper Silesia was now quite small; there were not more than 30,000 Jews in the ceded territories in 1918, and so they did not constitute a very large part of the German exodus. But their numbers continued to decline, and by 1931 only 7,200 remained in Poznania and 3,400 in Pomorze. This was in sharp contrast to the rest of Poland, where Jews made up 12-15 percent of the population of most wojewodships, and most cities and towns had Jewish populations ranging from 30 to 60 percent. At the time of the 1921 Polish census, 74 percent of those who were Jewish by religion also claimed Jewish nationality; 80 percent declared their native language to be Yiddish, and another 8 percent—doubtless those most affected by the Zionist movement—claimed Hebrew. In Prussian Poland, by contrast,

Jews were normally such by religion only and gave German as their nationality and native language.[8]

Reasons for the Exodus

The main source of controversy concerning the postwar exodus of Germans from Poland's new western provinces is not its scope but rather its causes. Specifically, to what extent was it natural and voluntary? To what extent was it a result of purposeful Polish pressure of one kind or another? There were certainly many good and obvious reasons why Germans, however long they had lived in this region, might now want to move to the Reich without waiting to see how they would be treated in Poland. Most fundamentally, given their deep-seated national feelings, many were simply unprepared to consider living in an alien country, whatever the conditions of life there. Many had also become accustomed to, perhaps economically dependent upon, the decades-long campaign by the Prussian state to keep the "Polish problem" in check. But even those Germans who remained aloof from this campaign were accustomed to life in a relatively stable and prosperous society where they were the dominant national group, a situation that was bound to change. A significant minority were employees of a state that promised them alternative employment elsewhere in the Reich, oblivious to the impact this policy would have on other Germans in the ceded areas. As a result, only those civil servants with especially strong ties to the region stayed; the rest were among the first to leave. Because they were a significant part of what passed for a German "intelligentsia" in Prussian Poland, their departure only encouraged other Germans to follow their example. According to a "stab in the back" theory constructed by Cleinow, the German government's facilitation of civil service transfers was primarily responsible for the loss of the Prussian East.[9]

The departure of most schoolteachers was especially unsettling. Of approximately 9,000 German teachers in the two provinces in 1918, about 8,000 left during the next few years, encouraged by promises of alternative jobs in the Reich and by the prospect of having to learn Polish if they wished to continue working in western Poland. One Prussian government study of the problems of public schools in the ceded areas discussed teachers mainly in terms of how long they would be "forced" to stay there before being permitted to leave; it was assumed that they would want to do so. By 1921, however, when 35 percent of the teaching positions in German schools in Poland were vacant, the focus had shifted to means of encouraging German teachers to remain at their posts. One teacher in Polish Upper Silesia agreed to stay only if given a one-third salary supplement, a guarantee of his personal property, and the right to future employment in the Reich should things not work out in Poland—and the Prussian Education Ministry felt obliged to meet such demands.[10]

Many Germans were also motivated by fears that in a Polish state the level of legal and personal security to which they were accustomed would drop. They worried that they would suffer popular violence or increased criminality under a government less inclined to protect them; that they might be subject to reprisals for the often heavy-handed Prussian suppression of Polish national aspirations during previous decades; that perhaps some new Polish equivalent of the Settlement Commission would seek to dispossess them. In the meantime, any family separated by the new frontier could reunite itself only by going to Germany, for Poland rarely permitted German immigration.

Language was another obvious factor in the exodus. Although the population of Prussian Poland had always been ethnically mixed, only Poles had been required by the schools to become bilingual. Few Germans had seen any reason to learn Polish, so they were in a difficult position when this difficult tongue suddenly became the sole official language. Within six months after the formal Polish takeover, officials stopped replying to oral or written submissions in German, and letters with German titles or place names were no longer delivered. In some predominantly Polish areas, Germans reported being shunned by Polish neighbors, and at least one *starost* (subprefect) told his subordinates that it was beneath their dignity to socialize in German homes. This kind of linquistic and social isolation was doubtless another reason for some Germans to leave.[11]

While some of these fears proved unfounded or exaggerated, they prompted many Germans to sell their property hastily and at very low prices, which were paid, moreover, in rapidly devaluing currency. The treatment of Germans during the Poznanian insurrection, continued reports of popular violence against minorities elsewhere in Poland, and Poland's inability to keep the Red Army from penetrating all the way to Pomorze in 1920 all seemed to lend substance to such fears. There probably was less personal security for many Germans under the new regime; whether this was a result of purposeful, nationalist actions or a function of ordinary criminality and turbulent social conditions was not always clear. It was usually played up as the former by the German government and press, which may have served German foreign policy interests but only added to the fears and insecurity of those still debating whether to stick it out in Poland.[12]

The Russo-Polish War of 1920-21 also contributed to the departure of many Germans from western Poland. Early Polish reverses led some Germans to fear that they might wind up under a regime worse even than the Polish. Just a few months after taking control of its new western provinces, Poland was compelled to call on them for conscripts to help the nation out of a crisis that was largely of its government's own making. Some Germans supported their new state, if only as the lesser of two evils. Others made no secret of their delight with the early Polish defeats; German intelligence reports described them as openly happy with Russian victories and, later, "depressed by the successes of the Poles." The overwhelmingly German "Free City of Danzig," whose foreign affairs had been entrusted to Poland, nonetheless declared its neutrality in this conflict; dockworkers in what served as Poland's principal port refused to handle western supplies destined for beleaguered Polish forces. Germany too banned the transport of military aid for Poland through the Kiel Canal and did other things to indicate its "tilt" toward Soviet Russia.[13]

Some Red Army units penetrated as far as the eastern counties of Pomorze, Działdowo/Soldau and Brodnica/Strasburg. Although there was little sympathy for Communism here, not a few Germans greeted the Russians as liberators from Polish rule; some even brought out their old German flags. In Działdowo, a majority-German East Prussian town awarded to Poland merely because of its importance as a railway junction, Red Army units were reportedly showered with flowers by the populace on September 3, 1920. One woman recalls in a recent memoir "how happy one was when Poland at first had to deal with defeat." Another witness, the local pastor, conceded that many Germans made what later turned out to be a "big mistake, . . . not only not responding to the Polish call to arms but usually even joyously greeting the enemy."[14]

Polish authorities responded to such evidence of disloyalty by imprisoning German leaders and war veterans. Kurt Graebe and Eugen Naumann, chief spokesmen for the minority in Promorze and Poznania respectively, were jailed for six to seven months. The Pomorze *wojewode* (governor) charged that "large auxiliaries of the 'Hakatists' [members of the *Ostmarkenverein*], our eternal enemies, sit along the border here. . . . They publicly threaten revenge. In their hearts they desire the victory of red Russia."[15] Other places witnessed violent demonstrations against the minority; in Chełmno/Culm, the *Starost* reportedly encouraged Poles, "If a German or Jew dares to say anything against the Polish state, [to] tie him up and drag him through the streets to the *starost*'s office or to the court."[16] Although the Versailles Treaty gave Germans until January 1922 to make their choice for Polish or German citizenship, many were compelled to declare right away, either for Germany (and explusion) or for Poland and induction into the Polish army. Officials clearly preferred the first choice; the threat of conscription was used to get still more Germans to leave Poland.[17]

After Polish forces stopped the Red Army in the "Miracle on the

Vistula," and it withdrew as quickly as it had arrived, Poles reoccupied these formerly German towns, bent on retaliation. In anticipation, many Germans crossed over into East Prussia, leaving only their property to be confiscated. In one such village, however, four Germans were killed in mob violence and numerous others arrested on the basis of denunciations by Polish neighbors. Mutual distrust between the two peoples in this particular part of Poland reached such levels that the *Oberpräsident* (governor) of East Prussia suggested the possibility of a formal, comprehensive exchange of minority populations.[18]

Germans who decided to stay on in western Poland also faced the almost certain prospect of reduced material circumstances in a country that was considerably poorer than the one they were used to. Even though Prussia's Polish provinces had been among the poorest parts of Germany, they were economically the most advanced parts of Poland and so seemed certain to be pulled down rather than up by the rest of the country. For example, the primarily agricultural economy of Poznania and Pomorze was considerably more market-oriented, made greater use of fertilizers and machinery, and had fewer mini-farms than other parts of Poland. Only 28 percent of the farms in these two provinces comprised fewer than 5 hectares (about twelve and a half acres), as opposed to about 80 percent in Galicia. Agricultural productivity was also notably higher in the western provinces: 15-16 tons of wheat were harvested from each hectare of farmland, twice the 7.5-ton average in some eastern provinces; similar disparities showed up in rye, sugar beet, and potato production. Figures compiled in 1921 indicated that the two western provinces contained from 16 to 28 percent of the cattle, pigs, and sheep in the entire country, Poznania alone, with 7.7 percent of the country's total arable land, accounted for 11.5 percent of its grain production and 21 percent of its grain exports in one representative year (1933 to 34).[19]

There were similar disparities between Prussian and non-Prussian Poland in other categories of "material culture." School enrollment, for example, amounted to 19 percent of the population of Pomorze and Poznania in 1919 but only 11 percent of the population of Congress Poland; illiteracy was less than 5 percent in Prussian Poland but 30-35 percent in Galicia and Congress Poland and as much as 70 percent in some eastern wojewodships. These discrepancies, incidentally, were less a function of ethnicity than of the dominant partitioning power: Germans in the central and eastern wojewodships had higher illiteracy rates (25 percent in Congress Poland, 57 percent in Volhynia) than Poles in Prussian Poland. Overall, the difference in standard of living between Germany and central Poland was probably no smaller in 1919 than it is today. Then as now, with even ethnic Poles attracted to Germany for economic reasons, Germans were bound to be affected even more strongly by the considerable economic gap between their previous country and the one to which they found themselves assigned.[20]

Poland was also plagued from the start by shorter-term economic problems, including hyperinflation and shortages. At first, the Polish mark was simply declared equal to the German mark; though the market exchange rate was closer to two to one, all citizens of Poland were required to exchange their German money for Polish money at par. This amounted to a form of confiscation for Germans and Poles alike, though in practice it affected primarily Germans who wanted to leave and had to sell out. Since the ruling applied also to debts and since Germans were more often creditors than debtors, they lost in this way as well. Of course, this exchange rate also made goods in Prussian Poland relatively (if temporarily) cheap for Poles from other regions. They soon emptied the stores in Prussian Poland, which did nothing to relieve concern about the economic conditions in the rest of the country. Poland's subsequent efforts to establish itself economically were further complicated by the several armed conflicts of the republic's early years; the result was an army of 300,000 men which consumed a third of the government's revenues. As in Germany, the currency had lost almost all its value by 1923; here too, an altogether new currency (złoty) had to be introduced at the rate of one to about 1.8 million Polish marks.[21]

Poland did move quickly to establish a network of social protection on a par with most other European states: unemployment insurance, public health care, and a forty-six-hour limit on the work week. But these measures benefited mainly industrial workers, whereas the bulk of the population consisted still of small farmers, artisans, and shopkeepers, and most of these remained very poor. Concern about the consequences of coexisting in the same state with such a large population of impoverished fellow citizens extended, by the way, to Prussian Poles as well as Germans. Whatever their resentment of prewar Prussian discrimination, the attitude of many Prussian Poles to things Germans was often ambivalent. Some saw themselves, in contrast to other Poles, as Polish representatives of the sterotypical Prussian virtues of diligence, order, and efficiency. One Pomorze wojewode, Kazimierz Młodzianowski, even recommended the otherwise despised Prussian bureaucracy to his own officials as "the school of order and legality." A National Democratic senator (and priest) from Pomorze complained about the posting in his province of eastern Polish officials speaking a "Polish-Russian-Kalmyk" dialect that locals could not understand. The arrival of large numbers of eastern Poles led to complaints that they were getting all the good state jobs; there were demonstrations against the newcomers and even some shouts that things had been better under Prussian rule.[22]

Polish workers in Polish Upper Silesia also expressed resentment of eastern Poles and their depressing impact on local wages. Most Polish expressions of preference for the previous Prussian-German order were probably just an attempt to get official attention (Polish national solidarity usually revived whenever Germans were present,) but Polish Germano-philia was never entirely absent, especially in times of economic difficulty. It was a reflection of deep-seated western Polish attitudes that Polish nationalists were often helpless to extirpate.[23]

The Role of Official Coercion

Each of the factors outlined above played at least some role in the German exodus from the ceded territories; taken together, they constitute the best explanation for it. Since few of these things can be attributed to the Polish government, purposeful government policies probably played only a secondary role in the exodus. For many German observers, however, the exodus was anything but natural, voluntary, or coincidental. Rauschning, in particular, argued that it was primarily a direct or indirect result either of purposeful official measures or of popular violence implicitly sanctioned by officials.

This was also how the German government saw it. A few months after the beginning of Polish rule, Germany charged that members of the new minority were being arrested arbitrarily, held without charge under "in-humane" conditions, pressured to choose Germany long before the dead-line for doing so, or drafted into the Polish army despite continued German citizenship. Germans in Poland, according to this complaint, enjoyed "anything but the solemnly promised equality of rights; rather, they appear almost everywhere to be free game" in a conscious effort to encourage them to emigrate. According to a second German protest, "the circumstances of this exodus, which has often meant impoverishment and misery for those involved, indicate that in the majority of cases they did not leave voluntarily."[24]

Rauschning, himself a West Prussian, argued that only about 10 percent of the Germans in the ceded areas were unwilling to remain in Poland regardless of how they were treated; only these could be said to have left "voluntarily." Another 10 percent were civil servants and their families, most of them without roots in the region and (as noted above) more or less invited by their employer to relocate to Germany. Most of the remaining 80 percent, in his opinion, would have preferred to remain in their home provinces but for the systematic de-Germanization policies of the Polish government. Other historians question the 80 percent figure but agree that at least "a large proportion of the emigration was involun-tary."[25] In support of this view, Rauschning cites numerous forms of official discrimination and legal chicanery as well as outbreaks of popular violence. Clearly, the departure of so many Germans was not unwelcome to official Poland, which did nothing to discourage German emigration and quite a lot to encourage it. The *starost* in Działdowo was quite explicit: he was not going to try to stop Germans from leaving and positively wanted Jews to go.[26]

Popular manifestations of hostility to Germans, far from uncommon, were doubtless also a factor in the exodus. For example, about 6,000 people turned out for an anti-German demonstration in Bydgoszcz (formerly Bromberg) in February 1921. It was followed by attacks on German-language signs, the town's only German newspaper, and German businesses—including a restaurant opposite the police station, from which no one attempted to intervene. When elements of the same mob subsequently attacked Polish authorities, however, troops were called in to suppress it, and official statements referred to a "Communist" rather than merely an anti-German mob. In the pseudonymous Upper Silesian town studied by Józef Chałasiński, March 22, 1922, was designated "payday": Germans (and Polish "renegades") were to be "paid back" for past transgressions against the Polish national cause by being made to join in nationalist cheers and kiss the Polish flag.[27]

The most serious outbreak of popular violence against Germans took place in June 1921 in Ostrów/Ostrowo. Polish workers at the local railway factory forced the dismissal of German co-workers and issued public warnings to them and to other Germans and Jews to leave town. Those who did not were subjected to a week-long mob assault; members of about fifty German families were beaten and their homes and businesses ransacked while police remained passive. A rally in Poznań shortly thereafter, attended by an estimated 20,000 people, demanded the expulsion of Germans and Jews in retaliation for the alleged expulsion of Poles from Germany. Leaders of the "Ostrów pogrom" addressed this rally and urged other Poles to follow their example by chasing the Germans away rather than waiting for the government to act.

Officials refused at first to condemn the violence or reassure the German population. One official in Ostrów, when asked for protection by Germans, replied with an "eye for an eye" remark and suggestions that such violence was a legitimate response to the alleged mistreatment of Poles in Germany. "Minister for the Formerly Prussian Partition" Leon Janta-Połczyński did not condone the violence, but in a conversation with a German vice-consul he expressed reluctance to confront a crowd of aroused patriots and "could not possibly have Polish workers fired upon to protect Germans." The provincial governor did belatedly condemn mob violence because of the harm done to Poland's larger interests, but he too brought up the subject of Germany's mistreatment of Poles as a mitigating factor.[28]

These allegations of mistreatment of Poles in Germany, though exaggerated, were not altogether without factual basis. Some German unions, for example, responded to reports of mistreatment of German workers in Upper Silesia during the Polish uprisings by demanding the dismissal of Polish co-workers. The Prussian state government also temporarily withheld some of the monies paid into state social funds by workers who returned to Poland (though in light of the much greater wealth belonging to Germans moving in the other direction, these funds were soon released). In addition to the several hundred thousand Poles who lived permanently in central or western Germany, another 100,000 or so were employed there seasonally, mainly as agricultural workers. Several German state governments (Bavaria, Mecklenburg, and occasionally Prussia) tried to force both groups to return to Poland. Many who did so arrived home with more or less fanciful accounts of mistreatment at German hands, which attracted support for their demand that room be made for them in Poland at the expense of Germans still living and working there.

Such allegations were cited as pretext for the formal expulsion of some Germans from Poland; for each Polish farm worker expelled by Germany, several Germans were expelled from Poland. After one group of Poles, without jobs, money, or housing (the official reason for their expulsion), was asked to leave Germany, eighty-five German citizens—twelve Evangelical pastors among them—were ordered to leave Poznania, some with only forty-eight hours' notice. Interior Minister Władysław Kiernik acknowledged the political considerations behind this action: "These pastors were known to Polish officials because of their hostile activities against the Polish state, especially because of their spread of separatism and hate" among their parishioners.[29]

Once the connection between certain German state actions and the situation of Germans in Poland became evident, German Foreign Minister Gustav Stresemann ordered a change in state policies. He noted that "Polish counter-expulsions . . . create a feeling of insecurity among the Germans of these [ceded] areas, which strengthens the tendency toward voluntary emigration. . . . For domestic-political, economic, and financial reasons too, such a continued influx of Germans from foreign lands into Germany is undesirable. . . . A large part of these returnees lose their basis of support and become a burden on public welfare." State governments were advised, therefore, to check with the Foreign Office before expelling any more Polish workers and then to do so in a way that did not embarrass the Reich.[30]

Meanwhile, the German consul visited Ostrów in the wake of the "pogrom" and urged Germans to stay put because their departure might encourage similar nationalist tactics elsewhere. But he found that most local Germans were quite discouraged; almost all were preparing to leave for the Reich.[31] Demonstrations against Germany and Germans continued in other places, including violent actions in Leszno, Wolsztyn/ Wollstein, and Września/Wreschen. In the last case, the threat of physical harm was used to compel Germans to sign a petition calling on Germany to stop its persecution of Poles. In Grodzisk/Graetz (Nowy Tomýśl County) the *starost* himself, accompanied by troops, obliged Germans to sign such a petition. In Chojnice/Konitz and elsewhere, nationalist mobs interrupted German church services and demanded the use of Polish. Other rallies were directed more specifically at Jews or at "settlers" (that is, those living on farms created by the former Prussian Settlement Commission). In some cases, settlers were forced to agree to leave Poland within the month, without their belongings; in others, they were rounded up at night and told to leave at once.[32]

Other official actions were designed to make it more difficult for Germans to remain in Poland by undermining their economic position. Such economic advantages as the state could dispense (government contracts, import licenses, supplies of scarce raw materials) went to ethnic Poles wherever possible. Many German professionals were denied the state licenses, including teacher certification, that they needed to continue practicing in Poland. A 1921 law required that all practicing physicians be citizens of Poland, but even ethnic German citizens of Poland were usually excluded from state-sponsored public health work. There was also apparently a policy intended to diminish the number of German innkeepers: in just two counties in a single year, fifty-five Germans lost their state liquor licenses, and so the ability to operate inns. The departure of some German workers too was less than voluntary; for example, the firm of Herzfeld & Victorius in Grudziądz/Graudenz asked for Reich help in relocating its German work force on grounds that physical threats and abuse by Polish co-workers made their continued employment there impossible. At the Liegnitz-Rawicz Railway and at a chair factory in Wejherovo/ Neustadt, German workers who were dismissed after Poles refused to work alongside them responded by leaving for Germany. Other forms of economic pressure designed to encourage German departure are discussed below; overall, there is a case to be made that at least some of the exodus was due to such factors and to "Poland's practice . . . of dispossessing the German minority."[33]

Polish opinion, on the other hand, has been pretty much of one mind in its insistence that this exodus had little to do with Polish pressure, that it was overwhelming voluntary and natural. Stanisław Potocki is representative; he argues that the exodus consisted mainly of returning officials and chauvinists and had a "mostly voluntary character." He agrees with Roman Lutman that "in the history of the world there is not a second example where in the course of two years such significant numbers of an immigrant, artificially imported element returned to its proper abode." Marian Drozdowski characterizes the Germans of Poznania and Pomorze as "an immigratory group" that left "of its own free will." Jerzy Krasuski too considers the "the mass exodus of Germans from Poland in the first years of the existence of the Republic [to be] completely natural. . . . One ought rather to wonder that so many Germans decided, despite everything, to remain in Poland as part of a national minority."[34] Others suggest that the German exodus from Poland was in some sense matched by the return of Poles from Germany, except that the latter were much fewer in number. Or they contend, incorrectly, that most Germans left before the onset of Polish rule, which cannot therefore be blamed for it; Lutman, for example, alleges that two-thirds of the exodus took place before January 1920 and that most of the others exercised their right under the Versailles Treaty to claim German citizenship and so moved westward as a matter of course.[35]

About 140,000 Germans in the ceded territories did choose German citizenship, and most of these had left Poland by 1924. Although that choice may have presupposed a desire to live in Germany, it was not always made under entirely free conditions. As noted above, a quick decision was sometimes the only way for young males to avoid conscription into the war with Russia. For others who were able to wait until the last minute, the decision was formally voluntary but reached only after concluding that they could not continue living in Poland under the new conditions. Most understood that their choice also meant a move to Germany, but some believed that they could retain German citizenship while living as resident aliens in what was now Poland; about 26,000 such people remained in the ceded areas of Poland in 1924. Once they learned that their choice required them to leave Poland, many tried to take it back, but Polish officials were seldom willing to entertain such requests. In this way and others, official Poland made it clear that it would not tolerate any more Germans in its western provinces than required by the Versailles Treaty. Most remaining German citizens were subsequently expelled from Poland, following an extended international controversy (discussed in the following chapter).[36]

Another common theme in many Polish accounts of the exodus is the argument that most Germans in Prussian Poland were not at home there in the first place; they were basically a transient element or recent transplants brought in as part of the Prussian campaign to Germanize the region. A contemporary tract by Czesław Andrezejewski exemplifies this attitude. Most Germans in Prussian Poland, he writes, were dependent upon the Prussian state: officials, members of the army, professionals or bank employees dependent upon state business, or settlers brought in by the Prussian Settlement Commission. "The German in Polish regions is only rarely of long residence, an element rooted in the soil of his fathers"; most are "aliens and intruders," artificially maintained by the state, "spongers strange to the land, transplanted to Poland from a distant homeland."[37] Kazimiera Jeżowa, in her point-by-point rebuttal of Rauschning, writes scornfully of the departed Germans as people who had never had any real feelings for the Polish lands, who had come only for the money and quick profits. She too alleges that 70 percent of them left before the Polish takeover, "tens of thousands of parasites and super- fluous characters, who got away as soon as they could; [perhaps] their bad consciences drove all these people away."[38]

This view permeates interwar Polish scholarship and has not disap- peared entirely even from more recent accounts. In fact, however, most Germans in Prussian Poland were there as a result of migration antedating the eighteenth-century partitions; they were there primarily because of Polish, not Prussian, state policies. Some students of this problem con- tend even that the percentage of Germans in Poznania was as high in 1793, when Prussian rule began, as in 1910; it clearly declined under Prussian rule from the 40 percent figure recorded for the 1860s.[39]

Related to the view of the German minority in western Poland as a recent development is the suggestion that it had developed mainly by displacing Poles or consisted primarily of state employees. Karol Grün- berg refers to the minority as mostly "bourgeois and bureaucrats," part of what Jerzy Tomaszewski terms the "repressive network" of officials, teachers, and state-subsidized landowners. Władysław Kulski, by includ- ing all military personnel, estimates the number of German civil servants in Prussian Poland at an incredible 378,000. Combining this figure with the number who chose German citizenship, he arrives at a figure reason- ably close to the number of Germans who left and so declares the great exodus almost completely voluntary.[40] But there were many Poles in both the army and the lower ranks of the civil service, and in any case, official figures for the number of state employees are much lower: 92,376 German and 10,781 Polish civil servants in Poznania and West Prussia before the war, and a military population, some of which was Polish, of 47,324. According to Rauschning, civil servants "from away" and their families accounted for only about 100,000 persons, or 10 percent of the German population of Prussian Poland. Others were natives of these provinces (and some natives were posted to other places in Germany). Thus one cannot simply subtract the number of German state employees from the German population itself and classify them all as outsiders whose real home was somewhere else and who were therefore bound to leave. Some state employees did stay on and choose Polish citizenship; if they learned Polish fast enough, they were theoretically eligible to join the Polish civil service, though it soon turned out that in practice this option was effectively closed to them.[41]

Even those historians who emphasize the voluntary nature of the exodus recognize that Germans were subject to some official chicanery and some popular pressure. Jerzy Krasuski comments on "an atmosphere unfavorable for the Germans" and acknowledges that "official and unofficial pressure was exerted upon them to leave for the Reich." Newly triumphant Poles often had little patience, for example, with Germans who failed to appreciate the full extent of the changed situation. When a mainly German school committee in Wąbrzeźno/Briesen tried to proceed with business as usual following the Polish takeover, it was informed that its meetings now constituted an "illegal assembly" unless approved by state officials.[42] Of course, adds Krasuski, this sort of thing was only to be expected after decades of Prussian discrimination; it does not alter the fact that the overriding reason so many Germans left was the inability to overcome traditional nationalist attitudes or behave in a way that would overcome legitimate Polish distrust. For most who left, becoming good citizens of Poland simply represented too great a challenge. Przemysław Hauser corrects the contention that most Germans left before the beginning of formal Polish rule—departures surged above all after January 1920—but concludes that "unwillingness to accommodate themselves to the changed conditions was the basic reason for the German exodus."[43]

The view that most of that exodus was essentially voluntary is not limited to Polish observers. Some German contemporaries, taking exception to Rauschning's interpretation, also argue that many Germans had no pressing reasons to leave Poland, before or after the formal Polish takeover. A pastor complained to the Foreign Office in 1920 that "most Germans are leaving their old homeland completely senselessly and without plans."[44] After visiting western Poland in 1923, a German official reported that Bydogszcz and other majority-German towns were being "abandoned" by their commercial populations, mostly without good reason. Those who remained seemed to be doing all right economically; while most teachers, lawyers, and other professionals had left, skilled German workers, artisans, and salaried employees were valued by their employers, even where these were Polish. "Economically," in the words of his report, "discrimination against German businesses and artisans is not taking place." But for the inability or unwillingnes to adapt to the new conditions, he concluded, most Germans could probably have stayed on.[45]

Jeżowa's work cites numerous other comments by Germans who were more critical of their own countrymen than of Polish officials. One speaks of "tens of thousands leaving the land of the eastern marches as in flight, abandoning their possessions, dumping their businesses and belongings. . . . Hundreds of thousands . . . [are] running away senselessly and headlong."[46] Another notes that "all too often Poznanian Germans lacked self-reliance; they were used to being always guided by the paternal hand of the government and to let it care for them. . . . Though many thousands of Germans were doubtless forced to emigrate against their will after 1918, it was primarily the rootless element which emigrated voluntarily."[47] In the opinion of a third observer, writing in 1925, 80 percent of the emigrants from western Poland had left voluntarily: "In addition, very many of those who were born in the ceded area or were resident there for years have shown by their option for Germany that they were not very bound to this area emotionally." Even Stresemann, while publicly protesting Polish pressure on Germans to emigrate, conceded privately that "many are dumping their property at any price without having to do so."[48]

To be sure, Germans who wanted above all to continue living in a German nation-state did not therefore lack attachment to home provinces now under foreign rule. But even some German observers believed that "the German population showed a regrettable lack of personal steadfastness; the great mass of Germans in the East lacked firm ties to and feelings for the land."[49] Otto Heike believes that those who stayed behind deserve some recognition for "courageous perseverance, . . . [but] most of the departed Germans cannot be spared the charge of insufficient steadfastness." Though some faced pressures to leave, "for most there was no sufficient reason to abandon one's homeland"; it was mainly a "collapse of spiritual resistance," complemented by the Reich's readiness to lend support and provide compensation, which caused the mass exodus.[50] Gotthold Rhode does not minimize Polish efforts to reduce German numbers, but he too reaches much the same conclusion: most members of the new minority, the young still more than their elders, simply did not believe they could live in a Polish state.[51]

Perhaps a glance at similar circumstances elsewhere during the twentieth century can shed some light on this exodus. For example, without equating Poles and Arabs, the departure of a comparable number of French from Algeria after that country became independent in 1962 suggests that the behavior of Germans in the lands ceded to Poland after World War I was not so exceptional. Krasuski may be right to argue that the focus should be not on why so many Germans left but on why so many stayed and tried to get along under drastically changed conditions.

Efforts to Stem the Exodus

Whatever the reasons, the exodus, was a most unwelcome development for the German government. It could only undermine the hope of keeping German claims to the region alive. It also undermined domestic economic stability, for Germany was in no condition just then to absorb such an influx of people. The German government called on Germans in the ceded territories, therefore, to elect Polish citizenship and remain in Poland. When so many ignored this injunction, it began to look for ways to stem the flow, for example, by promising to help Germans maintain their previous economic status in Poland. Alternatively, if Germany could not make it easier for Germans to live in Poland, its government could at least make it more difficult for them to come to Germany. Official "Guidelines for the Administration of Welfare for Refugees from the Ceded Frontier Districts of Prussia" (1920) ordered "all Germans in the . . . areas to be ceded . . . to stay in their previous homeland, even when it is given to a foreign state." The Foreign Office wanted to warn Polish Germans about the shortage of jobs and housing in Germany. The German consul in Toruń/Thorn proposed that "serious barriers" be erected especially to draft-age German males in order to persuade them to stay, serve in the Polish army, and so retain Polish citizenship. Others proposed that the Reich simply stop admitting "refugees" of any kind from western Poland.[52]

After most of its former officials and teachers had left Poland, the Prussian state government called on the remainder to stay put. Those who were willing to do so were given until 1929 to reclaim German citizenship and be taken back into the Prussian civil service without penalty or loss of seniority. This provision was further sweetened in 1921 when former teachers were offered a return to Prussian service at any time in the future; their pensions would be paid up and all moving expenses covered as well. The United Evangelical Church also urged its pastors to stay in Poland "so long as it is in any way possible, . . . even if they are compelled to make some personal sacrifice. We know how great this sacrifice is in some cases." A 1921 circular warned that those who left without compelling reasons could count on no special consideration in Germany.[53] One official statement warned that "whoever wants to sell his estate voluntarily to a Pole and then leave Poland, without being forced to do so through liquidation or other reasons, will normally receive neither a 'certificate of displacement' nor an entry permit to Germany from German consulates." Minority leaders were occassionally asked to certify that someone had indeed been required to pull out before he could count on receiving refugee compensation, but this policy was not implemented in any systematic manner.[54]

German minority leaders, interested naturally in keeping their group together, contended that Reich officials were undermining their efforts by being so concerned to help German emigrants from Poland. They thought that it should be more difficult for Polish Germans to acquire Reich citizenship or receive compensation for financial losses deriving from their relocation. Carl Georg Bruns, principal representative of the minority in Berlin, insisted that most Germans had no good reasons to leave Poland: "Every bank employee, every artisan, every physician, every farm worker is badly needed and will make a good living." He resented even the efforts of refugee organizations to provide help with state relief, temporary refuge, job referrals, and moving expenses; such assistance facilitated the decision to move to Germany, whereas it was in the interest of both the Reich and the minority for this decision to be made more difficult.[55] Meanwhile, German officials began to devise various positive inducements to get Germans to stay in Poland (discussed in Chapter 5).

Results of the Exodus

The German population in western Poland stabilized somewhat after 1926, though outmigration continued at the rate of several thousand per year until 1939. The great exodus, however, not only significantly reduced German numbers; it also drastically altered their social and demographic profile compared with prewar conditions. For example, before the war, 44 percent of the German population of Poznania and 38 percent in West Prussia lived in urban communities and pursued typically urban occupations. With the exception of Poznań, the principal cities of Poznania and Pomorze (including Bydgoszcz, Grudziądz, Toruń, Inowrocław, and Leszno) had been majority German; now Germans were only a small minority in these places. But while the German urban population declined by 85 percent between 1918 and 1926, the German rural population declined by "only" 55 percent. The best explanation for this differential is that farmland was more immune to official pressure than any other economic base, so farmers experienced less economic pressure to emigrate than other Germans. The result was that most of the remaining German population now lived in rural communities and earned its living from agriculture. Most of these rural Germans (61 percent in Pomorze) lived in places where they were the local majority, at least to begin with, though few districts anywhere in the two provinces were entirely without a German presence.[56] The postwar exodus of Germans, especially the unequal participation in it of urban and rural Germans, thus made the social and occupational structure of Germans in western Poland less urban/industrial/commercial and so less characteristically "German." Before the war, Germans in Poznania and Pomorze were "overrepresented" in the professional, civil servant, merchant, and artisan categories (as these terms were used by official census-takers). But these were the groups whose socioeconomic situation was most threatened by the change in sovereignty and who left for Germany in the largest numbers. As a result, the percentage of Germans engaged in "industry" fell by 25 percent, in trade/transportation by about 50 percent, and in the free professions or the civil service by 75 percent. Now Germans were seriously "underrepresented" in all these fields. Of the surviving German urban population, nearly half consisted of independent producers (artisans or owners of small businesses); white-collar workers made up only a small (8 percent) share; and most of the remainder fell into the "worker" category.[57]

The 1921 Polish census revealed that already 64 percent of the "Protestants" in Poland—a category that coincided roughly with "Germans"—now worked in agriculture. In Poznania and Pomorze, the figure was higher still and still growing: in 1926, 72 percent of the Germans there were engaged in farming, 13 percent classified as "industrial," and only 5 percent still worked in trade or transportation. The remaining 10 percent consisted of pensioners and members of such professions (clergy, physicians, teachers) as were needed to minister to a mainly rural population. By contrast, in Poland as a whole, one of Europe's less industrialized countries, only 58 percent of the population earned its living from agriculture, and the equivalent figure for Germany was only about 21 percent. As one would expect from this occupational structure, most Germans in Poland (80 percent) lived in the countryside, as opposed to 72 percent for the Polish population as a whole and only 33 percent for the German Reich. Similarly, the percentage of Germans in western Poland engaged in industry or crafts (13 percent) was not only far below the Reich figure of 41 percent but also below the figure for Poland as a whole.[58]

The relative immunity of German farmers to the urge to emigrate also meant that Germans remained a significant part of the rural population of western Poland even as overall German numbers declined. The German share of Poznania's population fell to less than 10 percent during the interwar period, yet Germans still made up 22 percent of that province's full-time, "independent" farmers. This disparity was even more pronounced in some individual counties: in Nowy Tomyśl/Neutomischel, Germans were 19 percent of the population but 53 percent of the farmers; in Wągrowiec/Wongrowitz, 13 percent and 40 percent respectively; and in Grudziądz county, 18 percent and 41 percent. The great majority (85 percent) of German farmers were full-time, independent producers, more

likely than Poles to have larger, "middle-class" holdings; 54 percent
owned at least twenty-five acres. By contrast, only 55 percent of Polish
farmers were full-time and and independent, and only 43 percent had
farms of twenty-five acres or more. Instead, Poles dominated the categories of part-time farmer and farm worker; only 5 percent of the province's
farm workers were German.[59]

Most of the German-owned land in these two provinces belonged to
this predominantly middle-class farming population, but a significant
proportion made up some nine hundred estates of 250 or more acres
apiece; in other words, Germans were also "overrepresented" among
owners of large estates in western Poland. In 1921 they owned 44 percent
of the large-estate land in Pomorze and 36 percent in Poznania. In the
following years, German large-estate holdings fell significantly (even
before the onset of the Polish land-reform program, which, as shown
below, took a large part of the remainder). Overall, in 1914 Germans
owned about 1,565,000 hectares of land in those parts of Poznania and
West Prussia subsequently ceded to Poland; by 1926, this figure had
declined by roughly one-third, to about 1,065,000 hectares).[60]

As Polish nationalists were quick to note, these holdings still constituted about 28 percent of the privately owned land in the two provinces, much higher than the German share of the general population.
They tended to attribute the continuing disparity to the Prussian regime,
specifically to the efforts of its Settlement Commission (established in
1886). Germans argued that this agency had enjoyed only limited success
in altering the ratio of German to Polish farmland in Prussian Poland and
had brought disappointingly few German farmers into the area. But in the
course of its thirty-two-year existence, the Settlement Commission did
buy up, at one time or another, about 8 percent of the total land in
Poznania and West Prussia. In Poznania, as many as one-quarter of that
province's medium-sized German farms were in villages plotted by the
Settlement Commission (and forming most of the isolated majority-
German communities shown on this book's ethnographic map, page 22).
But fewer than half of the "settlers" themselves remained in Poland in the
mid-1920s. The Settlement Commission doubtless contributed to the
preponderance of medium-sized holdings among the German farming
population of western Poland; it also stipulated that these were subsequently not to be divided up among heirs (the practice chiefly responsible
for the small average farm size elsewhere in Poland). On the other hand,
70 percent of the land the Settlement Commission purchased was taken
from German owners. When one considers in addition the rival Polish
parceling efforts, which also got much of their land from German owners,
it turns out that the prewar land policies of the Prussian regime had only a
marginal impact on the balance of land ownership between the two

nationalities. Indeed, Poles actually owned more land in these two provinces in 1918 than they had in 1886.[61]

The socioeconomic profile of the German minority in Polish Upper Silesia was quite different from that described above. To begin with, whereas 85 percent of Germans in Pomorze and Poznania were Protestant, 85 percent of the Germans in Silesia province (an amalgam of Polish Upper Silesia and Poland's share of Austrian Silesia) were Catholic. Moreover, 55 percent of them earned their living in industry and mining and only a small number in agriculture. At the beginning of Polish rule, Germans accounted for 60 percent of the industrial workers and roughly 90 percent of the white-collar employees in this province. According to a 1927 survey, they still constituted about 75 percent of the managers, engineers, and technical workers, though their share of the "real" working class had declined to about 30 percent. Even in the 1930s, more than half the private industrial capital in Polish Silesia belonged either to local Germans or to Reich citizens.[62] But as the following chapters make clear, neither industrial properties nor jobs in the Silesian industrial workplace were as resistant to politically motivated assault as the German-owned farms in Poznania and Pomorze.

Meanwhile, the point needs to be emphasized that as a result of the Great Exodus the German minority during most of the interwar years in western Poland was really only a minority of a minority. It constituted only the rump, and a significantly skewed rump, of the much larger German population that had lived in this area until 1918. At the time, a rational-minded observer might have held out hope that one result of the exodus would be improved relations between the remaining minority and the Polish government, that such a drastically reduced German presence might make the minority less of a threat in Polish eyes and so less of a problem. A Poland that would have had to feel menaced by a 35 percent German minority along its vital and contested western frontier might be less concerned about the 10 percent that survived to 1926. This lower level of concern might encourage a more tolerant approach toward the minority, for some of the economic consequences of the German exodus were negative from Poland's perspective. Perhaps Polish leaders would even find reasons to try to hold on to the remaining Germans.

As is usually the case in national conflicts, however, such rationalistic assumptions would have failed to anticipate the actual course of events. Germany's adamant refusal to accept the new frontier with Poland made even a small German minority seem intolerable to many Poles. Moreover, the relatively prosperous German agricultural population of Poznania and Pomorze and the prominent role of German capital, management, and skilled labor in Upper Silesian industry aroused the continued envy and suspicion of Poles and invited nationalist attack. For these and other reasons, official Poland soon embarked on a course designed to bring about a still more thorough de-Germanization of western Poland than had been achieved already by the quasi-voluntary postwar exodus.

3

Coming to Terms

The most important decision facing those Germans who remained in Poznania and Pomorze was whether they should accept their place in Poland (and Poland itself) as permanent or see themselves primarily as the Reich's lost children, waiting to be reclaimed. In the early years at least, most seemed to hold the latter view. Few saw anything positive in Polish rule or were persuaded by the arguments that made them subject to it. The lack of direct popular input into the drawing of the new frontier (on the wrong side of which they found themselves) was just one reason for seeing themselves as victims of a fundamental injustice. Though the area ceded to Poland by the Versailles Treaty was evidently (unlike Upper Silesia) majority-Polish in terms of national consciousness as well as native language, many Polish Germans continued to speculate about how their situation might yet be reversed by plebiscite or some other means. Most of them remained aloof from events of a Polish patriotic character, including the annual ceremonies marking Polish independence. In short, pragmatic acceptance of the new situation, not to mention sincere resignation to it, proved difficult for many Polish Germans, at least at first.

The Political Organization of the Minority

The national councils of 1918-19, the first German political organizations to appear in Poznania and Pomorze following the armistice, were concerned primarily to prevent the loss of these lands in the first place. Once this effort had failed, and as those most categorically opposed to Polish rule joined the exodus to Germany, the remaining minority proceeded to organize itself as such. One such effort was the Zentralarbeitsgemein-schaft der politischen Parteien (Central Coordinating Committee of the Political Parties), basically an extension of the parties of the Weimar Coalition. Its chairman was a Social Democrat, and most of its executive board was drawn from the SPD, Center, and Democratic parties. But though the

Zentralarbeitsgemeinschaft enjoyed the support of the new German government, much of the traditionally conservative German population of Poznania and Pomorze declined to fall in line behind a "red-black banner" (Graebe's phrase). Their sympathies were closer to the newly organized conservative parties, the Nationalists (DNVP) and the Populists (DVP), and so they formed rival organizations.

In Poznania, most of the German national councils united in a single *Deutscher Volksrat* under the leadership of the former *Landrat*, Eugen Naumann (1874-1939), who spent the first part of 1919 imprisoned by Polish insurgents at Szczypiorno. In West Prussia and the Netze region of Poznania, German national councils formed the Landesvereinigung des deutschen Volkstums in Polen (Provincial Union of Germans in Poland), first under Cleinow's direction and then, after his departure for the Reich, under Kurt Graebe (1873-1953), a career army officer until the drastic reduction of the German army persuaded him to remain in his now-Polish home province. In August 1919 the Poznanian and West Prussian groups merged under the *Landesvereinigung* name, with headquarters in Bromberg/Bydgoszcz. Naumann became chairman, and Graebe served as his deputy; other prominent figures included the estate owners Erwin Hasbach and Erik von Witzleben and Friedrich Heidelck, a teacher.[1]

In May 1920, when elections were held to add delegates from Poznania and Pomorze to Poland's constituent Sejm, the two German factions competed against each other. The result was a clear victory for the Landesvereinigung (82 percent) over the Zentralarbeitsgemeinschaft (18 percent). The traditional conservatism of most Germans in these provinces was evidently reinforced by resentment against the perceived failure of the Weimar Coalition to protect their interests. Despite the cool relations between the Landesvereinigung and itself, the Berlin government acknowledged the election results and told the Zentralarbeitsgemeinschaft to join forces with its more popular rival in order to maintain a united German front. When it hesitated to do so, the Foreign Office forced its hand by cutting off financial support. In December 1920, at a meeting arranged by Reich officials, the Zentralarbeitsgemeinschaft capitulated and agreed to merge with the Landesvereinigung.[2]

This led some months later to yet another organization, the Deutschtumsbund zur Wahrung der Minderheitenrechte (German League for the Protection of Minority Rights, or DB), supposedly an amalgam of the two but clearly dominated by the more conservative Landesvereinigung; no one from the Zentralarbeitsgemeinschaft (or from the parties of the Weimar Coalition) had an important role in it. Naumann became president; Graebe served as executive director and became the most prominent leader of the minority during the next thirteen years. He was politically close to the DVP and its leader, Gustav Stresemann; his period of greatest influence coincided with Stresemann's direction of German foreign policy. Carl Georg Bruns, previously "legal adviser" to the national councils and their liaison with the Berlin government, took over the same functions for the DB. The DB also formed auxiliary organizations to deal with school, welfare, and cultural affairs. The minority's principal women's, agricultural, artisan, trade/industry, teacher, and student organizations were also either established by the DB or soon made subordinate to it. The DB published its own newspaper, *Deutsche Nachrichten*, though the other influential German-language newspapers, specifically *Deutsche Rundschau* in Bydgoszcz and *Posener Tageblatt* in Poznań, also functioned as quasi-official voices of this organization. Among its eight regional subdivisions, one was in Polish Upper Silesia and three others in central and eastern Poland, but it remained essentially an organization of Germans in Poznania and Pomorze. A separate "League of Germans in Poland," also organized with Reich encouragement and financial support, did aspire to represent Germans throughout Poland, except that Polish government refused to recognize a nationwide organization of Germans. Therefore, the DB and other regional organizations remained most important.[3]

The DB saw itself as a "united front" substitute for regular political parties, which no longer played an important role in the minority's affairs. Only the Social Democrats remained aloof; reorganized as the "German Social-Democratic Party," they also remained outside the common German front at election time. But German socialists had only a small following in western Poland, and so their separate path detracted little from the vote for the German lists.[4]

In Silesia province, the minority's political organization was less tidy. Representatives of the principal liberal and conservative parties merged to become the Deutsche Partei (DP), but the Catholic Center was the traditionally dominant party here, and both Center and Social Democrats retained their separate identities. The Center reorganized as the Katholische Volkspartei (KVP) until 1927 and thereafter as the Deutschkatholische Volkspartei (DKVP). Its first chairman was Thomas Szczeponik, who was succeeded after his death in 1927 by Eduard Pant. Pant (1887-1938), an Austrian by birth, was a Christian-Social teacher in Austrian Silesia until 1918; his fate was linked to the ceded areas of Prussia when Austrian Silesia was combined with Polish Upper Silesia to form the Polish province of Silesia. Pant also headed the 25,000-member "Association of German Catholics in Poland" (VdK), exercised considerable influence over the largest German newspaper in Poland (*Oberschlesischer Kurier*), and became in general the most significant German-Catholic personality in interwar Poland.[5]

German socialists in Silesia also remained outside the DP. At first, they formed another "German Social-Democratic Party"; in 1923, they joined their counterparts in Poznania and Pomorze as the "German Social-Democratic Party in Poland" (DSP), which then merged in 1925 with kindred organizations in central Poland to form the "German Social-Democratic Labor Party" (DSAP). On most issues of importance to the minority, German socialists generally shared the views of other Germans. Perhaps they were more forthright in their acceptance of the new frontiers or in their willingness to depart from the nationalist attitudes of the past; the DSAP was the only group within the minority that agreed to forgo appeals of its grievances to international bodies as proof of its loyalty to Poland. It also tried to make common cause with Polish socialists; some even proposed that the DSAP merge formally into the "Polish Socialist Party" (PPS). In return, the PPS provided some moral support and backed the concept of "cultural autonomy" for national minorities. But closer cooperation between German and Polish socialists usually foundered on the deep-seated nationalism of the rank and file, especially in the PPS. In any case, the PPS had little direct influence over official policy and so could not provide much more than comforting words for German comrades.[6] German labor unions in western Poland—most members were in Silesia—also remained divided along the lines outlined above. In 1925 a "Free Union of Poland," associated with the DSAP, had 13,200 members; another 8,100 were in unions of the Hirsch-Duncker type, politically closer to the DP; "Christian" unions affiliated with the DKVP had about 7,200 members.[7]

While preserving their separate identities, the DP and DKVP generally cooperated on matters of interest to the minority as a whole; they ran a single slate at election time, the *Deutsche Wahlgemeinschaft* (German Electeral Community), and formed a single *Deutscher Blok* in the provincial legislature.[8] The DSAP ran separate campaigns, and two of the eleven German seats in the provincial legislature belonged to that party. The DP and DKVP also supported a new Deutscher Volksverband (later Volksbund) für Polnisch-Schlesien, (German National League For Polish Silesia) created at the behest of the German government to present a united German front on cultural and economic issues. The Volksbund was essentially the Silesian equivalent of the Deutschtumsbund (DB) in Poznania and Pomorze. Its director was Otto Ulitz (1885-1972), a former police official from southern Germany and the most prominent German leader in Polish Silesia throughout the interwar period. The Volksbund soon attracted a membership of more than 35,000 and, like the DB, ran numerous auxiliaries, including the provincial "German School Association," a "Culture League," and an "Economic League."[9]

The Polish Political Context

None of these several German organizations, and few representatives of Poland's other minorities, had much say in determining the constitutional structure under which they were to live. To some extent this was because most of the minorities, which later composed a third of Poland's population, were not yet under Polish rule in 1919 when the Polish constituent assembly convened. But even those minority populations already present in "core" Poland, including a large Jewish and a smaller but not insignificant German population in central Poland, had minimal representation and no discernible influence on the constitutional document that was ratified in March 1921.

Still, this constitution did contain many of the same promises as the Minorities Protection Treaty; moreover, they represented a voluntary affirmation of minority rights by Poland itself rather than obligations imposed by others. For example, every citizen of Poland was guaranteed "the right to preserve his nationality and to cultivate his language and national characteristics . . . by means of autonomous minority organizations of public-legal status" (Article 109); non-Poles were to have the same right as Poles "to establish at their own expense, to control, and to administer charitable, religious, and social institutions and schools and other educational institutions" (Article 110); they were also guaranteed the free practice of their religion (Article 111).

But the Polish republic, like its French model, was a highly centralized state, and this fact alone ran counter to the interests of the minorities, who were majorities in some parts of the country. The federal model favored by Piłsudski and others, in part because they thought it would make Poland more attractive to the neighboring peoples they hoped to incorporate, was never seriously considered. Silesia was the only province with any formal autonomy, a result of promises made during the plebiscite campaign. Interwar Poland's essential problem may have been that the country wound up between two stools: it failed to achieve the dimensions of the large federal state envisioned by Piłsudski, but it did manage by 1921 to become too large and too ethnically diverse to fit easily into the model of the centralized nation-state.

Also in keeping with the French model, Poland's executive, represented by the office of president, was quite weak. Government was dominated by an all-powerful bicameral parliament, consisting of the larger and more influential Sejm and the smaller Senate. (The Senate's powers were limited to the right to amend or veto Sejm legislation; its efforts, however, could be overridden by a mere 55 percent of the lower house.) Sejm and senate were both elected by proportional representation, which permitted many smaller parties, including minority parties, to win seats; thirty-one different parties were represented in the 1926 Sejm. Proportional representation also made it virtually impossible for any one party to win a majority of seats and so run the country by itself. The result was a series of multiparty coalitions that proved both difficult to assemble and short-lived.

In the first parliamentary elections under the new constitution (November 5, 1922), 38 percent of the seats went to the main parties of the right (National Democrats and Christian Democrats); two large agrarian parties, "Piast" (16 percent) and "Liberation" (11 percent), dominated the center of the political spectrum; the PPS, main party of the left and most liberal of the major parties on minority questions, won only a 9 percent share of the seats in parliament. Most disturbing to Polish nationalists, however, was the fact that an alliance of parties representing the national minorities, the Minorities Bloc, claimed 20 percent of the seats and so emerged as the second largest fraction. Of the eighty-nine seats won by the Minorities Bloc, seventeen were held by Germans, including ten from the lands in western Poland ceded by Germany.[10]

The Minorities Bloc was a logical consequence of the way the Sejm was elected; it was in the minorities' collective interest to run a single slate of candidates. The German government agreed and not only backed the Minorities Bloc financially but contributed directly to the campaigns of the other minorities as well. The Minority Bloc's 20 percent share of Sejm seats in 1922 was achieved despite a Ukrainian boycott campaign and official efforts to limit minority representation. For example, in predominantly Polish electoral districts one Sejm delegate was elected for each 40,000 people; in the mostly non-Polish eastern provinces, each Sejm delegate represented some 80,000 people. Predominantly Polish districts were also smaller; they might elect only five delegates, which meant that the Minorities Bloc needed 20 percent of the vote to claim a seat. Districts where Poles were in the minority were often larger; as many as ten seats might be at stake, which meant that a Polish party needed only 10 percent of the vote to get one. For the architect of this system, Kazimierz Lutos-ławski, this was simply a matter of common sense: those population groups with "somewhat less capacity for responsibility for the state" (that is, non-Poles) should also have proportionally less parliamentary representation.[11]

In the eyes of Polish nationalists, however, any system that resulted in a 20 percent share of Sejm seats for the Minorities Bloc had clearly failed. They became all the more convinced of this when minority representatives immediately made their presence felt by providing the center-left presidential candidate, Gabriel Narutowicz, with his margin of victory over the National Democratic candidate. The idea that Poland's first constitutional president should owe his position to non-Poles was too much for many Polish nationalists to tolerate. They boycotted Narutowicz's inauguration and disputed his legitimacy; finally, one young fanatic among them assassinated the new president within days after he took office. (The next president, Stanisław Wojciechowski, was elected by the same coalition, but was more acceptable to National Democrats.)

For the minorities, Narutowicz's assassination certainly marked an inauspicious beginning of their political lives in Poland. Nor did Poland's parliamentary leaders subsequently make any effort to include them in the life of the state. While they could not ignore altogether such a large segment of the population, Polish nationalists generally looked upon the minorities as, at best, an unavoidable inconvenience and, at worst, an affront to their perception of Poland as a nation-state. For them, Poland was the Poles' state; those who were not part of the Polish national community could not reasonably expect more than a grudging tolerance. This attitude was especially pronounced among National Democrats, whose approach to the problem implied the desirability of the departure of most Germans and Jews and the Polonization of the eastern Slav minorities. In his 1929 book, *Państwo Narodowe*, sometime Culture Minister Stanisław Grabski spelled out the National Democratic approach to the problem of minorities: sovereignty in Poland, he contended, belonged to the Polish people, not to the entire population. This implied, among other things, formal political inequality, with only ethnic Poles voting for president and Senate members.[12]

National Democrats were especially concerned to reduce the number of Germans in their own stronghold, the western provinces. Once the German population there had been reduced to a small remnant, toleration of individual Germans might be possible, but no formal or permanent political role for the German minority as such could be countenanced. Similar attitudes prevailed in most of the press, which regularly pressured the government to adopt tougher measures against the minorities in general and the Germans in particular. A representative editorial in *Kuryer Poznański*, the chief National Democratic newspaper in Poznania, warned that Germans in western Poland were "anti-Polish without exception," would never abandon thoughts of revenge, and constituted a strategic danger in case of war with Germany: "We must strive to get rid of this population as quickly as possible." The same paper charged that "the German population of western Poland is carrying on treason and espionage with the understanding of Germany and forms the avant-garde of the German army. All German properties in Poland are strategic footholds of Germany." A third editorial underlined the connection between minority policy and the security of Poland's borders: "It is as clear as day that a weakening of the German element [in Poland] will weaken the unhealthy appetite of Germany and its arguments in the international arena."[13] It is not always clear whether by "Germans" such statements were referring to German-speaking citizens of Poland or just those Reich citizens still living there. The failure to distinguish between the two in most contexts suggests that for Polish nationalists the distinction itself was not very important.

Although the most outspoken integral nationalists were usually National Democrats, the Christian Democratic, Piast, and other centrist or conservative Polish parties viewed Germans with no more enthusiasm or understanding. Leftist parties (PPS and Liberation) did occasionally call for greater toleration for national minorities, even democratic cooperation with them. Their Sejm representatives attacked the "chauvinism" of the National Democrats and occasionally rose to the defense of the minorities. The PPS program also included greater protection of minority rights; its 1924 congress called for an end to current "policies of religious and national persecution [and] decisive and energetic steps toward the complete and real equality of rights of all citizens of the Republic without distinction as to belief or nationality." The PPS further urged greater freedom for minority schools, the granting of state stipends and subsidies without regard to nationality, regional autonomy, and the inclusion of non-Poles in the civil service.[14]

The former socialist Piłsudski also distanced himself from time to time from the aggressive chauvinism of the National Democrats. He assured a delegation of Polish Germans in March 1920 that "during my whole life I have advocated the principle that every nationality has the right to the protection of its language and culture by the state to which it belongs. . . . The democratic Polish state desires to and must guard the cultural rights of all its citizens. . . . Whatever lies in my power to contribute to the peaceful coexistence in the Polish state of the two peoples, the Polish and the German, shall be done."[15]

But these remained minority positions among Polish leaders and people alike. National Democratic control of the government soon led to Piłsudski's resignation as army chief and (temporary) withdrawal from national politics. No other party was willing to express similarly explicit support for minority rights until the Christian Democrats, having experienced the wrath of the state themselves in 1930, added similar demands to their program shortly thereafter. Meanwhile, the PPS was weakest precisely in the three western provinces, including even heavily industrial Silesia. Instead, the predominantly middle-class Polish society of Pomorze and Poznania was National Democracy's strongest base of support in Poland, and the (then) similarly anti-German Christian Democrats had their strongest base in Silesia. On occasion, nationalist officials in these provinces frustrated even the rare conciliatory initiative from Warsaw. For example, when foreign Minister Aleksander Skrzyński offered (during a

1924 speech before the League of Nations) to set up bilateral "commissions" to deal with minority problems, officials in western Poland simply vetoed the idea.[16]

In May 1923, after a brief effort by the same left-center coalition that had elected the unfortunate Narutowicz, a Right-Center coalition took over, led first by Piast leader Wincenty Witos and then by a National Democrat, Władysław Grabski. The National Democrats remained the dominant force throughout the early years of the Second Polish Republic, especially where the national minorities were concerned. To ensure that minority representatives would not again play such a decisive role as in December 1922, the new coalition agreed (as part of its "Lanckorona Pact") that Polish cabinets would henceforth consist exclusively of ethnic Poles. Indeed, none of the approximately 350 ministers in the thirty-one coalition governments of interwar Poland was drawn from the non-Polish third of the population. The same was true of the chief provincial and county officials, *wojewodes* and *starosts*. In other ways as well, the minorities remained without effective leverage against their government. They retained significant representation in the Sejm, and thus the right to question ministers, but their efforts in that body were often awkward and generally ineffectual. Many German representatives could not even speak Polish, and Polish parliamentarians usually took their lack of loyalty to Poland for granted. German parliamentarians filed about 245 formal interpellations and complaints during the interwar period, but without discernible effect. Only twenty-seven received a reasonably positive or sympathetic response; seventy received no answer at all.[17]

In general, it is hard to fault Ezra Mendelssohn's conclusion regarding interwar Poland's minority policy: "Most Polish leaders adhered to the slogan 'Poland for the Poles.' . . . Non-Poles would have to conform, suffer in silence, and in the end either emigrate or undergo Polonization."[18] Germany's ambassador to Poland, Ulrich Rauscher, not a disinterested observer (but not a pronounced nationalist either), was also on target when he observed that Poland's stability would remain problematic "so long as cooperation with the national minorities is made to seem nationally scandalous, so long as Poland views a third of her citizens as objects and not as subjects of parliamentary activity"; similarly, "the fact that through denial of rights she forces her minorities to call constantly on international agencies (whereby Poland's reputation in the world is truly not improved) condemns the foreign policy of the Polish state to failure."[19]

The difficult situation facing Germans in western Poland was not just a matter of integral nationalist attitudes directed toward minorities in general. From the beginning, Polish Germans were the object of special suspicion and resentment on the part of public opinion and officialdom alike. The normal problems of different language, religion, and historical consciousness between Germans and Poles in western Poland were intensified, first, by the legacy of prewar Prussian policies. In addition, the perceived connection between the Germans in western Poland and Reich-German revisionism caused many Poles to see the minority primarily in terms of the security risk it posed. The problem of unsettled borders created especially unpromising conditions for peaceful coexistence between Germans and Poles. Continued talk of frontier revision, not only in Germany but in other western countries, including even rumors of a belated plebiscite solution to the Corridor problem, could only spur Poland's leaders on to eradicate the demographic basis for any reconsideration. So too did the plebiscites of 1920-21, which suggested that even strong Polish-speaking majorities were no guarantee of pro-Polish outcomes should other districts in the German-Polish borderlands be given the same right to decide their own fate at some future date. In the view of Jerzy Tomaszewski, most Poles "saw all Germans . . . as opponents, looked at Polish-German relations through the prism of eternal enmity or constant threats to Poland from the West"; under these conditions "there was no chance to find a place for Germans in the Republic of Poland."[20]

But given that a large German minority in western Poland was undesirable, what could Poland's nationalist leaders do about it? They might reasonably hope to assimilate much of their eastern Slavic population—many Ukrainians and especially Byelorussians did not yet have a pronounced national consciousness—but it was hard to entertain such hopes with respect to Germans. Offering Germans the prospect of some kind of cooperative role in the state might defuse the problem, but few Polish leaders were prepared to consider doing so. Aside from attempted assimilation and political co-optation, there was really no realistic alternative to policies designed ultimately to persuade Polish Germans just to leave the country.

Although most Polish leaders declined to accept the logic of this deduction, one who did was Stanisław Grabski. While serving as chairman of the Sejm committee on foreign affairs, he delivered a speech in Poznań in October 1919 (referred to thereafter as the "Poznań Program") which expressed the National Democratic vision of western Poland: "We want to base our relationships on love, but there is one kind of love for countrymen and another for aliens. Their percentage among us is definitely too high; Poznania can show us the way by which the percentage can be brought from 14 percent or even 20 percent down to 1.5 percent. The foreign element will have to consider whether it will not be better off elsewhere; Polish land for the Poles!"[21]

Some years later, Premier Władysław Sikorski, appealing for the support of National Democrats in their Poznanian stronghold, was greeted by

Poznań's mayor, Cyryl Ratajski, with these words: "The German danger . . . will not be removed until all German land has gone over into Polish hands and the enemy no longer has to be fed in one's own land. . . . Poznania cannot tolerate it any more that . . . each German interloper possesses ten *Morgen* [about 7 acres] of land more than the average Polish citizen." Sikorski had just met with two German churchmen in Poznań, neither of whom had been able to converse with him in Polish four years after the beginning of Polish rule, and this may have influenced the tone of his own remarks. In any case, he declared that it would be his policy, if reelected, to liquidate the German nationality in Poland's western provinces, regardless of international considerations. Because Polish Germans could not relinquish thoughts of revenge, it was actually in their own interest that "the great historical process . . . which one calls the de-Germanization of the western provinces be completed in the shortest time and at the most rapid pace. . . . Our previous considerateness, wavering, and lack of decisiveness must give way to a radical change. . . . It is always the case that the stronger is right, and the weaker counts as the vanquished and must take a back seat." Perhaps Sikorski did not intend his words to be taken literally; it has been suggested that he just wanted to get Polish Germans to stop thinking of Poland as something temporary. Perhaps he thought to force Germany to accept the new frontier by threatening tough Polonization measures. On another occasion he did specify the expulsion of resident Germans who had chosen German citizenship (in contrast to ethnic German citizens of Poland) as the recommended means of firming up the Polish element in Poznania.[22]

Whatever his intent, the record contains so many similar statements by politically influential Poles that one can only conclude that Poland's basic policy, at least during the period of National Democratic influence to 1926, was simply to encourage as many Germans as possible to leave the country. For example, Kazimierz Kierski, state's attorney in Poznań, later described his goals as having been "one, the greatest possible restriction of the number of Germans, and two, the liquidation of German property. . . . We were concerned to weaken the German element inside the country, to weaken it economically and quantitatively." In his view, most Polish Germans wanted only to be reunited with Germany, were unlikely ever to change their minds, and had little in common with Poles; the two peoples inhabited "two different worlds, unlike each other and fundamentally at odds." Moreover, Poland was obliged to undo the results of earlier Prussian Germanization policies, get rid of a population that was strategically dangerous, and try to reduce the share of the province's land owned by Germans.[23]

Mayor (later Interior Minister) Ratajski seconded this view in 1924: "I know the Germans, their tendencies and methods, and it is clear to me what a great danger threatens us from their side. . . . Thus I understand perfectly well that every German that we can somehow get rid of must leave Poland. . . . We can have no illusions about them; there is no reason to keep them here." Witos agreed that it was "high time that the German *Kulturträger* disappeared." And Furohjelm, the state police chief, added that "it is my duty to weaken the German nationality."[24] In the absence of significant countervailing statements, such remarks must be accepted as fair and accurate reflection of official attitudes during the early years of the Second Republic.

In many respects, Poland's treatment of its German minority resembled Prussian Polish policy before 1918: harassment of political organizations and the minority press, undermining of minority schools, attacks on the minority's landed property, and economic discrimination by the state. Poland did not explicitly declare a campaign against an internal "enemy of the state" à la Bismarck, however, or mount major legislative initiatives like the Settlement Law of 1886. In fact, Poland usually managed quite well without explicitly discriminatory laws; as one German contemporary observed, "Only prewar Germany was so honestly stupid as to make such laws and thus sanction injustice publicly."[25] Much of the pressure on Germans in interwar Poland came from provincial and local officials, who enjoyed wide discretionary powers and seemed confident that whatever they did to weaken the minority would find favor in Warsaw, provided only that it did not embarrass Poland internationally. They were also confident of the support of Polish public opinion; as one such official remarked in 1930, "the reaction of [Polish] society against the encroachments of its [German] enemies was so unanimous that in the actions I took for the government I had the entire society, regardless of political conviction, on my side."[26]

When such official attitudes were combined with the inflexibility of many Polish Germans, the result was what another contemporary called the "war after the war" in western Poland. Government and minority quarreled from the beginning about almost every aspect of their involuntary relationship, and overwhelming majorities of both nationalities across the entire political spectrum joined in. Several individual issues deserve special attention because they make clear how little official Poland appreciated having a German population in western Poland in the first place.

Citizenship and Language

One source of dissension had to do with which Polish Germans were entitled to Polish citizenship. According to the Versailles treaty, anyone who normally lived in the ceded lands and had either been born there or resided there since 1908 was entitled to Polish citizenship. Poland soon let it be known, however, by means of a citizenship law of January 20, 1920, that it would not be offended if most Germans chose to keep their German citizenship, for this would make them more likely to leave Poland.

Wherever possible, officials interpreted the wording of the Versailles Treaty in a way that would deny Polish citizenship to Germans who wanted to stay in the country. For example, the reference to "regular domicile" as of 1908 and in 1920 was interpreted to mean continuous residence between those two dates. This affected some politically influential members of the minority, including Klara Dittmann, principal owner of *Deutsche Rundschau*, who had resided in Bydgoszcz since 1874 except for three years spent in Germany proper during the war. Polish courts eventually took her side against the government, but in other cases absence even for military service or university study was cited as grounds for denying Polish citizenship. Officials also argued that "residence" meant exclusive residence—no second residence elsewhere in Germany. And "birth" in the ceded territories was interpreted to mean that one's parents had regularly resided there from 1908 to 1920. This issue was one of the first to find its way to the League of Nations; when Poland refused to accept the League's opinion that Polish citizenship should be granted to most of the Germans in question, the matter moved on to the Permanent Court of International Justice (PCIJ) at The Hague, where the German position again prevailed (September 15, 1923).[27]

A related issue was what it actually meant to choose continued German citizenship. As late as 1924, approximately 30,000 Reich-German citizens remained in western Poland, including about 3,800 who wanted to change their minds and adopt Polish citizenship. According to Article 41 of the Versailles Treaty, residents of the ceded territories who elected to remain German "might" move to Germany; Poland interpreted this to mean that they *must* do so, and within the year. (Polish Upper Silesia was not affected by this dispute, since the Geneva Convention gave Reich citizens the right to remain there for fifteen years.) These citizenship issues were the subject of lengthy German-Polish negotiations. They culminated in an agreement signed at Vienna, August 30, 1924, which endorsed the German interpretation of who was eligible for Polish citizenship but the Polish understanding that those who chose German citizenship could be made to leave. Under this agreement, Germans who owned no substantial property in Poland were required to leave within the year; owners of property in what Poland considered strategic areas were given fifteen months; other property owners could take up to two years. Poland agreed to buy them all out at a fair price.[28]

Poland's willingness to see so many presumably productive inhabitants depart, rather than grant them citizenship, was another bad omen for government-minority relations. It certainly made no economic sense to force these people out, nor did it enhance Poland's international image. Nonetheless, under the steady pressure of published opinion, the government began to implement the terms of the Vienna agreement by expelling most of them. Only after another year had passed, and fewer than 12,000 remained in Poland, did foreign Minister Skrzyński agree (in the course of the Locarno conference) to urge his government to forgo expulsion of the rest. Besides not wanting to appear intolerant in the eyes of its western friends, Poland could not really spare the funds necessary to buy out all these people. The issue receded somewhat during the following years, except when Polish nationalists brought up the continued sufferance of German citizens in the country as an indication of official weakness.[29] But as late as 1929, some Germans who believed that they possessed Polish citizenship complained that their property was being liquidated as foreign holdings. Only when Stresemann threatened to take the matter back to the League did the two governments agree to turn any additional questions of Polish citizenship over to the PCIJ, and the two countries came to a final agreement about citizenship questions in 1931.[30]

Poland's official language policy was another clear indication that its government was unprepared to accommodate a significant German minority in its western provinces. There was never any question, for example, of granting formal recognition to German as a second official language anywhere in the state. From the beginning, Polish was the sole official language in a region that had traditionally been one-third German-speaking, and few of the resident Germans had previously seen any need to learn Polish. But now all officials, including not only elected officials but officers even of nonpolitical and mostly German organizations (such as associations of artisans), were given only a brief period to demonstrate proficiency in this difficult language or be removed from their positions. According to 1920 guidelines, German-language submissions to officials were to be accepted but answered only in Polish. But as of March 1924, officials were no longer even to accept written or oral submissions in German.

The Poznanian *wojewode*, Witold Celichowski, forbade his officials to respond to correspondence that contained any German forms of address or terminology (such as *Landrat*), and the postal authorities announced that they would no longer deliver mail, even from abroad, that used the German spelling of place names. German newspapers had to use the new Polish forms (Bydgoszcz, Poznań) in their otherwise German-language articles. Even before the formal transfer of sovereignty, Celichowski advised the overwhelmingly German United Evangelical Church that it could request permission to use German "temporarily" in its internal correspondence, but each German communication would eventually have to be accompanied by a Polish translation. Public signs in German (on businesses, churches, and elsewhere) had to be bilingual, with a Polish translation. This hard line on the language question may have been partially prompted by the provocative behavior of some Germans. One pastor in Leszno announced, for example, that he was not going to respond to anything written or spoken in Polish. His attitude was condemned by both his superiors and minority leaders. Overall, however, no serious consideration was given to the need to accommodate this large and unilingually German population, however tactfully it behaved.[31]

To be sure, Poles in prewar Prussia had had to contend with an official language policy which recognized only German, but that policy dated only from 1876, by which time virtually every adult Pole in Prussia had been subjected to years of German instruction in the public schools. While there was nothing to prevent Germans from learning the language of their Polish neighbors during the period when Prussia ruled this area, the fact is that few of them did so. At the very least, then, Poland's official language policy was unrealistically abrupt.

"Liquidation" of German Property

Conflicting interpretations of ambivalent passages in the Versailles Treaty led to other government-minority problems during the first years of Polish rule. For example, Article 256 granted to Poland all the property and related rights that had belonged to the Prussian or German states or their ruling dynasty (the Geneva Convention contained similar language applicable to Polish Silesia). Under Articles 92 and 297, Poland was also given the right to "liquidate" (that is, purchase with reasonable compensation) any properties owned by German citizens in what was now Poland, Silesia excepted. It made little economic sense, of course, for the financially strapped Polish government to want to buy up all the German property in the country, but nationalist opinion insisted upon the full exploitation of every legal device for diminishing the German minority. The prevailing attitude, as expressed by State's Attorney Kierski, was that "the main purpose of liquidation was the de-Germanization of the western territories taken from the Germans. Poland had the right [to do so]— the moral right because of the extermination policies of the Prussian government, and the formal right based on the Versailles treaty."[32]

Problems began, however, when Poland passed an "Annulment Law" on July 14, 1920, which nullified all post-armistice property transactions by the Prussian and German states in what was now Poland. Poland's argument was that once Germany realized it would lose most of

Prussian Poland, it had begun to shift state-owned property into other hands in order to make them immune to Polish takeover. This law was used to acquire many German properties with no apparent political or even economic importance, including some school buildings and hospitals that had belonged originally to the state but were now the property of local German corporations.

This happened, for example, to the Bethesda Hospital in Gniezno-Gnesen, whose clientele was about 90 percent Polish but whose head physician and most nurses were German. Following the state takeover, the previous staff was dismissed and replaced by ethnic Poles; 47,000 złoty was offered as compensation for a building whose worth was estimated by the previous owners at 600,000 złoty. At another such hospital in Rawicz County, also owned by an association of local Germans and also serving both nationalities, several hundred Poles suddenly applied for membership in the association in 1924, and the courts ordered that their applications be approved. The German administration was then voted out and replaced by Polish officials, who promptly discharged the German staff.[33] The single most valuable property acquired by Poland under the Annulment Law was the Chorzów nitrogen works in Silesia. Germany appealed this takeover to the PCIJ and it was eventually declared illegal, but Poland was obliged only to provide financial compensation to the previous owners, not to return the firm to their control (see Chapter 5).

In addition to the state and domain lands, however defined, that fell automatically to Poland under the Versailles treaty, the government also "liquidated" about 200,000 hectares of privately owned German land in the early 1920s. Officials focused their attention especially on large German-owned estates, but they also took over factories, businesses, and other major economic holdings. Affected property owners often complained that Poland offered unfairly low prices as compensation and was then slow to make payment. Rauschning and "Polonicus" (the alias apparently of someone in the German Foreign Office) cite numerous examples of German landed estates compensated at only 10 percent of their prewar value; in some cases, back taxes, "emigration taxes," and other obligations consumed the entire purchase price. One group of former landowners claimed that they received only 1.7 million marks for properties whose combined prewar valuation was about 6.5 million. Of course, given the large number of Germans wanting to sell out and leave Poland, even property sold on the free market often fetched only a minimum. Prices were depressed still more by the effective restriction of the pool of prospective buyers to ethnic Poles. Overall, while the average estate price in Poland as a whole in 1924 was 36 percent higher than in 1913, in Pomorze and Poznania respectively it was 33 and 48 percent lower.[34]

There was often a significant lapse of time between the state's declaration of intent to liquidate a property and its actual purchase. Under a decree of November 6, 1919, officials could appoint an overseer to manage properties that the state intended to acquire, in order to keep the current German owners from transferring assets to the Reich or otherwise diminishing the value of their soon-to-be-Polish holdings. As overseers moved in and proceeded to run things, often badly, owners were reduced to bystander status. This situation could last for years if the state was not ready to complete the purchase; more often the procedure encouraged (and was doubtless designed to encourage) the owner to sell out quickly, often at a low price and often to the new overseer. One German estate owner related that a Polish administrator was assigned to his estate in Pomorze until he agreed to sell for a low price; the state then sold it to a Polish army officer for even less, about 10 percent of its prewar value.[35] When a large estate, factory, or other business property passed from German into Polish hands, most of the German work force was also replaced, sooner or later, by Poles. Given the frequent absence of alternative employment locally, the discharged German employees often followed the former German owners to the Reich (and so constituted another essentially involuntary part of the German exodus).

The same was true of many "settlers" who joined the exodus. The PCIJ decreed in 1920 that Poland could not confiscate farms simply because they had been created originally by the Settlement Commission; hence, the property rights of long-established settlers normally went unchallenged. But Poland refused to recognize property rights to farms created by the Settlement Commission during (or, in 1,100 cases, after) the war or any other post-armistice transfers of title to property that would otherwise have become Polish under the Versailles Treaty. About 26,000 settlers found their property rights challenged because the Prussian government had not got around to issuing formal title to ("registering") their farms by the time of the armistice, or because their mortgages had been transferred to private banks (including such specially created institutions as the "West Prussian Peasants Bank") during the following year. Poland eventually recognized the land titles of about 12,000 of these settlers; another 10,000 chose German citizenship and left the country. That left about 4,000 settlers and their families who asked for Polish citizenship and intended to stay in Poland, but whose rights to about 60,000 hectares of land remained in dispute. When they were ordered to vacate their lands in 1920, they appealed to the League; their case became the first of the many German-Polish disputes to occupy that body.[36]

Poland's position was that registration of formal title to these farms was not, as Germany contended, just a formality; rather, it counted for more than the original contract to purchase. Poland was convinced, of course, that belated title registrations were part of a post-armistice effort by German authorities to create additional economic *faits accomplis* in Prussian Poland and thus saw no reason to recognize them. But the League sided with the settlers; according to its September 1922 ruling, the mere absence of formal title registration before the armistice was not grounds for dispossession, and Poland was told to rescind its eviction of these farmers. But Polish officials found it difficult to accept the idea of outside restrictions on their efforts to erase the legacy of the despised Settlement Commission and refused to comply with the League's decision. Since settlers were not mentioned specifically in the Minorities Protection Treaty, they were not subject to League protection; this was strictly a matter of Polish law, and Poland intended to proceed with the removal of these settlers from their lands and (effectively) from Poland as well.

The dispute moved next to The Hague, where the PCIJ ruled on September 10, 1923, that the Prussian German government had retained sovereignty in Prussian Poland, including the right to transfer its property to private persons, until January 1920; thus, the land titles of the settlers were valid. But the decision came too late to be of much help to the settlers; most of them had long since been ejected from their lands, and only 227 of the 4,000 were still in Poland at the time of the PCIJ verdict. The court directed Poland to grant "full financial compensation" to the settlers who had been removed; it did not require the restoration of their farms, which already belonged to Poles. When Poland subsequently devised a slow and complicated compensation process, the PCIJ again intervened and suggested a lump-sum payment to an organization of dispossessed settlers, most of whom eventually received a modest compensation.[37]

Germans who held leases on Prussian or German state property at the time of the transfer of sovereignty had much the same experience. A Polish law of December 23, 1920, authorized officials to evict such lessees with six months' notice; many had longer-term leases, but these were not honored. A "Society of German Leaseholders of Properties in Poland," representing managers of about 100,000 hectares, claimed a violation of the Minorities Protection Treaty and took its case to the League and then to the PCIJ. Once again, the Hague court ruled that the Polish government's action was illegal; once again, the ruling came too late to help the plaintiffs stay in Poland, for most of them had long since been evicted and had departed for Germany.[38] Poland also claimed, as part of its inheritance from the Prussian state, the right to repurchase farms created by the Settlement Commission or to approve the sale of such farms to new owners. This system had been designed originally by Prussian officials, of course, to keep such farms out of Polish hands; the Polish state could now presumably use the same oversight rights to make sure that they went only to Poles. But only about five hundred farms created by the Settlement Commission were affected by state intervention under this clause before Poland agreed to abstain from the exercise of this right in 1929.[39]

A much more serious threat to the minority's economic underpinnings was Poland's assertion of an effective right of first refusal, designed to keep Germans from buying land on the open market. A decree of June 25, 1919, made subject to official approval the transfer of title to any farm of more than five hectares or any commercial/industrial property of more than one-eighth hectare in the formerly Prussian partition. Such permission was rarely granted to ethnic Germans, except in cases of direct inheritance within a family. The private parceling and farm-development enterprises that Prussian Poles had operated so successfully before 1914 were thus foreclosed to Germans in the new Poland. Once Polish rule began, it became almost impossible for Germans to acquire additional land. Whenever a German landowner died without direct heirs, or was forced to sell out, his property invariably wound up in Polish hands. Such efforts to reduce the level of German landownership were all the more ominous because the exodus of most of the German urban population had left a minority overwhelmingly dependent on agriculture for its livelihood.

The inability of German farmers to buy additional land, and their doubts about whether they would be able to pass even what they had on to their heirs, discouraged investment and so depressed a farm economy already struggling with numerous adverse changes. No longer could farmers (Polish and German alike) in the Prussian partition rely on a relatively secure and affluent market inside a major industrial state, with easy access to relatively cheap industrial goods, a well-developed banking and credit system, and a good transportation and education infrastructure. Though some of their former markets, especially Danzig and Polish Upper Silesia, came into Poland with them, most did not. Citizens now of an overwhelmingly agrarian country, they were forced to sell much of their produce on a highly competitive world market. Overall, approximately 500,000 hectares of privately owned German land in Poznania and Pomorze—one-third of the total—passed into Polish hands between 1919 and 1926. One contemporary student of the rural scene even predicted "the day . . . when a significant German farming population or land-ownership will no longer exist" in western Poland.[40] While most of this land was sold by Germans voluntarily departing Poland, a sizable share of the decline was due to the official measures outlined above.

Political and Cultural Restrictions

The minority's newly created political organizations, above all the Deutschtumsbund and the Silesian Volksbund, attracted official suspicion virtually from the start. Graebe, executive director of the DB, was arrested for political crimes as early as 1920. The list of formal charges included collusion with Reich authorities, acceptance of Reich financial support, participation in efforts to return Poland's western provinces to German rule, conveyance of libelous information and state secrets to foreign states, encouragement of "contempt for state institutions and decrees," and (finally) "treason" in general. According to Graebe's own account, he was offered his immediate freedom, despite the gravity of the charges against him, if he would only choose German citizenship and leave the country. When he refused, he was sentenced to six months imprisonment.[41]

He was publicly charged with disloyalty again in 1923, this time by Premier Sikorski, because of his retroactive promotion to lieutenant-colonel in the German army. In a personal confrontation with Sikorski in the Sejm, Graebe demanded a retraction on grounds that the promotion was merely part of the arrangement under which he left the army in 1919, at which time he was a resident and citizen of Germany. His contention that he was no longer subject to German military or political authority was somewhat disingenuous but sufficed to put this particular matter to rest.[42]

The DB itself came under official attack, especially when it began to submit grievance petitions to the League. Aside from the several complaints, discussed above, regarding citizenship and property questions, others charged Poland with violations of the language and school provisions of the Minorities Protection treaty and harassment of the Evangelical Church. For Poland, the DB was merely an arm of the German government, which had designated it the sole political representative of the German minority in western Poland and chief conduit for Reich financial aid. The German Foreign Office also used the DB to collect information on Polish Germans, to evaluate "expulsion damages," and to perform various quasi-consular chores. It allocated about three million German marks to the DB in September 1922, supposedly as payment for such services.[43]

Polish officials, convinced that the DB was essentially a Reich agency operating clandestinely in Poland, began to look for the right opportunity to move against it. The crackdown came on August 6, 1923: the government declared the DB dissolved and arrested Graebe and a dozen other leaders. There followed the suppression of organizations connected to the DB, including the German Farmers League and the Womens Association. The government justified its actions against the German minority's main political organization on grounds that it functioned as a Reich agency in Poland: it engaged in such quasi-governmental activities as the compilation of statistics, helped settlers confound state measures to eject them, helped would-be recruits avoid military service, sponsored meetings of Polish Germans with Reich political figures (for example, Hindenburg and the former Empress), conducted espionage, and made illegal contacts aimed at the return of German rule. The DB's complaints to the League, however, were clearly what made it truly insufferable; the decision to suppress this organization came shortly after its successful suit on behalf of the settlers before the World Court. A dozen members of the DB in Chojnice were tried quickly in October 1923; its leader was sentenced to four and a half years in jail, and the others received smaller sentences. In the other cases, however, many years were to pass before the charges against the DB and its leaders were brought to trial (see Chapter 4).[44]

The DB was soon replaced by an organization more difficult for officials to attack: the German Union in Sejm and Senate (Deutsche Vereinigung in Sejm und Senat, or DViSuS). This was formally an association of German members of parliament who, as such, were entitled to parliamentary immunity, but there was little attempt to disguise the degree of continuity. The DViSuS was in most respects just the DB under a different name, and Polish officials reported that "the [German] movement is just the same as it was formerly in the Deutschtumsbund." Like its predecessor, the DViSuS claimed to represent all Germans in Poznania and Pomorze; it had essentially the same leadership (Graebe, Naumann, Hasbach, Heidelck) and was housed in the same building in Bydgoszcz. It was loosely supervised by a broadly representative *Hauptwahlausschuss* (Main Elections Committee), with delegates from two dozen Polish-German organizations and interest groups under Naumann's chairmanship. A Committee of Five managed day-to-day affairs.[45]

Before long, even the local socialists returned to the fold. When the DSAP decided to run a joint campaign with the PPS in 1928, its Pomorze-Poznania branch refused to go along; it broke away, reclaimed its old DSP name, and adopted many of the same nationalist positions as other Polish Germans. Polish officials described the new DSP as "completely directed by the DViSuS," but by this time organized German socialism in western Poland had declined to the point of political insignificance. Even in industrial Silesia the DSAP had only about 3,200 members in 1930; more remarkable still, PPS membership in this province was not much larger.[46]

Most of the other auxiliary organizations of the DB, insofar as they were suppressed in 1923, reappeared in slightly different form. For example, in place of the *Hauptverein* of German Farmers in Poland (established 1919), there appeared several provincial farmers' associations, including the West Polish Agricultural Society (*Westpolnische Landwirtschaftliche Gesellschaft*, or Welage) in Poznań and its Pomorze counterpart, the Landbund Weichselgau (Vistula District Farmers League).[47] Many farmers also belonged to one of several cooperative societies: the Verband deutscher Genossenschaften (Union of German Co-operatives) (Raiffeisen) in Poznań, with 31,000 members in 360 individual co-ops (1924), the Verband landwirtschaftlicher Genossenschaften (Union of Agricultural Co-ops) (Offenbach), also in Poznań, with 17,000 members in 219 locals, which gradually merged with the first *Verband* after 1925; and the Verband Ländlicher Genossenschaften (Union of Rural Co-ops) in Grudziądz with 4,600 members in 205 locals. Leo Wegener was head of the larger Poznań organization until 1925, when he was succeeded by Friedrich Swart. The highly successful Polish co-op movement of the pre-1914 period served Wegener and Swart as an example of how a national minority might survive and prosper even under hostile political conditions.[48]

Organized German cultural life in Poznania and Pomorze, traditionally in the shadow of Berlin and so not especially vigorous, was weakened still further by the change of sovereignty. Gone were the state-subsidized German theaters, museums, and libraries, which had provided the economic basis for a modest local intelligentsia. Only one regular theater survived, the Deutsche Bühne in Bydgoszcz. Most of the remaining cultural institutions were supported by Reich funds and controlled by the DViSuS. Individuals active in the prewar historical and cultural societies had largely joined the exodus to Germany, but a "Historical Society for the Province of Poznania" carried on. Its first postwar director was Hermann Rauschning, author of the key work on the postwar exodus; Rauschning also edited the Historical Society's *Deutsche Wissenschaftliche Zeitschrift für Polen* and the more popular and literary *Deutsche Blätter in Polen* (1924-31). The society operated a German library in Poznań and sponsored a series of scholarly monographs ("East German Research"). A Central Association of German Public Libraries ran a network of several hundred small libraries and reading circles. In Silesia, the Volksbund sponsored an equivalent German Cultural League as well as its own German library. Rauschning wanted the Historical Society to do still more. He proposed, for example, that it compile a "dynamic inventory," an actual card file of the several hundred thousand remaining members of the minority in Poznania and Pomorze which would permit their more effective mobilization. When DViSuS leaders dismissed his ideas as impractical, Rauschning resigned and left for Danzig and a career in politics that brought him considerable prominence in the 1930s.[49]

Polish suspicion of organized German political activity extended logically to the German-language press. At the beginning of Polish rule there were about one hundred German-language journals in western Poland, including fifteen daily newspapers. Officials believed that most of them, as recipients of Reich subsidies, were also subject to Reich directives and so helped keep resentment of the peace settlement alive and otherwise hindered the minority's adjustment to the new conditions. Most influental among the German-language papers were the *Deutsche Rundschau* in

Bydgoszcz, edited by Gotthold Starke with advice from a consortium that included prominent DB and then DViSuS leaders; *Posener Tageblatt*, edited by Johannes Scholz; *Kattowitzer Zeitung*, politically close to the German Party in Silesia; and *Oberschlesischer Kurier* in Królewska Huta, associated with the German-Catholic Peoples Party.[50]

The supply of news from Germany was subject to official controls; a German-Polish Press Service, set up by Berlin to supply minority newspapers with material, was banned in October 1920. The minority press was also limited in its ability to air Polish-German complaints and frequently fined or confiscated for doing so. During the year 1920 the *Thorner Zeitung*, for example, was censured or confiscated approximately every other day for violating official directives banning criticism of the Versailles Treaty. In 1924 the editor of *Pomereller Tageblatt* was sentenced to fifteen months in jail for criticism of government minority policies. *Deutsche Rundschau*, the most influential German paper in Poland, was the object of four major trials, and editor Starke was imprisoned or physically assaulted several times. During one five-year stretch in Silesia, the *Kattowitzer Zeitung* was seized 124 times and the *Oberschlesischer Kurier* 190 times. Most of the alleged offenses did not reach the point of actual court proceedings; official interventions were chiefly designed to suppress particular stories or to weaken the papers economically.[51]

Minority Schools

No aspect of German life in Poland was more important to most members of the minority than securing a German education for their children. Few things were more important to Poland's leaders than exposing their diverse citizenry to the right kind of civic education. These two goals conflicted early and often. Under the Minorities Protection Treaty, Poland was required to establish and fund German-language elementary schools in the formerly Prussian partition (secondary schools were not covered by the treaty, however, and most public German secondary schools soon disappeared). Specifically, the treaty required the establishment of a minority school wherever a "considerable proportion" of the population was non-Polish. Unfortunately, those who drafted this provision did not have the foresight to define "considerable." Some Poles argued that it must mean at least 50 percent of the local population. (In the wake of the great exodus, Germans no longer constituted 50 percent of a single county in western Poland and so were presumably not covered by this treaty to begin with.) Poland's education minister suggested in 1923 that 20 percent might be sufficient; some years after that, the League defined "considerable proportion" as 10 percent.[52]

Chief architect of Poland's minority school policy was Stanisław Grabski, author of the "Poznań program" of 1919 and head of the Culture Ministry in 1923-25. His school law of July 31, 1924, was guided by the desire to turn minority schools into instruments for the gradual Polonization of the minorities and to Polonize the schools themselves. Instruction in the Polish language was obligatory, beginning in the fourth grade. The hours devoted to the minority language were then gradually reduced in favor of increased attention to Polish as one reached the higher grades. History and geography were taught from the Polish point of view and later, in the higher grades, in the Polish language as well. As Marian Drozdowski concedes, this law "abridged considerably the previously normal development of minority schools" and was "incompatible with the spirit of Article 110 of the Constitution."[53]

The designation "German-minority school" did not mean that teachers or administrators were German, only that German was the language of instruction for most subjects. Teachers were required to take a loyalty oath to Poland and demonstrate mastery of the Polish language within a specified period in order to retain their positions. Officials retained the right to veto the election of school board members and frequently prevented boards from hiring ethnic Germans. Most vacancies were filled by Poles, whereas ethnic German teachers working in these schools were subject to re-assignment to Polish schools anywhere in the country. Before long, a teacher in a German-minority school was just as likely to be Polish as German. Some Polish teachers had only a rudimentary command of German and little sympathy for their pupils' nationality. (According to one presumably exceptional complaint brought before the Sejm, such a teacher in the minority school at Żnin/Znin treated his pupils to the observation that "Germans stink like dead dogs and scabby sheep" and should be chased from their jobs and replaced by Poles.) By the mid-1920s all German teacher-training institutions had been closed, and it was difficult to be certified to teach in Poland with a degree from a foreign university. Would-be minority-school teachers were more or less compelled to get their training at a Polish university, which was yet another disincentive for them to enter this profession.[54]

These measures only exacerbated the already serious shortage of qualified German teachers. As noted previously, most of them, given the choice of continuing in the Prussian civil service or continuing to teach in what was now Poland, took the first option and emigrated to the Reich. Of the minority that chose at first to continue working in Poznania or Pomorze, about one-third were dismissed on political grounds. Some refused, for example, to sing the Polish national anthem or take a vow to "stand up consistently for the greatness of Poland." It took some time for such teachers to realize that they could serve the German cause better by keeping quiet (and keeping their jobs) than by senseless acts of nationalist defiance. Minority-school teachers were also Polish civil servants, of course, and as such they were subject to the supervision of officials on the lookout for signs of insufficient "Polish spirit." Most of them lived in fear of being transferred to some distant part of the country if they exposed themselves politically.[55]

Under the Polish school law of March 10, 1920, each public school in Poland, whether Polish or minority, had to have at least forty pupils; if enrollment fell below that number, the school could be closed, its school board dissolved, and its property turned over to the state. This minimum would not in itself have been discriminatory or unreasonable had it not been up to state officials to determine the size and shape of school districts. Germans alleged that some districts were gerrymandered in order to push the number of pupils below the minimum. Even the fact that a minority school exceeded the forty-pupil minimum did not prevent its being closed if officials believed that it would fall below that level in the foreseeable future. Requests of smaller schools to combine in order to meet the forty-pupil minimum were usually denied, nor were children in districts without minority schools permitted to travel to a school outside their district. One group of German parents, according to another complaint brought before the Sejm, was fined for sending their children to live in a town that had a German-language school after being denied a permit for one of their own. The buildings that had housed German schools before 1920 usually became the new Polish schools, so minority schools were left to set up shop wherever space could be found. This often invited additional trouble from officials on grounds that such places failed to meet state requirements for school buildings.

Officials were also careful to keep "Polish" children—those who spoke Polish or had Polish names—out of the minority schools; they were also effectively foreclosed to children whose parents worked for the state and sometimes even to German Catholics. One particularly zealous official explained his intervention this way: "S. is of Polish origin, a Polish citizen who has married a Pole, raised his child to date in the Polish spirit, given her an education in a Polish school, and solemnly declared on several occasions to be Polish himself; he does not have the right arbitrarily and without motive to change nationality" and enroll his child in a minority school. As this case headed for the League, Culture Minister Grabski intervened and ordered S.'s daughter admitted to the German school in Nakło. In most cases, however, local officials had the last word in determining whether a pupil was sufficiently German to attend a German-language school. Germans regularly complained that these and other regulations were used to limit the number of German schools and so compel their children to attend Polish-language schools.[56]

For the 1921-22 school year, official sources listed 1,250 German-language elementary schools in Pomorze and Poznania, including 150 that did not then meet the forty-pupil minimum; combined enrollment exceeded 80,000. Year by year thereafter, the number of German schools and the percentage of German children with access to them declined. A growing minority of German schoolchildren (37 percent in 1926-27) were enrolled in Polish-language schools, though few were actually able to follow instruction in the usually unfamiliar language. Officials attributed the decline in the number of minority schools to declining German numbers, but most Germans attributed it to official manipulations and chicanery, and school conditions remained the greatest single source of minority-government friction during the interwar period.[57]

Religious Issues

Second place on the list of sources of discord belongs probably to church-state questions. Aside from Silesia (where Germans and Poles alike were usually Catholic), most Germans in Poland were Protestant, whereas Poles were overwhelmingly Catholic. In many areas, German nationality and Protestantism were considered as inseparable as Polish nationality and Catholicism. The already substantial national differences were therefore reinforced by religious differences, which created yet another source of conflict between Poland and the German minority. Roman Catholicism enjoyed a quasi-official status in Poland; though the Minorities Protection Treaty promised equal protection to other denominations, a 1925 *concordat* recognized the Catholic Church's special position in public life. This position was manifested in numerous ways: in one representative year (1925), 16.8 million *złoty* in public funds went to the Catholic Church compared to 1.6 million for all other religious organizations combined. Some of Poland's national holidays and official ceremonies also had a specifically Catholic content, yet all citizens were expected to take part in them.[58]

In the formerly Prussian provinces the peculiar traditions and structure of Prussian Protestantism created additional problems. The United Evangelical Church here was the result, strictly speaking, of an amalgamation of Lutheran and Calvinist (Reformed) doctrines and congregations, fashioned by Prussian kings to bridge the gap between their own Calvinism and the Lutheranism of most of their subjects. Prussian monarchs had always been the titular heads of what was a classic state church, but suzerainty over this church was among the rights that the Polish state, despite its own close association with a rival confession, inherited from the Prussian state under the Versailles Treaty. A Polish decree of July 1,

1920, demanded that "any connection should and must . . . cease" between the United Evangelical Church in western Poland and the rest of this organization, headquartered in Berlin; at least one church official was removed from office by Celichowski for appearing before a synod in Berlin. Minister for the Formerly Prussian Partition Bernard Chrzanowski announced that membership in the church's governing body, the Evangelical Consistory in Poznań, "can only be determined by the Polish government." He also declared the church's previous constitution invalid and refused even to look at a new draft constitution presented by church leaders on grounds that the government intended to devise one of its own.[59]

Officials also claimed the right to appoint or ratify delegates to church assemblies and to be heard at these councils. Evangelical pastors were informed that they were now, in effect, Polish state employees; those who continued to provide information about emigrants to German authorities, for example, could be charged with unlawful foreign contacts. Officials banned the hiring of Reich-German pastors, denied the importation of key texts from Germany, and discouraged would-be pastors from getting their training in that country. So many pastors took part in the exodus that there was soon a serious shortage; as they left or died, their positions often remained vacant. By 1925, forty of 292 positions were vacant, and forty more were held by men over retirement age; many of the remainder were staffed by pastors whose German citizenship made them liable to summary expulsion on various pretexts.[60]

Officials were concerned above all to inject greater Polish influence into what had always been an overwhelmingly German institution. The departure of so many officials, professionals, and other German "authority figures" only increased the role of the remaining pastors in the minority's affairs. Pastors usually presided over local school committees or were in the forefront of efforts to establish private German schools. Welfare associations too, even those not connected officially to the church, were usually run by pastors. The Evangelical Church was considered part of the minority's organizational structure; DB and DViSuS leaders took it for granted that pastors would remind their congregations of their national duty to turn out on election day and vote for German candidates. Church officials urged pastors to remain at their posts and acquire Polish citizeship wherever possible, for national as well as pastoral-religious reasons. The Versailles Treaty provided some protection for pastors who had worked in the ceded territories before January 1919 but could not become Polish citizens; Polish officials, however, did what they could to encourage their departure—by forcing them, for example, to apply for expensive residence permits.[61]

Paul Blau (1861-1939), an erudite theologian and political conservative, was the formal head, or superintendent, of the United Evangelical Church in Poznania and Pomorze. Though a German citizen and of advanced age, he remained at his post throughout the interwar period, if only to keep Polish officials from trying to determine his successor. But he also encouraged his clergy to adapt to the new conditions and tried to overcome some of the official suspicion of his church. He urged his pastors in 1923 to "distance themselves strictly from any political activity" and to avoid topics in their sermons that could be interpreted as political: "Spiritual and political affairs should not be mixed. . . . Our church is concerned with the peaceful development of its relationship with the state," and pastors should always show "a certain restraint" in political matters. He did not even want pastors to serve on the Main Election Committee of the DViSuS because it was "not in the interest of our church that colleagues expose themselves politically without compelling reasons." He also urged all pastors who were not already "too old" to "devote themselves with enthusiasm to learning the Polish language." [62]

When the president of Poland paid a visit to Poznań in 1924, officials were pleasantly surprised that Blau asked to meet him and presented him with a loyalty declaration. When the situation recurred in 1928, Blau was even able to speak his piece to the president in Polish. On resurrected Poland's tenth anniversary (November 1928) he ordered special prayers in all services "for the land in which we live, the state to which we belong, and the authorities who stand over us." [63] He even called on pastors to subscribe to state bond campaigns to make it "clear that citizenship obligations are being met in an unmistakable way by members of our church," who have an "obligation to contribute to a solution of the state's economic emergency." [64]

In an effort to remedy the shortage of pastors, Blau established a new theological seminary in Poznań. But it could provide only three semesters of work, after which the seminarians had to continue their studies elsewhere, presumably in Germany. Officials frustrated this strategy by requiring would-be pastors to study in Poland for at least two years—and that created yet another problem. The only Polish university with a program in Protestant theology was the University of Warsaw, and it was run by the Augsburg Lutheran Church, the Lutheran organization of formerly Russian Poland. United Evangelicals insisted that they were not the same as "regular" Lutherans; officials contended that they were merely seeking a pretext to boycott a Polish university. To make matters worse, though the membership of the Augsburg Lutheran Church was 82 percent German, its state-appointed hierarchy was largely Polish. Its superintendent, Juliusz Bursche, was not just a Polish nationalist but a member of the openly anti-German "Union for the Defense of the Western Regions" (ZOKZ) and so seriously at odds with the views and interests of most of his flock. In effect, then, the government gave to Bursche and his equally nationalistc faculty at Warsaw University the exclusive right to train Protestant pastors in Poland. Many of the pastors hired by Bursche were Polish or Polonophile, and Germans became convinced that he was using his church to Polonize its membership. In 1921, Evangelical leaders—including Otto Dibelius, later the well-known bishop of Berlin-Brandenburg—called on Lutheran congregations in the United States to stop supporting the Augsburg church financially so long as it served as an instrument of national suppression. American Lutherans dispatched a team to investigate these charges but took no formal action. A subsequent investigation by a Dutch churchman, however, published as *Kirche, Volk, und Staat in Polen,* was highly critical of Bursche and of Poland's treatment of Protestants generally.[65]

Even though most Poles were Catholic, the number of Lutheran Poles, particularly in central Poland, was not insignificant. As some of these moved into western Poland, additional problems arose. Sometimes they formed separate denominations under Polish clergy, but where their numbers began to approach the number of German Protestants, as in Silesia, officials encouraged them to join existing German denominations and perhaps take control of them. Silesian officials, equating language with nationality, claimed that two-thirds of the Protestants in their province were already Polish and charged German church authorities with failure to meet their needs by providing Polish-speaking pastors and services. (There were only thirty pastors in the United Evangelical Church in Silesia, but none was Polish.) Superintendent Hermann Voss countered that Poles in the subjctive political sense constituted no more than 10 percent of his flock (in elections to church bodies, 90 percent of the membership's vote normally went to German candidates) and that the church's constitution gave congregations the right to elect their own pastors. Citing doctrinal differences, but seeking also to confound official efforts to create a Polish majority, Voss resolved not to accept adherents of the Augsburg Lutheran Church coming in from central Poland. But the government simply vetoed this resolution, charging that it was motivated more by nationalist exclusivity than by doctrinal considerations.[66]

While Protestant Germans naturally looked with some trepidation on life in a predominantly Catholic state, the smaller number of German Catholics in western Poland anticipated some improvement in their status. According to the 1931 census, there were 118,000 German Catholics in Poland, including 68 percent of the German-speakers in Silesia, 9 percent in Poznania and 13 percent in Pomorze. but they too were disappointed. Polish became the sole official language of the Catholic Church throughout Poland, and German priests were systematically replaced by Poles.

Polish priests were often prominent in anti-German organizations; some priests in Silesia pronounced it a "sin" to enroll a "Polish" child in a German school. Polish Silesia belonged traditionally to the Archdiocese of Breslau (Wrocław); in 1925, a new Bishopric of Katowice was created and made subordinate to the Archbishop of Gniezno-Poznań. The church cut back the number of German-language services in Silesia, leaving many Germans without services in their own language—a situation that even sporadic "church strikes" failed to change.[67]

DKVP leader Eduard Pant denounced the complicity of Catholic authorities in the regime's nationalist policies; he objected especially to the fact that the minority's own priests sometimes held leadership positions in such anti-German organizations as the ZOKZ: "What these people are doing is a crime against religion. They are burying religion and the moral foundations of the people. . . . They seem to be concerned only to rage against Germans. . . . The population has lost its faith in the clergy here, and the clergy itself is to blame."[68]

Prominent German priests who chose to stay in western Poland were isolated and ostracized; in 1923, Polish clerics in Poznań demanded the removal of the remaining German members of their cathedral chapter "in the interest of the Church and of the Polish state." One of these, Josef Klinke, though fluent in Polish, was a German Sejm representative and otherwise prominent in minority affairs. In 1928, Archbishop August Hlond ordered the *Demherr* to decline reelection to the Sejm, but Klinke remained a member of the Committee of Nine, which managed many of the minority's economic and cultural affairs.[69] In 1934, the church's "German chaplain" (*Deutschen-Seelsorger*), Venantius Kempf, was expelled from the country. According to a colleague, Kempf "always avoided carefully anything that could be interpreted as political. . . . He never uttered a word against Poland." But officials were always "quick to raise the charge of 'disloyalty' . . . whenever someone just stands up openly and honestly for his German nationality."[70]

Kempf was succeeded by Hilarius Breitinger, whose recent memoirs suggest what it was like to be a German priest in western Poland. Breitinger, who had never been to Poland, was greeted by superiors and colleagues speaking only Polish; only Polish and Latin were acceptable for written submissions, and those in Latin received replies in Polish. At first, only Cardinal Hlond was halfway congenial and willing to converse a little in German with his new staff member. Breitinger describes his Polish colleagues as generally unfriendly at first, and heavily involved in Polish nationalist organizations. Once he learned some Polish himself, however, and was willing to try to use it, his colleagues warmed up to him—and then condescended to converse with him in German, which they spoke fluently.[71]

Forms of German Adjustment

The foregoing survey covers only the most significant of the many issues that divided the Polish state from its German minority. Official intolerance and aggressiveness were clearly a major reason for the rapid development of one of interwar Europe's classic nationalist conflicts, but the psychology of the remaining German population of western Poland also played a significant role. For example, just as the refusal to concede any official status to the German language speaks volumes about Poland's long-term intentions, so too does the attitude of many Germans toward their new country's official language suggest an underlying reluctance to accept their place in Poland. For many years after the beginning of Polish rule, many Germans conceded, even flaunted, their lack of Polish, hoping apparently to force Poland to deal with them in their own language. One German elected to the Sejm eight years after the beginning of Polish rule tried to resign his seat "in consideration of [his] complete lack of knowledge of the Polish language." (The government, curiously, refused to let him do so.) Two years later Eugen Naumann announced that he would decline another term in the Sejm in favor of Bernd von Saenger on grounds that at least one member of the German delegation ought to be fluent in Polish. On most German-run farms and in most German-owned businesses, German remained the language of administration, even where Poles made up most of the work force. Whether or not there was provocative intent, such situations made the minority that much less popular in the eyes of a Polish majority already hypersensitized by the long period of Prussian rule.[72]

Two recently published memoirs provide especially interesting insight into the thinking of presumably representative (albeit upper-class) members of the German minority in western Poland. Oda Goerdeler, raised in Działdowo County, formerly part of East Prussia, recalls the contempt of many Germans for the new order and the "feelings of mutual dislike, the reaction of perceived injustice on both sides" in this ethnically mixed region. Germans were "haunted by feelings of superiority, which had previously been taken for granted. People simply had no time to come to terms with what came over them." All that remained to them was pride in their nationality, to which they clung ever more tenaciously after 1920.

Goerdeler's father was jailed briefly for political reasons and the family home searched by police. Her parents were also hurt economically by the collapse of farm prices, diminished access to new agricultural technology and up-to-date farm machinery, and the reduction of their holdings by the Polish land reform program. Goerdeler's attitude—reportedly the attitude of most of her peers as well—was one of aloofness from, if not outright refusal to accept, the new political situation. "One sealed oneself off from the Polish element," she writes; a Polish spouse was "completely unthinkable." In particular, the better situated members of the two nationalities avoided each other socially as much as possible: "Poles were neither invited to, nor would they have even thought to participate in" German social events. Goerdeler enjoyed private schooling at home before attending secondary school in Danzig, so she had little exposure to Polish even as a subject of instruction. She concedes that she was not especially interested in learning her country's official language, aside from the fragments traditionally exchanged with Polish farm workers: "The unpronounceable language of sh-sounds was the language that one was now supposed to speak?" As a result, "our Polish language abilities remained at the lowest level" throughout the interwar period.[73]

Many of the same attitudes show up in Walburg Lehfeldt's account of life as the politically uninvolved mistress of a large Poznanian estate. She denies feelings of superiority or hostility toward the Poles who made up 75 percent of her home village. Though German-Polish relations were "not affectionate," they did exist; the two nationalities participated jointly in the annual *Erntedankfest*, and a Pole was foreman of her estate. But she agrees with Goerdeler that upper-class Germans and Poles seldom socialized with each other; her own family specifically discouraged her from riding or playing tennis with Poles her own age. And Lehfeldt clearly always considered herself a German, politically as well as ethnically. She followed closely (and took pride in) what was happening in the Reich in the 1930s; during a 1934 visit to Berlin she was even treated to a three-hour visit with Hitler and Julius Streicher (testimony presumably to her Aryan good looks and not to her half-Jewish husband).

Though Lehfeldt managed, through private lessons, to learn some Polish, her father continued to use German as the language of his estate; indeed, he "did not speak a word of Polish" and would leave the room if someone else began to speak it. German children attended a minority school in nearby Wolsztyn and maintained separate social clubs. The two nationalities rarely intermarried (in part, to be sure, because of religious differences). Lehfeldt and her family understood that the regime under which they lived sought less to Polonize them than to persuade them to leave the country. But Germans who submitted to this pressure and prepared to leave for the Reich were treated as shirkers, if not traitors, and shunned socially. Only a few German stores remained in Wolsztyn in the wake of the great exodus, and they struggled to survive amid a Polish population that often refused to patronize them. It was therefore a matter of patriotic obligation for Germans to do so, regardless of the shortcomings of these often marginal enterprises. Whatever their religious feelings, the Lehfeldts also considered it a national obligation to support the local Evangelical Church, which Germans and Poles alike viewed as a symbol of German national culture.[74]

There were, on the other hand, some Germans who not only chose to remain in Poland but also saw positive aspects to life in that country. Numerous first-person accounts dating from 1919-20 reflect a cautious optimism based on Polish promises of fair and equal treatment and a willingness to overlook the contentious past. A pastor reported, for example, that most of his congregation wanted "to adapt to conditions and cooperate" with the Poles. Others saw economic opportunities in a large but economically underdeveloped state, a tempting market for the mostly German businesses of Prussian Poland. Conservative Germans might also appreciate the fact that Poland had a more conservative government than Germany and could offer the kind of military career in its large army that post-Versailles Germany could not.[75]

Other memoirs of this period, including many of the post-World War II recollections deposited in the Bundesarchiv, focus more on the essential normality of German-Polish relations especially among the nonpolitical classes and at the level of everyday life, than on national enmity. Wilhelm Pieper, for example, recalls that, with certain exceptions, Germans "who minded their own business" were left pretty much alone by Polish authorities. To be sure, his list of "exceptions" is rather extensive, including occasional house searches, the inability to buy farmland, restrictions on travel to Germany, and official hostility in general. Axel Weiss, who grew up in interwar Poland, became fluent in Polish, and served in the Polish army, reports having had few problems as the only German in his secondary school. Claus von Jonanne recalls life on a large estate as relatively unaffected by national-political events right through 1939. Some of these accounts suggest that real national hostility was peculiar to the formerly Prussian partition, that Germans and Poles got along better elsewhere in Poland. Others see the national problem in class terms: some German landowners report having been on good terms with their Polish farm workers, who allegedly preferred German to Polish employers; some argue that the lower classes suffered most from nationalist envy, accepted nationalist myths most readily, and were most likely to resort to mob violence. It is curious, however, that even those accounts that recall mostly harmonious national relations report little in the way of direct personal or social interaction with Poles. Some combination of temporal distance, the trauma of expulsion, and homesickness is doubtless partially responsible for their relatively benign tenor.[76]

Whatever the individual feelings of Polish Germans, important developments were under way which forced them to stop thinking of themselves as the Reich's temporarily misplaced children and start thinking about strategies for getting along in Poland over the longer term. For example, the tariff war between Poland and Germany, which broke out in 1925 (see Chapter 5), interrupted many of the minority's economic connections with the Reich. Restrictions on trade and travel between the two countries, combined with the fading prospects of frontier revision, encouraged a mood of resignation as well as some new ideas for adapting to the new situation.

One effort at adaptation was spelled out in a forty-one-page memo, "The Political Task of the German Minority in Poland," drafted by a group of Germans in Pomorze and presented to the German Consul in Toruń in 1925. They claimed to have overcome the original shock at being turned over to Poland and to be ready to look beyond thoughts of revanchism. They wanted to think of themselves as Germans in Poland, not just as irredentists: "What we want is not political reunification with Germany but cultural autonomy within the frontiers of Poland, which will preserve our nationality and guarantee us the possibility of positive cooperation in the state." They saw no future in serving as tools of German foreign policy; it was better to cooperate with Germans from elsewhere in Poland to secure the minority's cultural and economic development and ameliorate the admittedly hostile Polish political climate. The German government could help most by improving its own relations with Poland, if only out of appreciation of the Polish role as a bulwark against Soviet Communism.[77]

The Catholic People's Party in Silesia was also relatively quick to come to terms; it cited religious doctrine as the rationale for its declaration of loyalty to the Polish state, adding already in 1921 that it "eschewed any irredenta."[78] Some of the minority's young intellectuals likewise readily accepted the Polish state as the context of their work, turning, for example, to German issues throughout Poland rather than to Reich-German topics. Most prominent were Kurt Lück (1900-1942), who had a Ph.D. in Slavistics (albeit from a German university) and became head of the German Library Association in 1934; and Alfred Lattermann (1894-1945), Rauschning's successor as director of the Historical Society.[79]

There was also a spate of new ideas, more or less utopian, which sought, in effect, to transcend the unpleasant new boundaries so long as they could not be changed. Among these were new concepts of "co-nationality" and campaigns to make "nationality law" an aspect of international law. Given the demonstrated impossibility of homogeneous national states in most of eastern Europe, it was proposed to make the ethnic group an alternative basis of social organization, alongside or even in place of the territorial state.[80] Where territorial solutions to national problems were impossible, members of ethnic minorities should at least be accorded some kind of formal "cultural autonomy." Some Germans in Poland talked of creating a virtually self-contained society, complete with their own secret tribunals in order to avoid using Polish courts.[81] The idea was to establish the concept of civil rights for national groups as well as for individuals and secure the right of such groups to maintain relations with their "core states" across political frontiers.

There were several attempts by European-wide organizations of German minorities or minorities in general to implement these somewhat hazy concepts in the 1920s. For example, the Verband Deutscher Volksgruppen in Europa was founded in 1922, headed (until his death in 1931) by Carl-Georg Bruns. A "European Nationalities Congress" convened annually in Geneva beginning in 1925 and issued its own journal, *Nation und Staat*. The secretary-general of this organization was Ewald Ammende, former editor of the *Rigasche Rundschau*; he was instrumental in getting at least one of the successor states, Estonia, to adopt some of the notions of cultural autonomy advocated by German minority leaders around Europe. His assistants included the Polish-Jewish leader Izaak Grunbaum, and the leader of the Polish minority in Germany, Stanisław Sierakowski.[82]

Territorial and frontier issues were banned from the agenda of these organizations, which focused instead on genuine legal equality and cultural autonomy for minority groups within existing states. They tried, with mixed success, to get the German government to throw its weight behind these concepts and persuade other states to adopt them. But only a few smaller states (such as Estonia) could be persuaded to do so. The German Foreign Office did subsidize attendance at League sessions by representatives of the Nationalities Congress, but this only reinforced Poland's view that the Congress was essentially a tool of German policy.[83]

Differences of opinion on the key question of coming to terms with the new situation sometimes threatened to shatter the facade of political unity within the minority. Chairman Naumann of the DViSuS, for example, seemed to share the views outlined above; he argued (in the words of German Consul Alfred Lütgens) that "Germans must establish themselves in Poland for an indefinite period; the preservation of German nationality there should be the most important consideration." But some of his DViSuS colleagues, especially Graebe and others of the "Pomorze camp," disagreed; they continued to favor the role of temporarily displaced Reich Germans who were obligated to orient themselves to the needs of German foreign policy. Naumann reacted angrily to reports that Graebe and others were going behind his back to oppose Germany's halfhearted search for compromise solutions to some of the outstanding German-Polish problems. In Naumann's somewhat naive formulation, Graebe's belief that the minority's political strategies should remain "subordinate to the 'Corridor question' . . . brushed very close to irredentism." More important, it constituted "no basis for a healthy German national policy," under which "adherence to one's own nationality" had to be combined with the minority's "integration into the Polish state as citizens."

When Naumann concluded that he was in a minority in the DViSuS leadership, he resigned his chairmanship and his Sejm seat as well. At this point, however, the German consulates intervened, fearing that such internecine strife might undermine Reich financial support for the minority, administered chiefly by the DViSuS's Committee of Five. The German consul in Poznań proposed that this committee be reorganized to guarantee parity between Poznania (Naumann) and Pomorze (Graebe) and to "standardize" the distribution of Reich support. At a "unity meeting" called by Lütgens, Graebe and the others denied (untruthfully) that they had operated on their own in Berlin, were wedded to irredentism, or wanted to prevent better German-Polish relations; Naumann, in turn, agreed to withdraw his resignation. The Committee of Five became a Committee of Nine, with four delegates from each province and Naumann continuing as chairman.[84]

Whether the aggressive nationalism of the Polish regime or the nationalist obduracy of many Germans in western Poland was more to blame for the rapid decline in relations between them would be difficult to determine, for both factors were present in abundance. On one hand, an official report on minority attitudes was doubtless correct that "while preserving the appearance of loyalty to the Polish state, the attitude of the majority of Germans [in Poland] is strongly nationalistic, and they sympathize more with the German Empire."[85] On the other hand, it is hard to deny the validity of Paweł Korzec's observation that "it was a political absurdity to expect and demand patriotism from millions of people who had been added to the Polish state against their will, were discriminated against by this state, and robbed of the rights that had been formally granted them by the [Polish] Constitution and international agreements."[86]

There were occasionally signs that government-minority relations might improve (or could *only* improve) from their level during the first half-dozen years of Polish rule. One possibility was the sort of evolution of German-minority attitudes outlined above, especially a willingness to accept a national-minority role in Poland as something permanent. Another possibility was that changes at the top of the Polish government might produce a more conciliatory approach to the German minority or to minorities in general. It was from this perspective that many Germans in Poland viewed the return of Marshall Piłsudski to power in 1926.

4

The Piłsudski Era and the Economic Struggle

The period of National Democratic dominance in Poland came to an end, along with parliamentary government itself, in 1926 after seven crisis-plagued years. Although the national minorities figured prominently among the many problems that made parliamentary rule unworkable, it was a financial crisis that brought matters directly to a head. The attempt to stabilize Poland's finances by introducing a new currency in 1924 proved only temporarily successful; within a year, both the new *złoty* and the government were in serious trouble. Persistent doubts about Poland's long-term viability, related in part to minority problems and the friction they caused with neighboring countries, undermined efforts to attract foreign financial support and forced the Polish state to pay stiff interest rates for such credit as it could find. In May 1926, with the currency again near collapse, unemployment rising, and angry demonstrators in the streets, the current government came apart. As party leaders tried to stitch together yet another coalition, Józef Piłsudski, supported by the army and some labor leaders, carried out a bloody but successful *coup d'état*. For the next nine years, Poland was effectively subject to his personal dictatorship.[1]

The Piłsudski Regime and the Minorities

Many Germans in Poland welcomed Piłsudski's seizure of power, if only because it came at the expense of the National Democrats. They expressed hope that it would mean more tolerant minority policies and thus an improvement in their own situation. For one thing, Piłsudski drew most of his support from central and eastern Poland, where the deep-seated anti-German feelings of the National Democrats (many of whose leaders hailed from the formerly Prussian partition) were less pronounced. The new premier, Kazimierz Bartel, promised that the his government would not "permit the reasonable rights of citizens of non-Polish nationality to be violated. . . . I think that attacking Polish citizens because of their language or religion stands in contradiction to the Polish spirit."[2] Another of the new ministers, Felicjan Sławoj-Składkowski, expressed a desire to tie non-Poles closer to the Polish state by "respect for the national character of each minority," though they should not expect to get anything from the state "by force."[3]

Unfortunately, it was not always easy to determine exactly what Piłsudski himself thought about minority policy in general or the German minority in particular. He served only briefly as minister-president, exercising control instead from the position of war minister, and so was seldom required to take public positions on minority issues. He described his regime vaguely as a "moral" dictatorship, dedicated to the moral renewal and "cleansing" (sanacja) of public life. (He is putative author of the oxymoronic phrase "guided democracy," which found renewed currency in the "Third World" after 1945.) The facade of constitutional government was preserved, but the constitution itself was changed so that Piłsudski could dissolve the Sejm and rule by decree when it was not in session. Despite his PPS background, he governed in alliance with conservative forces, including an amorphous "supraparty," the "Non-Partisan Bloc for Cooperation with the Government" (BBWR). But both his programmatic statements and his stewardship of Poland betrayed a lack of substance; he devoted most of his attention to foreign and military affairs while remaining somewhat aloof from domestic politics, including those questions of greatest concern to Germans and the other minorities.

Shortly after the coup, Piłsudski, Bartel, Foreign Minister August Zaleski, Interior Minister Kazimierz Młodzianowski and several others met to discuss policy toward the minorities. Piłsudski expressed some criticism of the previous approach and conceded that "the mass [of the minorities] are defiant and mistrustful toward the state." He doubted that much could be done to change this if the government relied on force; Polish Germans, for example, constituted in his view "a fully mature national community . . . represented in all social classes, in the country as much as in the city, . . . a self-sufficient national organism . . . not subject to having its strength broken." He believed, however (presumably on the basis of his experience in Imperial Russia), that they had "demonstrated in the course of their history an ease of assimilation and possess an innate streak of loyalty toward the state. The utilization of this minority for the state, with the prospect of political assimilation, is possible and probable. The government should be just but powerful toward the Germans, for, God knows, this population must sense the strong hand of authority over itself."[4]

Młodzianowski condemned previous policies aimed at forced assimilation as, "in some senses, exterminating"; moreover, "the lack of consideration, and often the malice, of local administrators contributes to the fact that the Polish state has lost a number of cases [before the League], which discredit it . . . [and] make of her an 'old client'" in Geneva. He described Polish Germans in the same positive terms Piłsudski used: they were "an industrious and prosperous society, socially a positive element; very well organized, they represent a major force which will submit to no dissolution." But he was less sanguine than Piłsudski about the prospects for mutually beneficial co-existence: "Germans, concerned for the preservation of their property, generally preserve a position of formal loyalty toward the state. But a series of experiences shows that [they] act basically in favor of their former mother country; given this situation, the virtues of the German population can represent a dangerous factor." New "guidelines" for handling the German minority emerged from this conference, urging the "strict but loyal and circumspect application of treaty provisions" combined with an "assurance of impartial behavior by local administrative authorities toward the concerns of the German population."[5]

Another product of this reappraisal of the minority problem was the official Institute for the Study of Nationality Questions (Instytut Badań Spraw Narodowościowych), which suggested a more serious effort by the government to understand the minorities and their concerns. But its executive committee consisted exclusively of Poles, and an editorial in the first volume of its journal, *Sprawy Narodowościowe*, took the unpromising—indeed, threatening—position that "the minorities must adjust to the needs and changing demands of the state of which they are a part; they must renounce those aspirations which are particularist from the state's standpoint in favor of the whole, the state. As the state draws them into the sphere of its leveling activities, it crushes one minority, bends another, and transforms them all, including the main nationality, according to its common and general needs."[6]

Subsequently, when the Minorities Bloc tried to publish its own journal, *Natio*, in 1927, authorities suppressed it within a year. The bloc's Jewish leader, Izaak Grunbaum, was then beaten up in front of his Warsaw home, and the German representative, August Utta, a teacher, was transferred from Łódź to a remote village in another province.[7] Provincial officials continued to criticize Germans' tendency to lead (in the words of one *wojewode*) a "too pronounced life of their own," based on their own social and economic organizations, instead of pooling their energies with other citizens for the good of Poland.[8] For Education Minister Sławomir Czerwiński, the problem was simpler still: Polish Germans just could not "stand the fact that they are not in charge any more; the process which is now being carried out [in the western provinces] is one of de-Germanization of Polish territories that were Germanized in the course of one hundred years."[9]

Even after 1926, the government made few attempts to gain the support of Polish Germans, and these lacked credibility. For example, the loyalist *Deutscher Kultur- und Wirtschaftsbund* (DKWB), established in Silesia in 1929, was all too clearly a government front. It issued a newspaper, the *Neuer Schlesischer Tageblatt*, which had little impact. After just a year (and about one million *złoty* in state subsidies), officials conceded its failure and stopped funding it. In central Poland, DKWB leaders included an associate of Bishop Bursche (Johannes Danielewski) and a former Polish agent named Bruno Gebauer. Aside from some schoolteachers, who as civil servants found it difficult to refuse invitations to join, the DKWB failed to attract much of a following. Its Silesian leader, Rolf Weber, soon ran afoul of a fraud conviction, suggesting that the quality as well as the quantity of the Germans attracted to this organization left something to be desired.[10] In Poznania and Pomorze, official observers conceded that "the interest of the German population [in the DKWB] was . . . almost nil"; reports for both 1935 and 1937 found "no significant activity," and its total membership never rose much above two hundred.[11]

The small number of Germans willing to align themselves with openly collaborationist organizations mirrored the even smaller number of prominent Poles who advocated better treatment of the minority. Most Poles remained convinced that German attitudes toward Poland were essentially fixed, that there was little they could do to assuage German revanchism. Only rarely did a prominent political figure warn that Germany's growing strength, Poland's poor relations with virtually all its other neighbors, and the remoteness of French support made the nation increasingly vulnerable, and that some nonterritorial concessions to Germany or to the German minority might therefore be worth considering.[12] But this suggestion was never seriously pursued—at least not before 1934, when a regime toward which such ideas made no sense had taken over in Berlin. Throughout the life of the Weimar Republic, the vision of a nationally homogeneous Poland and the prevalent view of Polish Germans as security risks combined to stifle this train of thought.

Perhaps Polish-German differences did indeed defy resolution, but the question of just how hostile democratic Germany would remain in the face of a more conciliatory Polish attitude toward the German minority was scarcely posed, much less answered. Instead, public opinion in Poland continued to be monopolized by integral-nationalist ideas and organizations, whose pressure on government was directed at the intensification, not the relaxation, of the de-Germanization effort. This agitation became, if anything, more vocal and better organized after 1926. The most important of these organizations was the "Union for the Defense of the Western Provinces" (*Związek Obrony Kresów Zachodnich*, or ZOKZ), which published *Strażnica Zachodnia* (1922-34.)

The ZOKZ evolved from a Poznanian organization set up to support the Polish cause in the Upper Silesian plebiscite; its headquarters were in Poznań, with branches in Toruń and Katowice. It received financial subsidies as well as information from the state; in fact, it was described in a 1929 legal action (against the *Posener Tageblatt*, which had "offended" it) as an organization that "enjoys the special protection of the state." Membership stood at 23,500 in 1928, including 10,000 in Silesia, 6,000 in Poznania, and 3,000 in Pomorze; by 1934, it had increased to almost 50,000, about half in Silesia. Teachers and civil servants were the most prominent occupational groups, National Democrat the preferred party affiliation.[13]

The ZOKZ agitated against what it termed the "privileges" enjoyed by Polish Germans (for example, minority schools) and disproportionate German levels of land ownership in western Poland. It denounced the "anti-state spirit" of Germans and their ties to the Reich as a "danger which threatens the state." Its efforts were supported by kindred associations of "insurgents" in Silesia and Poznania, similar in composition and goals; they staged anti-German rallies, organized boycotts of German businesses, pressured employers to give preference to ethnic Poles, removed monuments and other surviving symbols of Prussian rule, and lobbied in general for a still tougher posture against Germany and the German minority in Poland. In place of the Prussian monuments, new Polish monuments appeared; one in commemoration of the 1907 school strikes in Września displayed the less than conciliatory words: "Poles! Let us not forget that during our imprisonment the arch-enemy tortured our children here because of their strong attachment to the faith and language of their fathers."[14]

ZOKZ projects included publishing the names of ethnic Germans holding "good" jobs (suggesting their removal) and of allegedly Polish families who sent their children to German schools. One broadside warned: "Mothers! See that your children are entered in the Polish schools. . . . Only children from Polish schools will find easy employment in Poland and so provide for your old age." Other parents received threats: "We know that you are sending your child to the minority school. . . . We ask you: do you wish to bring down upon yourself your child's curse and that of the Polish population for the denationalization of a Polish child? . . . Do you know that German schoolchildren will find no employment in Poland?"[15] There was also a sharp public reaction in Poland, sometimes spontaneous but usually organized by the ZOKZ, whenever German officials spoke of regaining the Corridor or Polish

Silesia: for example, Chancellor Hans Luther in 1925, Minister Gottfried Treviranus in August 1930, and Prussian Minister-President Otto Braun in November 1930. Since German politicians themselves were out of reach, however, ZOKZ demonstrations were often directed at the more accessible German minority. In particular, Treviranus's remarks triggered an outbreak of anti-German violence, including the destruction of the offices of the *Volkszeitung* in Łódź (though that newspaper was affiliated, ironically, with the anti-revisionist DSAP).[16]

The exodus of Germans proceeded at a slower pace during the Piłsudski years not because of any relaxation of the pressure to leave but because most Germans had already done so. A census conducted by the minority itself in 1926 found 240,000 Germans in Poznania (11.5 percent of the population) and 130,000 in Pomorze (12.5 percent). Five years later the 1931 Polish census counted only 193,000 Germans in Poznania (9.2 percent of the population) and 105,400 in Pomorze (9.8 percent); it counted only 731,000 Germans in all of Poland. According to this census, the German population of western Poland had fallen to about 30 percent of pre-1918 levels. Not one county or important town retained a German majority; indeed, the German population exceeded 25 percent of the total in only two counties, Sępólno and Chodzież/Kolmar.[17] Once again, minority representatives challenged the accuracy of the census, and in this case their doubts were subsequently confirmed when the chief of the Main Statistical Office, Edward Szturm de Sztrem, admitted after the war that officials had been directed to undercount minorities, especially those in the eastern provinces.[18]

In fact, one cannot readily compare the 1931 with the 1921 census figures, because the key question in 1921 asked about one's "nationality," whereas in 1931 it was a question of "mother tongue." There remained, of course, a considerable discrepancy between the number who were German by native language (and recognized as such by officials) and the larger number who were German in terms of national-political consciousness (and so claimed as such by minority leaders). Though not limited to Silesia, the discrepancy was greatest there: the vote for German parties was sometimes twice as high as the number of Germans of all ages according to the 1931 census. On the basis of election results, German publicists claimed as many as 350,000 "subjective" Germans in this province. Walter Kuhn, using a figure of 300,000 for the German population of Silesia, argued that the actual size of the German minority in the three provinces of western Poland in 1931 was closer to 630,000 than to the 367,000 figure produced by the official census. A subsequent German "self-count" in 1934 claimed a more modest 492,000, including 205,000 Germans in Poznania (9.7 percent of the population), 108,000 in Pomorze (10 percent), and 180,000 in Silesia (16 percent). One area of agreement between the official census and the minority's own figures was the fact that Germans in the ceded territories were now only a minority of the German population in Poland as a whole.[19]

In short, despite isolated indications of greater sensitivity to minority concerns by Piłsudski and others, Polish minority policies changed little after 1926. Indeed, in some respects they changed for the worse: in Silesia, for example, Piłsudski's coup was followed by the appointment of an outspokenly anti-German *wojewode*, Michał Grażyński. It was apparently just not possible for a Polish leader, even one with Piłsudski's authority and charisma, to be seen as "soft" on the minority question. As it was, Piłsudski's interest in minority questions was limited, and he showed little desire to revise the aggressive policies he had inherited from the National Democrats. Especially with the onset of the great Depression, which stirred up Polish as well as non-Polish opponents, his regime became increasingly arbitrary and notably harsher in its methods.

Election Fraud and Show Trials

Despite the decline of the German population in Poland, Germans managed to increase their Sejm representation to nineteen seats in 1928 (not counting the two German socialists who ran on the PPS ticket). With an official 3.7 percent of the state's population, Germans held 4.8 percent of the seats in the lower house of parliament. For Polish nationalists, this merely illustrated the ability of Germans to lure Poles to their cause by exploiting their unwarranted socio-economic position. More likely explanations for the discrepancy include the higher German voter turnout and the undercounting of minorities by the 1921 census.[20] In August 1930, however, Piłsudski dissolved Sejm and Senate and arrested leaders of the center-left opposition, including Witos and Korfanty, as well as many Ukrainian leaders. He confined them either in a military prison at Brest Litovsk or at one of the first modern concentration camps for political prisoners: Bereza Kartuska in eastern Poland. The subsequent election campaign was less than free and fair; the regime used gangs to break up opposition rallies and encouraged all "loyal" Poles to cast "open" (public) votes.

Included in the general campaign against opposition forces in Poland was a specific effort aimed at German political organizations and newspapers. Following a series of anti-German demonstrations in Poznań, officials closed the Concordia Publishing Company, publisher of the *Posener Tageblatt*, allegedly because of "technical inadequacies" and a "lack of cleanliness." German newspaper editors were charged with making the Polish state "contemptible" (a formal offense) as a result of stories on the plight of minorities in Poland. In Starogard/Preussich-Stargard, twelve local leaders were arrested on political charges during the election campaign, and the candidate himself fled to Danzig. Many Germans were also prevented from voting in the 1930 elections; in Grudziądz, where Germans stood a good chance of electing a candidate to the Sejm, about 30,000 voters were disfranchised when the German list was declared invalid on grounds that one or more persons whose Polish citizenship was under legal challenge had signed the nominating petition.[21] The eastern Slavic national movements doubtless had even greater reason for complaint than the Germans. The Byelorussian nationalist organization (Hramada) was effectively suppressed in 1928, and during the next two years, most of the aboveground Ukrainian opposition was also silenced by means of an often violent "pacification" campaign. Official pressure kept the Minorities Bloc from campaigning as such in 1930; with each minority running on its own, they all lost a significant share of their parliamentary seats.

The 1930 campaign was especially violent in Silesia province. As the result of a promise made during the plebiscite campaign, Silesia was the only Polish province with its own *sejm*, which meant an additional cycle of elections. Germans were allowed (at first) to use their own language in this body and were also able to claim a substantial share of the seats. In the first Silesian Sejm, elected in 1922, 29 percent (14 of 48) of the seats were held by Germans; this was less than the 44 percent that had voted for Germany in the plebiscite but well above the share of German speakers in this province. Aided by a voter participation rate of close to 90 percent (versus about 60 percent for Poles), Germans were over-represented in city councils and other elected bodies as well. They also clearly benefited, however, from disillusionment with the new regime on the part of Silesians who had supported Poland in the plebiscite. Despite the exodus of Germans to the Reich, the vote for German parties began to climb back toward 1921 levels. German candidates did particularly well in the local elections of 1926-28: they received 37 percent of the vote overall, including an outright majority on the city council of Katowice, the largest city. The new *wojewode*, Michał Grażyński, tolerated this situation for nine months, then dissolved the council and appointed a replacement body that was two-thirds Polish. After German candidates also did surprisingly well in 1927 elections in Rybnik, a runoff election was conducted under what an official German observer described as "the most serious terror"; the German vote fell by 25 percent, compared with the first round.[22]

Hundreds of individual acts of "terror" directed at the minority, including even bombings, were ignored by police or remained unsolved. After seventy members of the DKVP were injured in a bomb attack in Królewska Huta, the perpetrators marched away singing, and the police arrested only the editor of *Oberschlesischer Kurier*—for printing the story the next day. DKVP leader Eduard Pant, himself a near-victim of a 1923 bomb attack, responded with an impassioned speech in the provincial *sejm*, charging that "injustice based on brutal force triumphs among us in Silesia. . . . The law serves [only] . . . the de-Germanization of this area." The lives and property of Germans, he claimed, were "little respected; membership in the Association of Insurgents [*Związek Powstańców Śląskich*, or ZPS] or the ZOKZ suffices to be granted immunity or 'mitigating circumstances.' " [23]

The Mixed Commission protected the Volksbund, the main German organization in Silesia, from the kind of direct suppression that befell the Deutschtumsbund in 1923; however, Volkbund leader Otto Ulitz was charged in 1927 with some of the same infractions—for example, helping Polish Germans avoid the draft. His immunity as a member of the Silesian Sejm saved him from immediate prosecution, though it did not prevent Foreign Minister Zaleski from attributing "crimes" to him before the League Council in 1928. The following year, after the Silesian Sejm refused a request by Grażyński to lift Ulitz's immunity, President Ignacy Mościcki simply dissolved that body. Ulitz was arrested a few hours later; on the basis of a clumsy forgery, he was convicted and sentenced to five months in jail. His conviction was later overturned on appeal, but the trial itself revealed a concerted official campaign to compromise German leaders in Silesia by planting spies in their organizations and offering bribes to their employees. [24]

In May 1930, the election of a new provincial *sejm* turned out especially badly from Grażyński's perspective. Despite the continued decline of the German population, German parties received 34 percent of the vote (versus only 17 percent for Grażyński's own *sanacja* list). Thanks to the division of the Polish vote among several parties, the German Electoral Union actually became the largest party in the Silesian Sejm. In Pszczyna/Pless the vote for German parties exceeded even the vote for Germany in 1921. At a time when the official census recognized only 67,000 Germans of all ages in Polish Upper Silesia, the vote of the German parties was 183,000. [25]

But Grażyński treated the provincial legislature much as Piłsudski treated the national *sejm*: when it refused to endorse his program, he dissolved it and ordered new elections. These were held in November under even harsher conditions than those that prevailed in the national campaign of the same month. There were numerous cases of violence by Sanacja partisans and threats of physical harm directed at Germans and especially pro-German Poles. A campaign by the civil servant unions encouraged public voting; those who declined to make their vote public were branded as "enemies of the state" in the pro-government press. The

Chief of the District III election commission (Katowice) announced that eight to ten uniformed Insurgents should appear at each polling station; election commission members should also wear their ZPS uniforms. Although no voter was to be molested inside the building, this directive disclaimed responsibility for what happened outside; anyone who insisted on keeping his vote secret could be considered an opponent and treated accordingly. "Circular #8" from the Insurgents Association in Rybnik included the passage: "Do not allow a single German vote to be cast! Away with all that is hostile to the state!" (Grażyński, though not a Silesian himself, had commanded an Insurgent unit during the 1921 revolt and was now honorary head of the ZPS.) An election poster put up by the ZOKZ declared that "every Silesian man and woman who votes for a German list becomes a traitor. . . . No one will have any mercy on those who dare to vote for the German lists." A ZPS election poster accused some Poles of taking "Judas money" to work for the German cause; it demanded also that German newspapers be "banned from Polish houses. . . . We must be informed of any Poles who read German newspapers." A German complaint to the League of Nations detailed about two hundred beatings and other acts of violence against Germans in Silesia, especially during an "Anti-German Week" proclaimed by the ZPS, October 19-26.[26]

Many Germans were prevented from voting at all on election day. Any citizen could challenge the right of another to vote, usually on grounds that he was not a citizen; such challenges were facilitated by printed forms distributed by officials. Would-be voters, however often they had voted previously, could prove their citizenship when challenged only by means of a certificate obtained within three days from the *starost's* office (which then remained closed for this period). Entire lists of German candidates (for example, in Rybnik, source of about a quarter of the German vote in the province) were nullified because they allegedly contained the names of noncitizens.

Of course, Polish opposition parties did not fare much better in 1930; ironically, as the regime began to treat Polish opposition groups as harshly as the minorities, it became harder for the latter to make the case for persecution on national grounds alone. Wojciech Korfanty, long-time leader of the Polish national movement in Silesia but also head of the Christian Democrats, and so the chief obstacle to Sanacja hegemony, was among the many leading Polish opposition politicians imprisoned at Bereza or Brest Litovsk.[27]

Despite all these efforts, however, the Sanacja list failed to achieve a majority in the Silesian Sejm. Still, the German share of the vote was depressed to 21 percent: 16 percent for the Electoral Union and another 5 percent for German socialists (who, however, outpolled the PPS). The number of German delegates to the forty-eight-member body fell from sixteen to seven.[28] Nationally, Piłsudski's BBWR was able to claim the desired majority in the Sejm (though this institution no longer counted for very much) but only at the price of considerable harm to Poland's international image and the alienation of many Poles as well as non-Poles inside the country. The number of minority seats in this body fell from eighty-four to thirty-three; with about 35 percent of the state's population, minorities now had only about 7 percent of the seats in parliament. The number of German representatives in the Sejm fell even more sharply, from twenty-one to only five. Similarly, the number of Germans serving on town councils in Poznania fell from about one hundred in 1929 to thirty-three in 1933, some 2 percent of the total. In Pomorze the decline was from seventy in 1929 to twenty-four in 1933, about 4 percent of the town councillors in that province. Clearly, official pressure—not changed voting habits or demographics—was responsible for these sharp declines.[29]

The increasingly repressive political atmosphere evident in the campaign of 1930 was manifest also in a series of political trials of minority leaders. One of these involved leaders and members of the German Scout movement in Poland, arrested upon their return from a festival sponsored by the German Sports School in Berlin. They were put on trial in May 1930 for participating in "paramilitary" exercises and traveling illegally to Germany in the first place. One Scout leader was sentenced to fifteen months in prison for spying and conspiracy; 130 Polish German youth, having been photographed by Polish agents while participating in the festivities, were sentenced to fifty days in jail. All these sentences were reduced on appeal, however, and then set aside altogether, pending a retrial that never took place.[30] Another group called "German Youth in Poland" (Deutsche Jungenschaft in Polen, or DJiP), established in 1926 on the basis of several older youth organizations, also held illegal joint meetings with kindred groups in Germany and Danzig (the high cost of Polish passports was usually cited as the main reason for crossing the frontier illegally), conducted seminars on more or less political subjects, and organized excursions to isolated German communities in eastern and southern Poland. Increased official scrutiny in 1929-30 was at least partially responsible for the DJiP's subsequent decline.[31]

A second major legal action was aimed at the leadership of the DViSuS, chief political organization of the minority in Poznania and Pomorze. In October 1929, Graebe's parliamentary immunity was specially lifted to permit his arrest. The Bydgoszcz headquarters of the DViSuS were searched and locked up for a week, and numerous documents were confiscated—an action that the Deutsche Rundschau was warned not to write about. The homes of several other German Sejm representatives as well as the offices of the main association of German farmers in Pomorze, Landbund Weichselgau, were also searched. DViSuS offices in Poznań as well as were entered again by police in February 1930; the records of the German Welfare Association, of which Graebe was chairman, were seized, and additional arrests were made. Those arrested were accused of training would-be insurgents, maintaining illegal ties with a foreign power, collecting census data without authorization (that is, the minority's "self-count" of 1926), and gathering "intelligence" for "treasonous" use against Poland in the League of Nations. But the point of these actions was apparently not to secure convictions but to find additional evidence for use in the long-delayed trial of the Deutschtumsbund.[32]

That trial finally got underway in April 1930, almost seven years after the suppression of the DB. The *Manchester Guardian*'s account concluded that "as in the case of Ulitz, there is no doubt about the complete innocence of the accused [or] about the loyal behavior of the German minority population vs. the Polish state." Nonetheless, all the accused were convicted of "participation in an anti-state association," part of an unauthorized "state within the state" that frustrated state policy by encouraging settlers to resist attempts to eject them, advising Germans to choose Polish citizenship and remain in Poland, and carrying complaints to the League of Nations. Heidelck and another former DB leader were sentenced to twelve months in jail; eight others received sentences of one to six months. Because of his restored parliamentary immunity, Graebe's trial was delayed until after the Sejm was dissolved in 1931. Amidst considerable international attention, he was acquitted of the main charge of treason but given a six-months sentence on a lesser charge of moving children from one school district to another to keep minority school enrollment above the forty-pupil minimum. The Polish supreme court affirmed all the verdicts and ordered the eleven minority leaders to begin serving their sentences; a short time later, however, those convicted were all amnestied in the wake of the German-Polish Non-Aggression Pact of January 1934 (see Chapter 6).[33]

As a result of these less than satisfactory legal actions against the minority's principal leaders, the Polish criminal code was amended in 1932 to improve the state's chances in future encounters. Maintaining contacts with foreign powers and causing "hostile action" against Poland now constituted a crime punishable by ten years' imprisonment (Article 99). Article 109 made it a crime to spread information "hostile to Poland," and Article 152 threatened with three years in prison anyone "publicly scolding or ridiculing the Polish state or people." These amendments, an effort above all to limit the minority's ability to appeal for support from Berlin or Geneva, ended by having little impact, for the government declined to follow through on its intentions after the signing of the 1934 non-aggression pact.[34]

Other forms of official pressure on politically active members of the minority continued unabated, however. One lengthy report by the German consul in Poznań cited many examples of police house searches, opened mail, arrests and detention for months without charge, restrictions on the right of assembly, proscriptions on the use of the German language in public, harassment of German co-ops and hospitals and charitable institutions, and a refusal to sanction a nationwide organization of Germans.[35]

Undermining Minority Schools

Another measure of the Piłsudski regime's treatment of the German minority was the status of the minority-school system. The number of German public schools in Poland declined from 544 to 200 between 1926-27 and 1933-34. The dip was even sharper in Poznania and Pomorze: in 1926-27, there were 254 such schools in these two provinces, plus 160 primarily Polish schools with individual classes taught in German; in 1937-38 there were only sixty of the former (a decline of 76 percent) and ninety-two of the latter. The percentage of German children in these formerly German provinces who were forced to attend Polish-language schools increased from 37 percent in 1926-27 to 57 percent by 1937-38; 43 percent of German pupils attended schools where German was not even available as a subject of instruction. The 43 percent of German children who did enjoy instruction in their own language included only 27 percent in the publicly supported minority schools guaranteed by the Minorities Protection Treaty; the other 16 percent were in private institutions.[36]

The undermining of the minority-school system was especially pronounced in the politically sensitive Corridor, where fewer than 25 percent of German children attended such institutions in the 1930s. In one Pomorze county, Świecie/Schwetz, the decline of German schools was absolute, from forty-one and 1925 to zero in 1939. Germans claimed that these numbers were proof that Poland was not living up to its obligations under the Minorities Protection Treaty; the official responsible for most of the Reich support programs for the minority contended that the "systematic de-Germanization policy of the Poles in Poznania and Pomorze is unmistakable. . . . The numbers show that Poland . . . is pursuing the destruction of the German nationality, [especially] in the Corridor area."[37]

Yet the decline of the German school system was even more precipitous in central Poland, which was not on Germany's revisionist agenda and where the German population remained fairly steady. Here the number of German schools fell from 564 in 1919 to only eighty-three in 1930; in Łódź, whose German population actually registered a modest increase during the interwar period, the number of schools available to it fell from twenty to nine. In Koło County, which had thirty German schools at the end of Russian rule, there were none at all to serve the county's 8,800 German inhabitants in the 1930s.[38]

In Silesia, minority schools enjoyed somewhat better protection than elsewhere in Poland. The state was required to fund minority schools at the same level as majority ones, and parent councils were formally invested with a supervisory role. In districts with fewer than forty but more than eighteen German pupils, otherwise Polish schools were obliged to offer instruction in German (Article 107). Where none of the prerequisites for public instruction in German obtained, Germans had the explicit right to establish private schools, provided only that they were up to state standards and did not engage in "anti-state" activities (Article 98). A German-language secondary school was also supposed to be set up wherever there were at least three hundred prospective students (Article 108). In contrast to the rest of Poland, Silesian minority schools were also able to employ noncitizens (Reich citizens) as teachers. What mattered, however, was not that the Geneva Convention's school guarantees were different from those in the Minorities Protection Treaty but that President Calonder and his Mixed Commission were on hand in Silesia to provide some enforcement. This was also the reason why the struggle over minority schools became most heated in this province.

Another reason was the continuing disparity between the modest number of Silesians who spoke German from birth and the considerably larger number whose native language was Polish but who had acquired a German national consciousness and so wanted their children to have a German education. The question was whether these people themselves or state officials should decide the language in which their children were to be educated. According to Article 131 of the Geneva Convention, the "subjective" concept of nationality was clearly supposed to prevail; parents were to have the exclusive right to decide whether their children would attend a German or a Polish school and thus, in effect, the national group with which they wished to identify. Officials did not have any apparent grounds for second-guessing this decision. Yet at the beginning of Polish rule in 1922, when more than 50,000 parents petitioned to have their children assigned to German-language schools, officials approved only about 18,000 of these petitions.

In the eyes of Polish nationalists, anything short of complete agreement between objective and subjective nationality—that is, between native language and political orientation—was unnatural and could only be the result of conditioning or coercion during the years of Prussian rule.

Officials acknowledged only the approximately 7 percent native German speakers as the "real" German minority in Silesia province. They were particularly upset when interest in German schools subsequently began to grow, despite the establishment of Polish rule and a steady decline of the German-speaking population. They were convinced that some kind of coercion, however subtle—perhaps promises of economic advantage, or just anachronistic assumptions about German social superiority—was behind the desire of so many "Polish" parents to send their children to minority schools. They charged that "certain persons supported financially by the Reich [that is, the Volksbund] . . . were trying to draw large numbers of children who are undoubtably Polish to the minority schools." There were even some Polish officials who considered this step, in the apparent belief that a German education still meant social or professional advantage.[39]

Minority leaders claimed that they had no reason to enroll children in their schools who did not understand German. They did, however, run programs to prepare Polish speakers for study at German schools. And Polish as well as German schools experimented with various incentives to attract more pupils: free lunches, Christmas gifts, cheap excursions to Poland or Germany respectively. The German government was aware of the advantages deriving from traditional Germanophile attitudes and channeled funds toward Silesia in order to keep them alive. In 1928 the consulate in Katowice urged the continued flow of Reich funds on grounds that "there is a very close connection between the financial capability of a Reich-German office and the attraction of the German cause in elections."[40] But even absent coercion or bribery, the fact (and, for officials, the problem) was that a significant percentage of Polish-speaking Upper Silesians continued to identify with German political nationality.

When the right of parents to enroll their children in the school of their choice was appealed to Calonder, he cited the explicit wording of the Geneva Convention: "Legal guardians exclusively shall determine the language of a child, and this declaration may not be examined or contested by school authorities." He supported the German argument that minority schools should be open also to those for whom German was a second language but who wanted to acquire better command of a major world language, and for those Silesians to whom written Polish was almost as alien as German to begin with. He came out strongly in support of the right of parents to choose schools without official interference: "The pedantry that leads officials to disregard the wishes of the applicants and to declare hundreds of applications null and void on purely formal grounds if unfair . . . and wholly irreconcilable with the Geneva Convention, which aimed not at placing obstacles in the way of minority schools but at facilitating their establishment." This unequivocal statement was probably responsible for a slight increase in minority-school enrollment in Silesia, to about 24,450 pupils in ninety-nine schools, by 1926.[41]

Especially after Grażyński's arrival in 1926, however, Polish officials ignored Calonder's opinions and began systematically to reject the applications of Polish-speaking children to attend minority schools. They considered that they had a national obligation to eradicate traditional conceptions of German cultural superiority and reclaim nationally ambivalent Poles, even if doing so meant going against the letter of the Geneva Convention or interfering with the rights of parents. In 1928, Grażyński decreed that parents could declare only one "mother tongue" for their children, instead of "both German and Polish" as some were wont to do, and had to swear formally to the truth of their declaration. In pursuit of their mission to re-Polonize autochthonous Silesians, some officials went so far as to address minority-school pupils in Polish on the streets and, if they answered in that language, order them transferred to a Polish school.[42] Mothers of illegitimate children were added to the category of those not considered qualified to select their children's schools. Nationalist organizations, with official backing and financial support, conducted periodic campaigns against Silesians of Polish background who persisted in trying to enroll their children in German schools. Parents who ignored these pressures complained of being "terrorized," and German newspapers that printed their stories were confiscated.[43]

As a result of these actions, the number of minority schools in Silesia declined sharply under Grażyński (and Piłsudski). After 1933 the Volksbund itself relaxed its efforts to enroll autochthones, a consequence presumably of the new ideas of "racial" purity emanating from the Reich. Minority school enrollment fell to about 7,600 in 1936-37, primarily because of official efforts to keep Polish speakers out. Whereas about 15 percent of the province's children had attended German schools in 1922-23, only about 5 percent did so in 1938-39. Enrollment in the two surviving public German secondary schools (Katowice and Królewska Huta) declined by 38 percent (from 1,626 to 1,007) during the first three years of the Grażyński regime, and both institutions were closed soon thereafter. By the 1930s there were only two German secondary schools in Silesia, both privately run, plus some German-language classes in otherwise Polish institutions.[44]

Meanwhile, the teaching staff of the surviving minority schools became progressively less German. The normal practice whenever a vacancy occurred anywhere in western Poland was to fill it with a nationally conscious Pole, provided only that he had a rudimentary command of German. Silesian officials ignored the Mixed Commission's opinion that minority schools should be staffed primarily by minority teachers. They argued that it was Poland's business who was hired to teach in the public schools, for minority schools too were state institutions, as subject to state authority as Polish-language schools. The percentage of minority-school teachers in Silesia who were Polish rose from virtually zero to 57 percent in 1936-37, and all but two of the forty surviving minority schools had Polish principals.[45]

Disillusioned with public minority schools in Poland, minority leaders turned increasingly to private schools as an alternative. These were run by a "German School Association" (*Deutscher Schulverein*, or DSV), established in Bydgoszcz in 1921 and directed throughout the interwar period by Otto Schönbeck (1881-1959). Schönbeck remained a Reich citizen and so was ineligible to teach in his own schools, but on orders from the Polish Foreign Ministry he was given a wide berth by officials, most likely out of consideration for an equivalent Polish organization that operated in Germany. The private schools were supported financially by the Reich, which provided the DSV with money for teachers' salaries and pensions, below-cost books, and scholarship aid for poor students and for those who agreed to become teachers in Poland. A "Kant Association," modeled perhaps on the successful nineteenth-century Polish Marcinkowski Association, also provided financial aid to help needy students with tuition payments. Financial support from Germany further allowed the DSV to supplement low teacher salaries in Poland; as a result, some German teaches made several times as much as their Polish counterparts at the same institution.[46]

The DSV's annual budget eventually approached four million *złoty*; it used the influence that came with this financial clout to assert its control at the expense of local school boards. DSV documents show Schönbeck functioning as a sort of superintendent over the entire private-school network, offering detailed advice to parents and school boards on how to deal with officials, when to display the Polish flag, and whom to hire for teaching and administrative positions.[47] According to the account of one disgruntled teacher, a Dr. Jacob (published in *Das Andere Deutschland* in 1930 under the title "Pirates of Patriotism"), Schönbeck insisted that his teachers toe the line politically; he "demanded an anti-Polish position" from them and kept a "black list" of antinationalist classroom comments reported by pupils (which Jacob blamed for his own transfer from Grudziądz to Chojnice).[48]

Private German schools were not exempt from official requirements and restrictions. For example, only Polish citizens fluent in the Polish language could teach in them; history and geography had to be taught from the Polish point of view; and Polish officials administered the school-leaving examinations for private secondary schools. Teachers in private schools also required official certification, which was provided for only one year at a time; approval to teach could be denied for vague or arbitrary reasons, and sometimes just before the school year began. The number of private German schools in Pomorze and Poznania had climbed to 117 by the school year 1926-27, including four secondary schools (in Grudziądz, Bydgoszcz, Poznań, and Leszno).[49] Officials viewed private minority schools with greater suspicion even than the public ones; they were reluctant to approve their establishment where public minority schools were available or in sensitive areas such as the Corridor. Additional growth was slowed by a 1927 law that made it easier for officials to deny approval of or to dissolve a private school if, for example, they suspected that "ulterior motives" were behind its founding. A 1932 law established special loyalty tests, unusually strict building codes, and other obstacles for groups wanting to operate private schools. Thereafter, German applications to establish private schools were denied more often than not, and the DSV found itself in a "bitter and unequal struggle with Polish officials" to replace closed public minority schools. Nonetheless, in 1937-38 one hundred private German schools with a combined enrollment of 7,205 (16 percent of all German pupils) were still operating in Poznania and Pomorze, and there were twenty-five private schools in Silesia with about 100 pupils each, including the secondary schools in Katowice and Królewska Huta.[50]

The memoirs of two former minority-school teachers suggest what it was like to work in such institutions. Thea Wohlgemuth tells the story of the public German-language *Gymnasium* in Toruń. Founded in 1568, this was the only public German secondary school in Pomorze and Poznania to survive until 1939. By then, however, it had been fundamentally altered. First, the large building in which it had previously been housed became home to a new Polish school, and the German school had to make do with temporary quarters and only occasional access to the laboratories and physical education facilities in its old building. Its work was then disrupted by the departure of most of its teaching staff for Germany during the first years of Polish rule. Vacancies were invariably filled by ethnic Poles, even to teach German classes, and they soon constituted a majority of the faculty. Polish was also the obligatory *lingua franca* of teachers' conferences and internal administration. In 1927, the German principal was dismissed, and his job too went to a succession of Poles. By 1936 only two German teachers, including Wohlgemuth, remained. She reports that German and Polish teachers got along well enough but that there was little "closeness" between Polish teachers and their German students.[51]

The Toruń German Gymnasium's curriculum, traditionally rigorous, became still more so after 1920. In addition to the two foreign languages normally required in Poland (not German, curiously, but French and Latin), students at this school had to learn a third: Polish. And they had to do so quickly, for this was the language used to teach classes in history and geography. Polish was the most difficult subject for most students, not only at first (when few young Germans had been exposed to it) but later as well, suggesting that most Germans continued to have little exposure to Poles and their language even while living in a Polish state. Many students even in the 1930s, despite having lived most of their lives under Polish rule, still required private tutors to pass this subject—and no diploma was possible without a passing grade in Polish. Under these conditions, the Toruń German Gymnasium gradually lost its appeal for many students, who gravitated instead toward the private German secondary schools in Bydgoszcz and Grudziądz.

Dietrich Vogt published his recollections of life at the largest of the private German secondary schools, the Schiller Gymnasium in Poznań, where he served as principal. This school was established with twenty teachers and 680 students in 1920, after it became clear that none of the four public German secondary schools in Poznań would survive the transfer of sovereignty to Poland. Only those students certified as German by officials were eligible to attend. Parents provided about half the school's expenses; the other half came from the DSV or Reich agencies. From the start, the Schiller Gymnasium suffered a high rate of teacher turnover. In order to be certified, teachers had to pass an examination in Polish within a specified time. This proved a difficult hurdle for many and is one reason why so many teachers joined the exodus to Germany. (As noted above, an unfortunate consequence of Prussian Polish policy was that a unilingual German population came to share these provinces with a bilingual Polish one, which created few problems so long as Germans were in charge but became a real handicap when Polish rule began.) Despite these difficulties and a steady decline in student enrollment during the next two decades, Reich subsidies later permitted the construction of a fine new building, though Voigt denies that such subsidies allowed Reich agencies to dictate policy to him or that they attempted to do so.[52]

Officials supervised the private Schiller Gymnasium just as closely as the public one in Toruń. Only the Polish form of the school's name was permitted on the outside of the building. Instruction and examinations in history, geography, and Polish were conducted in Polish, and Vogt felt obliged to hire ethnic Poles to teach these courses. He recalls only good relations, however, with the seventeen Polish teachers whom he employed at one time or another. As in Toruń, Polish was the most difficult subject for most students; in an average year, 30 percent had to repeat, most because of difficulties with that subject. The school served a wide geographical area, obliging most students to board locally; Vogt encouraged them to room with Polish families to improve their proficiency in the

Polish language. After 1924 the school's faculty lost the right to administer its own school-leaving examinations; that task was taken over by a committee of Polish school officials. While the Schiller faculty was giving the examinations, 89 percent of the students passed in an average year; from 1925 on the success rate dropped below 60 percent. That school officials applied different standards to Polish and German graduates is suggested by the following figures: in 1931, 96 percent of the students at four Polish *Gymnasia* in Silesia passed their school-leaving examinations; 75 percent did so in the public German Toruń Gymnasium; the success rates at the private German *Gymnasia* in Poznań and Bydgoszcz were only 52 percent and 49 percent respectively.[53]

Vogt describes official school inspectors as generally "correct," though an increasingly hostile attitude became apparent in the 1930s. They were favorably impressed with the physical plant and the qualifications of the faculty and seldom found real grounds even for political objections. Their most frequent complaints concerned the low level of student fluency in Polish, the paucity of Polish books in the school library, and other signs that this institution was trying to ignore its place in a Polish state. Schiller Gymnasium was never granted full certification (at a time when 78 percent of the private secondary schools in Poland were "fully certified," only one of the seven German institutions in western Poland enjoyed this status). Only during the years 1928-31 were those attending this school even recognized officially as "students" and so made eligible for such state benefits as reduced-fare rail travel.[54]

The records of the private German *Gymnasium* at Leszno, preserved in the state archives in Poznań, provide yet another perspective on the problem of minority schools in western Poland. This school was run by a "German School Association in Leszno" and had about 250 students in the 1920s, 75 percent from outside Leszno itself. The many requests for tuition abatement suggest that many families found it difficult to finance a German education for their children; the school itself was constantly forced to straddle a narrow line between social exclusivity and financial insolvency. Especially in the wake of the 1932 law on private schools, officials watched the Leszno school ever more closely and enforced regulations ever more strictly. Annual visitations turned up numerous deficiencies: most of these could be remedied, but some (corridors too narrow or ceilings ten centimeters too low) called in effect for a new building. German Sejm representatives claimed that school building codes were being applied unfairly to prewar structures; the application of unrealistic construction standards forced the closure of nine private German schools within a single year, and "the agitation of the German population in Poland . . . reached a high level as a result."

In some desperation, the Leszno school board hired Ludwik Roehr, a Polish lawyer in Warsaw, and made a direct appeal to Piłsudski to save the institution: "We are prepared to make any sacrifice" to prevent its closing, but the present school building "really meets all reasonable demands" and it would be "incomprehensible" to close a *Gymnasium* dating back to 1555 for such trivial reasons. Roehr reported that the key to this problem was not in Warsaw but at the provincial level, "where everything was cast"; the most he could achieve was a three-year grace period during which the school board would agree to build or buy a new building. A short time later the provincial *wojewode* did grant such a reprieve. He also complimented the school board for having had the good sense to hire a Polish lawyer (which, however, it could not apparently afford: Roehr submitted at least six requests for his 2,500 *złoty* fee, reminding the school board that it "made out much better than others, thanks to my intervention").[55]

Officials also monitored the teachers and administrators at private German schools for signs of political incorrectness. In 1931 the chairman of the school board in Leszno reported having received an "incomprehensible decree" removing the school's acting head two weeks before the start of the school year and depriving him of his teaching certificate as well. The official visitation report for 1933 complained that too many of the teachers at the Leszno school still could not converse in Polish. Other objections included "blemishes" (that is, the old frontiers) on some of the maps used and the students' weak performance in Polish class. On the other hand, the report was pleased to note that Polish national holidays (including Piłsudski's "name day") were properly observed and that students had voluntarily formed a "Polonists" club. A surprise visitation in 1936, however, turned out much worse: only an assistant principal named Dorien was on hand to greet and guide the school inspector, and he was unable to do so in Polish. Meanwhile, the rest of the staff and most students were found assembled in a large room listening to the radio broadcast of a Reichstag speech by Hitler. (Even Schönbeck sympathized with official annoyance on this occasion and ordered Dorien's removal as assistant principal.) Just before the beginning of the school year in September 1936, officials revoked the teaching certificates of three more teachers and vetoed the proposed new principal on grounds that he did not know enough Polish. Finally, at the end of the 1936-37 school year the Leszno German Gymnasium, faced with official chicanery, declining enrollments, and the need to construct a new building, was forced to close.[56]

Another DSV effort to deal with the growing number of German children without access to instruction in their own language was a program called "Parents Aid" (*Elternhilfe*). Beginning in 1927, "traveling teachers" *(Wanderlehrer)* were recruited from youth organizations and from the ranks of teachers excluded from the classroom for political reasons (the DSV claimed to have sixty-seven such teachers by 1930 and 119 in 1936, though others put the number much lower). *Wanderlehrer* could not pretend to be "real" teachers; they were permitted only to coach parents in the education of their own children or preside over small educational-social functions. Even so, and though their numbers remained modest, they met with strong opposition from the government, which pursued them with fines and even jail terms.[57] Blau suggested that church members help out by conducting German-language religion classes for children without access to such instruction in the schools, but officials watched these carefully to make sure no one tried to teach German language or history under the guise of teaching religion. In 1932 some of the church's religion classes were declared illegal, and a school-teacher was sentenced to jail for two weeks for including material about the German language in the religion classes he conducted in his own home.[58]

The Economic Conflict

Precisely during the Piłsudski years, the more conventional forms of official harassment, aimed at the minority's political and cultural institutions, were supplemented by a concerted effort to weaken the German population economically. This included, most prominently, an attack on its main economic foundation, its landed property. By 1926, German private land-ownership in Poznania and Pomorze had already fallen by about 35 percent, mostly as a consequence of the German exodus. A sizable additional amount was lost after 1926, but most of this decline was the result of state measures, especially "land reform."

The first Polish land reform law of July 15, 1920, was mainly a crisis measure, passed in the midst of the Red Army's advance. As that threat disappeared, the law was allowed to lapse and was trumped altogether by the 1921 constitution, which required the state to pay full compensation for any land taken. A second effort to deal with the chronic problem of peasant "land hunger" by breaking up large estates was initiated in 1925. Under this law, estates of 180 hectares or more (300 hectares in the eastern provinces) were subject to "reform." A "land supply" (the sum of private holdings in excess of 180 or 300 hectares) was determined for each province, and a small part of this was put on the list of properties earmarked for state purchase each year. Affected owners were given a year in which to sell their "excess" property before they were subject to forced purchase. Any such properties put up for sale voluntarily were then subtracted from the year's list of earmarked holdings and only the difference was forcibly taken by the state. Under the law, up to 200,000 hectares could be taken nationwide each year; as a result of "voluntary" sales from the land supply and other factors, the amount actually taken in most years was considerably less (only 57,000 hectares in 1934). In fact, only after 1929 (and then primarily in the western provinces) did this modest land reform program reach the point of actually forcing owners to sell some of their lands.[59]

All together, about 154,000 new farms were created throughout Poland under the 1925 law; an additional 500,000 small holdings were made somewhat larger. Stated differently, the number of peasant holdings in the country increased by only 4.5 percent, a paltry advance more than canceled out by a 20 percent increase in Poland's rural population between the two world wars. In western Poland, most of the new "settlers" came from overpopulated Galicia; many of these failed to prosper under unfamiliar circumstances on farms that were usually still rather small. Insofar as this program had an economic impact, it was to weaken larger and often more efficient producers and discourage investment by others in property that they might not be able to keep very long.

The program's major drawback, however, was that it was motivated as much by national-political as by social considerations. It was clearly aimed at German and other minority landowners and thus saw its most extensive implementation in Poland's western provinces. When it came to assigning the farms created under this program, certain social groups were entitled to preferential treatment: previous employees of the estate itself, veterans, the offspring of fallen soldiers, graduates of agricultural schools, and political refugees from the Soviet Union and other countries (refugees made up 39 percent of the early settlers). But even if one qualified according to any of those criteria, one had also to be ethnically Polish.[60]

In Poznania and Pomorze together, Germans were owners of 39 percent (262,000 hectares) of the "land supply" subject to requisition under the 1925 law. The first annual list of properties to be reformed included, however, 10,800 hectares from thirty-two German landowners and only 950 hectares from seven Poles. The following year (1927), Pomorze, with about 3 percent of the large-estate property in Poland, was tapped for 14 percent of the land to be reformed nationwide.[61] Germans charged that Poland's land reform was really just another form of national discrimination and a violation of the Minorities Protection Treaty. Poles replied that Germans must give up proportionately more because they owned a disproportionate share of the land in these provinces to begin with. As noted previously, the minority's share of farmland in these two provinces did considerably exceed its share of the total population; in effect, the nonagricultural German population of western Poland was so diminished by the great exodus that the remnant minority became overwhelmingly agricultural and its share of the region's farmland therefore disproportionately large.

The Polish land reform program soon joined the list of German-Polish disputes brought before the League of Nations; perhaps because of the League's attention, the two nationalities in western Poland were treated more equally in 1928. This result only provoked a backlash from Polish nationalists, however, including some local officials. A confidential memo from the Pomorze *wojewode*, Wiktor Lamot, to the district land office in Grudziądz left little doubt about the national-political considerations guiding land reform: "Political concerns as well as the needs of state security are not being considered," he argued; it was necessary to consider the "loyalty of the affected citizens, their nationality, their religion, and their general attitude toward the vital interests of the state." Land reform ought to be applied in a way that also took into consideration the special strategic position and significance of this province. For example, "the part of Pomorze through which the so-called Corridor runs must be cleansed of larger German holdings." The coastal region "must be settled with a nationally conscious Polish population, capable of withstanding the agitation of both domestic radicals working toward insurrection and agents of the neighboring country. Estates belonging to Germans must be taxed more heavily" to encourage them voluntarily to turn over land for settlement. "Border counties, . . . particularly a strip of land ten kilometers wide, must be settled with Poles. German estates that lie here must be reduced without concern for their economic value or the views of their owners."

German property in Chełmno County and along the Bydgoszcz-Tczew-Dirschau railway were also to be targeted because this region constituted "the largest, economically most developed salient of German influence." The provincial capital Toruń too would need to be surrounded by a Polish peasant population. Lamot further asked officials to focus "especially on those personalities among German landowners who by their political activity have a negative effect and who encourage the tendency toward separatism. . . . The most extensive ruthlessness must be applied to these Germans. Under no circumstances can the retention of their current level of property ownership be permitted." The estates of Erwin Hasbach, Nordewin von Koerber, and other prominent minority political figures were indeed included on the first land reform lists; many subsequently found themselves in some economic difficulty because of the state-induced shrinking of their holdings. But "under no circumstances," added Lamot, were "the considerations that have really exercised influence" over this policy to be made public; instead, "principles of an objective nature must always be found" to explain which landowners were called upon to give up land.[62]

Publicly and before the League, Poland maintained that it took relatively more land from Germans because it wanted first to tackle the largest estates, which were more often German. In fact, there were 630 Polish estates of more than 500 hectares in Poznania and Pomorze (1928) versus 347 owned by Germans. Yet during the same period when thirty-five German estate owners with less than 500 hectares were called on to part with up to 50 percent of their land, three-quarters of the Polish-owned estates of 1,000 hectares or more remained unscathed. On other occasions, Poland maintained that Poles were less subject to mandatory land reform because they contributed more to voluntary parceling schemes, or because Reich financial support helped German landowners to resist the normal economic pressures encouraging them to sell off "excess" land. According to one set of figures brought before the League, Germans in Pomorze (owners of 44 percent of the "land supply") were required to contribute 73 percent of the land taken under compulsion but only 66 percent if one includes land voluntarily parceled. The figures of Poznania, where 36 percent of the land supply was in German hands, were 63 percent and 50 percent respectively. In other words, this explained only a small part of the disparity. Of course, German landowners were also less likely to be interested in voluntary parceling schemes because ethnic Germans were excluded from acquiring privately created small farms as well as those created by the state land reform program. According to Land Reform Minister Witold Staniewicz, the policy was that "only Germans whose loyalty toward the state is beyond doubt can count on land from the parcelization project." In fact, however, Germans were generally and apparently categorically excluded from the benefits of the land reform program, regardless of their political orientation. Younger children of German farmers and employees of estates broken up by land reform usually had no alternative but to leave Poland if they wished to remain in farming.[63]

The negative impact of land reform and other official measures on the agricultural economy of Germans in western Poland came on top of the difficulties of economic adjustment in the national economy of which they were now an integral part. Most of the Polish economy had developed as part of the Russian, based on a large Russian market that was now closed to it. Germany would have been the logical replacement had not political hostility prevented such an adjustment. For this and other reasons, Polish agriculture and Polish industry alike grew at a rate below the world average during the interwar period. Reasonably good economic times did not arrive in Poland until about 1927, fueled by increased demand for coal, the country's principal export product, especially in the wake of the 1926 general strike in Great Britain. Agriculture also began to improve, and overall domestic consumption rose. But then, just as the economy was approaching 1913 production levels, the great Depression descended. By 1932, Polish industrial production was only 59 percent of 1928 levels, which were not again reached during the interwar period. In other words, Poland's overall industrial production in 1938 was probably no greater than in 1913; per capita, it was 18 percent less. According to the most knowledgeable students of the interwar Polish economy, at least half the period 1918-39 saw it in a condition of serious weakness if not outright crisis.[64]

This relative economic decline was felt most sharply in the more highly developed western provinces. For example, while the number of industrial workers in Poland as a whole increased somewhat, it fell by 16 percent in Poznania and Pomorze and by 23 percent in Silesia. The transfer of considerable wealth by means of the tax system from Poland's western provinces to other parts of the country caused the level of economic development in the former to decline still further in relation to Germany, without however making much of an impact on the remaining regional disparities. One illustration of disparity was the per capita tax burden, which in 1933-34 stood at 20.3 złoty in Poland as a whole but at 52.4 złoty in Poznania. Another illustration: 60 percent of the automobiles registered in Poland in 1939 were in the three western provinces.[65]

There was evidence of fundamental regression in the agricultural economy of formerly Prussian Poland as a result of its transfer to Polish rule. The share of land devoted to more intensive agriculture ("fields, gardens, and pasture") declined, while the amount of acreage in the more extensive "meadow, woodland, and fallow" categories increased accordingly. Per capita production of four major grains in Poznania fell in the course of the interwar period from 3.8 tons per million inhabitants in 1909-13 to 3.6 tons (1934-38.) Productivity fell more sharply still, from 19.3 tons of wheat per 1,000 hectares in the mid-1920s to about 15 tons in the mid-1930s. Yet even such a decline failed to erase the huge agricultural surpluses that continued to depress farm prices in Poland. Low farm prices—wheat fell by nearly half from 1925 to 1938—discouraged production and investment precisely in the more intensive western areas. Farmers in western Poland (both German and Polish) also faced tighter credit conditions and the higher interest rates characteristic of less developed, weak-currency countries. One compensation, at least for those larger operations that had struggled with farm-labor shortages before the war, was the ample supply of labor now available in Poland's eastern provinces. Indeed, hundreds of thousands of Poles continued to leave Poland each year in search of work in other countries; half of them found only seasonal work in agriculture, mainly in Germany.[66]

In addition to land reform and other policies aimed at German land-ownership, Poland found other ways to inhibit the minority economically. For example, the state licenses required to practice some professions, though not denied to Germans across the board, were denied to specific groups of Germans on more or less explicit political grounds. In one case, 40 percent (fourteen of thirty-five) of the German physicians and pharmacists working as *Kassenärtze* (employed by state health insurance agencies) in Pomorze lost the right to engage in this practice in a single year (1933). The last two German dentists authorized to do state-financed work (without which professional survival was often difficult) were also dropped from the rolls. Ten years after the beginning of Polish rule, there was no longer a single German notary in Poland. Hundreds of German innkeepers complained that their state liquor licenses had been withdrawn for political reasons; they too took their case all the way to the League of Nations but found no redress there, and most wound up having to leave Poland for economic reasons. One Pomorze *wojewode* refused a liquor license to a German social club (the Deutsches Heim in Toruń) on grounds that the government granted such licenses as a "favor"; German businesses that agreed to advertise in the quasi-official *Dzień Pomorski* could expect more favorable consideration, he added.[67]

German firms were normally excluded from state contracts, but officials also kept a watchful eye on the national orientation of ethnic Poles when deciding such matters. For example, the file of one entrepreneur describes "a Pole of German orientation" who was married to a German, spoke German at home, and sent his children to German schools; therefore he was to be excluded from the preference normally shown to ethnic Poles.[68] Ethnic Germans were no longer hired by the civil service. Some German railway and postal workers remained from the previous regime but were ordered not to participate in minority organizations, send their children to minority schools, or use their native language "ostentatiously." Some of these remaining German state employees were forced out anyway by pressure from Polish colleagues. There was an apparent purge of the civil service in western Poland in 1928, focusing on state employees who spoke German at home or read German newspapers or were thought to vote for German candidates. Those who fell into any of these categories were transferred to remote parts of the country where few Germans lived. Also caught up in this house-cleaning were several hundred police officers recruited from among Poles who had returned from Germany; because they had become bilingual, they were now considered politically suspect.[69]

Nowhere was official economic pressure on the minority so persistent and so central to the state's strategy as in Silesia. Grażyński declared that his program for Silesia was the same as that of the ZPS: to increase Polish power, to get rid of the remaining Germans, and to keep open the question of that part of Upper Silesia still ruled by Germany. Andrzej Chojnowski has accurately summarized his goals as "the consolidation of the Polish position . . . [while] combatting the 'privileged' German position . . . by means of administrative measures not always consistent with the stipulations of the Upper Silesia Convention."[70] In addition to his integral-nationalist ideology, Grażyński was also driven by economic and strategic concerns to reduce the German minority in Silesia. This small and strategically exposed province accounted for 73 percent of Poland's coal production and 71 percent of its steel. In addition to the German minority, Grażyński also had to worry about a significant "autonomist" movement among local Poles. The ambivalent national orientation of much of the "Polish" population of this province also remained a source of constant concern. Korfanty and his colleagues had felt obliged (and not just by the Geneva Convention) to work with economically powerful local Germans before 1926; Grażyński did not. He accused Korfanty, no mean nationalist himself, of catering excessively to German economic interests. And he did not hesitate, as noted above, to defy Calonder and the Mixed Commission when they suggested that his policies were in conflict with the Geneva Convention.[71]

Grażyński's greatest advantage in his campaign against the German minority in Silesia was the fact that most of them were not (as in Poznania and Pomorze) self-sufficient farmers, relatively immune to official pressure, but industrial workers or salaried employees. The most effective weapon against them was denial of employment. Although the Geneva Convention (and the Mixed Commission) forbade economic discrimination between eastern/Polish and western/German Upper Silesians, virtually all 23,311 of the latter (most of them Germans) who continued to commute to jobs in Polish Silesia after 1922 were gone by 1926. Grażyński also declared publicly that two-thirds of the remaining Germans in his province would have to leave, for they would find no work there in the long run. He steadily extended state control over German-owned industrial enterprises and used this control to reduce the number of Germans in their work forces; he also intervened to get German executives removed, allegedly in the name of labor peace. Plant managers were under constant pressure to Polonize their operations; even Polish firms were told that they might have trouble getting state contracts, or face difficult tax audits, if they did not replace ethnic Germans in key positions with Poles.[72]

In one significant case recounted by Neal Pease, the American firm of W. Averill and Co., in coalition with Anaconda Copper, purchased the large zinc foundry of Giesche's Erben AG in 1925 and created a new "Silesian-American Corporation." This company received tax breaks, special export quotas, and other economic considerations from the government because this was just the kind of foreign investment Poland most wanted and needed. But Harriman disappointed nationalist officials by leaving much of the previous German management in place; he took up membership (for business reasons, he claimed) in the local association of German industrialists; and he turned back official suggestions that he purge Germans from management on grounds that there were "simply not enough trained and experienced Poles . . . to run the plants." Harriman soon became an object of attacks in the nationalist press for his allegedly Germanophile sentiments; this press campaign probably cost him the contract to provide one-quarter of Poland with electrical power in 1929. It certainly helped alienate one of the few major foreign firms to show serious interest in interwar Poland and so was clearly self-defeating. Grażyński, however, was evidently interested in economic development less for its own sake (as a disillusioned Harriman reported to U.S. Ambassador John Stetson) than as part of his "hidden war against the German minority."[73]

A number of cases of purposeful and (under the Geneva Convention) impermissible Polonization of the Silesian labor force reached the League of Nations. In one such case a German claimed to have been fired by the quasi-private Spółka Bracka, the miners union's insurance fund, in response to official pressure because he insisted upon sending his children to a minority school. His grievance included a 1925 letter to twenty-two German employees from the fund's director, ordering them to remove their children from German schools: "Anyone who . . . continues to send his children to the minority school does not intend for his children to be brought up as Polish citizens and prefers to educate them in the German spirit as enemies of Poland." Four German employees who disregarded this warning were told by their supervisor the following year that they would be fired if they persisted: "You must make your choice: either the Volksbund or your daily bread." The head of the Central Mines Administration in Katowice admitted in court that he had pushed the insurance fund to Polonize its management: "It was my official duty to see that . . . the institution assumed a definitely Polish character."[74] Poland defended this practice before the League on grounds that the employee in question was a member of the PPS, had previously identified himself as a Pole, and so should not be sending his children to a German school or petitioning the League for protection as a member of the German minority. The League declined on this occasion to intervene; it determined that the insurance fund was essentially private, which meant that the Polish state could not be held responsible for its actions.[75]

This same insurance fund was the subject of a second complaint when it terminated the contracts of thirty-two German physicians on grounds that their command of the Polish language was inadequate. The physicians' complaint to the League presented evidence of an official campaign to diminish the number of German professionals in Silesia, including the comment by a state official on the fund's board of directors that there were too many unemployed Polish "academics," and "we must therefore dismiss Germans in order to make their posts available for Poles." Calonder supported the grievance of these physicians and tried to effect a compromise: the fund would rehire all but one of the fifteen still on the scene, provided that those under age sixty were Polish citizens and could converse at least in the Upper Silesian dialect. But Grażyński refused to agree to this compromise; those on the fund's board who did agree were attacked by the nationalist press, and one member was arrested on the day of the key vote. As the League showed signs of taking up this issue, however, the Warsaw government overruled Grażyński, agreed to Calonder's recommendations, and ordered the reinstatement of fourteen of the German physicians.[76]

The largest German conglomerate in Polish Silesia, the largest owner of both mines and land, and the largest employer of Germans was the Pless concern. Grażyński kept up a steady pressure on this company to Polonize its work force, especially its white-collar staff. When its owner, Johann Heinrich von Pless, who also functioned as titular head of the Volksbund, attempted to appoint a German legal adviser in 1928-29, he was told by the (Polish) head of the provincial Department of Commerce and Industry that the government had not worked to get rid of the previous (German) legal adviser just to see the post filled by another ethnic German; reprisals were threatened if Pless did not agree to hire more Polish executives. In 1930 the state cut back its purchases of coal from this firm and, after a special tax audit, presented it with a $2,000,000 tax bill, payable at once. Pless hired a couple of French tax-law experts to plead his case to the League; they contended that Polish tax law left too much to the subjective determination of officials who were motivated by considerations "of a political rather than fiscal nature . . . aiming to ruin the undertakings of the leader of the German minority in Upper Silesia . . . [and] amounting indirectly to an expropriation of his property." Faced again with a rash of unwelcome negative publicity in this world forum, Poland agreed to suspend its efforts to collect the back taxes—so long as the matter remained before the League.[77]

In 1934, however, Pless was arrested on charges of employing an alien (a citizen of Danzig) and presented again with a huge tax bill. He was forced to sell about 20,000 hectares of land to meet it and was then compelled to accept a Polish manager for his remaining holdings. His work force had traditionally been about 80 percent German; most of these employees, including some with Polish names but with children in German schools, subsequently lost their jobs and were replaced by Poles.

Pless's renewed appeal to the League elicited some expressions of sympathy but no effective support; Germany, his chief protector, was by this time no longer a member of that organization. The firm's headquarters employed 148 Germans in 1934, of whom 134 had been dismissed by 1937; all those hired to replace them were ethnic Poles. A firm that had previously employed almost 4,000 Germans now had almost no German employees left.[78]

In sum, German hopes that Piłsudski might make a difference and that his government might break with the minority policies of his National Democratic rivals were pretty thoroughly dashed. Precisely after 1926, the usual methods of political chicanery were supplemented by new economic weapons that threatened the landed property and the jobs of the rump minority, and thus its very survival over the longer term. Under these conditions, the minority was more or less forced to turn increasingly to Germany and to international organizations for support.

5

The Minority in the International Arena

For Germany, even for a then democratic Germany that had no plans (and no capability) to wage aggressive war to revise its frontier with Poland, there was never any question of watching passively while its former citizens were treated so roughly. The condition of the German minority in Poland necessarily became a problem for the German government, not solely a domestic problem for Poland. In the course of the 1920s the German minority came to loom ever larger as a problem in the international arena as well, exacerbating already poor relations between Germany and Poland and challenging the League's ability to back up its promises of support for minority rights.

The Minority and German-Polish Relations

Germany could not reasonably be expected to remain indifferent to the fate of its former citizens, especially under the conditions outlined above. Yet Poland was bound to see whatever Germany did on behalf of the German minority in Poland as interference in its internal affairs and an attempt to retain control over what were now Polish citizens. In the wake of Germany's refusal to accept its changed eastern frontier, Poland was also bound to view virtually anything done for Polish Germans in the context of German revisionism; the same revisionist specter that spurred Polish officials on to diminish the size and economic influence of the German minority also determined their attitude toward German aid programs designed to slow this process. Yet it would be wrong to see this issue exclusively in the context of German revisionism and Polish fears of same. Just as Polish minority policy stemmed from underlying motives far beyond the question of whether Germany was satisfied with the 1919 settlement, so Reich efforts to soften the blow of this settlement on the German population of western Poland were motivated by more than just revisionism. Quite apart from the desire for different frontiers with Poland, the question for German leaders was always how, not whether, they should help Polish Germans survive under the new conditions.

There were several different approaches that Germany could take toward this problem. One called for direct dealings with Poland, leading perhaps to a formal bilateral agreement to secure better treatment for the minority in exchange for some other consideration. Germany retained significant leverage over Poland; the substantial German role in the Polish economy and the fact of a remaining Polish minority in Germany might be exploited to get Poland to pull back from its Polonization policies. Germany remained Poland's principal market and principal supplier as well; in 1923, Germany absorbed 51 percent of Poland's exports and provided 44 percent of its imports. Poland's role in the German economy, by contrast, was relatively insignificant; only 4 to 5 percent of Germany's trade was with that country. Thus Germany might threaten to disrupt the close but unequal economic relationship in order to win concessions for the German minority in Poland.[1]

Such a strategy was attempted sporadically in the early years of the Weimar Republic, but it bore no fruit. For one thing, given the extent of popular German resentment of Poland, no German government could afford to venture very far in the direction of compromise, regardless of the anticipated payoff for the German minority. For another, German-Polish relations remained on an essentially cold-war footing throughout the life of the Weimar Republic. Even when German interests were not directly involved—for example, when Poland moved into the Ukraine in 1919—Germany seemed almost reflexively to adopt an anti-Polish position. During the ensuing Polish-Soviet war, Germany imposed a ban on military exports to Poland and otherwise demonstrated a clear tilt toward Soviet Russia.

In the wake of the Polish liquidation law of July 14, 1920, which seemed to point to the eventual expropriation of all German "settlers," additional economic sanctions were imposed: the export ban became more comprehensive; Polish journals were banned from Germany; and deposited funds belonging to some formerly German, now Polish towns were confiscated. There was already a general consensus within the German government that neither Poland nor its German minority could be allowed to think that Germany was indifferent to the fate of its former citizens in Poland or helpless to aid them. One minister, warning that "the Poles are pursuing, systematically and ruthlessly, the complete displacement of the Germans" in western Poland, feared that this goal would soon be achieved if Polish actions met only verbal protests. Another believed that the July 14 law, which indicated "a lack of any feeling for law or justice," demanded "the most rigorous position by the German government." Several cabinet members called for a comprehensive trade ban, hoping that Poland's economic vulnerability would force accession to "our justified demands for the protection of the German minority."[2]

Economics Minister Ernst Scholz dissented, questioning whether such a ban was enforceable. Poland would get what it needed from other countries, or illegally from Germany itself; Germany would risk losing a market that its industrial economy needed for its own recovery. Since Polish-German trade was mostly in German hands on both sides, German businesses in the ceded lands would be hurt more than Polish enterprises. Several Polish-German firms, including Gebr. Koerting AG in Poznań, made the same point, complaining that they were more adversely affected than anyone else by existing trade restrictions. But even after a Breslau firm blamed its own bankruptcy and the loss of some 7,000 jobs on the loss of its market in Poland, the cabinet majority remained convinced that its trade ban, "the only weapon that Germany has in hand versus Poland," would bring Poland around to a deal regarding the German minority. Even before the conclusion of the Polish-Soviet war, however, the Foreign Office was forced to concede that economic sanctions were having no discernible impact on Polish policies and doing nothing for the German minority.[3]

Poland never really considered responding in the desired way to German economic pressures. Caught in a life-and-death struggle with its huge eastern neighbor, Poland viewed German sanctions as an expression of fundamental hostility, not just a bargaining ploy in behalf of the German minority. Moreover, influential Germans were known to be opposed not just to the German-Polish frontier but to Poland's very existence; they seemed prepared to consider any means and associate themselves with any partner, including Soviet Russia, to bring about Poland's demise. Chief of the General Staff Hans von Seeckt was a prominent representative of this school of thought: "Poland's existence is unbearable, incompatible with Germany's vital needs. She must disappear and will disappear, through her own internal weakness and through Russia, with our help."[4] Others hoped to achieve much the same goal by means of improved relations with western powers, whose governments might be won over to the German point of view. Chancellor Joseph Wirth, one of the architects of the German "fulfillment" policy toward these countries, declared at the same time that Poland "must be finished off [erledigt]; my policies are oriented toward this goal."[5] Stresemann did not go that far, but he did include among the positive results of the Locarno Pact the "preservation of the possibility of the reacquisition of German territory in the east."[6]

With the successful conclusion of its war with Soviet Russian, however, Poland clearly showed more resilience than many in Germany had hoped or thought possible. As it became apparent that Poland would be around for a while, the two countries moved toward somewhat more normal relations. A 1921 agreement covered traffic through the Corridor, permitting essentially free German passage between east Prussia and the Reich. The following year, the Wirth-Rathenau government negotiated several other treaties with Poland, covering border traffic, joint operation of some Upper Silesian mines, and the normalization of water traffic between the two countries. Despite continuing political tensions, about twenty additional treaties were concluded between Germany and Poland during the next few years, most of them dealing with frontier or economic issues.[7]

In 1925, however, relations again took a turn for the worse with the outbreak of the "tariff war" between the two countries. German duties on Polish agricultural imports increased in steps to reach 27 percent by 1927; Poland responded by increasing to 56 percent the tariffs on manufactured goods coming in from Germany. Moreover, as Poland sought to persuade other countries to help in the severe financial crises of 1924 and 1926, it found that Germany was campaigning behind the scenes to dissuade them from doing so. Treatment of the German minority in Poland was at least one of the reasons for this German policy of economic confrontation, and renewed efforts to use economic pressure tactics to get a better deal for the minority was one of the reasons the tariff war lasted into the 1930s. Germany paid a considerable economic price for the hard line against Poland, but German leaders were convinced it was a price that had to be paid. In the words of the German consul in Poznań: "The rigorous persecution of the tariff war seems to be the last opportunity to save local Germans from complete and final decline. . . . Hatred of Germans is a national religion here, and fighting Germans is equated with 'building up the fatherland.'" Foreclosing the German market to Polish goods might yet persuade Poland to back off from additional discriminatory measures, reign in local officials, and intervene more forcefully to control outbreaks of popular anti-German hostility.[8]

High atop the list of German objectives during these economic battles was a Polish agreement to forgo the "liquidation" of remaining Reich-German property in that country. As of 1925, about 55,000 hectares of German property, worth about 60 million German marks, remained subject to state takeover, and the legal status of another 15,000 hectares was in dispute. Even though liquidating the property of Reich citizens did not seem to be directed at the minority as such, these properties provided a living for about 7,000 German-speaking Polish citizens who were unlikely to retain their jobs if the land came into Polish hands. Stresemann also thought that getting Poland to stop the liquidation of German property would help dispell the "panicky mood" among Polish Germans and "encourage these people to hold out."[9]

Minority leaders also asked Germany to intervene more forcefully in behalf of the threatened property rights of the "settlers." About 9,000 of these remained in Poland, most of them Polish citizens but many also quite old. The state was poised to take over their lands when they died; their survivors could expect only minimal compensation and would most likely have to leave for Germany. Unless Germany was able to secure clear title, including the right of free inheritance, many of these people would probably pull out sooner rather than later. During a 1927 meeting with Graebe, Chancellor Wilhelm Marx expressed support for this position, but he declined to make it a prerequisite for ending the tariff war.[10] Germany's ambassador to Poland, Ulrich Rauscher, contended rather that Germany was more likely to achieve its goals by being conciliatory than by waging economic warfare and publicly berating Poland at every opportunity: "However indispensable [the latter approach] might be for propaganda purposes," he wrote, "it has proved ill suited so far to the achievement of practical advantages for the minorities." He cautioned that the government was letting domestic-political considerations get in the way of agreements that were both achievable and vital to the minority. A treaty limiting the liquidation of German property was "not just a matter of some desirable treaty which one can conclude or not; rather, it must be concluded if at least 50 percent of the German property in Poland is not to be hopelessly lost."[11]

The two countries did finally come to terms on a liquidation treaty on October 31, 1929. They agreed to drop all outstanding claims against each other dating from World War I and its aftermath. In return for a payment of one billion German marks, Poland agreed not to liquidate any more German property; more important, it also agreed to stop contesting the property rights of the remaining settlers and to relinquish rights of repurchase stemming from Prussian Settlement Commission contracts. Rauscher called this pact "the greatest service . . . the German Reich has been able to perform for its minority in Poland thus far. . . . It leaves completely untouched the basic territorial disputes between the two states. . . . We are making only financial sacrifices . . . while the compensations granted by the Poles are of a national-political nature. . . . In particular, we have kept our hands completely free for the future representation of minority grievances. In return, we have normalized our relationship with Poland and thereby opened the way for the economic penetration of this country."[12] Adding the property covered by this agreement to what settlers still owned, Rauschning figured that the 1929 liquidation agreement preserved up to 180,000 hectares of German-owned land from Polish takeover and kept as many as 80,000 Polish Germans from having to leave for the Reich.[13]

Unfortunately, the very idea of German-Polish agreement remained anathema to significant sectors of public opinion in both countries. In awareness of this fact, each side agreed to let the other present the Liquidation Treaty to its respective public in the most favorable light. Nonetheless, the agreement was attacked with equal vigor by German and Polish nationalists. Many Poles agreed with Rauscher that Germany had got the better of the deal. Alfons Krysiński lamented his government's abandonment of the right of repurchase and with it the prospect of being rid of an additional 80,000 ethnic Germans. *Ilustrowany Kuryer Codzienny* (Cracow), for whom the minority constituted an "immigrant formation, . . . a German-covered part of the Polish organism," considered it a "crime to give up the liquidation effort, since it is a matter of aliens who were sent to liquidate Poles and Germanize the land."[14]

Neither government was confident that it had the votes to get this agreement through its respective parliament. Stresemann's successor, Julius Curtius, supported it as "guaranteeing the existence of our German countrymen on the other side of the border" but confided that, "as things stand today, I have the most serious concern that we will not be able to get the treaty through the Reichstag." Increased focus by the nationalist press on the anti-German thrust of Poland's agrarian reform program made his task still more difficult; the Center Party, in particular, cited this as reason enough to withhold its support from the government of which it was a part. Curtius appealed to his Polish counterpart, Zaleski, to help the cause with some kind of written promise that Polish land reform would henceforth treat the two nationalities more equally, but Zaleski was unable, because of Polish nationalist pressures, to oblige.[15] The Liquidation Treaty was eventually ratified by the Reichstag (1930) and the Sejm (1931), but the political difficulties it created for the two governments hardly encouraged the search for additional agreements. Moreover, German-Polish relations were exacerbated just then by the long-delayed trial of the leaders of the *Deutschtumsbund*; Poland was cautioned that a show trial of its "ridiculous" charges against the German government as the alleged manipulator of the DB would affect German-Polish relations negatively and cause Germany to protest Polish violations of the Minorities Protection Treaty even more forcefully.[16] The violent election campaign of November 1930 also strained German-Polish relations. Poland was cautioned that "the German public sees in these incidents . . . a systematic struggle against Germans, conducted with the toleration and cooperation of official Polish agencies. . . . The necessary restraint with respect to domestic-political events in a neighboring country ends where it becomes a matter of the vital concerns of one's own people, the crude disregard of which seriously threatens the peaceful coexistence of peoples."[17] The growth of political extremism, especially in Germany, furthered the general deterioration of relations in the early 1930s. Whenever the Reichstag took up an issue related to Poland, the government was subject to harsh attacks from the right. The Reichstag climate was so hostile that Curtius became reluctant to submit treaties even on such strictly technical questions as railroad traffic through the Corridor.[18]

The conclusion of the Liquidation Treaty coincided also with the onset of the Great Depression. Germany moved to protect its home market by raising most tariffs even beyond the levels of the previous tariff war; by 1931, agricultural imports from Poland faced a rate of 83 percent. Germany continued to play a fairly significant role in the Polish economy, ranking third (behind France and the United States) on the list of countries holding Polish debt, and still took about 15 percent of Poland's exports. But the reverse was hardly true: Poland accounted for only 1.2 percent of Germany's imports in 1934, and the share of German exports going to Poland dropped even below the 1 percent mark. By this time, two dozen other countries ranked ahead of Poland on the list of Germany's trading partners. Given the geographical proximity, historical interdependence, and obvious economic complementarity of the two countries, this represented a remarkable triumph of political considerations over economics.[19]

It was, above all, Germany's continued refusal to back away from revisionist demands that made Poland unreceptive to overtures regarding the German minority. In a 1932 interview Curtius reiterated his belief that "without the return of the Polish Corridor to Germany, a solution of the German-Polish problem is not possible or conceivable."[20] Moreover, international support for German revisionism, especially in Britain and the United States, seemed to be on the increase during the early 1930s. U.S. Senator William Borah openly embraced the German position, arguing that the best way to neutralize National Socialism was to liquidate the Corridor and make Poland treat its German minority fairly. U.S. Secretary of State Henry Stimson also offered some thoughts on the Corridor and European peace but was effectively deterred from pursuing the issue by Polish vows to fight rather than revise. New books by British and American writers (some of them subsidized, to be sure, by the German Foreign Office, if not ghostwritten by its employees) supported German demands for the return of the Corridor or Polish Upper Silesia or both. The German Foreign Office also sponsored escorted tours of the Corridor region for prominent foreign visitors, stressing the disruptive effects of the frontier and highlighting the downed Vistula bridges and neglected dikes. Some 5,000 people participated in these tours, including U.S. Ambassador

Frederic Sackett, who in 1930 pronounced the German-Polish border "impossible."[21]

Piłsudski's belligerent response to this revived German revisionist agitation—for example, his scarcely veiled threats to move into East Prussia—culminated in a brief "war scare" in July 1932, defused only after Poland denied such designs and blamed the scare itself on National Socialist campaign rhetoric.[22] It was this specter of a Polish move against East Prussia that helped Chancellor Heinrich Brüning's opponents undermine his ban on public demonstrations by Nazi Stormtroopers on grounds that they offered some insurance against a scenario with which the Reichswehr would be at a loss to deal.

Ambassador Rauscher remained reluctant to abandon efforts to reach an understanding with Poland; he was reluctant even to pass along the Bülow note cited above. In his opinion, Germany had already lodged too many protests, including four official *démarches* within the fortnight. He was convinced that most of these were motivated by domestic-political considerations, part of the effort to placate growing nationalist feeling in Germany, but unlikely to provide tangible relief for the minority. He questioned whether Poland had done anything even during the 1930 elections (except perhaps in Silesia) worth protesting to the League and reminded his own government that Poland did have an authoritarian government which tolerated little opposition of any kind, Polish or non-Polish. He believed that truly "terroristic" official actions against the minority, or open collusion between officials and the nationalist mobs responsible for most of the violence, were rather uncommon outside Silesia. In reply, Bülow acknowledged the domestic-political pressures but insisted that they were a secondary consideration; Germany could not stop interceding in behalf of Polish Germans just because the Piłsudski regime suppressed Polish as well as German opponents. Treviranus made the same point: certainly the government was under growing domestic pressure to "do something" about the treatment of Germans in Poland, but the many "acts of terror" during the recent campaign would demand a forceful response under any circumstances.[23] Curtius hoped that Germany would be able to "break off the fight" and get along with Poland, but only while "repudiating, of course, all encroachments against the German minority."[24]

On the whole, then, though some slight improvement was perceptible from time to time, German-Polish relations never became really "normal" at any time during the life of the Weimar Republic. As a result, Germany's ability to secure relief for the minority in Poland by means of direct negotiations with that country's government remained quite limited.

The Minority and the League of Nations

Many German-Polish issues found their way to international organizations, especially the League of Nations in Geneva and the PCIJ in The Hague, and several were resolved in the minority's favor. The Minorities Protection Treaty stipulated that its guarantees were "obligations of international concern . . . under the guarantee of the League of Nations. . . . Any member of the [League] Council . . . shall have the right to bring to the attention of the Council any infraction . . . of these obligations and the Council may thereupon take such actions and give such direction as it may deem proper and effective." Alleged violations were submitted to the secretariat, which passed them on to a "Minorities Section" to determine whether they were actionable. The complaint had then to be sponsored by a member of the League Council; many complaints by Polish Germans died for lack of a sponsor until Germany became a member in 1926. A complaint that made it this far was then submitted to the accused government for its response; this and the original complaint were next submitted to a minorities subcommittee of (usually) three delegates from disinterested states. The subcommittee's goal was to bring about voluntary compliance with what it understood to be the requirements of the minorities treaty. If such compliance by the accused state was not forthcoming, the complaint might be referred to the full Council, which normally turned it over to the representative of yet another disinterested state for formal arbitration. But the weapons at the disposal of such arbitrators included only moral suasion and negative publicity; if the accused state remained adamant or the minority remained dissatisfied, the only recourse was to take the issue to the PCIJ.[25]

The first list of German complaints from Poland was filed just a few months after the Versailles Treaty took effect. Among other things, it objected to the dispossession and expulsion of settlers, the dissolution of German organizations, harassment of the minority press, and the refusal to recognize elected German public officials on grounds that they did not speak Polish. In subsequent years, most of the major issues treated in the two previous chapters of this book became subjects of complaints to the League. The most frequent sources of formal grievances were Polish land reform and other forms of economic discrimination, school policy, election irregularities, and anti-German popular violence. Germany also began filing petitions in the minority's behalf in 1922 and soon became the League's most frequent plaintiff on minority questions. By the same token, Poland's minority policies generated more complaints than any other country's, not just from Germans but from the other minorities as well. Specifically, of the 525 complaints that reached the League's Minorities Section between 1920 and 1931, 155 concerned Poland; 104 of the 525 came from German minorities, in Poland and elsewhere in Europe. A Brazilian diplomat active in League minority affairs characterized Poland as his "best client" and the chief testing ground of the idea of internationally sanctioned protection of minorities.[26]

Germany's ability to intercede at the League in behalf of the German minority in Poland was enhanced, of course, by German membersip on the League Council after 1926. Being able to do more for German minorities in neighboring countries was one of the reasons Stresemann cited for joining in the first place: "Poland and others . . . will not be able to disregard their obligations so reprehensibly if they know that Germany can bring all these lapses before the League of Nations."[27] He assigned the nine million Germans living outside the Reich in central Europe an important role in his overall strategy, as is evident from a memorandum of January 13, 1925, which largely prefigured Reich policy vis-à-vis the German minority in Poland during the following eight years. German minorities in central Europe would be "called on politically . . . to influence the policies [of their home states] in a way favorable to the German Reich. They represent, and encourage the spread of, German culture and world views; economically, they serve as an important market and supplier for Reich businesses; they live in those regions of Europe [the Baltic and Danubian realm and along the frontiers of the Reich] in which the vital questions of German policy and economy must be decided. . . . [Of course,] they will always be viewed by the majority peoples as an irredenta, whose eventual destruction or absorption must be pursued by all means. [Especially those living along Germany's eastern frontier,] the most important group for the German Reich, . . . are engaged . . . in a life-and-death struggle with the peoples who control their states. . . . This endangered position, together with their invaluable significance, compels the Reich to do everything to support them in the struggle for the preservation of their German nationality and to leave no means untried."

Stresemann recognized that Germany, unable at the time to do much by "power-political" means, had to try to "interest world opinion in the fate of the suppressed German minorities in such a way that the majority peoples [would] be forced by international pressure to grant vital cultural freedoms." Germany should try to win world opinion over to the principle that "the right of every minority to cultural autonomy represents a natural right completely independent of all political considerations and concerns, the denial of which cannot be excused and is synonymous with suppression. Its general realization can take place without the shifting of political boundaries and should clearly have a healing, conciliatory effect precisely there where the principle of the self-determination of peoples was violated." Minority protection treaties had been "only minimally effective [to date], and the supervision of the League, though still better than nothing, [had been] rendered almost illusory by the problems of procedure." Still, it would be foolish to ignore the League's "undeniable significance as a permanent means for the influencing of public opinion in the world." Already, "the minorities problem is a question of international interest, and a generous solution of this problem in Europe is seen as a precondition for lasting peace." [28]

Membership in the League seemed to offer the prospect of pursuing a tangible German interest while framing it as a concern of the entire "world community." As Stresemann told the Reichstag, "whoever commits himself to the idea that human rights of language, race, and religion should be respected and honored despite state boundaries, he speaks up for the preservation of peace and for the avoidance of violent disputes. Peace among peoples will be all the more secure the less often the cries of minorities whose cultural survival is threatened reach the ear of the public. That assumes, however, that the leaders of the minority states will let themselves be persuaded that it accords with the most fundamental interests of the state when it seeks a positive, legal solution to the minority question(s) within its boundaries." [29] In this context, Stresemann regularly insisted on Germany's right to question Poland's treatment of the German minority and the right of German parliamentarians to comment on the subject in the Reichstag. He frequently had German diplomats lodge protests against strictly internal Polish practices, such as the membership of ministers in the ZOKZ or the appearance of officials at anti-German rallies. He repeatedly made the point that improved German-Polish relations were contingent upon "exact compliance" with the Minorities Protection Treaty. When Poland tried to follow Germany's suit and become a permanent member of the League Council, Stresemann made his approval conditional upon "effective protection" for minorities in Poland. But "since protection of minorities in Poland without international checks is ineffectual," what was required was a system of ongoing international supervision, which Poland was bound to reject out of hand. [30]

Protection treaties and their enforcement by the League achieved some relief for minorities. They were saved, at least, from the kind of open repression practiced by Italy and some other states not subject to such constraints. Ultimately, however, the League's efforts proved disappointing. One problem was the difference of opinion among the major powers about what the minority treaties were supposed to achieve in the first place. Minorities spokesmen assumed that they were meant to facilitate the continued existence of minorities as such in the new sates. Others, such as British Foreign Secretary Austen Chamberlain, interpreted them as an attempt to ease the gradual but inevitable assimilation of minorities, not block that process indefinitely. French Foreign Minister Aristide Briand observed that the League, without "destroying the unique character of the minority," ought nonetheless to promote "a kind of assimilation" of the "small family" into the "larger [majority] family" in each state.[31]

The League was not inclined, of course, to alienate its own members by prying too much into their internal affairs. Member states enjoyed more status in the League than minority petitioners, and the League always tried to resolve disputes by appeasing the accused states or granting them the benefit of any doubt. The cumbersome procedure for dealing with minority complaints itself provided ample room for subterfuge and delay. In most cases, the best that could be achieved for minority petitioners was a promise by the accused state to mend its ways; specific remedies, not to mention penalties or compensation, were seldom proposed. The more serious issues wound up at the PCIJ, but by the time that court was prepared to render a verdict, new *faits accomplis* usually rendered the verdict itself of only academic significance for the minority. Approximately fifty complaints by the German minority in Poland (of the 314 submitted) found their way into the League's grievance machinery. Some were successfully mediated before the procedure was exhausted; others made it all the say to the PCIJ. Only a few, however, were taken up by the League Council, and none of these was resolved to the satisfaction of minority leaders.[32]

Poland, it should be added, did not respond very gracefully to League efforts to enforce the Minorities Protection Treaty or (in Silesia) the Geneva Convention. At first, it argued that only member governments, not minority organizations or individuals, should be entitled to petition the League in the first place. Poland always contended that minority peoples needed no protection from their own government and that it was "disloyal" of minority organizations to seek redress before the League. Poland's League representative denounced the Deutschtumsbund, sponsor of the first German petitions, as an "illegal" organization that got both its funding and its orders from Germany and existed primarily to further German revisionist goals.[33]

In succeeding years, Polish spokesmen became increasingly impatient with German complaints and threatened to restrict minority rights if what they saw as unfounded allegations and frivolous complaints to the League did not stop.[34] During a major League-sponsored debate on minority policies held at Lugano in December 1928, attended by both Stresemann (who initiated it) and Zaleski, the latter denounced the stream of "petty" complaints, especially those coming from Otto Ulitz and the Volksbund. In his view, these constituted abuse of the League Council, threatened European peace, and "bordered on treason." The last remark elicited an impassioned, table-pounding rejoinder from Strese-mann, who was under growing domestic pressure to do more for Ger-mans outside the Reich. He had received intelligence reports suggesting that Poland was about to dissolve the Volksbund and prosecute its leaders on charges of treason, and so his outburst was probably not entirely spontaneous. Eugen Naumann also denounced Zaleski's remarks in a speech to the Sejm (delivered, of course, in German). He argued that the Volksbund, chief representative of the "German collective personality" in Silesia, was precisely the kind of organization protected by Article 109 of the Polish Constitution; the government's desire to suppress it could only reflect a desire to "break the back of German nationality itself in Po-land."[35]

Among the German-Polish issues that came before the League, none proved more vexing than Polish school policy. This was particularly true in Silesia, where the disparity between language and national conscious-ness created special problems. As one of the League's minorities experts complained, no one could have foreseen that "a portion of the majority would attempt fraudulently to pass itself off as belonging to the minor-ity."[36] This awkward formulation only illustrates, however, how difficult it was for many outsiders to comprehend the problem. It came before the League in 1926, after Grażyński's officials examined the minority-school applications of 8,500 pupils and rejected 7,114 on grounds that these applicants were of Polish ancestry and would be unable to follow instruc-tion in what was for them a foreign language. The parents of some 1,500 of these children felt sufficiently strongly about the issue to organize a boycott of the schools to which they were assigned; the Volksbund took the matter to Geneva, citing the exclusive rights of parents under the Geneva Convention to determine the language in which their children would be educated. The League tried to find a compromise by hiring Swiss "educational expert" Wilhelm Maurer to determine on a case-by-case basis whether the children were sufficiently fluent in German to follow instruction in that language. Maurer seemed to aim for a middle position between minority and government: of the first 964 pupils he examined, 441 were approved for admission; 523 were judged deficient in German. When Silesian officials refused admission to another large groups of children on the same grounds in the following year (1927), and Calonder again sided with the parents, the matter was again referred to Maurer. This time, he determined that the majority of children (435 of 720) were qualified to attend a German school.[37]

The German government, however, agreed to this procedure only as a temporary expedient and only on condition that the League affirm the sole discretion of parents over the longer term. When the League hesi-tated to do so, Germany took the issue to the PCIJ. In rulings dated April

26 and December 15, 1928, the court ruled that officials had no right under the Geneva Convention to override parents' choice of schools for their children; it ordered that even those children whom Mauer had previously pronounced unqualified for German instruction be admitted to minority schools. Of course, the PCIJ was no more able than the League to enforce its decisions against a determined, sovereign state. Both before and after the PCIJ decision, a stream of Volksbund petitions told the same basic story: a minority school would be closed down, or refused permission to begin operations in the first place; the matter would be appealed to the Mixed Commission, which usually ordered the school opened; officials then rejected so many would-be pupils that the forty-pupil minimum could not be achieved, leaving appeal to the League as the only recourse.[38]

One such appeal concerned a woman who was jailed for two weeks for refusing to send her child to a Polish school while officials sat on her application to a minority school. In this case, the League not only backed the petitioner but also ordered financial compensation for her.[39] But when Calonder, citing the PCIJ decision, ordered the admission of a group of children whose parents had declared their language to be German but who failed an exam administered by officials, Grażyński simply refused to comply. In response, Calonder tendered his resignation (August 1930) to indicate his exasperation with Grażyński's readiness to disregard his opinions. Neither Poland nor Germany could imagine a replacement for Calonder; they issued a joint appeal to him to withdraw his resignation, and he complied.[40] But nothing could persuade Grażyński to change his approach; this question was clearly too vital for Poland to permit its hands to be tied by concern for "world opinion."

The League also spent a lot of time on German complaints about Poland's nationally discriminatory land reform program. The figures produced by the League's minorities subcommittee (chaired by Japan's Baron Adatci) differed from those advanced by minority leaders but still revealed "a considerable disparity" in the treatment of Germans and Poles: Germans owned 35 percent of the large estates in Poznania but contributed 50 percent of the reformed land between 1926 and 1929. Polish figures showed that Germans, who constituted one-eighth of Pomorze's population, received only one in sixty of the new farms created in that province (and minority leaders could not find even this one-sixtieth part). Adatci's committee conceded that the figures "revealed discrimination against the minority" but declined to recommend any specific action in consideration of Polish promises to correct the disparity in the future.[41] Germans also complained about the low levels of compensation under the Polish land reform program. Those whose land was taken were offered only low depression prices and then paid not in cash but in state bonds, which promised 5 percent annual interest but were trading on the open bond market for only 35 percent of their face value.[42]

Adatci returned to the land reform problem the following year (1932), by which time the contribution of Poznanian Germans had dropped from 50 percent to 47 percent; he judged this "a partial rectification of the disparity" but still not enough and proposed that the League ask Poland to stop taking German land until the disparity disappeared altogether. But the Council declined to act on this recommendation, and so this issue too came before the PCIJ.[43] After Poland announced land reform quotas treating the two nationalities more equally, the PCIJ decision of July 29, 1933, denied the main German demand: an order to Poland to stop taking minority land until parity had been achieved.[44] Thereafter, Germany largely abandoned this issue in the wake of its withdrawal from the League and rapprochement with Poland.

Long before mid-1933, however, German leaders had begun to acknowledge that the best to be hoped for from all these minority grievances was the embarrassment of Poland before an interational forum. This, more than the prospect of real relief for the minority, determined Germany's increasingly confrontational style toward Poland in the League after 1929. Curtius, in particular, began to file grievances without even waiting for minority spokesmen to take the lead, for example, in the issue of widespread antiminority violence during the Polish election campaign of 1930.[45] On this particular occasion, the League's response was unusually forceful and explicit: it called on Poland to punish the perpetrators, to report back on measures taken to prevent a recurrence, to limit its ties to such chauvinistic organizations as the ZOKZ and the ZPS ("which are moved by a spirit not designed to facilitate rapprochement" between the two peoples), and to undertake other measures to help the minority regain its "feeling of confidence," which had been "profoundly shaken."[46]

Curtius expressed satisfaction with this outcome; he believed that Germany had won a significant "moral victory" by subjecting Poland's treatment of the German minority in general, and Grażyński's regime in particular, to almost universal criticism before a world forum.[47] Poland's response was unusually forthcoming; it reported that fifty-two people had been fined or jailed, nine officials reprimanded, and 114 victims given some compensation because of criminal acts against the minority during the 1930 election campaign. Even Grażyński (doubtless with some encouragement from higher up) reaffirmed his respect for minority rights before the Silesian Sejm and in a circular to all *starosts*. He claimed that the ZPS and the ZOKZ no longer enjoyed official status; indeed, both were on a list of political organizations to which police officers were not to belong.[48] This represented a major retreat, rhetorically at least, for the Silesian *wojewode*, and Adatci could only express his satisfaction with the Polish response.

Encouraged by international criticism of conditions in Silesia, and under growing pressure from nationalist public opinion, Germany continued to press its case against Poland in the League. It filed a complaint about conditions in Pomorze and Poznania, despite Rauscher's objection that suppression of opposition forces was now so general in Poland that it was hard to make a case of specifically national persecution. In Silesia, Grażyński's retreat was only rhetorical and only temporary; new complaints soon arrived in Geneva, claiming that the disciplined officials had been reinstated, the ZPS again carried arms in public, and police officials were still to be found among its members.[49] Germany's League representatives demanded increasingly radical sanctions against Poland, including formal censure, punishment of officials, and the breakup of the ZOKZ. Konstantin von Neurath, Curtius's successor as Foreign Minister, suggested that Germany make its continued membership in the League conditional upon that body's acquiescence to these demands. Even if Germany did not get its way, he argued, bringing such issues repeatedly before the League would gradually increase British and French sympathy for the German side of German-Polish issues.[50]

Poland's strategy was essentially to wait the League out and let it tire of the impossible task of trying to adjudicate every minor national quarrel (not just in Poland but in the numerous other countries subject to minority protection treaties). Eventually, this strategy paid off; the League declined more and more frequently to take up matters not specifically addressed by the Geneva Convention or the Minorities Protection Treaty. Volksbund complaints about the hiring of Poles as teachers in minority schools or the exclusive use of Polish in minority-school administration elicited only a passive response. Complaints about the lack of personal security in Silesia—one petition cited seventy-five examples of violence by state-subsidized nationalist organizations in early 1928 alone—died somewhere in the League's bureaucracy.[51] A growing weariness with minorities issues was apparent among League officials; some of them doubtless regretted the world organization's decision to enter into such a morass in the first place.

This decline in attention coincided with a growing sense of disppointment on the part of minority members with the results of all their appeals to the League. Perhaps Stresemann had originally simply overpromised what the League would be able to do for the minority in order to build support for German entry. The cumbersome procedure for dealing with minority complaints and the League's reluctance to alienate its own member states certainly played a role in the disappointing outcome. With the few exceptions noted above, League mediators almost always recommended accepting the promises of member governments to mend their ways; rarely was the full Council even asked to take action. Even when the League found fault with a policy that had led to a minority complaint, it was almost never able to get a member state actually to rescind it.

On occasion, the readiness of Adatci's committee to look into a minority grievance may have encouraged a compromise solution or some kind of compensation; many German complaints about the inability to buy land in Poland or the continued assertion of the state's right of repurchase after the 1929 liquidation agreement seem to have been settled behind the scenes in this way. On the other hand, virtually none of the many complaints concerning the denial of business licenses to ethnic Germans were taken up by the League; for example, officials could always find some reason other than an innkeeper's nationality to justify their refusal of a liquor license. Individual petitioners to the League stood little chance of prevailing against their government; indeed, it is surprising that so many kept trying right into the 1930s. Ultimately, after a decade of petitions, the investment of much time and effort by League officials, and even some favorable League findings, Polish Germans could point to little in the way of real amelioration. This view was prevalent even before the German "League strategy" for supporting the minority came to an abrupt end in 1933 with Hitler's seizure of power and German's withdrawal from the League.

The Polish Minority in Germany

Polish leaders soon discovered that one way to parry German complaints in the League was to draw attention to the Polish minority in Germany. There was, however, considerable disagreement about its exact size. Polish estimates ranged as high as 1.5 million persons, which would make the Polish minority in interwar Germany larger than the German minority in Poland; the 1925 German census, which counted Poles, Masurians, and Polish-German bilinguals separately (though virtually all of them were ethnically Polish), came up with a combined total of only 674,000.[52]

The main problem, however, was that many if not most of these Polish speakers did not describe themselves as Polish when the question went to their national-political consciousness. Only about 100,000 votes were cast for Polish candidates nationwide in the 1925 Reichstag elections, and Polish nationalists were never able to elect even one delegate to the Reichstag. In 1928 the vote for minority parties in Germany—Poles and others—amounted to only 0.3 percent of the total. Attendance at the sixty-four Polish public schools in Germany averaged only twenty-three in a typical year; the only secondary school (in Beuthen; a second was established later at Marienwerder) graduated only sixty-four students during a seven-year period in the 1930s. The Polish press in Germany consisted of just five daily papers. As one Polish newspaper lamented in 1932, "the national foundations of the Polish people [in Germany] are breaking up. . . . The level of national and political development has fallen enormously. . . . The clearest proof of this is furnished by . . . the [recent] elections. The number of votes is falling steadily [and] national consciousness is practically nonexistent."[53]

Under the German Constitution (Article 113), "equality of rights for the non-German-speaking peoples of the Reich" was guaranteed, and they could not be "restricted in the use of their mother tongue for education." But Germany was not obligated in the same way as was Poland by the Minorities Protection Treaty, and there were occasional suggestions that Germany restrict the rights of its Polish minority in retaliation for Poland's treatment of Germans. Radical nationalist groups like the DOV urged the government to use the threat of reprisals against the remaining Polish minority in Germany to win concessions for Germans in Poland. Prussian Minister-President Braun (SPD), himself an East Prussian, did take back some of the promises his government had made during the 1920 plebiscite campaign, such as the right of Prussian Poles to establish private schools or to have Polish-language classes in otherwise German public schools. He responded to Polish complaints in 1923 by charging that Poland, "since achieving political independence and freedom through the weapons and blood of others, has displayed such a degree of intolerance and such terror toward members of other nations that she has forfeited any moral justification for complaining about repression by others."[54]

But a tit-for-tat approach was consistently rejected by the government in Berlin on grounds that it was bound to harm Germans more than Poles. There were (doubtless) more Germans in Poland than Poles in Germany, and the former figured in German policy to an extent that the latter did not in Polish. In fact, Poland would probably welcome German reprisals against German Poles as justification for what State Secretary Edgar Loehrs assumed to be its ultimate goal: "the complete ejection of Germans from Poland." Even if German-Polish relations were to deteriorate to the point where a population transfer à la Greece and Turkey became the only solution, he reasoned, this would probably suit Poland just fine.[55] To the extent that Poland's interests would be served by simply liquidating both minorities, German efforts to link treatment of the two groups in bilateral negotiations or threats of reprisals against Poles in Germany were unlikely to bear fruit.

Indeed, Stresemann argued that the interests of German minorities in other countries required Germany to turn sharply away from the repressive minority policies of the prewar era. He pressured both his own government and individual German states (which controlled the key education sector) to adopt minority policies that would be perceived as models of toleration. He also offered Poland a bilateral agreement under which each state would grant identical school rights to its respective minority. He reasoned that this approach would provide more relief than the Minorities Protection Treaty, whose guarantees had proved to be "pretty theoretical"—in part because they were one-sided, involuntary obligations which Poland sought to circumvent wherever possible. Given the generally low level of national consciousness among the Polish-speaking population in Germany, Stresemann was confident that an agreement to afford the same rights to both minorities promised substantial relief for the beleaguered Germans of Poland while posing no danger for Germany.[56]

Stresemann acknowledged that powerful forces were at work to weaken German minorities in neighboring countries; in the words of an anonymous Foreign Office memorandum from this period, for states like Poland and Czechoslovakia "a strengthening of the German minority will always be viewed as a threat to their own political existence. [Such states] may not be able to abstain from suppressing German minorities under their rule [merely] out of consideration for the [relatively] few Polish or Czech co-nationals living in the Reich." Germany should therefore grant its own minorities maximum freedom out of respect for "natural law," and not tie its minority policies to what other countries were doing. There might also be some *realpolitische* advantages "Should the opportunity arise later to reincorporate all Germans in the Reich, which would mean including a lot of non-Germans as well, this would go more smoothly if by then the Reich (in contrast to Imperial Germany) had built up a record of dealing fairly with minorities."[57]

Bruns, who ran the Berlin office of the Verband der deutschen Minderheiten in Europa, also played a role in persuading Prussia (above all) to change its minority policies in the 1920s. In his view, most minority problems were "not to be solved by political frontier-drawing alone . . . [for] each change of the political boundaries only manages to make ruling peoples out of subject peoples and vice versa." The point was rather to persuade states with minority populations to abstain voluntarily from the full exercise of their sovereignty in those cultural and economic spheres considered most vital to ethnic minorities. Despite his association with the German minority in Poland, Bruns seemed genuinely concerned to find a better system for all minorities, not just Germans. Only by "standing up for our own ideas of minority rights [and] realizing them in our own country," he argued, could Germany put effective pressure on Poland to ease up on its German population. Minorities in the Reich must at least have their own schools; these should be fully supported by tax funds, free of unnecessary restrictions, and open to all children whose parents wanted to enroll them.[58]

Leaders of the German minority in Poland also expressed support for more liberal Reich minority policies. In a discussion with Chancellor Hans Luther in 1925, Naumann urged the German government to guarantee its own Polish minority the same rights that Germans in Poland were demanding. He called on the Reich to launch a "moral-political initiative" that would raise the minority question to "a higher level" throughout Europe. Bruns, who accompanied Naumann to this meeting, added that Germany would find it hard to complain about Poland's treatment of Germans so long as Germany itself "basically denied [its minorities] the right to national schools." At this time, there were twenty-eight public and three private Polish-language schools in German Upper Silesia, where school rights were guaranteed by the Geneva Convention. Elsewhere in Germany, however, the picture was less positive; the significant Polish population in the Marienwerder district had access to only eleven public and no private schools. "In the school area," Bruns wrote later, "not only is the situation not ideal, but a comparison with the situation in other states, including Poland, is unfavorable to Germany." Luther, however, seemed to have little interest in this issue and terminated the conversation without committing himself to specific actions.[59]

Stresemann continued to press the issue nevertheless. At a February 1926 meeting with Prussian officials, who were in charge of the school system in all the regions with significant Polish populations, he argued that "in order to be able to conduct the struggle against the denationalization efforts directed against the nine million Germans living outside our borders in Europe, it is essential that we ourselves do something exemplary for our minorities in the Reich. . . . In the interest of our German brothers in the ceded eastern territories, it is essential that we inaugurate a liberal cultural policy" toward Reich minorities.[60] Prussian officials were concerned, however, that such liberalization might interrupt the gradual process of Germanization that had long been under way among Masurians and Upper Silesians. Culture Minister Carl Becker opposed granting Poles (and Lithuanians) even such rights as were already enjoyed by the Danes of southern Schleswig. State Secretary Friedrich Meister in the Interior Ministry contended that the "domestic danger created by the granting of full cultural autonomy [to Poles] was greater than the prospect of the achievement of the [foreign policy] goals" outlined by Stresemann. East Prussian *Oberpräsident*, Ernst Siehr, warned that the proposed changes might well "break the back of East Prussian defenses" against Polish efforts to recruit Masurians for their national movement, have a "depressing effect on local Germans, . . . and create a chasm between Masurians and Germans."[61]

The Prussian concern was doubtless nourished by periodic reminders that Germany was not the only state unhappy with the German-Polish border. Polish nationalists also entertained notions of revising it—in Poland's favor. Few of them accepted the results of the several postwar plebiscites; they still had designs on German Upper Silesia and East Prussia. Under these circumstances, Prussian officials were reluctant to relax efforts to solidify the pro-German sentiments of their Polish-speaking populations. For example, an expensive new theater was built in Allenstein (Olsztyn) in 1925 "in the interest of keeping the Masurian population German." The same train of thought was evident in both the *Osthilfe* program (which subsidized struggling East Prussian agriculturists) and in Brüning's subsequent proposal to parcel bankrupt eastern estates and settle them with unemployed German workers.[62] Despite Prussian doubts, Stresemann eventually won the argument in cabinet, which declared its support for his position in April 1926. New Prussian minority school policies emerged (belatedly) in December 1928; they fell short of what Bruns and others had advocated, but they did guarantee publicly supported Polish-language schools wherever enough parents requested them. At the time, there were thirty-nine Polish-language schools outside German Upper Silesia (twenty-seven in the *Grenzmark* [Border Province] Poznania-West Prussia and twelve in East Prussia); three years later, in 1931, the number had risen to fifty-eight. There were still no Polish-speaking schools in the Evangelical districts of Masuria, however, supposedly (as officials insisted) because most Masurian parents were committed to full assimilation into German life.[63]

Meanwhile, with the encouragement of the Polish government, the "League of Poles in Germany" began to submit complaints of its own to the League. Since German Upper Silesia, under the Geneva Convention, was the only part of Germany subject to League supervision, all Polish complaints concerned that province. Most complained about the actions of individual officials rather than state policies, which no longer provided many openings for attack. For example, a German teacher was accused of slapping a child for speaking Polish on the schoolground; Stresemann himself spoke to this incident before the League, conceding the truth of the complaint but assuring the world body that the teacher had been transferred and the principal reprimanded. He also produced a circular from the Upper Silesian *Oberpräsident*, Alfons Proske, urging all teachers to show respect for the language of the Polish minority and denouncing as "reprehensible" any effort to discourage them from speaking Polish outside the classroom. In response to another Polish complaint about an insulting police official, State Secretary Carl von Schubert reported that the official had been fined. A third complaint involved a Polish opera company invited to perform *Halka* in Oppeln (April 1929); after much press agitation against the performance itself, members of the troupe were attacked by a nationalist mob at the railway station, with no police in sight. Once again, the response of the German government (formal apology to Poland and demotion or early retirement of three police officers who had remained passive during the assault) seemed to be above reproach.[64]

There was clearly a concerted effort to preserve the League as a venue for German minority complaints: hence the all-too-exemplary German replies. The trivial nature of some of the Polish complaints and their extreme length (sixty to eighty pages each) suggests, on the other hand, that they may have been part of a purposeful effort to cripple or discredit the very idea of the League's effort to fine-tune relations between minorities and their governments.

Direct Financial Support for the Minority

Given the meager results of bilateral negotiations and appeals to international agencies, Germany turned increasingly to a third means of defending the German minority in Poland: direct financial support. Such support had begun to flow eastward almost as soon as the terms of the Versailles treaty were revealed. In October 1919 a program of compensation for war losses included also preliminary compensation for Germans whose property had been (or would be) liquidated by Poland. Another significant amount (117 million German marks) was authorized to keep German schools, newspapers, and social organizations running in the areas due to be ceded. In 1920 the Konkordia GmbH was established under the direction of Max Winkler (1875-1965), a former West Prussian official and German Democratic Party (DDP) delegate to the National Assembly, to subsidize German newspapers in Poland. Konkordia came to own or control many minority newspapers and also served some of the functions of a wire service.[65] As long as they lasted, German national councils also received monthly support payments from the Deutsche Zentrale für Heimatdienst, operating out of the chancellor's office. Other funds were soon established to support schools, charities, meeting halls, and the like, during the transition to Polish rule.[66]

At first, little thought was given to the need for the longer-term support of Germans in the ceded areas, and emigration was still believed to be necessary "only in the most unusual cases." But as it became clear, with the formal beginning of Polish rule in January 1920, that the German population of these areas was moving to Germany in distressingly large numbers, the government looked for financial incentives to encourage them to stay and to help them retain something of their prewar material and cultural position. In 1919 the National Assembly set up an "Inter-Party Eastern Committee" to keep track of conditions in the ceded territories and to coordinate financial support for their German populations. In November 1920 this committee was transformed into the primary Reich agency for the support of Polish Germans: the Deutsche Stiftung ("German Foundation," or DS).

The stated purpose of the DS was the "provision of subsidies for the cultural and economic support of Germans in foreign countries": specifically, in the areas ceded to Poland, plus Danzig and the Memel District. It was later given primary responsibility for such programs throughout Poland and so assumed a pivotal role in relations between the minority and the German government. Though outwardly a quasi-independent "foundation," the DS was controlled by the Reich and Prussian governments which funded it; it was formally subject to the Foreign Office and to a Reichstag *Beirat* (advisory council) consisting of representatives of the major parties. (Not all parties, however; Independent Socialists, Communists, and, later, National Socialists were considered too "unreliable" to have a voice in this project.) Five parliamentarians, each with personal experience in the ceded territories, made up the executive committee of the DS: Max Winkler (DDP), Paul Fleischer (Center), Richard Wende (SPD), Otto Everling (DVP), and Otto Hoetzsch (DNVP). Most of the DS's activities were kept from the view of the general public, however, which meant that this parliamentary oversight remained remote.[67]

The Deutsche Stiftung was managed by its executive secretary, Erich Krahmer-Möllenberg (1882-1942), a civil servant who had served during the war as adviser on eastern matters to the Prussian Interior Ministry. He tried to create the impression that the DS was not just a state agency and not just an obedient instrument of Reich policy. In the opinion of Norbert Krekeler, however, who has researched the DS most thoroughly, it was "outfitted with almost all the criteria of a Prussian bureau, . . . [employing] officials excused from [regular] Prussian service, . . . with complete retention of their civil service claims." It was originally supposed to operate on the interest from a capital grant (100,000 German marks) provided by the government, plus whatever it could attract in private contributions. But when the hyperinflation of 1923 wiped out this capital base (and also destroyed the private fortunes of many who were expected to contribute), the DS came to rely primarily on the German Foreign Office for its funds; a confidential annual allocation for it was hidden somewhere in the Reich budget.[68]

Krahmer-Möllenberg was left to run things pretty much on his own, with only distant supervision from the Foreign Office. To rationalize the Reich's aid effort, he encouraged the DViSuS to set up the "Committee of Five" in 1924 to serve as primary conduit. Krahmer-Möllenberg's role in the everyday life of the minority was substantial throughout the interwar period. He had a hand in such matters as setting the salaries that could be paid to teachers in minority schools, supplying them with textbooks, deciding whether a specific building should be purchased, reimbursing minority members for the cost of legal actions against the Polish government, organizing the payment of veterans' benefits, subsidizing minority economic organizations, and enforcing political unity within the minority.[69] Polish Germans who did not conform—for example, those who married Poles, sent their children to Polish schools without having to do so, or were deemed "politically unreliable" in some other sense—were usually ineligible for DS-administered aid.

A school committee, comprising representatives of the DS and other interested organizations, subsidized and essentially controlled the German School Association (DSV) in Bydgoszcz, which operated the minority's private schools. Thanks to this support, the minority was able to construct thirty-two new school buildings in western Poland, including large regional secondary schools in Poznań, Grudziądz, and Bydgoszcz. In appearance and facilities these schools compared favorably with local Polish schools; the buildings themselves became objects of pride and centers of German social life—and thus objects of Polish resentment. Reich subsidies were also used to enhance the salaries of German (but not Polish) teachers in minority schools, and the often significant salary differentials created another source of Polish resentment.[70] Sending a professional statistician to help the minority conduct its own census in 1926 was another form of Reich aid. And when August Utta, prominent German leader in Łódź but also a public schoolteacher, was ordered transferred to a remote part of the country, Krahmer-Möllenberg, citing his indispensability to the German cause, arranged for him to quit teaching and work for the *Freie Presse* in Łódź, on a salary to be paid by the Reich.[71] Similarly, Hermann Rauschning received a monthly DS stipend of 200 German marks (plus another 300 in state funds from a *Notgemeinschaft*) over an eighteen-month period while writing his book on the de-Germanization of Poznania and Pomorze.[72]

A representative DS budget (1929-30) included under "cultural expenses, Polish Silesia," 45,000 German marks for the theater in Katowice, 10,000 for a choral society, 33,600 for the German coal miners union, 8,000 for school construction, and 4,000 for the German retail sales union. The "Economic Union for Upper Silesia" received an additional annual subsidy of 7,000 marks from the Foreign Office on grounds that it was "one of the best . . . sources of economic information" for the German government. The German Foreign Office also covered 9,500 marks in election costs for German parties in the 1927 Silesian elections and 80,000 for the national elections in 1928 and 1930. It contributed another 4,500 marks toward a new headquarters building for the Volksbund and to cover Ulitz's travel expenses to Geneva.[73]

Other forms of DS assistance included a monthly stipend of 150 marks for German priests and 100 for vicars in Poland; the VdK was supported to the tune of 6,000 to 8,000 marks monthly from the DS and other Reich sources in the early 1930s.[74] The major German "think tanks" concerned with minority problems in east-central Europe (the Deutsche Börse in Marburg, the "Institute for East German Economy" in Königsberg, Boehm's "Political College," the "Baltic Society," and the Deutsches Auslands-Institut in Stuttgart) were all subsidized by DS as well.[75] Little wonder that, in Schönbeck's opinion, "if the Germans in Poland owe[d] gratitude to anyone in the Reich, . . . it [was] to Krahmer-Möllenberg and his colleagues" in the DS.[76]

Despite the numerical decline of the German population itself, the scale of DS support grew steadily into the 1930s. The largest subsidies went to threatened German industrial firms in Polish Silesia. In 1925, after several large firms were forced out of business and many German workers found themselves out of work in a society that was seldom willing to provide replacement jobs, the German government approved a program of confidential support payments to remaining firms totaling about 10,000 marks per day.[77] In 1927, a special import quota was made available to two large steel firms, Bismarckhütte and Baildenhütte, in order to save the companies themselves and the jobs of about 2,000 mostly German workers; these companies were allowed to export 260 tons of steel per month to Germany at pre-tariff war rates.[78] Unemployment benefit supplements, distributed through German unions, amounted to 60 to 70 million marks annually from 1926 to 1933.[79]

There were, of course, some political conditions attached to this support. One typical agreement obliged the management of a Silesian firm to buttress German "cultural influence" inside the business (for example, by sticking to German as the language of administration) and in the community at large.[80] When the German consul complained that the management of the German-owned Ballestrem corporation was permitting a Polish personnel officer to fire Germans and hire Poles to replace them, he was informed that this executive and the firm's other Polish management were politically protected, and little could be done about them. The consul was convinced, however, that management was all too willing to "betray German nationality for materialistic reasons and in order to be left alone by Polish officials as much as possible." He recommended that the firm's import quota be canceled, since it was failing to do what this benefit was designed to achieve: protect German workers.[81]

The cost of the Reich's financial commitment to Silesian industry only grew with the onset of the Great Depression. In 1932, Foreign Minister Neurath proposed an additional allocation of 37 to 40 million German marks just to keep major German firms from going bankrupt. The "catastrophic condition" of German industry in Polish Silesia threatened the minority's very existence by "depriving it of its strongest economic support and creating the conditions for the unrestrained Polonization of this area." A further weakening of the German economic position there would also undermine Germany's efforts to recover this region ("one of our main demands") and would add thousands of jobless refugees to Germany's horrendous unemployment rate. The German government, though financially strapped, agreed to an additional grant of 23 million marks in order to save the most endangered firms, which provided a living for about half the German population in Polish Silesia. Major recipients included the Pless concern (11.5 million marks), Laura/Kattowitzer AG (8.5 million), and the Ruda anthracite union (4 million).[82]

A Foreign Office review in 1935 noted that "minority policy in eastern Upper Silesia has been conducted so far by means of quite considerable financial expenditures." In addition to industrial subsidies, "schools, unions, . . . and the cultural amalgamation of the minority in the Volksbund have been financed almost exclusively by Germany, [and] 162 million RM have been invested in the IG Kattowitz/Königs- u. Laurahütte alone."[83]

Elsewhere in western Poland, most Germans were farmers or employed in businesses dependent upon a farming population. Their major concern was not unemployment so much as the lack of the affordable credit needed to run their farms and businesses. Low prices and the poor outlook for advanced agriculture in Poland discouraged private lenders from making farm loans. Not much money was available for lending in the first place; interest rates were relatively high; and whatever credit help the government could provide was channeled first of all to ethnic Poles. Germans complained that private Polish banks either denied them credit on political grounds or attached impossible political conditions.[84] Reich support focused therefore on the provision of affordable credit, some of it open and direct but the larger amount clandestine and indirect. At first, these funds were moved into Danzig banks, which already provided much of the credit for Polish Germans, to encourage them to make still more available. In 1925 the German government established a special bank registered in the Netherlands, the Hollandse Buitenland Bank (HBB), to serve as intermediary between credit sources in Germany and Germans in Poland and to attract additional capital in the open market for their use. This bank was launched with 11.8 million German marks in capital, virtually all of it German and most of it taken from the central Prussian co-op bank. The bank's officers were Dutch but served as a facade behind which a three-German "credit commission," including Krahmer-Möllenberg, had actual say over the bank's funds.[85]

The HBB provided some large loans to Polish Germans, including 8 million marks to the Pless concern, but the modest amount of outside capital it attracted left it unable to perform its task adequately. The following year, therefore, the German government approved an additional project, proposed by Krahmer-Möllenberg and endorsed by Stresemann, to provide 30 million marks in direct grants and credits to Germans in other countries; 16.5 million were to go to Polish Germans. The stated purpose of the program was to keep German enterprises afloat, because when they foundered, their employees and owners alike were usually forced to join the exodus to the Reich. These credits were to be distributed by the Ossa Vermittlungs- und Handelsgesellschaft, run by a steering committing that included the ubiquitous Krahmer-Möllenberg, Winkler, and eight others. Like the DS, Ossa was outwardly a quasi-independent operation subject only to the loose control of a Reichstag committee; essentially, it was an arm of the German Foreign Office. Ossa subsidiaries included an Ost GmbH, which controlled the HBB and conducted other operations in Poland and neighboring states; the Vereinigte Finanzkontore, which handled other "special tasks" in the same region; and a Südost GmbH, which operated in countries to the south of Poland.[86]

When the original 30-million RM budget for Ossa quickly proved insufficient to meet the minority's credit needs, Krahmer-Möllenberg and the Foreign Office returned with a request for an "emergency program" of block grants; a first installment of this aid (50,000 marks) was approved by the cabinet in October 1927.[87] The following year, when Krahmer-Möllenberg reported that Ossa was once again out of money, the cabinet provided another financial boost and declared its satisfaction with Ossa's efforts to date: "The activities of Ossa . . . are known to the Reichstag parties and have been approved by them previously."[88] The HBB and other banks, "in order to give this aid the character of normal economic credit," remained the principal conduits for Ossa funds. Other German credits reached the minority by way of credit cooperatives in Danzig and, later, through a special division of the Danzig Landwirtschaftliche Bank. Loans were provided at 10 percent interest at first, later at an effective 8 percent, which was lower than the going rate in the Reich.[89]

A 1930 Foreign Office assessment of the impact of this program on the German economic situation in Poland contended that the minority had been able to hold on to much of its land thanks only to such credit, which "Polish strangulation policies" had made unavailable in Poland itself.

According to this summary, Ossa credit had been vital to the survival of as many as six hundred larger German landed properties. Most loans had been granted according to strict economic criteria; as a result, interest payments were arriving on schedule, and there had been almost no losses through default.

Nonetheless, Ossa funds were again exhausted. With the onset of the Great Depression and the reluctance of the Polish government to do much for ethnic Germans, the authors of this report proposed a new five-year program of 45 million German marks in economic credits and another 15 million for cultural projects. Ninety percent of the economic credits would go to Poznania and Pomorze, including 15 million to buy off additional heirs and so keep farms intact, 6.25 million for urban and rural business credits, 6 million to prop up HBB loans threatened by land reform, 4 million for new settlements, 2 million for occupational retraining, and 1 million to meet remaining settlers' obligations to the Polish state. Most of the 4 million intended for Silesia were to go to eleven "peoples banks." Ossa would continue to distribute the economic credits; DS would distribute the funds for cultural projects. This extention of the Ossa program was approved by all the Reichstag parties except the Communists and National Socialists (who were not asked) and the Social Democrats (who declined to support this expensive project any longer). In a continuing effort to keep the Ossa program confidential, its allocation was buried in a request to cover the costs of implementing the 1929 Liquidation Treaty. When Poland hesitated to ratify this treaty, the Reichstag, without publicity or debate, in October 1930 approved a government request to include this program in the budget of the "war burdens" fund.[90]

According to a summary of Ossa activities for 1926-31, 37.5 million marks' worth of credit were provided to Germans in Poznania and Pomorze; an additional 8 million was earmarked for 1932. Polish Upper Silesia received 5.5 million under this program through 1931 and was to receive another million in 1932. Three million in Ossa funds went to German co-op banks in Poland (the main co-op bank in Poznania was saved from failure in 1931 only by the injection of Reich funds), 3 million to DS-sponsored school projects, 740,000 to the DS itself; smaller amounts were spent for legal expenses, labor unions, social funds, vacations for children, propaganda among the Cashubes, and an array of other projects.[91]

One might well ask why Germany went to such lengths to keep this aid program secret. Polish authorities evidently knew almost everything worth knowing about it; if they did little to impede it, this was probably because they were providing many of the same kinds of help to the Polish minority in Germany, also "clandestinely." Financial support for minority schools in Germany began flowing by way of Polish consulates as early as 1923. In 1925, the Sejm approved standing allocations to several ministries for such purposes, though the exact amounts remained confidential. Poland also subsidized the election campaigns of the small Polish political party in Germany. The "World Union of Foreign Poles" raised funds for schools and cultural institutions in Germany; its funds, like those of DS, came from a combination of private contributions and state grants.[92]

More to the point, there was nothing really illegal or even improper about such programs, Polish or German. As one (Polish) recipient put it: "If we call on the help of our motherland to preserve our national identity," this is only "quite natural, legal, and ethical."[93] Krekeler states that Ossa's activities had to be kept secret "for reasons of international law," but he cites no sources to substantiate this assertion.[94] By contrast, German consuls who served as conduits for some of this aid claimed to be operating "on the basis of legality, by legally unassailable means."[95]

In any case, German officials and minority leaders did do all they could to obscure the extent of Reich financial support. After the 1923 raid on the Deutschtumsbund exposed aspects of its relationship to Reich authorities, Krahmer-Möllenberg worried that Reich-minority relations had grown still more "bureaucratic" and that another such raid might have "catastrophic consequences." He urged that written correspondence between Reich agencies and minority leaders be kept to a minimum. Minority leaders normally avoided the Polish mails, communicating with Berlin instead by means of the consulates—a "*Passtelle* [passport agency] Bromberg" served as the major point of contact—but not even the consulates were informed of all DS activities.[96] Whenever German intelligence picked up word that Poland might be planning a new crackdown on minority organizations, minority leaders were advised to destroy any compromising correspondence in their files and to limit contacts with Reich agencies for a while. The 1929 raid on the headquarters of DViSuS turned up, among other things, a letter detailing Reich support for German schools in Poland and citing the German Foreign Office as its source. But as Graebe reported to Berlin, nothing more vital was discovered; "as agreed," all documents that might be "in any way incriminating" had been destroyed.[97]

The reason usually given for this secrecy was not that the activities themselves were illegal but that Polish seizure of key records might interrupt the flow of vital support to Germans in Poland. If the aid effort was both legal under international law and unexceptional, however, treating it so secretly could only fuel Polish suspicions and lead to exaggerated notions of its scale. Polish nationalists argued that Reich support for the minority was so lavish that it meant a substantial competitive advantage for Germans; they began to pressure the Polish government to provide equivalent help for Polish enterprises.[98] Moreover, with so much money changing hands under clandestine conditions, the suspicion, perhaps the reality, of corruption was bound to develop. In 1931, Heidelck was unable to account for 63,000 złoty belonging to the German Welfare League and was "transferred" to the Reich soon thereafter. Exposés in the Polish press charged that numerous minority leaders, including Naumann, Witzleben, Georg Busse, and Georg von Massenbach, reaped important financial benefits from the Reich support programs they administered.[99]

In addition to DS, Ossa, and the other sources of direct Reich financial support, several quasi-private organizations played a role in sustaining German minorities in other countries. The oldest of these was the Verein für das Deutschtum im Auslande (VDA), established in 1881 as the "German School Association." The VDA was financed by donations, membership dues, and state subsidies; it used these monies to support schools, cultural organizations, libraries, youth groups, scholarship programs, and travel for German minorities around the world. In the areas ceded to Poland, the VDA focused mainly on minority schools, providing textbooks and other kinds of support. The government provided the VDA over 2 million marks from funds left over from the wartime German administration of occupied eastern Europe for this purpose.[100] Though the VDA had a large membership and was solid financially, left-leaning politicians often expressed concern about its conservative coloration. Paul Löbe (SPD), head of a rival group of Deutschtum organizations, and the Prussian Interior Ministry (also SPD) did not want to assign the VDA a major role in Reich relations with the new minorities because they considered it "too reactionary." But Chancellor Wirth and Foreign Minister Walther Rathenau decided to stand by this organization, provided that it suppressed any political agenda of its own and stuck to school and cultural matters.[101] In the lands ceded to Poland, the VDA usually took a back seat to the DS, but even here its role as a conduit of Reich support, especially for schools, was significant.

A second organization that figured prominently in Reich relations with Germans in foreign countries was the Deutsches Auslands-Institut (DAI), established in Stuttgart in 1917. Also supported by donations, dues, and subsidies from public funds, the DAI worked to maintain ties between Germans abroad and their putative motherland. It was concerned especially with economic ties and with the economic role of German minorities in other countries. The DAI was somewhat more "academic" than the VDA, also closer to the parties of the Weimar Coalition, but it generally enjoyed broad multipartisan support.[102]

A third organization concerned with Germans in other countries was the Deutscher Schutzbund für das Grenz- und Auslanddeutschtum

(DSb), established in 1919 by a group of nationalists who believed the older VDA to be "obsolete." The DSb was actually a loose confederation of about 120 local, regional, and special-interest associations, many of them of the *Landsmannschaft* (or emigré-patriotic) type. Most members of DSb-affiliated organizations were former members of German minorities, now living in Germany itself. They were less concerned with the situation of remaining minorities in other countries than with their own refugee interests, especially their demands for financial compensation.[103] This was also true of the Bund der Auslanddeutschen (BdA), another organization primarily of German immigrants from other countries who were now Reich citizens. There were many other such organizations, especially during the immediate postwar period, but most were of only passing importance. Some were openly revanchist and so were shunned by most of the Weimar Republic's many governments. The once prominent DOV, for example, enjoyed little official favor after 1918 and went into a sharp decline before merging into the DSb-affiliated Deutscher Ostbund in 1922.[104]

The problem soon arose of sorting out the numerous *Deutschtum* organizations and coordinating their role in the campaign to help the German minority in Poland. In 1920 the government offered to allocate 15 million marks annually to these organizations, most of it to the VDA and DAI, provided that they agreed to coordinate their efforts. But negotiations to bring this about were unsuccessful. Interior Minister Adolf Koester (SPD) blamed the failure mainly on the VDA, which "refused finally to dissolve its formal relations to openly revanchist organizations," whereas the Foreign Office and the DAI "felt they had to stand by this demand." The VDA did join with the BdA, DSb, and various smaller organizations in 1923 to form the Zweckverband der freien Deutschtumsvereine, but the DAI and other groups aligned more closely with the Weimar Coalition remained aloof. The Foreign Ministry expressed opposition to the Zweckverband and refused to support it financially.[105] Prussian state officials also expressed misgivings about the allegedly right-wing orientation of the VDA and suggested that it was not so much a representative of Germans in other countries as part of the conservative opposition to the Weimar Republic.

In the government's own opinion, the amount of financial support that went to these organizations remained "within very modest limits." According to a 1929 survey, the VDA received 165,000 to 195,000 marks annually from Foreign Office and Interior Ministry funds for organizational expenses and for the support of German schools abroad; the DAI got 75,000 to 100,000 from the Interior Ministry. By contrast, the DSb received only 50,000 marks, the BdA only 12,000, and some of the other *Deutschtum* organizations no government support at all. The Ostbund, a major constituent organization of the DSb, was not only refused a financial subsidy but was told by officials to stay out of Polish-German affairs. The DSb itself also lost its government funding, temporarily at least, after a 1929 story that some of its funds had found their way into the antirepublican campaign of the Austrian *Heimwehr,* a paramilitary organization close to the Christian Social Party.[106]

By the late 1920s there were indications of growing official impatience with the multiplicity of *Deutschtum* organizations and their frequent requests for financial assistance. Chancellor Marx turned down VDA requests for funds to cover the costs of its annual meetings, and Chancellor Hermann Müller (in contrast to his predecessors) refused even to let his wife serve as the VDA's honorary chairman. The BdA was unable to get a member of the cabinet to put in an appearance at its annual meeting, though it was still considered politic for the government to send a representative to the annual meetings of VDA and DAI.[107] The fact is, Weimar leaders did not seem to have much time for these groups; they regularly turned down invitations to address their meetings, undeterred by complaints from the nationalist press about the "shoddy" official treatment of such patriotic organizations. With the exception of the VDA, none of these organizations figured prominently in Reich policy toward the German minority in Poland, and most of them fell on hard times, financially or politically, in the early 1930s. The DSb faded in consequence of reports of financial irregularities and its inability to establish ties to the NSDAP. The BdA was officially classified as "superfluous" in 1931 and stopped receiving state support. The DAI prospered throughout the Weimar period, supported by all the main factions in the government, but this fact only left it especially vulnerable after the National Socialist takeover in 1933. Even the VDA was in financial difficulty by 1932 and had to appeal to Polish Germans to submit testimonials to its effectiveness in order to avoid a sharp cutback in state support. It remained prominent during the first years of the Hitler regime, but then fell victim to *Gleichschaltung.*[108]

The Minority's Relationship with the Reich

German efforts to sustain the minority in Poland financially led necessarily to ever closer ties between minority leaders and agencies of the German government. They also raised the question, at least in Polish minds, whether such a relationship was compatible with the obligations of German minority leaders as citizens of Poland. And in fact, dispatches on general international questions which Graebe submitted to Krahmer-Möllenberg from Geneva are indistinguishable in content and perspective from what a Reich diplomatic official might produce; there is certainly no indication that they are from a citizen of Poland.[109]

At regular meetings in Berlin, minority spokesmen not only presented their case for increased Reich support but also tried to shape Reich policy toward Poland. In 1926, for example, Graebe and others visited the Imperial Chancellery to lobby against the kinds of concessions that might permit a quick end to the German-Polish tariff war. He urged German leaders not to end this conflict until Poland agreed to some of the minority's demands, including guaranteed rights of inheritance for settlers, the right of Germans to buy land, an end to national discrimination in the land reform program, and greater "cultural autonomy." He predicted, indeed looked forward to, Poland's imminent economic collapse, provided only that Germany persevered. An early end to the trade dispute, on the other hand, would only enhance Poland's international credit-worthiness and thus help it recover financially. In Graebe's view, as the price of recovering its fiscal health, Poland should be made to pay in the form of concessions to the German minority.[110]

Simultaneously, Reich financial support provided German officials with the means to influence the thinking and behavior of Polish Germans. The German government closely followed and exercised a good deal of control over the internal affairs of the minority, especially concerned to keep it united and in line with Reich policies. Whenever an internecine dispute threatened the common front, consular officials were told to intervene "energetically" to resolve the dispute and reinforce the leadership favored by Berlin. One threat came from a group of unhappy settlers, led by Heinrich Reineke, who organized the Interessengemeinschaft Deutscher Ansiedler in opposition to the minority "establishment." They were upset that their property rights remained in limbo after so many years of Polish rule; at that time (prior to the 1929 Liquidation Agreement), they did not think they would be able to pass their farms on to their offspring. They charged that Naumann, Graebe, and the others in the DViSuS were not fighting hard enough for settler interests and were too concerned about large landowners.[111] A second, less substantial threat to minority unity came from the short-lived Deutsche Bürgerpartei in Bydgoszcz; leaders of this 150-strong faction charged that the "Graebe-Heidelck clique" was corrupt and took their case to Prussian state officials. The German consul conceded that there was some truth to the charges (which led to Heidelck's removal in 1932) but urged continued support for the DViSuS leadership.[112]

There was also the case of the Deutscher Unterstützungsverband, which complained that Reich financial aid was not being directed to the "truly needy" among the minority. Because the point of most Reich aid was to preserve German economic strength in Poland, it did in fact offer less to economically weaker segments of minority society. But with elections drawing near, the local consul first suggested a nominal grant of 10,000 marks to keep the group quiet. Later, however, it turned out that this organization was a Polish government front, seeking to mobilize the Polish-German "lower classes" against the DViSuS, and Reich officials were told to have nothing to do with it.[113] In general, consular officials did all they could to support the DViSuS and its auxiliaries against such insurrections, and those who disturbed the facade of unity among Polish Germans could expect no support from Berlin.

The fact that all this Reich aid, though dispensed by the DViSuS and its affiliates, was really administered by Reich "outsiders" was also a source of friction. DViSuS leaders wanted the money to be turned over to them in large block grants, which they would distribute according to their own criteria and their own understanding of minority needs. They asked that their own Main Elections Committee, as the legitimate representative of Germans in western Poland, be recognized as the chief conduit for Reich aid. At least one consul sympathized with their resentment of a situation where a "distant *Hofkriegsrat*" (Krahmer-Möllenberg) gave the orders about every detail. He suggested that Rauschning's resignation was due in large part to frustration with support programs steered from Berlin and warned that other minority leaders might follow suit if they were not given greater autonomy.[114] Such advice was generally disregarded, however, and Polish Germans continued to complain that they were being treated like so many welfare recipients. Graebe repeatedly protested Berlin's slow response to his urgent requests for help and Krahmer-Möllenberg's imperious administrative style. Nine months after the government's approval of a 1927 "emergency" aid program, for example, there was still no sign of it in western Poland, and the Committee of Five felt itself sufficiently compromised by the delay to threaten to resign in protest.[115] In 1929 both co-op leader Swart and Welage chief Massenbach also threatened to resign if things did not improve.[116]

But those on the other side of this relationship also had their dissatisfactions with the aid program. Officials in Berlin complained that the minority's needs seemed to grow as fast as new programs could be approved and soon outstripped the ability of the government to fund them. In 1927, Graebe asked for a 150,000-mark "social fund" to support the neediest Germans in Poland and discourage their emigration to the Reich; he was granted only 30,000.[117] The following year, despite Graebe's pleas, Chancellor Müller cut the 200,000-mark annual budget for the German Welfare League in Poland (chairman: Graebe) and an equivalent fund administered by the consulate in Katowice for the "control of exceptional need of Germans in the ceded areas" to a combined total of only 82,000 marks. (Similar programs in Germany itself, by contrast, were being enhanced at this same time.) Graebe warned government leaders that their apparent indifference was undermining his efforts to keep "the poorest of the poor" in Poland, which is where the government presumably wanted them to stay.[118] Krahmer-Möllenberg, on the other hand, worried about the growth of a "subvention mentality" among Polish Germans; their desire to be spared any financial risks at all only reminded him of the unfortunate results of prewar Prussian *Ostmarkenpolitik*. Graebe's 1929 suggestion that the Reich guarantee the property of German landowners against Polish land reform, the cost of which he estimated at "only" 5 to 10 million marks, struck the DS chief as both hopelessly expensive and bound to encourage Poland to proceed even more aggressively against German land ownership. The Foreign Office also rejected this idea after estimating that it would cost some 63 million marks and benefit only about 550 large landowners. As one blunt Foreign Office memo noted, the point of the Reich's aid program was not to preserve the wealth of Polish Germans but to keep them in Poland.[119] Just as the onset of the great depression caused demand for Reich aid to jump, the German government was forced to reduce spending levels in most programs. Support for the VDA was cut by a million marks in 1930, for example, just as its own collections dropped by a like amount; the DS budget was also cut in 1931.[120] Aside from the tight fiscal situation, however, there was growing Reich resistance on more general grounds to minority requests for assistance. For example, minority leaders thought that the credits they needed should be provided at below-market interest rates, whereas the Foreign Office wanted "to preserve in the eyes of the Poles the character of strictly business transactions"; it feared that subsidized credit would only distort economic judgment and discourage good economic practices by recipients.[121] A 1930 request for Reich help in restructuring existing debt also found little sympathy in Berlin, despite Graebe's drastic warning that "without help from Berlin [he mentioned cheaper credit, refinancing of current debt, and import quotas] the collapse of the German nationality in the Corridor is unavoidable."[122]

At a November 1930 meeting, described as "stormy," between Reich officials and minority leaders in Danzig, the latter expressed general dissatisfaction with current levels of support and asked for a direct meeting with Chancellor Brüning. The Foreign Office was opposed, however, to such continued high-level contacts; they were not "expedient for foreign policy reasons" and only provoked Poland by making still more explicit the close ties between minority leaders and the German government. State Secretary von Bülow warned that such a tight relationship, "whereby every door in Berlin is open to gentlemen who present themselves as representatives of the minority, . . . has contributed to ever harsher measures by the Poles against the minority, and so threatens its future."[123]

Graebe, Naumann, and other minority representatives were granted a meeting with other key Reich officials, including Curtius and Trevir-anus. They made another urgent request for help and received support for at least one of their demands, a special wheat import quota. But they were unable to persuade the government to relieve them of their current debt burden, much of it owed to the HBB.[124] Despite Foreign Office misgivings, Graebe and his colleagues Koerber and Hasbach were able to meet personally with Brüning in January 1931 and express their disap-pointment with a proposed cut of 20-25 percent in the Reich's support for German minorities. They also submitted their "Ideas for Practical Work for Eastern Revisionism," which warned that "a considerable number of Germans in city and country are about to succumb to the economic catastrophe; those still in good shape are bound to falter too if aid is not forthcoming. . . . Poland helps only the Poles." They urged a more de-termined Reich effort to sustain "a German population in the Corridor (a) to prevent Poland from creating *faits accomplis* and (b) so that later, after the revision, Germany would not have an almost exclusively Polish popu-lation inside its borders." In the meantime, "Poland is unable to solve the minority problem or live up to the obligations she assumed in 1919." Letting Poland "wear herself out" against minority outposts in the ceded areas would further demonstrate the Polish state's "incompetence in minority affairs," encourage the Masurians and Cashubes to remain faithful to Germany, and forestall a Polish offensive against East Prussia, Danzig, or Pomerania.[125]

Graebe criticized the current system of distributing credits by way of intermediary banks (the HBB and the Landwirtschaftlicher Bank); the loans which these banks offered, at 8-10 percent, led "not to salvation but to ruin." What the minority needed was cheaper credit, including at least some loans at 4 percent, to get rid of the existing burden of high-interest debt. He also wanted minority leaders to be given a greater role in the running of this program; "It is not right that farmers or urban entrepre-neurs are asked by a Danzig consortium to sell their businesses without [minority] political leaders hearing anything about it. Nor is this compati-ble with current policies discouraging emigration to the Reich. But unless decisive measures are taken in a very short time, numerous businesses will surely succumb. Land and history will be lost. . . . Without [Reich] financial *sacrifices* [his emphasis], the embattled Germans in Poland sim-ply cannot be preserved economically. . . . We have to know where we stand. . . . We cannot justify leading our followers to ruin any longer." Graebe closed with the threat that if something were not done soon, he would give his followers "the green light" to leave for Germany "adjust

our policies, which so far have been in full conformity with the Reich's,"
in the direction of rapprochement with the Polish government.[126]

In response to this agitated appeal by minority leaders, Brüning
acknowledged that his government had a "moral obligation," based on
the 1929 Liquidation Agreement, to German landowners in western Poland. If it could no longer support them, it should at least inform them
of this fact and so free them to sell their estates and pull out. He agreed
to Graebe's suggestion that a cabinet subcommittee (composed of Treviranus, Curtius, and the Finance and Agriculture ministers) be set up to
oversee relations between Berlin and the minority and to determine how
much Germany could do to "encourage Germans in Pomorze to persevere
in their difficult situation." A subsequent February 5, 1931, draft by
Curtius, "Measures for the Support of Germans in Pomorze and Poznania," proposed a wheat import quota for German farmers in western
Poland.[127] Under this arrangement, Germany agreed to forgo 1,850,000
marks (500,000 of which would come out of Ossa's budget) of the duty on
10,000 tons of wheat from German farmers in Pomorze. Giving this
advantage only to Pomorze represented a break with previous guidelines,
expressed in Ossa's charter, whereby Reich aid was to be made available
to Germans throughout the ceded areas of Poland on an equal basis. In
practice, Ossa had begun previously to favor Pomorze and the Netze
region, fearing that its funds would be stretched too thin otherwise;
German farmers in Poznania received token consideration only so that
they would not think they were being "written off." Following the granting of the wheat import quota, however, the government reaffirmed that
"the monies allocated to Ossa for mortgage purposes will be distributed
without regard to regional limitations to Germans in the formerly German
eastern areas."[128]

The Brüning government was less willing to accommodate Graebe's
other requests, including subsidized interest, debt refinancing, and a
loosening of Ossa's control over the process. Bülow suggested that minority leaders lacked sufficient appreciation for all that had already been
done for them, including the 60-million-mark Ossa program and an
altogether reasonable 8 percent interest rate; there was simply no money
available for debt refinancing or for subsidized credit. He reasoned that
the wheat import quota was a partial substitute for the latter, equivalent to
a 1 percent reduction in interest rates, but this was all Germany could do
under current circumstances: "If some Pomorze landowners take the
position that the Reich is obliged to preserve them as state pensioners and
relieve them of every material worry, then this sort of attitude must be
resisted with all necessary bluntness." The Ossa program was already
being denounced by some Social Democrats as a "support program for
larger landowners," and the Foreign Office suggested that dissatisfied

minority leaders spoke chiefly for these interests, whereas it was more important to Germany's interests to save the smaller German farmers of western Poland. "Any linking of this action with the [domestic] *Osthilfe*," warned Bülow, "would hopelessly discredit it, expose the Reich to serious foreign political involvements, and end with the destruction of the remaining German landholdings in western Poland."[129]

In December 1931, Graebe, Ulitz, and minority leaders from elsewhere in eastern Europe met again with Brüning to submit a new list of requests and repeat their fears for the future of the German minority in Poland. Graebe warned that the minority was growing weaker economically, partly because of declining Reich support; it needed firm, long-term commitments as protection against economic crises. He was especially unhappy with the management of the Ossa program; one Polish German farmer, whose estate employed about thirty other Germans, claimed that his request for Ossa help to forestall bankruptcy was met with the suggestion that he simply sell out. Graebe proposed that a prominent German political figure, one who enjoyed the confidence of the minority, be installed as a permanent intermediary between the Reich and Polish Germans and be given control of all aspects of the financial support system. (He mentioned Treviranus, whose revisionist talk during the 1930 campaign had made him especially unpopular among Poles and, perhaps for that reason, all the more popular among Polish Germans.) This meeting with Brüning lasted only about ten minutes, however, and no additional commitments were forthcoming from the chancellor.[130]

Graebe continued his campaign for additional Reich support in 1932 with a rather windy memo, "On the Significance of State-Supported International National-Political Work," stressing the strategic importance of the German minority in Poland and its readiness to cooperate with a more active German policy in eastern Europe: "East-central Europe is disordered and thus open in a quite different sense than before the war. An eastern policy without the cooperation of the German populations there and without their support is unthinkable. . . . Germany is the only nation in Europe that sees everything that takes place in the east-central European region with its own eyes."[131] The minority was granted an additional concession that year when the wheat import quota was supplemented by one for butter: minority dairy farmers could send 3,750 tons of butter to Germany at a tariff of 25 marks per 100 kilograms instead of the standard rate of 170 marks. The Foreign Office supported this measure on grounds that otherwise the "considerable financial sacrifices of recent years would have been in vain and one of the salient aims of Reich policy buried."[132]

Graebe returned in January 1933 with additional thoughts about the geopolitical role of the minority and a request for "comprehensive credit aid for economic operations in town and country" at a cost 30-35 million marks.[133] He was supported by Germany's ambassador to Poland, who vouched for the minority's depressed economic situation: "The German population is excluded almost completely from the Polish government's aid measures, yet the collection of taxes from them is pursued much more rigorously. . . . German merchants and businesses suffer besides from an often systematic boycott, which a large part of the Polish population, at the direction of the ZOKZ, carries out against everything that is still German or imported from Germany. . . . The economic crisis, now three and a half years old, is facilitating to a large degree the de-Germanization policies of the Polish government directed at these areas. . . . In my opinion, we would be guilty of a major political mistake if we abandoned these Germans in their struggle for economic survival." The pressure on Polish Germans to emigrate was growing stronger, he pointed out; another wave of emigration like that of the early 1920s would weaken the German population to the point where struggle against the Polish majority by those remaining would become senseless; if the Reich did not help now, everything done in the past would have been in vain.[134] Graebe and Naumann wanted to follow up this latest initiative with a meeting with interim Chancellor Kurt von Schleicher, but German political leaders had more pressing things on their minds in January 1933. The Foreign Ministry assured the minority leaders that their request would be treated seriously but warned that they "should not be under any illusions about this matter" in light of its proposed costs.[135]

Despite the unavoidable frictions, despite inevitable feelings of disappointment with the amount of aid that depression-plagued Germany could provide, the Reich's support program was clearly the most effective approach to the problem of sustaining the German minority in Poland. Without such aid, there is little doubt that the loss of German economic substance in Poland and the exodus of Germans would have been substantially greater. True, this support served German foreign policy as well as promoting its stated aim of sustaining a vulnerable minority, but this is no reason to view the entire project exclusively or even primarily in the context of revisionist motives. There was clearly much more than revisionism behind the felt obligation of German government and public opinion to come to the aid of countrymen left behind in Poland, nor did the readiness of Polish Germans to accept outside aid necessarily turn them into tools of a foreign government—although much of the historical literature, and virtually all Polish accounts, would argue that Reich aid was essentially an aspect of German revisionism, and the willingness of the minority to accept it was a sign of its active role in the revisionist project. For Christoph Kimmich, the support program permitted the German government to "help the minorities maintain themselves; in return, it gained control over them."[136] This view finds even stronger expression in the work of Norbert Krekeler, whose central theme is that Polish Germans existed primarily to serve Reich interests and were artificially sustained mainly for that purpose. They were simply an "extended arm of German foreign policy . . . [and] oriented themselves in their actions to the preservation of the demand for revisions."[137]

From this perspective, however, it is only a short jump to the attempt to justify Polish suppression of the minority on grounds that it was a threat to Poland's very survival. Thus Krekeler indicates little interest in or understanding of the conditions of minority life in Poland which compelled Polish Germans to look to the Reich for support. He refers to "Polish displacement measures" only in quotation marks, as though they were imaginary; he observes somewhat cavalierly that but for Reich efforts to sustain the minority and tie it to revisionist objectives, Germans would have been able to find a satisfactory place in Poland "somewhere between national self-assertion and assimilation"—without specifying what this might mean.[138] In his view, it was primarily the refusal of Polish Germans to accept their new state, together with Germany's refusal to accept its new frontiers, that not only poisoned German-Polish relations during the life of the Weimar Republic but also led to Hitler, World War II, and the loss of the German East in 1945.[139]

No one can deny the connection between German revisionist aims and Reich financial support for the minority in Poland, and the fact that specific programs such as the wheat import quota for Pomorze were directed exclusively at places high on the list of revisionist goals further underscores the connection. As State Secretary Schubert acknowledged while making the case for Ossa, "The Reich government has always viewed it as an essential object of our foreign policy to preserve by all means those Germans still living in the ceded territories, for this is a prerequisite for the favorable solution of the Corridor and Upper Silesian qustions."[140] Krahmer-Möllenberg also noted the connection between the program he administered and the minority's relationship to the German government: "Because Germans in Poland were bound to the German government by material ties, they were also bound, despite the new political frontiers, to continue to see this government as their master and to support its goals, which undeniably conflicts with their duties as Polish citizens."[141] The Foreign Office accompanied a 1932 request for additional support with the words: "We have no choice currently but to provide for the preservation of all those German positions in the ceded territories which can in any way be preserved . . . [as] the only possible way to create a foundation which an active revisionist policy can follow later."[142] On another occasion it conceded that the only reason for Germany to come to the aid of the Pless concern was the expectation of regaining Polish Upper Silesia.[143]

Hans-Adolf Jacobsen's observation that "justified worries about the fate of the brothers and sisters outside [the Reich] blended in a dangerous way with undisguised revanchism" is doubtless true.[144] But it is equally important to distinguish between these two impulses and to remember that the worries themselves were indeed "justified." Moreover, revanchism appears much less frequently in recorded discussions of the aid program than do other motives, such as the desire to keep Polish Germans from coming to the Reich and claiming jobs or public services. Discouraging German emigration from Poland, not maintaining the revisionist option, is the most frequently cited argument and justification. One consul justified spending money to help German farmers remain in Poland on the simple grounds that to do so was cheaper than putting them up in the Reich.[145]

To the extent that projects were "targeted," it was less at regions the Reich wanted to regain than at individuals who were thinking of leaving Poland. As noted, special considerations granted to the Corridor or to Silesia were the exception; in most cases, aid went equally to all the ceded territories, and no explicit differentiation was made between those parts of Poland that might be reclaimed by Germany at some later date and those that would not. In contrast to Tadeusz Kowalak's assertion that Germans in central and eastern Poland "did not get major sums,"[146] many of the Reich's programs aided Germans all over Poland, whether or not they had ever been Reich citizens. Even the scattered references to revisionist goals that do occur in relation to the Reich's support program do not mean that these were the primary consideration rather than a means of garnering additional support for an expensive project. In short, the overlapping of German foreign policy interests and aid to the German minority in Poland is only part of the story; there was sufficient justification, unrelated to German territorial designs, for the Reich's assistance. Nor was there necessarily anything underhanded or devious about a program that grew naturally out of a recognized obligation to countrymen left behind in Poland.

Of course, these observations and this justification of Reich financial aid for the minority apply only to the period of the Weimar Repubic. With the National Socialist seizure of power in 1933, the nature of the German revisionist threat changed dramatically; so too did the implications for Poland of a German minority population that took its cue from Berlin. Hitler's Germany faced the same choice of approaches to the problem of sustaining the minority as had the Weimar Republic, except that Germany's withdrawal from the League meant the effective abandonment of the first: reliance on international agencies. The second approach, the aid program initiated by the Weimar Republic, continued after 1933, though more often than not it did so at reduced levels and with an eye to manipulating rather than sustaining the minority. Ironically, it was the third option, the bilateral negotiations with Poland that paid so few dividends before 1933, which soon became Nazi Germany's preferred approach. Moreover, the German government was no longer content to exploit the dependency relationship created by its subsidies merely to impose a superficial political unity upon the minority; after 1933 its support programs became a tool in the thoroughgoing ideological *Gleichschaltung* (coordination) of the German population of Poland.

6

The Impact of National Socialism

There are no statistics showing the precise degree of support for National Socialism among Germans in western Poland, but it is clear that a substantial majority of them embraced this movement and its attendant ideas without much hesitation. Even though there had not been much of a National Socialist movement in Poland before January 1933, the major German newspaper in Poznania declared just a few months later that "we Germans in Poland are all National Socialists."[1] This was an exaggeration, perhaps, but only a slight one; a 1937 article in *Slavonic and East European Review* estimated that 70-80 percent of the minority was committed to Hitler and his ideology, and among young Germans the figure was higher still.[2] Indeed, the percentage of Germans who genuinely sympathized with Nazism was probably greater in Poland than in Germany itself, which is all the more remarkable when one considers the absence in Poland of the totalitarian state apparatus that compelled adherence to Nazism inside Germany.

One does not have to look far to find reasons for this quick and positive response. Poland had certainly done little to win the allegiance of its German-speaking citizens, and there was also widespread disappointment with the system of international guarantees and organizations just then; many Germans saw the more assertive Reich promised by Hitler as the only effective means of easing their situation. Moreover, the supra-state, non-territorial concept of nationality advocated by National Socialism accorded well with ideas of national solidarity across political boundaries which German minorities had long advocated as the best means of long-term survival in the diaspora. Polish Germans also expressed the hope that Germany would now see them less as a moral obligation, an object of charity, and more as the equals of Reich Germans in the all-German *Volksgemeinschaft*. The fact that Hitler himself was an *Auslanddeutscher* of sorts only enhanced their readiness to see him as their savior.

Of course, Polish Germans had only an imperfect understanding of the changes taking place in Germany after 1933. Their accounts reveal more wishful thinking than firm knowledge of developments; and the minority's own press rarely discussed the less savory aspects of Hitler's rule. Superintendant Blau, spiritual leader of most Germans in Poznania and Pomorze, declared his own support for the "new currents in the Reich." The "spiritual movement in Germany," he said, was "healthy for our area and so must to be approved unanimously." But he defined it in the most benign terms, as little more than an attempt to mobilize national resources more efficiently under a more unified leadership. In guidelines prepared for his pastors, Blau described Nazism as a movement promising renewal, diligence, cleanliness, the suppression of subversive ideas, and improved relations between people and their churches. He showed no awareness of those aspects of Nazi ideology that bothered other churchmen: its neo-paganism, its racial anti-Semitism, its glorification of political dictatorship.[3]

The ready adoption of National Socialism by most Germans in Poland was encouraged by their close and dependent relationship to various Reich agencies. Just as Hitler came to power, the minority's own resources were being strained by the Great Depression. Many wondered how much longer they would be able to hold out in Poland before having to join the exodus to the Reich—which seemed reason enough not to get on the wrong side of the new rulers there. Moreover, Berlin had become the source of the financial support upon which many of them relied, and it was likely to be dispensed only to those who went along with the new political line.

Hitler's accession led to significant changes in this system. The nominal role of the parliamentary *Beirat* in overseeing the Deutsche Stiftung was assumed, first, by the Foreign Policy Office of the NSDAP and then, in November 1933, by a new Volksdeutscher Rat (VR). The VR was put in charge both of Reich relations with German minorities in other countries and of the numerous quasi-private organizations concerned with *Ausland-deutschen*. The noted geopolitical theorist Karl Haushofer served as VR chairman; Hans Steinacher, who had just become the new head of the VDA, was its director. Rudolf Hess served as a distant titular head, empowered to screen all contacts between *Auslanddeutschen* and Hitler himself. Of the eight members of the VR's governing council, only one, Robert Ernst, was a member of the NSDAP, but given what the others had to say for the record, this was not an important distinction. In addition, the NSDAP had its own Gau Ausland (later *Auslandsorganisation* or AO/NSDAP) under Ernst Bohle, which often involved itself in minority affairs, as did the Foreign Office.[4]

The quasi-priate organizations set up to serve Germans in other countries, (VDS, DAI, BdA, DSb, and others) quickly declared their support for Germany's new rulers and tried to get on good terms with them. Some were not very well positioned to do so, however. In February 1933, Hitler became the first chancellor to refuse the honorary chairmanship of the DAI, and he let it be known that this had something to do with the "racial" background of its director, Fritz Wertheimer, a "Lutheran of Semitic ancestry." Despite years of work in behalf of German minorities abroad and strong testimonials from Graebe and others, Wertheimer soon found himself locked out of his Stuttgart offices by members of the SA. In September, DAI Chairman Theodor Wanner was also eased out in favor of Stuttgart Mayor Georg Stroelin, and the swastika soon graced the DAI's letterhead.[5] In April the VDA's executive committee concluded that "only complete agreement between the leading men of the VDA and the leading men of the national movement" could assure the organization's continued effectiveness. The *Verein* now became a *Volksbund*, and Steinacher became its new director. The BdA proposed the Prince of Waldeck as its new head, but when the regime indicated its disapproval the position went instead to Fritz Thyssen; Robert Ernst became the new *Führer* of the DSb, but neither organization played a significant role in the affairs of the minority in Poland. Indeed, both were now ordered to limit their activities to Germany itself.[6]

Steinacher was the most interesting and (temporarily) the most influential of these new players. He was a native of German-Slovene Carinthia, had attended school in German-Polish Austrian Silesia, and then taught school at Meran in German-Italian South Tyrol. He was a decorated Austrian officer in World War I and played a leading role in Austria's successful postwar plebiscite campaign in his native Carinthia. He then worked for the German cause in other plebiscites and participated in the antiseparatist campaign in the Rhineland. After earning a Frankfurt Ph.D. in 1925, he joined the VDA and became its head in 1933.[7] Under Steinacher, the VDA became the clear favorite among the many organizations concerned with Germans abroad; it took over most of the DAI's overseas projects. In western Poland, however, it continued to take a back seat to the DS, whose chief, Krahmer-Möllenberg, seemed to have no trouble switching his allegiance from the Weimar Republic to Hitler.

The same was true of the minority's political leadership, represented by the DViSuS in Poznania and Pomorze and by the Volksbund in Silesia, although some prominent individuals were not sufficiently fast on their feet, or identified too strongly with other views, and so had to go. For example, Eugen Naumann, the senior German leader in Poznania since 1919, chairman of the Main Elections Committee and the Committee of Nine, was replaced in Febuary 1933 after he went public with a plan to put relations between the minority and the Polish state on an altogether new foundation. Germans in Poland, he suggested, should relinquish whatever political rights they enjoyed as Polish citizens in return for guarantees of their equal-but-separate cultural and economic development. Several historians have described this initiative as "inspired by the NSDAP" or containing "NS thoughts"; they attribute Naumann's removal to the unwillingness of other minority leaders to embrace National Socialist ideas so quickly. In fact, Naumann was evidently dropped not because he leaned toward Nazism too soon but because he was not able to do so convincingly.[8]

Kurt Graebe, chief minority leader in Pomorze and director of the DViSuS, also lost most of his real power in the wake of Hitler's accession. He quickly praised the "national revolution" in Germany and expressed confidence that it "would get rid of everything bad and damnable in the German people"; German-Polish relations, he said, would also benefit from the fact that both peoples now had authoritarian governments.[9] Nevertheless, local Nazis denounced Graebe to Reich officials as a former associate of Stresemann and friend of socialists; Steinacher dismissed him as a "frustrated Reich German," at home only in the military chain of command but now largely superfluous. Graebe was persuaded to withdraw from his position in the DViSuS, though he remained active in minority affairs and in the European Nationalities Congress. In 1937, he left Poland and was stripped of his Polish citizenship; not especially welcome in Germany, however, he remained formally stateless until 1941, when he regained German citizenship by volunteering for military service in World War II.[10]

These two individuals aside, most members of the minority political establishment made the necessary adjustments and retained their positions after 1933. Otto Ulitz, for example, principal leader of the German minority in Silesia and director of the Volksbund, publicly embraced the "National Socialist idea" in 1933, though he does not seem to have understood all that this idea entailed. He too was attacked by local Nazis, and some in the Reich as well, for trying too hard to keep all Germans in the fold, regardless of political persuasion.[11] He even retained some Jews on the Volksbund's membership rolls until, in 1936, this fact was leaked to Der Stürmer, which denounced the Volksbund as a "Jewish organization" and forced removal of the Jewish members.[12] By this time, however, Ulitz and the Volksbund seemed to be fully in line with Reich thinking. The annual report for 1937 included Ulitz's long paean to National Socialism as "the German ideology, . . . an idea which encompasses the soul, . . . (where) the future of our people lies, . . . encompassing as one all the parts of the people"; it was the "national duty of Germans to profess" this creed.[13] Most minority leaders were "conservative-bourgeois," but they kept any philosophical reservations they had about National Socialism, especially its social-revolutionary and anti-establishment aspects, to themselves; most made the switch with little apparent struggle. Those who indicated any ambivalence did so less because National Socialism clashed with their own principles than because they wondered about its relevance for those who could not be part of the new Reich.

Only a small minority of Germans in Poland resisted National Socialism categorically. As in Germany itself, the two significant political movements that remained most immune to its appeal were social democracy and political Catholicism—neither of which had ever enjoyed much support among the Germans of Poznania and Pomorze. In Silesia too, among Poles and Germans alike, the socialist movement remained surprisingly weak, considering that this was Poland's most industrialized province. The DSAP did take a hard line against National Socialism, harder, in fact, than did the Polish government; after a harsh attack on Hitler, the editors of the DSAP's *Volkszeitung*, in Łódź, were jailed by Polish authorities for "offending the leader of a friendly state." The DSAP also helped shunt SPD exiles from Germany to other countries and smuggle exile literature into the Reich. It responded to the *Reichskristallnacht* in 1938 by declaring it a duty of "every decent German, and German socialists in particular, to protest the disgrace which has been inflicted on the German people by these events."[14]

Despite these brave words, German social democrats were seriously weakened, especially in western Poland, by the defection of much of their already small movement to pro-Nazi organizations. In Pomorze and Poznania, Arthur Pankratz's small DSP came out itself in favor of the National Socialist "idea" in 1935.[15] In Silesia, the DSAP went into a sharp decline; its paper ceased to appear daily and was later just a local edition of the Łódź *Volkszeitung*. And although some outside observers estimated that social democracy was still supported by as many as 10 percent of Germans in Poland in 1937, Polish government observers noted no significant DSAP activity at all in Silesia that year.[16]

By contrast, political Catholicism had long been dominant in Upper Silesia, among Poles and Germans alike. Eduard Pant, a native of Austrian Silesia, remained the most prominent German Catholic leader in Poland. He was a member of the Silesian Sejm (1922-35) and the Polish Senate (1928-35), and head of both the DKVP and the VdK. Though closer to the Austrian than to the Prussian tradition, Pant got along well enough with the mostly Protestant minority leaders from the Prussian partition, at least until 1933.[17] And like most other minority leaders, Pant expressed qualified approval of the Hitler/Papen government in early 1933: "We reject national socialism, though we must concede that it possesses a certain value; . . . this consists of its Christian foundations."[18]

Unlike the others, however, he soon became disillusioned and, moreover, said so publicly. At a meeting of the "German-Christian Peoples

Party" (DCVP), as the former DKVP was now called, in January 1934, Pant criticized as "godless" the Reich's new rulers; at a meeting of the VdK he stressed the fundamental incompatibility of Christianity and National Socialism. He also supported the regime of Engelbert Dollfuss in Austria as it headed for its bitter showdown with Austrian Nazism. It was not easy, of course, for Pant to take up a position in such sharp opposition to Hitler's regime at a time when the Catholic Church in Germany was still trying to get along with it, but he persevered. He denounced the excessive nationalism and militarism on both sides of the Polish-German divide but also made clear his preference for coexistence with Poles rather than with Nazis, and he was the first major German politician to vote for a Polish state budget.[19] When the *Oberschlesischer Kurier*, which traditionally represented political Catholicism in Upper Silesia, was taken over by an opposition faction influenced by National Socialism, Pant started up a new paper, *Der Deutsche in Polen*, and used it to continue his attacks on Hitler's regime and those Germans in Poland who took their cue from it.

German authorities became increasingly annoyed with Pant's attacks; in the words of the German consul in Toruń, "it would be desirable if this nuisance to our German nationality could soon be put out of business."[20] Krahmer-Möllenberg passed the word that those who stuck with Pant would receive no more financial support from his agency, and numerous Pant supporters were in fact cut off. Minority members who wanted to remain in good standing with the Reich were told to boycott any organization with which Pant was associated. After the consul in Poznań informed the Poznanian branch of the VdK that Pant was guilty of undermining German unity, the organization agreed to his ouster in order to continue receiving Reich financial support. The German Party (DP) in Silesia, which had traditionally formed a joint parliamentary delegation with Pant's DCVP, now shunned him and refused to attend any business meetings of the faction so long as he remained its chief. The largely ceremonial *Zentralausschuss der Deutschen in Polen* (Central Committee of Germans in Poland) declared in August 1934 that it too would shun Pant for "offending national feelings [and] for attacks on German leadership in Poland."[21] Nothing that Pant did upset Reich officials more than his trip to Vienna at the head of a VdK delegation to honor the slain Dollfuss.[22] One newspaper even reported an SA plot to arrest Pant during a visit to German Upper Silesia, but he canceled the trip.[23]

These pressures were effective in reducing Pant's DCVP following from about 7,000 members in 1933 to about four-hundred by mid-1934; the circulation of his new newspaper did not rise above a thousand. He continued, nonetheless, to enjoy the support of most of the executive committee of the VdK, whose goal he defined simply as "fighting National Socialism."[24] As this or that member of the VdK threatened to cave in to the pressure, Pant ousted him or, as in Pomorze, dissolved the entire section. But at a meeting of the VdK in Katowice in December 1934 (the travel costs of all the opposition delegates were covered by the DS), he finally lost out to advocates of a "Papen course" of good relations with the Reich's new masters. Pant thereupon denounced the *gleichgeschalteten* VdK and founded a new organization, the Verband der Deutschen in Polen (Union of Germans in Poland). Though he attracted only a small membership, he stuck to his guns—campaigning against Nazism, encouraging the Polish government to crack down on Nazi activities in Poland, and trying to organize an anti-Nazi league of German minorities in Europe—until his death in 1938.[25] By then, however, the DCVP (whose head he remained) had only about 900 members *vs.* 26,000 in the *gleichgeschalteten* VdK, and official Polish observers were using the same phrase in reference to Pant's group as they did for the DSAP: "no significant activity."[26]

Pant was indeed a remarkable exception (and the only notable exception) to the rule among minority leaders in western Poland. The rest, out of conviction, calculation, or fear, went along with the new regime in Berlin and its ideas. The Evangelical Church, for example, presented few obstacles to the process of ideological *Gleichschaltung.* To be sure, Superintendent Blau's internal correspondence with pastors did indicate some awareness of the basic contradictions between Christianity and National Socialism. In 1934, he warned against the growth of "neo-heathen" ideas among German youth. In his annual report for 1936, he pointed out that the "new world view" (National Socialism) touched on some religious issues that could not be ignored in sermons. For example, he asked rhetorically, was religion a matter of blood and race or of the Holy Spirit? Was Christianity really "Aryan-German" or a faith with a foundation in the Semitic world, a "Christ from the seed of David," and a "Bible to which the Old Testament belongs?"[27] Blau doubtless also had National Socialism in mind when he warned of a threat to the "truth" of Christianity from "anti-Christians" inside and outside the church and urged his pastors to stick to this truth above all other political and national considerations.[28] But he indicated none of these misgivings in public. Instead, his church distributed copies of openly National Socialist works (such as *Volk and Kirche* by Heinrich Grothaus) as the basis for synodal discussions; it cooperated with requests by Reich authorities for proof of the "Aryan" ancestry of former parishioners; it went along with the Reich's new official definition of a Jew and ordered that "the religious marriage ceremony is to be denied" to those Christians who fit this definition.[29]

Jungdeutsche Partei and Deutsche Vereinigung

The most intriguing aspect of Nazi Germany's campaign to establish firm control over the minority in Poland is that the principal obstacle was not the meager anti-Nazi elements cited above but the minority's own indigenous NS movement. National Socialism had assumed organizational form in Poland long before Hitler came to power in Germany. The Deutscher Nationalsozialistischer Verein für Polen was founded in 1921 by the engineer Rudolf Wiesner; a decade later it was renamed the Jungdeutsche Partei in Polen (Young German Party in Poland, or JDP) but still had only a few hundred members at this time. Its home base was Bielitz in formerly Austrian Silesia, a majority-German town surrounded by a Polish-speaking countryside. (Wiesner and his followers emerged, in other words, from the same Austro-Bohemian milieu that gave birth to what there was of pre-Hitler National Socialism.)[30] There was also a separate NSDAP in Poland in the 1930s, tolerated by the Polish government but with the understanding that it would enroll only Reich citizens. This organization had fewer than 2,000 members, about 15 percent of the German citizens in Poland, but its significance for the minority itself—that is, Polish citizens of German nationality—was slight.[31]

Besides the JDP and the NSDAP itself, there were some more ephemeral manifestations of National Socialism in western Poland: for example, several sightings of underground SA or SS formations. The consulate in Katowice believed that these illegal Nazi groups consisted primarily of Young Germans (JDs), though Wiesner denied any involvement and promised to expel any JDP members who joined them.[32] The Foreign Office discouraged German involvement in such organizations, in part because they were so readily infiltrated by Polish agents and in part because they undermined German-Polish relations.[33] German officials also suspected that they might be Polish fronts designed to ensnare the minority; several such underground groups were revealed to consist mainly of ethnic Poles, who apparently saw them as an outlet for frustrations of a more general nature. Some Cashubes were arrested for distributing fliers with the slogan "Hitler is coming!" (one of them died of unexplained causes while in police custody), and crowds of unemployed Poles were not above brandishing swastika flags or shouting pro-Hitler slogans as a surefire way of attracting official attention.[34] In 1935 the Gestapo warned Nazi sympathizers in Polish Silesia to beware of an "NSDABund"; the NSDAP knew nothing about it and thought it might be a Polish creation aimed at "the destruction of the German minority." Its leader, Paul Manjura, was reportedly recruiting unsophisticated Upper Silesians to wrest this province forcefully from Polish rule; he claimed to have Reich support for the project and as many as 10,000 members already enrolled. In January 1936 the Gestapo managed somehow to acquire the records of this organization and found that it consisted of only five cells of about 150 members each; these were thoroughly penetrated by Polish police, who arrested their leaders a few weeks later. Of the 120 Upper Silesians identified as members, most were Polish-speaking; Manjura himself committed suicide before he was able (or forced) to reveal much else about the origins of his organization.[35]

The JDP, also active first in Polish Silesia, expanded north into Poznania and Pomorza and then into the rest of Poland. Its appeal was strongest among German workers and other urbanites in nationally exposed situations. Before long, it found itself in a contest with established minority organizations for the support and control of Polish Germans. The Young Germans were "socialist" in their appeal to class envy, even against other Germans; in particular, they exploited widespread dissatisfaction with the minority "establishment" and its distribution of the Reich's limited and always insufficient subsidies. The official program of the JDP, with its promise of a great pan-German *Volksgemeinschaft* (national community) governed by the principle *"Gemeinnutz geht vor Eigennutz,"* was indistinguishable from that of the NSDAP. It claimed to embrace Christianity, if only to underscore its rejection of Jews as a component of German nationality; for more obscure reasons, Freemasons were also banned.[36]

In some respects, the JDP went further even than the Reich party in enforcing some of the more arcane items on its ideological agenda. For example, the JDP used only the new "German" names for the months in its internal correspondence; (thus the historian who would work with this material needs first to find out what *Hartung, Hornung, Lenzing,* and so on, refer to).[37] Once Poland lifted its ban on Hitler's *Mein Kampf* in 1935, copies of that work were made available at a reduced price to all JDP members. They were also urged to become regular readers of *Der Stürmer* (published in Nuremberg), "the only and greatest polemical journal against this Jewish plague."[38] JD efforts to fashion a "uniform" out of black pants and white shirts and to incorporate the swastika into its emblem were firmly rejected, however, by the German Foreign Office as well as by Polish officials.[39] Wiesner himself was a "true believer," characterized by those who knew him as a "fanatical" supporter of the Nazi world view. His inner-party communications, however, dealing mostly with the party's chronic financial problems, reveal an unimaginative and pedantic mind. Steinacher, who knew him and tried to work with him, described him as "soft and inexperienced" but also "stubborn" on occasion, which was the basis for such *Führer* qualities as were attributed to him.[40]

Although the Young Germans described their goal as the unification of all Polish Germans in a single ideological movement, the actual result of their campaign was the most serious schism in the ranks of the interwar minority. They presented themselves as a movement of German youth and workers in opposition to a "reactionary-bourgeois" DViSuS and Volksbund establishment. They portrayed the latter as an unresponsive clique, too concerned with the economic interests of their mostly upper-class supporters but neglectful of the needs of the bulk of Polish Germans, and too slow to adjust to the post-1919 situation and to transcend the former partition boundaries in the interest of a common German front throughout Poland. For the benefit of Reich observers, Young Germans liked to portray their struggle with the Polish-German establishment in NSDAP and DNVP terms; one JDP broadside described a contest between "Young German hearts and German-National capital."[41]

The attitude of the German government toward this schism was simply that it should end. But how? The different Reich and party agencies that took a hand in Polish German affairs during the early years of the Hitler regime often worked at cross purposes. The VR's Steinacher thought more highly of the established leaders and wanted them to remain in place, whatever their past ideological shortcomings. He praised Ulitz, for example, as "a real man," strong, direct, and honorable, and thought he would make a good head of the Verein Deutscher Volksgruppen, the organization of German minorities throughout Europe. Steinacher was also impressed with Swart's competence; the German co-op network over which he presided was "one of the most significant national achievements [in Poland] since 1918," and its director was too valuable to be cast aside for ideological reasons. JDP leaders, by contrast, struck Steinacher as less capable; he suspected that they were looking primarily for "advantages" from the Reich's support program.[42] He met with Wiesner personally in June 1934 and asked him not to do anything that would disrupt the system of Reich financial support. According to Steinacher, Wiesner promised to leave the existing German-Polish organizations alone and respect directives from the VR. It soon became evident, however, that Wiesner either would not or could not restrain his followers.[43]

The Foreign Office and its DS subsidiary also continued to favor the traditional minority leaders and did what they could to persuade others in the Berlin government that their ideological conversion to National Socialism was genuine.[44] The consular officials who were closest to the intraminority quarrel took the position that the JDP's adversaries were not any less National Socialist in their sympathies but simply opposed to JD "excesses" or unimpressed by JD leaders. "Both camps want the same thing," wrote the consul in Poznań, "but through different means, and are not therefore worse Germans." He testified to the sincerity of the ideological conversion of the traditional leadership, some of whom he considered indispensable. A few were perhaps too conservative still and thus might have to be eased out along with Naumann and Graebe (he mentioned Swart, Massenbach, and Saenger by name, though all three managed to hold on to their positions during the following years), but JDP leaders were simply less capable and had few substantial individual achievements to their credit.[45]

The Foreign Office also encouraged minority leaders to fashion new organizational structures to bridge the gap with the Young Germans. One such effort was the Deutscher Jungblock in Polen, (German Youth Block in Poland) self-described as an organization of "loyal citizens of the Polish state," without "political connections with foreign states," who sought the "union of all Germans on the basis of National Socialist ideology," while avoiding the "partisanship" of the Young Germans. Its "statement of principles" resembled the JDP program: it opposed materialism, class-consciousness, Marxism, and capitalism; "earned private property" deserved respect, but Gemeinnutz came first; membership in the greater-German national community was a matter of personal sentiment rather than language—except that one had to be "Aryan."[46] A second such effort was the "Jägerhof Circle" of January 1934, a group of "young intelligentsia" in Poznania who wanted "to work in conformity with the National Socialist idea." Its leaders included some who were identified with the DViSuS (such as "Führer" Erik von Witzleben) and some Young Germans (such as his assistant, Hans Wiese). The German consul in Poznań described Witzleben as "the leader approved by the Reich" and the Jägerhof Circle as the best vehicle for "infusing the minority with the ideas of the Third Reich" while preserving its political unity.[47] A comparable effort to overcome the breach between JDP and Volksbund in Silesia was the Deutscher Volksblock für Schlesien established in January 1935 and supported by Ulitz and some Young German dissidents. But none of these efforts to bridge the gap between the factions succeeded in persuading Wiesner and the JDP to drop their opposition.

In July 1934, principal Polish-German Leaders (Ulitz, Swart, Hasbach, Graebe, Starke) as well as some of the more moderate Young Germans (Wiese, Hans von Rosen, Günther Modrow) were invited by the VR to unity talks at Zoppot on the territory of the Free City of Danzig. Under pressure from Reich representatives, a deal was concluded under which the minority's Committee of Nine would be reconstituted to include four Young Germans alongside four representatives of the older organizations. Hans Kohnert, considered acceptable to both camps, would be chairman and ninth member. In return, the Young Germans agreed to merge into a new organization to be called the Deutsche Vereinigung für Westpolen (DV), the aim of which would be the "great German Volksgemeinschaft." The leadership of the new DV—Witzleben as *Führer* and Wiese as his Young German deputy—was inherited from the Jägerhof Circle, and it was granted official recognition by Polish officials in September 1934. Like the DViSuS, the DV had its headquarters in Bydgoszcz, and it controlled most of the other minority organizations in western Poland.[48] Witzleben soon turned out to be not much of a "leader": he was criticized first for giving Wiese too much latitude to carry on his feud with Swart and Graebe; then, after he dismissed Wiese, Young Germans charged that Witzleben was just a creature of the Old Guard, after all. He was replaced by Kohnert (1905-1965), who remained head of the DV until the war. Kohnert was a native of Poznania; in contrast to most other minority leaders, he was also young enough to have attended Polish schools and served in the Polish army before graduating from the Technische Hochschule in Danzig.[49]

The DV's constitution and by-laws of December 28, 1934, made clear the extent of the minority's quasi-voluntary *Gleichschaltung*. The DV declared itself to be just as National Socialist as the JDP, only a little less "revolutionary"; it stood for "true National Socialism" in all areas and called on all other minority organizations to work "in the National Socialist spirit." At its first annual meeting, June 1935, Kohnert declared that "the great idea which has led tens of thousands to the banner of the DV is the idea of the National Socialist renewal of our German nationality."[50] The DV stressed the "great sacrifices" it had made in the interest of unity, for example, by persuading Witzleben to step aside for Kohnert, "an open adherent of the NSDAP."[51] The German consul in Toruń recommended that the Reich back the DV as the "sole German agent" in western Poland. He testified that it stood "absolutely on the ground of the National Socialist German renewal movement. . . . It is absolutely not . . . to be equated with the former DNVP, and thus with reactionaries." The contest between the DV and JDP was less a matter of two competing ideological movements than a quarrel between the "right" and "left" wings of the same National Socialist movement.[52]

But Wiesner and the JDP did not go along with this and other efforts to resolve the schism. The Young German interlocutors at Zoppot had operated apparently without Wiesner's authority to strike such a deal, and he quickly repudiated it. In his opinion, Witzleben and Kohnert were merely stalking horses for the former DNVP, and those Young Germans who stood by the pact were expelled from the party. The DV remained limited to Poznania and Pomorze; the Volksbund continued to assert its claim to speak for the German minority in Silesia province and faced the same kind of Young Greman challenge. Ulitz and Pless, titular head of the Volksbund, tried to stay above "partisan struggles"; the Volksbund was a "national-cultural" organization in which no party or political ideology could assert exclusive dominance. Like Ulitz, Pless claimed in 1934 to have accepted the National Socialist idea "as he understood it"; like Blau, he seemed to misunderstand it as something akin to Christian democracy: a movement to transcend class and confessional differences, help the disadvantaged, and create a "national community." He also denounced the (Nazi-inspired) violence in Austria during the summer of 1934, including the attempted coup that led to the death of Chancellor Dollfuss.[53] Thus the "war" (Steinacher's word) between the two factions in western Poland continued with even greater intensity. In other words, the most significant short-term consequence of Hitler's seizure of power in Germany was the development of a major schism within a minority society that had previously remained surprisingly free of such divisions.

Complicating things was the fact that each faction was getting support from different agencies in the Reich. Many in Germany did see the struggle as the Young Germans wished, as analogous to the NSDAP and DNVP competition of 1932-33. Reports from the Poznań consulate lent support to this view and suggested that the adherence to National Socialism of Germans in western Poland was being restrained somehow by their conservative leaders. Consul von Tucher was especially critical of Swart, whom he described as "a bank magnate, . . . a cold businessman, unsocialistic, and . . . a member of the opposition in Reich terms"; efforts so far to bridge the gap were merely fronts for the "Swart group." Witzleben was a bad choice as compromise leader, for he could not choose between Swart and the Young Germans and so was unlikely to attract the support of "true National Socialists." Tucher suggested that the Reich intervene by appointing a "true leader" to oversee its support network, one who would enjoy the confidence of the Young Germans and prevent their drift toward more radical, perhaps pro-Polish positions. While asking for further directions from the VR, he clearly anticipated that these would call for "cooperation with the Young Germans" at the expense of the traditional leadership.[54]

Even after the Foreign Office worked to set up the DV, then, Wiesner continued to be encouraged in his defiance by others in Germany's labyrinthine political system, specifically the AO/NSDAP and the "Hitler Youth."[55] Bohle, the AO/NSDAP chief, seemed to want to impose a pro-JD solution. For example, when leaders of the principal organization of German farmers in Poznania (Welage, associated with the DV) refused to admit Young Germans, Bohle tried to cut off that organization's financial support on grounds that only forthright National Socialists within the minority were worthy of such aid.[56] He was blocked, however, by the Foreign Office and Kramer-Möllenberg, who got Haushofer to persuade his former student, Rudolf Hess, that the support system for German minorities abroad could only be run by people who knew what they were doing and who understood that "the cliché of Reich-German National Socialism cannot be applied as is to the very different circumstances of our minorities in other countries." Poland, moreover, would never tolerate the Reich's imposition of an openly Nazi leader of its German minority.[57]

But other party officials also identified with and encouraged the Young Germans. The *Völkischer Beobachter,* the rest of the official press, and the state radio usually described the struggle within the German minority from a one-sided, pro-JDP perspective, at least at first, and Reich research and propaganda institutes turned out pro-JD pamphlets. A story on the *Posener Tageblatt's* firing of a Young German writer spoke of "economic terror . . . by reactionaries against the Young German movement in Poland." The term "reactionary" was regularly attached to the DV, which was assumed to lack the support of younger or ideologically more committed members of the minority.[58] The AO/NSDAP remained on its different track for quite a long time, receiving Young German delegations and pressuring the DV to be more conciliatory to Young Germans.[59] The new German consul in Toruń, (Johannes Bernhardt, who came to that position by way of the AO) confided to a delegation of Young Germans in 1935 that whereas he had to be pro-DV as a representative of the Foreign Office, as a member of the NSDAP he remained definitely pro-JDP. (He was soon transfered.)[60] The Foreign Office complained that the controlled Reich press paid too much attention to Wiesner and not enough to the leaders of the DV and the Volksbund. The Young German newspaper in Silesia, *Der Aufbruch,* continued to receive Reich funds, which kept it operating (and attacking the Volksbund) into 1937.[61]

Young German pamphlets assailed the DV and the Volksbund for insufficient ideological rigor and for previous expressions of disagreement with Hitler. Kohnert was reported to have declared at one point (however improbable this seems today) that he "could go through fire for [Franz von] Papen, but never for Hitler."[62] Because he worked to bring local socialists into the DV fold, Kohnert was also accused of "harboring Marxists"; in reply, he testified (accurately) to the new *völkisch* convictions of remaining DSP adherents and reminded everyone of the large number of former SPD and KPD members now enrolled in the NSDAP.[63] The publisher of the *Deutsche Rundschau* (edited by Starke, who was one of the behind-the-scenes powers in the DV) was castigated for also publishing the works of Emil Ludwig and other anti-Nazis. Young Germans made an issue of any works by Jewish or emigré authors which they found in the libraries run by the DV-affiliated Deutsche Bücherei, despite the protestations of its director, Kurt Lück, that such texts served only "scholarly purposes." The Young Germans were convinced that DV leaders were just opportunists masquerading as National Socialists and that the DV itself—an "organization only of reactionaries, whom nothing positive, only resistance to the evolving new thing, has brought together"—was an obstruction to the unification of the minority on the basis of true National Socialism.[64]

Young Germans also liked to call for greater self-reliance by Polish Germans and less dependence upon Reich subsidies. To some observers, however, the very crux of their hostility to the established leadership seemed to be its refusal to grant them equal access to the Reich's financial trough. Rauschning thought the whole quarrel boiled down to a contest for the "lavish funds" provided by the Reich. Steinacher suspected that the more generous assistance provided to formerly Prussian areas, as compared with Bieltiz (Wisener's home base) and the rest of Poland, also played a significant role. Of non-Prussian background himself, he sympathized with outsiders resentful of the "highly developed Prussian concern" for its own former territories, combined with a reluctance to provide similar help for Germans elsewhere in Poland; minority leaders in western Poland were primarily former Reich citizens who were "paid by Berlin practically according to the Reich salary scale and received pensions which were not available to younger Polish German leaders."[65] The JDP, by contrast, was perennially short of funds to wage its campaign. Wiesner, declaring that "it takes money to wage war," periodically ordered special assessments from the membership to fund special projects. Members were also obliged to take out subscriptions to the party newspaper, *Deutsche Nachrichten*, unless they were unemployed (as was true of a significant percentage).[66]

The DV-JDP schism soon introduced some unpleasant new behaviors into the political life of the minority. Opposition speakers were heckled into silence and assemblies disrupted; there were also street brawls and other signs that the political culture of the late Weimar years in Germany was spilling over into Poland. Local Nazis, spurred on by Young German allegations, even prevented Ulitz from delivering an address to the VDA in Königsberg, on German territory.[67] Young Germans sometimes trucked in rowdy "Bolsheviks" (as opponents described them) from other areas to disrupt DV assemblies; in some cases, they carried weapons. When one especially serious clash took place in Grudziądz on May 13, 1934, at what was billed as a "unity assembly," a Young German (Fritz Makus, age twenty-two) was killed. Now the JDP had its own martyr, and the anniversay of his death became the object of solemn ceremonies on the model of Reich observances of Horst Wessel's death (which the JDP observed as well).[68] Both factions regularly denounced rivals to Reich authorities; some JDs, in their determination to get at the "big shots" in the DV, even denounced them to Polish officials—alleging, for example, financial irregularities in Swart's highly successful but pro-DV co-op network.[69]

DV supporters replied in kind to such attacks, or in other ways unavailable to the JDs. For example, DV supporters used their superior economic or political positions to purge Young German employees and subordinates. Wiese, Heidelck's replacement in the DViSuS, and Erich Jaensch (whose thesis from the staunchly republican Deutsche Hochschule für Politik in Berlin became the pseudonymous book by "Stanislaus Mornik") both claimed that they were fired because of their Young German sympathies. At the DV's first annual meeting, June 1935, Kohnert launched a long attack on the Young Germans, quoting Bismarck as well as Hitler against them. After first trying to include JDs in their organization, the DV now invoked an "exclusivity clause" that forbade simultaneous membership in DV and JDP. The Volksbund also purged JD members, about 5,000 out of a total of 35,000, in April 1935.[70]

The private minority schools run by the DSV and affiliated with the DV were also occasional targets of Young German attacks. When the financially strapped German school board in Leszno stopped granting tuition waivers to every parent who requested one, the JDP accused it of excluding children of poorer JD families from its *Gymnasium*. The school board denounced this allegation as untrue and harmful to the school; it asked DSV head Otto Schönbeck to warn the five JD teachers employed by the school ("who have not expressed their disapproval of this attack with sufficient force") about the "dubious" nature of their behavior and the possibility that their party's attacks might cost them their jobs.[71] The Evangelical Church also lined up clearly behind the DV. Superintendent Blau admonished his pastors to stay out of the quarrel: "Politics do not belong in the pulpit. . . . Our congregations have a right to hear on Sunday something different from what they can read in any newspaper, and precisely that which they will not find there." His real sympathies became apparent, however, when he forbade pastors to join "political parties," but classified only the JDP, not the DV, as such a thing.[72] Wiesner complained about this pro-DV posture and even threatened the church with "consequences" if it did not become more evenhanded, but Blau stuck to his position.[73]

The DV held on to the support of the minority's principal economic organizations, with the exception of the Verband Deutscher Ansiedler und Bauern, known after 1932 as the Verband Deutscher Bauern (VDB). Its chairman, Heinrich Reinecke, remained dissatisfied with the large-landowner biases of the minority establishment and took several different positions on the DV-JDP issue. He turned first to the JDP and declared his conversion to National Socialism; when his supporters were expelled along with other Young Germans from Welage, Reinecke sued that organization and denounced Swart for trying to block the growth of the National Socialist "spirit" among Polish Germans. (German agents reported, however, that while Reinecke was writing fawning letters to Hitler, he had only harsh words for him in the VdB meetings they infiltrated.)[74] Reinecke had a falling-out with the JDP in 1934 and turned next to the Polish government as the only way "to save German farmers." Finally, in response to the DV's offers of financial support, he turned back to that organization. By this time, however, his supporters had tired of him; he was accused of financial irregularities and voted out of power in favor of a slate headed by the JD leader in Poznania, Ulrich Uhle. When it turned out that Uhle was a large landowner himself, he was quickly deposed, despite his spirited condemnation of such narrow "caste thinking." But Max Wambeck, also of the JDP, became the VdB's new head; thus this small organization of about 4,000 members remained under effective Young German control.[75] But it was the exception to the rule; all the larger economic (and subsidy-dispensing) organizations remained in the hands of DV supporters.

Aside from disrupting everyday life within the minority, the JDP-DV feud also threatened to weaken it vis-à-vis the Polish government. Polish officials, needless to say, were delighted to see this quarrel develop. One police minister gloated that he was now saving the money he had used previously to spy on German organizations because everything worth knowing was being leaked by one side or the other.[76] Officials who were charged with keeping an eye on minority activities confessed that they did not understand the point of the feud, since both sides seemed to be abundantly National Socialist. Poland seemed to favor the JDP, however: perhaps because it seemed weaker, the JDP was permitted to operate throughout Poland, whereas all applications by the DV to "go national" were denied. JDP delegations were also more likely than DV groups to receive official approval for travel to the Reich. Reich officials suspected a purposeful Polish effort to buttress the JDP in order to undermine German unity and pressure the more entrenched DV to relax its opposition to the government.[77] When two German representatives were added to the now-appointive Senate in 1935, the Polish government was careful to give one seat each to a representative of the DV (Hasbach) and the JDP (Wiesner.)

In the first quarter of 1935, Young Germans held 460 meetings in Pomorze and Poznania in an effort to increase (or demonstrate) their strength. They held another 497 meetings in the second quarter, at which time Polish officials estimated JDP strength in the two provinces at 8,800. The DV held fewer meetings (351 in the second quarter) but attracted a much larger membership. The German consul in Poznań estimated DV strength at over 50,000 and believed that it enjoyed the support of most Germans in his region.[78] Eventually, most Reich agencies came around to the Foreign Office's position in support of the DV. While JDs hoped that

Germany's rulers would see their struggle in the NSDAP/DNVP terms of 1932/33, the Röhm/Hitler analogy may have become prevalent after the June 30, 1934, "Night of the Long Knives." This was reflected, for example, in a sharp change of course by the *Völkischer Beobachter,* which began to criticize the JDP in late 1934.[79] In 1935 the Gestapo weighed in with the suggestion that Poles rather than Germans were the main support of the JDP.[80] But this choice was never made explicit or public, and the feud itself continued unabated.

As much as it wanted to see a quick end to the rivalry, the German government seemed unable to bring it about. Despite numerous attempts over a period of several years, and despite the clout its financial subsidies were thought to provide, it found that precisely the most outspoken National Socialists were most difficult to bring into line. One frustrated consul blamed the failure of his efforts to quell the controversy on the fact that there was still "too much freedom of opinion" in Poland to permit a "true leader" to emerge.[81] Hitler himself claimed not to be very disturbed by such intraminority quarrels; in a comment recalled by Rauschning, referring apparently to the situation in Poland, Hitler rationalized that "it is useful to have at least two organizations of Germans in each country. One must always be able to appeal to its loyalty [to its state of residence]; it should handle social and economic relations. The other can be radical and revolutionary," though it might occasionally have to be sacrificed for reasons of state.[82] Krahmer-Möllenberg, on the other hand, was increasingly concerned about the feud's impact on the support network he administered and called for a more forceful Reich intervention to stop it. Although "the minority must decide for itself who leads it," such quarrels could not be permitted to harm the Reich's "image" or lead to situations that would tempt one side or the other to turn to the Poles or Polish courts; anyone who did that should be "dropped" by the Reich. A more determined Reich effort to resolve the minority leadership issue might cause problems with the Polish government, but the Poles already knew that both sides "look to Berlin for support of their actions" and saw Reich directions behind anything the minority did.[83]

Steinacher's repeated efforts to bring the two sides together were frustrated finally by the "agitation" of the Young Germans and especially Wiesner's "crazy" policies.[84] Though the government had supposedly settled on the DV by 1935, Steinacher continued to come across party agencies working at cross-purposes with his VR. He also faced growing criticism for his refusal to limit VDA support for German minorities abroad to National Socialists. His position on minority issues seemed indistinguishable at first glance from those of "real" Nazis, but his belief in the intrinsic value of German minorities in other countries contrasted with Hitler's more opportunistic perspective. Steinacher pursued minority politics more for their own sake than as a rationale for changing frontiers; he did not expect that the "core state" would ever coincide with German nationality in general and so did not look to territorial conquest as the solution to the minority problem. He took seriously the concepts of "peoples transcending frontiers" and "cultural autonomy" and believed that German minorities (new official designation: *Volksgruppen*) were valuable in their own right, not just because of their use to German foreign policy. *Auslanddeutsche* deserved to be treated as the equals of Reich citizens—or, in the newly sanctioned terminology, *Volksdeutsche* should count for as much as *Reichsdeutsche*. (For Hitler, by contrast, the "core state" had to have primacy, and minority considerations had to take a back seat). For personal reasons, Steinacher also took exception to the harsh treatment of Germans in the Italian South Tyrol, even after Hitler effectively sanctioned it under the 1936 agreement with Mussolini.[85] For these and other reasons, Steinacher found himself outmaneuvered and was gradually pushed aside. His VR evolved into the Volksdeutscher Arbeitskreis (VA),which had a larger membership but less clout. Finally, after being held under arrest briefly by the Gestapo in 1936, Steinacher was removed as VDA chief in 1937, after which that agency lost all independence.[86]

Meanwhile, in 1935, an agency headed by Otto von Kursell was put in charge of German minorities in other countries and tried to end the dispute in Poland by imposing a "four-point program" on the minority. But this effort too remained without real effect.[87] The Büro Kursell evolved into the *Volksdeutsche Mittelstelle* (VoMi) in 1936 and was soon gathered into Heinrich Himmler's growing SS empire. In January 1937, Kursell, the VA, and Bohle's AO/NSDAP were all relieved of primary responsibility for minority affairs by VoMi's new leaders, Werner Lorenz and his assistant Hermann Behrends, both of the SS.[88]

At a meeting in Berlin in April 1937, which included Kohnert, Ulitz, and Hasbach as well as some Young Germans, Lorenz threatened a crackdown if the German feud in Poland was not mended. Kohnert argued that any attempt to impose a unified leadership by force would only provoke the Poles, and Lorenz backed off. A year later, however, as the schism persisted, he became more insistent and announced his own unity plan: a Bund der Deutschen in Polen was to be organized under a *Führer* appointed by the Reich, and any member of the minority who rejected it would be ostracized. The DV was to merge into the JDP in order to "inherit" from the latter organization the right to operate throughout Poland; a committee of six (Kohnert, Ulitz, and Ludwig Wolff of the central Polish *Deutscher Volksverband*, plus Wiesner and two other Young Germans) would run things. Once again, however, too many minority leaders, and Wiesner above all, refused to cooperate, and VoMi's confident orders had little impact.[89] Behrends also tried to get Wiesner to clear his public statements in advance with VoMi by way of the German Embassy in Warsaw "in order to bring about agreement with Reich policy" (the point was mainly to get him to tone down his speeches), but Wiesner often failed to comply and remained something of a loose cannon. (Hasbach, the other German senator, did clear his major speeches with the embassy before delivering them.)[90]

In short, that the intra-German feud in Poland did recede after 1937-38 was due more to the clear victory of the DV-Volksbund faction than to the efforts of Reich officials. Ultimately, the best explanation for the JDP's failure to dislodge traditional conservative leaders is the speed with which the latter embraced the same ideas. By 1936-37, it was clear that the JDP had lost the struggle against the DV; Kohnert declared as much and announced that he would no longer engage in public argument with Young Germans.[91] By this time, DV membership in Poznania and Pomorze stood at about 60,000; the JDP had only about 12,000, down from a peak of 17,000 in late 1934.[92]

The JDP was further weakened just at this time by a split in its own ranks, a result of "differences of opinion" about Wiesner's cooperation with the Polish government, his authoritarian style, and his general lack of success as JDP leader. Wilhelm Schneider and others led a sizable group in Silesia and central Poland out of the party and back into association with "establishment" organizations.[93] In the 1938 campaign for a now toothless parliament, the JDP agreed to a common front with its German rivals, whereupon the government awarded Wiesner's Senate seat to Max Wambeck. Wambeck enjoyed little stature as a minority leader, and such reputation as he had was damaged by his business partner's charges of fraud. Wiesner ordered him to decline the nomination; when Wambeck accepted, he too was expelled from the JDP.[94]

Part of the failure of the Reich's unity projects can be attributed to turf disputes and administrative confusion in the Reich itself, but it is hard to avoid the conclusion that things would have turned out differently had Hitler's agents really been in effective control of the minority. After all, the victory of the DV faction (backed by Neurath's Foreign Office and Steinacher's VDA) over the JDP faction (favored by key NSDAP agencies) manifested itself in the same year (1937) that those two agencies and those two men were purged and replaced by Nazis of a purer sort. Both the length and the outcome of the JDP-DV feud and the often helpless role of Reich agencies points up the limited ability of even this German regime to exercise close control over German minorities in neighboring countries even when these were strongly influeced by Nazi ideology.[95]

The German-Polish Non-Aggression Pact of 1934

The same considerations that made Hitler a symbol of hope to the German minority in Poland led understandably to increased vigilance on the part of Polish government and society. When Hitler was reported to have said something about the "impossibility" of the Corridor and the need to resolve this problem quickly, Poland responded speedily and emphatically. Piłsudski was apparently even prepared to consider a "preventive war," a military foray into Danzig, East Prussia, or German Upper Silesia, in order to force Hitler to renounce any revisionist aspirations while he was still too weak to resist. Nothing came of this idea, perhaps because Poland's chief ally, France, withheld its support.[96] Piłsudski settled, therefore, for a more modest demonstration of Poland's determination to defend its borders. In March 1933, he demonstratively increased the size of the small garrison that Poland was authorized (under existing treaties) to maintain at Westerplatte on the territory of the Free City of Danzig. The increase of troop strength (from 82 to 202) was largely symbolic, but Poland's friends in western Europe were unwilling to support even this demonstration of resolve and the League of Nations forced Piłsudski to rescind the increase.[97]

Popular Polish concern in the wake of Hitler's seizure of power manifested itself in part by increased violence against the German minority. The offices of both the *Deutsche Rundschau* and the DViSuS in Bydgoszcz were attacked by a nationalist mob in March 1933.[98] April saw a rash of hostile demonstrations, leading to broken windows, the burning of bundles of German newspapers in the streets, and the scrawling of *Szwab* or "Jew" on German businesses. In Grudziądz, businesses were attacked, newspapers destroyed, and German-language signs defaced for an entire day while police remained inactive; perpetrators were either not prosecuted at all or let off with light sentences.[99]

The most serious outbreak of violence took place in central Poland; the principal minority institutions in Łódź, including the offices of the *Freie Presse* and the main German publishing house, book store, and high school were partially destroyed on what became known as "black Palm Sunday." This particular mob, however, though organized by the ZOKZ, consisted mostly of Jews who were doubtless motivated by something besides the usual Polish nationalism.[100] There was also a huge ZOKZ rally in Poznań, proclaiming a boycott of all things German; a spokesman for the ruling BBWR addressed the crowd and urged it not to resort to violence against the minority, but his reasoning was not very reassuring: the government, he said, already had the "tax screw," its land offices, and the boycott, and "these methods have proved themselves very well."[101]

The "war scare" manufactured by Piłsudski in March 1933, though frowned upon by France, may have made the desired impression on Hitler. At any rate, Germany and Poland began to move toward better relations, the former because of its continued military weakness and the latter because of fears that French support might be weakening. In May 1933, elections were held in the Free City of Danzig, and the NSDAP—led now by Hermann Rauschning—took over the government. Rauschning, a native of Pomorze and veteran of the early struggle against de-Germanization policies there, had joined the NSDAP in 1931 and was viewed as the party's agricultural expert. He was not the purest of Nazis ideologically—he was probably closer to Papen than to Hitler—but he was an educated man, a good publicist, and the kind of "respectable" conservative that the local party needed for the position of president of the Danzig senate.

Despite his problems with Polish officialdom in the 1920s, Rauschning had since evolved into a leading proponent of German-Polish understanding. In the course of several visits to Warsaw in 1933, he tried to persuade Piłsudski that his National Socialist government in Danzig, and by extension the one in Berlin as well, might be easier for Poland to live with than their predecessors of more conventional German-nationalist bent. Before long Piłsudski came around to the position that German National Socialists were indeed no worse from Poland's perspective than the democratic revisionists of the Weimar Republic or the Prussian-conservative Germanizers before that. Poland's problems had traditionally stemmed from Prussian, North German, Protestant Germany, whereas Hitler and most other top Nazis seemed to represent another Germany: Austrian, South German, Catholic. Neurath, the conservative German foreign minister, continued to express the traditional "rejectionist" attitudes; he declared in April that "an understanding with Poland is neither possible nor desired. The tension with Poland must be maintained, if only to keep the world's interest in a revision of the German-Polish frontier from dying out."[102] Rauschning, however, was more responsible than anyone else for weaning Hitler away from this position and persuading him of the wisdom, or at least the expediency, of a different approach.[103]

Thus the minority's early fears that Hitler's accession would make their own lives in Poland that much more difficult were soon eased by signs of German-Polish rapprochement. Despite Hitler's radical-nationalist rhetoric, he was the first German leader since 1919 to entertain the idea even of superficial accord with Poland. Encouraged by France's weak reaction to Germany's withdrawal from League-sponsored disarmament talks, Piłsudski's Poland moved closer to an understanding with Germany than ever before. Zaleski was replaced as foreign minister by thirty-two-year-old Colonel Józef Beck, who aimed to free Poland from its excessive dependence on France; he proposed to make Poland the leader of a "third force" in east-central Europe, between Germany and the Soviet Union but independent of both. This strategy eventually foundered on Poland's own weakness and on its inability to get along with the likely candidates for such an alliance, Czechoslovakia and Lithuania. In the meantime, however, this reorientation of Polish foreign policy was accompanied by hints of a more conciliatory approach to the grievances of the German minority.

The fall election campaign of 1933 witnessed another rash of anti-German violence. In Silesia, meeting places of the Volksbund came under provincewide attack on October 7-8, 1933; windows were broken and individuals assaulted, and Germans claimed to recognize some school-teachers and even police officials among the leaders of ZPS mobs.[104] In Grudziądz, a nationalist mob broke up a German campaign rally and then attacked individual participants on their way home; two Germans, Krumm and Riebold by name, died as the result of their beatings that evening. Polish officials made clear their disapproval, however, by attending a funeral service, together with about 4,000 Germans, for the two victims. Beck apologized formally for this and other "excesses" committed in the course of the campaign and promised firmer measures against nationalist "rowdies" (his word) in the future. Ten people were convicted for their part in the Grudziądz attack and given unusually tough sentences of one to three years in jail. And when ten Poles were arrested for a subsequent attack on Germans in Świecie, even German embassy officials described the measures taken against them as "energetic."[105]

The process of German-Polish rapprochement culminated on January 26, 1934, with the signing of a ten-year non-aggression pact, and German-Polish relations entered what seemed an "era of good feelings," compared at least with the previous fifteen years. The new and certainly quite different German view of Poland was outlined a short time later by Rauschning in a speech before the Danzig senate. He made every effort to see things from the Polish point of view: true, Poles tended to glorify their state a little too much, but only because they had been without one for so long; true, they discriminated against other nationalities in such matters as land reform, but that was just part of their effort to become economically independent. Rauschning suggested that Germans, rather than harping on the nationalist excesses of the Poles, should take a lesson from them and also show greater appreciation for Poland's role as a "glacis" of European civilization against "eastern-Asiatic cultural forces." Besides, Poland's leadership, predominantly from the gentry, was probably descended from Germanic tribes, contained "a lot of Nordic stock," and so deserved more respect on this account as well. In short, Rauschning argued that Germany and Poland were mutually compatible, indeed complementary. Poland had come a long way in fifteen years; Germans should come to terms with it, accept it as a permanent factor in European politics, and become better acquainted with its culture.[106]

In addition to these kind words, there were also some conciliatory German actions. In September 1934, when Poland finally acted on a long-standing desire to be rid of its obligations under the Minorities Protection Treaty, Germany scarcely bothered to object. Strictly speaking, Poland unilaterally renounced not the treaty itself, just Polish willingness to let the League interpret or enforce it. But this was a distinction without a real difference: it meant the effective end of complaints to international agencies by Germans and the other minorities in Poland. Given the contentious history of the Polish government's efforts to satisfy the League's notions of its obligations under this treaty, the desire to be rid of them is understandable. Poland hesitated as long as it did only out of concern for "world opinion" and arguments echoing Paderewski (see Chapter 1) that the Minorities Protection Treaty was a condition of the acquisition of formerly German territories in the first place.

But these considerations were overshadowed after 1930; international reaction to Poland's "pacification" of the western Ukraine was particularly intense and unfavorable. Above all, just as Germany removed itself as a source of torment at Geneva, the pending admission of the Soviet Union to the League meant that another hostile state would be in a position to support the complaints of Poland's other minorities, the Ukrainians and Byelorussians.[107] German indifference to this Polish step reflected not just a desire for better relations between the two countries but also Germany's own departure from the League and the disappointing results of the League's efforts on behalf of the minority prior to 1933. Neurath reckoned that Germans lost about 700 schools, 2,700 churches, and 1 million hectares of land in western Poland while under the League's protection; "in the final analysis," he concluded, "the League has been just the executor of the will of the victorious powers" of World War I.[108] There was another reason as well: Germany itself was coming under increasing fire from international bodies because of its anti-Semitic measures. At the Congress of European Nationalities in September 1933, Graebe, after restating the grievances of Polish Germans, was challenged to defend the Reich's policies. He tried, but could do so only weakly: "Germans have always fought most rigorously against national assimilation. . . . We consider the exclusion of people of a different national and especially racial type from a national body to be basically justified, to be 'dissimilation' rather than 'discrimination.' "[109]

Poland repaid Germany's acquiescence in the destruction of the Minorities Protection Treaty by remaining surprisingly passive in the face of

Hitler's unilateral renunciation in March 1935 of the Versailles Treaty's limitations on German armed forces. Piłsudski chose to believe that Germany's rearmament, like his own military planning, was directed first and foremost against the Soviet Union. When Germany struck its most serious blow against the Versailles system by remilitarizing the Rhineland in March 1936, Poland did agree to cooperate in French efforts to devise a suitable response, but probably in the knowledge that none would be forthcoming.[110] Under Beck's direction, Polish foreign policy became increasingly unpredictable; Poland, like Italy, often behaved like one of the restless revisionist states rather than a principal beneficiary of the Paris settlement.

The final disappearance of democratic pretense in Polish politics after 1935 encountered no criticism, of course, from Nazi Germany or even from the minority in Poland. Polish Germans did not believe they had benefited much from Polish democracy even when it was real (that is, before 1926). Some speculated that an authoritarian regime, less sensitive to public opinion, might be more likely to grant them what they most wanted: cultural and economic autonomy. The possibility for Germans to win seats in the rubber-stamp Sejm had disappeared along with proportional representation; they had to be satisfied with the two appointive seats, filled by Hasbach and Wiesner, in the upper house. Poland's newest constitution was designed (like that of the Fifth French Republic) to fit a particular politician: Piłsudski. In Poland's case, however, the leader for whom it was intended died a few weeks after ratification. Minister-President Walery Sławek (briefly), President Ignacy Mościcki, and the army chief, Edward Rydz-Śmigły (increasingly) exercised greatest influence over the government thereafter. The place of Piłsudski's "Non-Party Bloc" was taken by the Obóz Zjednoczenia Narodowego ("Camp of National Unity," or OZN.) The new electoral system permitted one-party rule by the OZN, which (like the BBWR) was a welter of interests and personalities offering few new ideas for dealing with Poland's minority and other problems. Its leader, Colonel Adam Koc, tried to spell out a program in his "ideal-political declaration" of February 1937, but it was hopelessly imprecise. For this reason, perhaps, it was embraced enthusiastically by Senator Wiesner; Senator Hasbach combined tentative approval with a reminder of the minority's continuing grievances.[111]

National Democrats (now the "National Party") predominated increasingly over Piłsudski followers after 1935, though on most issues of interest to the German minority the distinction between them, never very pronounced, virtually disappeared. Both groups held increasingly authoritarian and corporatist views and found their chief base of support in an "intelligentsia," broadly defined to include the bureaucracy and army (and consisting to a considerable extent of lineal descendants of the old gentry). As the personal power of Rydz-Śmigły increased, he was officially proclaimed "Number Two" in the state; civil servants were told to follow his orders as well as those of "Number One," the president. There were even attempts to make him the object of a "leader-cult" à la those of Mussolini and Hitler. Moreover, in addition to the OZN (which was not free of "fascist" tendencies itself), an explicitly fascist "National Radical Camp" (ONR) appeared, supported by alienated younger members of the same "intelligentsia." Older nationalists like Dmowski, convinced that Poland was threatened more from within—especially by its large Jewish population—than from without, declared that the "national revolution" was "the only salvation for Poland. It has triumphed (so far) only in Italy and Germany, but everything suggests that its victory in all of Europe is unavoidable."[112]

Minority leaders in Poland did their part for German-Polish rapprochement by becoming ever more outspoken in their declarations of loyalty for the Polish state. To some extent, their new attitude was prompted by the new German policy toward Poland; as Graebe conceded, it was not necessarily something DV leaders wanted to do but something they did "in order not to put us at odds with current Reich policy."[113] To some extent, however, the new rhetoric stemmed also from indigenous hopes within the minority that abstention from political matters might be the best way to gain some breathing room on the more vital economic and cultural fronts. DV leaders consistently denied any conflict between their National Socialist convictions and their obligations as citizens of the Polish state. Hasbach assured the Senate that "no one thinks that a program created for the Reich can be transferred to a foreign country. Whoever in Poland wants to embrace National Socialism . . . can only do so in a way that does not conflict with the laws of the state."[114] Kohnert described the "diligence and labor power of the German farm population in the western territories" as a "state-supporting factor" and a contribution to Poland's strength, which the state should be encouraging rather than trying to snuff out.[115]

Bernd von Saenger sometimes delivered his speeches in Polish even when Germans predominated among his listeners. In 1935, after reiterating the minority's traditional complaints, he gave a generally upbeat speech to the Sejm, urging all citizens of Poland to pull together to confront the continuing economc crisis. He promised Polish-German loyalty in return for equal treatment; as a sign of good faith the German delegation would vote for the government's budget request.[116] The DV also called on its followers to support the government's official list of candidates in 1936 and 1938, even after its refusal to grant Germans a token place on it. Apparently as a reward, however, Wiesner and Kohnert received official permission to attend the 1937 NSDAP rally in Nuremberg as Hitler's personal guests.[117]

The JDP was still more consistently and outspokenly loyalist than its rivals; Young Germans regularly stressed their loyalty to the Polish state and denied having any formal ties to other countries (that is, to Germany). Wiesner advised his followers that "everything in our work that might tend to disturb our good relations with [Polish] officials is to be avoided."[118] Before officials had a chance to intervene, he ordered Young Germans to stop wearing emblems containing the swatika or "uniform-like" clothing. He even saw to the removal from the party songbook of songs offensive to Poles, such as "Nach Osten geht unser Ritt" ("We're Riding Eastward").[119] According to another JDP circular, it was "self-evident for every Young German that he does not behave provocatively toward the Polish public."[120] Party members were urged to enroll in Polish civil defense leagues, to participate enthusiastically in annual celebrations of Piłsudski's birthday, and to decorate their meeting places with Polish flags. One JDP group in Inowrocław was even reported to have laid a wreath at the local grave of the "unknown Poznanian insurgent."[121]

Polish officials who watched over the minority's activities remarked (with some skepticism, to be sure) minority leaders' "loud and demonstrative insistence on loyalty toward the state," which were "in a few cases perhaps even sincere." Piłsudski's death in May 1935 had "strongly moved the national minorities; . . . his greatness is generally respected," and there were numerous "polite or perhaps even sincere condolences" from German leaders.[122] One of Blau's assistants at the Evangelical Consistory described Piłsudski as "an exemplary patriot [whose] greatness and humanity . . . guarantee him a lasting memory . . . also among Polish citizens of other nationalities."[123] Senator Sobolewski expressed his satisfaction that the German minority had indeed become more "sober," that a "significant part" of it (he mentioned specifically Catholics in Silesia) had "assumed for some time now a completely loyal position toward the state."[124] Other officials also took note of the "ever more evident realistic currents [and] a growing sobriety" in the public statements of minority leaders.[125]

At the same time, however, government agents had infiltrated virtually every German organization of any importance in Poland; if officials remained skeptical about the depth of German loyalty, it was because of the unguarded and less "loyal" remarks that minority leaders continued to make in private.[126] Nor could their leaders keep individual Germans from occasional displays of provocative behavior, including Nazi salutes, belligerent songs, or threatening remarks such as "Hitler is coming!" These demonstrations enjoyed no legal protection in Poland—the price for such outbursts was often several months in jail, and there was a fine for use of the straight-armed salute—but they persisted and so further diminished the credibility of the leadership's declarations of loyalty.[127] Polish Germans clearly found little reason to feel loyal toward Poland, and most of their protestations were doubtless insincere. Krahmer-Möllenberg, following a 1936 visit among the Germans of western Poland, described their prevalent attitude in rather different terms: most still felt that they "belonged to the Reich, from which they were only temporarily separated"; they remained in a "definitely combative posture vis-à-vis the Polish government and at core, despite all current assurances, toward the Polish state as well."[128]

The new expressions of loyalty were rarely credited by Polish nationalists; indeed, some argued that the minority's sudden conversion to loyalism in the wake of the 1934 pact only demonstrated how thoroughly it was controlled by the Reich.[129] The non-aggression pact between the two governments had little impact either on Polish public opinion or on the anti-German feelings of many Poles. One railway official, in a "secret" speech heard by German agents, passed the word that, non-aggression pact or no, war was still to be expected with Germany and the German minority in Poland was still to be viewed in this context.[130] Other officials noted that German words coincided with "actions that clash with the idea of loyalty," such as performing services for Reich consulates, complaining (in Silesia) to international bodies, spreading rumors about pending frontier revisions, and proselytizing among the "nationally undecided population in Silesia and Cashubia" (efforts which, it was conceded, had achieved "certain successes").[131] Minority leaders denied the last charge and cited National Socialist principles for their lack of interest in assimilating other nationalities, but officials remained unconvinced. When they discovered that quite a few Cashubes had joined the JDP, they could attribute this only to some kind of German economic lure. In the words of one report, "vocal public loyalty . . . did not keep the [JDP] from . . . catching in its nets nationally insufficiently conscious Poles . . . [who] had lost their national resistance due to the economic crisis."[132] The JDP leadership finally issued orders to Young Germans to stop accepting ethnic Poles as member because it created so much additional friction with officials.[133]

Ties between Polish Germans and the Reich were another sore point with Polish officials, especially now that these were being used to enforce conformity to the Reich's ruling ideology. Krahmer-Möllenberg set up seminars on Nazi ideology in Danzig, which teachers on the DSV payroll were encouraged to attend.[134] The Deutsche Bücherei kept its member libraries from straying too far from the new orthodoxy in Berlin; in 1937, the Rawicz branch library was warned that "while looking through your catalogue, we find still the following books [five were listed] by Jewish authors. . . . Please remove these books promptly. You have, after all, the *Handbuch der Judenfrage*" to serve as a guide. An inventory of books confiscated from a presumably representative library in Piotrowo (Szamotuły County) in 1939 revealed nothing at odds with National Socialism amid the collected works of Hitler, Goebbels, Rosenberg, and Grimm.[135] Some Evangelical pastors drew a reprimand from Kohnert for criticizing Hitler's failure to fulfill a supposed promise to "make Germany Christian"; their remarks suggested that some pastors remained insufficiently programmed, but the tone of the warning itself only testified to the church's subordination to the DV and thus to the Reich.[136]

The minority's "excessive" interest in Germany's reacquisition of the Saarland and in the reintroduction of conscription in the Reich were a further source of annoyance to Polish officials. They also objected to the numerous political excursions to Germany to attend, for example, ceremonies honoring German war dead or conferences of German minorities from around Europe—including one in Königsberg where delegates swore a formal oath of allegiance to the "German idea."[137] Kohnert's trip to Berlin to congratulate Hitler on his birthday and the occasional display of Hitler portraits in the minority's meeting halls also provoked official ire.[138]

German-Polish Rapprochement and the Minority

Germans in Poland seemed to read considerably more into the 1934 pact than did the more skeptical Poles, especially when it came to anticipating improvements in their own situation. A 1934 editorial in the *Deutsche Rundschau* was headed "Germans in Poland: The Bridge to German-Polish Understanding," and the *Posener Tageblatt* suggested that the stage was now set for Poles to reject previous assimilationist policies and join with Germans in the fight "for the Nordic cultural sphere and against the carriers of the idea of Jewish world rule."[139] The minority press devoted a great deal of attention to manifestations of the new German-Polish relationship, such as the opening of a Polish-German Institute in Berlin (1935), a Polish-German Society in Warsaw (1936), and a *Handelskammern* (Chamber of Commerce) designed to promote German-Polish trade in Breslau (1936). Each of these was inaugurated by joint German-Polish delegations amid much fanfare, and a new economic treaty of November 4, 1935, restored mutual most-favored-nation status for the first time since the beginning of the tariff war in 1925.[140]

In fact, however, the price Germany had to pay for its more cordial relations with Poland included an implicit willingness to pay less attention to Poland's treatment of its German minority. Under a new bilateral press agreement, Poland promised to prevent "any attempt [by its press] to tarnish the good reputation of the *Reichskanzler,* of the *Führer,* and of the prevailing conditions in Germany."[141] In return, the controlled Reich press was enjoined not to dwell on the treatment of the German minority in Poland. A 1938 Foreign Office memo reaffirmed, "after consulting with the *Führer,* . . . the order to publish nothing negative about Poland; this includes also incidents concerning the German minority."[142] Goebbels refused to permit a ceremony in honor of Volksbund leader Arthur Lamprecht, who died in a Polish jail in 1936, on grounds that it might display an "anti-Polish tendency" and upset the new "friendly relationship" with Poland.[143] In 1937, Hitler told Neurath that "general German-Polish relations should not be seriously burdened by the minorities question. . . . The fate of the German minority in Poland should not influence . . . the larger foreign policy of friendly relations with Poland."[144] Minority leaders were advised to tone down their complaints to international agencies in the interest of German-Polish rapprochement, and also because of Hitler's belief that such appeals were beneath German dignity; he personally reproached Graebe for continuing to present Polish German complaints before meetings of international minority organizations. Under orders from Berlin, minority organizations withdrew any petitions still pending before the League at the time of Germany's withdrawal.[145]

Some Reich officials even began to suggest that Polish Germans might be as much to blame as Poland for their inability to get along together. The German consul in Toruń thought the time had come to tell the minority to be less noisy, less provocative, and less ambivalent about their loyalty to the Polish state. Germans were also advised to make fewer trips to the Reich; their meetings with Reich officials seldom remained confidential and led only to Polish legal action, provided grist for Polish nationalist propaganda, and burdened German-Polish relations.[146] The consul in Katowice suggested that Reich agencies such as the Labor Front stop inviting Polish Germans to its functions in Germany, which only meant trouble with authorities when they returned.[147] Neurath intervened to stop members of the *Auslandsabteilung* (Foreign Section) of the Reich Youth Leadership from crossing illegally into Poland to meet with minority youth, generating in the process a lot of official attention and problems for the minority.[148]

Poland's response to improved intergovernmental relations and minority declarations of loyalty included a new willingness to tolerate the minority's political organizations. It continued to view the DV and the Volksbund essentially as arms of Reich policy, but during the period of the non-aggression pact they enjoyed a limited immunity from official harassment; Germany did as much for the equivalent Polish organization in that country. Beck also promised to take "energetic steps" to halt the systematic firing of German workers in Silesia, though he had no direct authority to do so.[149] In an unusually conciliatory speech before the Sejm, Interior Minister Bronisław Pieracki observed that "our powerful state in the past was based on its ability to bring together . . . alien nationalities in the context of its state idea. . . . No act of terror or individual or collective violence [against minorities] will be tolerated. . . . No physical expression of racial or national hostility will be tolerated."[150]

Minister-President Felicjan Sławoj-Składkowski, Sławek's successor, denied that ethnic Poles needed any special "majority rights"; his government expected to stand above majority and minorities alike rather than participate in their conflicts. He condemned expressions of hatred or intolerance toward Poland's minority peoples: "The majority should preserve calm, moderation, and equanimity . . . not only because the interest of the state demands it . . . [but] because only then can the majority . . . gain cultural and economic influence over the minorities." He expected, of course, that the minorities would in turn be loyal to the state and cautioned that "this cannot be a passive, formal loyalty. . . . If the minority . . . is merely loyal from a strictly formal point of view, it pushes itself down to a lower level . . . less useful, and so for the state less desirable, citizens."[151]

There was also a small number of Poles, including conservatives who wanted a joint German-Polish front against the Soviet Union, who hoped that the 1934 pact would develop into genuinely close German-Polish relations. The influential Cracow newspaper *Czas* was one such voice; it occasionally crticized the regnant chauvinism in Polish public life, recommended Poland's acceptance of its multi-national character, and urged a more serious effort to appease the minorities. Stanisław Mackiewicz and Władysław Studnicki, associated with the Wilna (Vilnius) journal *Słowo*, were more specifically Germanophile.

Studnicki, survivor of eight years of Siberian imprisonment before the war, was driven to his position by a strong dislike of Russia; he criticized Poland's treatment of the German minority on grounds that it interfered with German-Polish cooperation against Poland's real enemy, the Soviet Union. Better treatment of Polish Germans, he said, would also permit them to play their "prominent and fruitful role in the de-Judaizing process" in Poland.[152] He castigated Bursche and especially Grażyński, whose policies he described as "a scandal and a provocation"; he described Grażyński himself as "the greatest enemy of Poland"—which earned him a libel conviction after a much-publicized trial. He argued against a Polish foreign policy directed primarily against Germany, warning (prophetically) that war with Germany could only mean defeat for Poland and that "Russia alone will emerge as victor from a war of central Europe verses eastern Europe." Mackiewicz charged that "acts of retribution against the German minority [were] mistaken and harmful for both domestic and foreign-political reasons." Polish Germans, in his opinion, were the minority most willing and likely to be assimilated politically, if only they were given the time and the opportunity; their outspoken anti-Semitism was an additional positive feature, in his view.[153]

But these and other advocates of closer German-Polish ties were clearly at odds with prevailing opinion in Poland. Whenever *Czas* or *Słowo* called for better relations with Germany or better treatment for Polish Germans, they were attacked by most of the rest of the Polish press. Not even Polish anti-Semites found it easy to see Germans as natural allies in the 1930s, probably because of their older belief in the underlying affinity between Germans and Jews.

Poland's post-Piłsudski government returned to the continuing problem of the minorities in 1936. A Committee for Nationality Questions was set up, consisting of the minister-president and five other ministers; it oversaw an Office of Nationality Policies under Stanisław Paprocki, head of the older Institute for Nationality Questions and author of a standard book on the subject. Its immediate tasks included the development of new guidelines, dated July 9, 1936, to govern the state's approach to the minorities.[154] One of these proposed that the rights of the German minority in Poland be linked to whatever rights Germany was willing to grant its Polish population. Concerns receiving special attention included the need to diminish ties between the German minority and the Reich and to solidify the Polish national consciousness of ambivalent groups such as the Upper Silesians and the Cashubes. A "secret decision" by the Council of Ministers dating from the same period promised that "all means will be used to recover Germanized elements of the Polish peoples."[155]

German authorities urged the minority not to recruit among such groups, not just because it upset the Poles but because of the more exclusive National-Socialist view of nationality.[156] But Polish nationalist opinion remained agitated by reports that Germans were recruiting among the still-significant population of Polish-speakers whose subjective national orientation remained unresolved. Many Poles were convinced that Germans, however disadvantaged their current political status in Poland, retained significant social and economic advantages— including jobs and Reich-subsidized benefits, which minority organizations used to lure especially Polish Protestants and Cashubes and others disillusioned by the contrast between the Polish economy and its unfree but dynamic counterpart next door. Much nationalist anger was directed at Polish "renegades" who were thought to identify with German nationality for reasons of material advantage.[157] Officials closed several units of the VdK in Poznania on grounds that they accepted "Poles" as members;

as *Ilustrowany Kuryer Codzienny* editorialized, "every nation has the right to fight for the souls of individuals who are on the margins of national consciousness."[158] Some critics charged that Nazi Germany itself was trying to "buy Polish souls" by enrolling members of the Reich's Polish minority in the Hitler Youth.[159]

On one hand, the 1936 conference on minority policy ruled out, for the time being at least, additional efforts to diminish the German minority, out of concern for Poles in Germany or for Polish foreign policy; on the other hand, it failed even to consider the relaxation of discriminatory policies already in place. Improved German-Polish relations after 1934 were not matched, in other words, by any improvement in the situation of the German minority. Indeed, the Polish government appeared to believe that better relations with Germany meant a freer hand to do as it liked with the minority. Minority leaders soon gave voice to their disappointment. *Deutsche Rundschau*, while acknowledging some official restraint in the immediate aftermath of the non-aggression pact, claimed in 1936 that "this politeness has long since been abandonned."[160] The consul in Toruń also concluded that Poland had turned its back on a policy of "reconciliation and understanding . . . and is once again openly preaching hostility toward the Germans, including their ruin and destruction."[161]

An examination of the condition of minority schools, for example, shows only continued decline during the period of the non-aggression pact (1934-39). A 1936 cabinet resolution proposed that "the general policy with regard to schooling for the German minority should be directed to the gradual limitation of German as the language of instruction to the advantage of Polish."[162] Newly hired teachers had now to be the products of Polish teacher-training institutions and were usually ethnically Polish as well. As a result of the steady Polonization of minority-school faculties, most classes were taught by teachers for whom German was at best a second language. Politically sensitive subjects such as history and geography were taught not only from a Polish perspective but, after 1933, in the Polish language as well.[163]

In Silesia, the end of the Geneva Convention in 1937 meant the loss of international protection for minority schools. By this time, only about 6 percent of the province's children attended minority schools, but Grażyński sought to depress this number further still. Children wanting to attend German schools had now to pass a rigorous language exam before an all-Polish board; virtually no ethnic Poles surmounted this hurdle. In some cases, officials also vetoed applications from children with Polish names and fined their parents for trying to enroll putatively Polish children in minority schools. When hundreds of parents staged sporadic "school strikes" to protest the forced enrollment of their children in Polish schools, authorities responded with fines and even jail sentences: six to twelve weeks for one group in Rybnik.[164]

The purpose of the 1936 guidelines' call for the preservation of German-language public schools was primarily to keep Germans from turning to private schools, which were more difficult to control. It was the opinion of the officials who reported regularly on them, for example, that all but one unnamed member of the Poznań branch of the DSV, which operated the private Schiller Gymnasium, were "stubborn enemies of Polish nationality."[165] Visits by officials to DSV schools sometimes uncovered evidence to support these suspicions, such as swastikas scratched on school walls or maps showing the prewar boundaries. They were also concerned that these schools were still educating minority children in a German-national spirit. Thus an official visitation to the private German *Gymnasium* in Katowice took exception to the the year's required reading list on grounds that it contained too few works about Poland, Polish literature, or German-Polish cultural ties; though the school year had already begun, the list had to be withdrawn in favor of an alternative list proposed by officials. They also rejected the text used to teach the German language at this school on grounds that it contained too much material on Frederick the Great and other German historical figures, who (in the words of the report) "embody a feeling of antipathy for the Polish people and the Polish state."[166]

DSV chief Schönbeck urged German teachers to stay out of politics, including the DV-JDP quarrel, because "our private German schools are under the closest supervision by state officials" who do not approve of political activism by minority teachers. To ignore this advice, he warned, would mean that "the teacher risks his profession and the school its existence."[167] Albert Breyer, for example, a noted local historian who volunteered for the Polish army in 1920 (and died as a member of that army in 1939), was denied the necessary "loyalty certificate" in 1937 because of his resistance to the Polonization of the Lutheran Church.[168]

As a consequence of official measures dating back to 1920, only a minority of German children in Poland still had access to German-language schooling in 1939. According to one survey, 53 percent of the 127,000 German schoolchildren in Poland attended Polish schools where there was no instruction in their own language; another 24 percent enjoyed some German-language instruction in otherwise Polish institutions; only 23 percent were enrolled in public or private schools that used German to teach most subjects. This last figure was somewhat higher in Poznania and Pomorze, lower in Silesia.[169] The state archives at Poznań contain some interesting essays by a group of Polish-German children, ages eleven to thirteen, who were asked after the German invasion in 1939 to record their experiences at Polish-language schools. The point of the exercise was doubtless to generate propaganda, but what is most remarkable about these essays is the ungrammatical, scarcely intelligible German in which they are written.[170] Overall, the number of German-language schools in Poznania and Pomorze, private as well as public, fell from 200 (1933-34) to 152 (1937-38) and German Ambassador Hans von Moltke believed that "the closing of German schools is proceeding at such a rate that the complete destruction of the German school system is just a matter of time."[171]

The years of the non-aggression pact were also difficult for the Evangelical Church in western Poland. The government wanted to create a single nationwide Lutheran church under its own control, most likely under the direction of Bishop Bursche, who ran his own Augsburg Lutheran Church in an increasingly authoritarian and anti-German manner. In 1936, when the mostly German membership of the Augsburg church refused to ratify his proposed new constitition on grounds that it would increase state control and sanction Polish as the sole official language, the government simply imposed it and made Bursche "bishop-for-life." After officials vetoed 70 percent of the delegates elected to its 1937 synod, and others boycotted the session in protest, the remaining rump elected a mostly Polish consistorial council to run what remained an overwhelmingly German church.[172]

Grażyński moved in a similar manner to take control of the much smaller United Evangelical Church in Silesia; just two days after the expiration of the Geneva Convention (July 15, 1937), he forced a new constitution for this church through the provincial *sejm,* all three (required) readings taking place within one minute. German governing bodies were dissolved and replaced by mostly Polish boards, and police compelled the surrender of church records to them. Superintendent Voss's position was taken by a Polish lawyer; many of his pastors were fired for resisting the takeover, and those without Polish citizenship were expelled from the country. The new Polish pastors were left with largely empty churches, however, as parishioners retreated to their own homes, where former pastors conducted private services.[173]

The United Evangelical Church in Pomorze and Poznania remained a substantial organization of about 280,000 members, but it too faced an uncertain future. The government's 1936 guidelines called for additional measures to reduce ties between this church and its Prussian mother church. A decree of November 27, 1936, permitted the hiring only of pastors who were Polish citizens and had graduated from a Polish university (even though, as noted previously, the only program in Protestant theology in Poland was run by Bursche at Warsaw University). Superintendent Blau seemed to go out of his way to avoid conflicts with Polish officialdom. He urged his pastors to refrain from what officials might consider "undesirable political activity" in behalf of the minority. He also urged them to learn Polish; as members of a "corporation of public law," he wrote, "it is justifiably expected of [pastors] . . . that they command the national language," and he offered study leaves and residencies in Polish-speaking areas as encouragement.[174]

Bursche nevertheless accused Blau's church of "disloyal behavior toward the Polish state" and encouraged a "Union of Evangelical Poles" to push for a greater Polish role in it; Blau responded by withdrawing from the Polish Council of Protestant Churches.[175] As of early 1939, only 198 out of the 406 Evangelical pastoral positions in Poznania and Pomorze were filled; 25 percent of these were staffed by men over the age of sixty and 21 percent by Reich citizens, subject to expulsion if they aroused the ire of officials.[176] Blau himself was in his seventies by this time and often ill; he spent months at a time undergoing medical treatment in Germany. But he refused to relinquish his position, if only because to do so might permit the government to impose a Bursche-like successor.

The array of official restrictions and petty decrees also grew year by year during the 1930s. Continued efforts to enforce the status of Polish as the only acceptable language did not, like economic and cultural repression, threaten the minority's very existence, but they did testify to official Poland's continued unwillingness to recognize the German presence in the western provinces as something natural and permanent. Though there was no law to this effect, some individual officials now declared that bilingual public signs were no longer sufficient; they had to be exclusively Polish.[177] The use of German names for places in Poland, even in otherwise German texts, was frowned on by officials and could mean the rejection of an entire submission.[178] Farmers claimed that they had been told to cover even the proverbs—*Sich regen bringt Segen* (Industry leads to abundance), for example—carved into the beams of their houses.[179]

The series of political arrests and trials continued, concentrating especially on minority youth, who seemed most attracted to the new ideas emanating from the Reich. Though the DV enjoyed general official tolerance, it was not allowed to enroll youth under age eighteen; five DV cells in the Corridor were suspended for "exceeding their charter" in this way.[180] The leader of an outwardly apolitical DV auxiliary for young women received a ten-month sentence in 1938 for running a "secret organization" with ties to the Bund deutscher Mädel (League of German Girls) (charges which, she conceded after the war, were essentially true).[181] Another DV unit, whose members "marched" on field trips, was ordered disbanded for engaging in "military" activities. A Scout camp in Tarnowice/Tarnowitz, Silesia, was broken up on grounds that its members wore (Scout) uniforms and carried weapons (Scout Knives).[182] Young Germans who attended meetings or courses in Danzig or the Reich were photographed by Polish agents and faced charges upon their return. On the basis of such surveillance, twenty-seven members of a youth group in Tarnowice were sentenced to jail terms of eight to thirty months in 1936; a 1937 trial of twenty-six members of a pro-Nazi Wanderverein resulted in sentences of two to twelve months. Efforts to establish work camps for unemployed minority youth in Silesia were blocked by Grażyński, suspicious of their resemblance to the *Arbeitsdienstlager* in Germany. In Chojnice, twenty-two Germans age seventeen to twenty-four were charged with "political education . . . unfavorable to the Polish state" in connection with such a work camp and sentenced to eight to twenty-four months in jail.[183]

In an effort to reduce regular contact between the minority and Germany in the 1930s, Poland made it more difficult for Reich citizens to enter Poland or for Polish Germans to travel legally to Germany. Polish visas and passports were extremely expensive. Visas permitting study at German universities cost 3,000 to 4,000 German marks and were available only if a particular course of study was not offered in Poland.[184] A passport cost 400 *złoty* in 1933, about as much as a schoolteacher earned in two months. At these prices, most travel between Germany and Poland took place by means of illegal border crossings. On the other hand, passports to do things of which the state approved cost little or nothing: beginning in 1932 the government offered free passports to Poles who wanted to visit members of the Polish minority in Germany. Moreover, an emigration visa allowing a German to leave Poland for good cost just one *złoty*.[185]

On those occasions when officials agreed to receive minority complaints about all these things, they readily conceded that aroused public opinion left them no choice but to adhere to a hard line on national questions. Stimulated by unchallenged German foreign policy successes and growing evidence of the leadership deficiencies of Piłsudski's successors, popular anti-German feeling only increased during the period of the non-aggression pact. Some officials went so far as to suggest that the government itself was no longer in complete control of this aroused feeling, especially in western Poland, and that it threatened the government as well as the German minority.[186] Beck, while expressing his own support for equal treatment in the land reform program and for permitting the use of German in the courts and other aspects of public life, believed that such concessions were foreclosed by "strong resistance from the chauvinists"; provincial officials, especially in Silesia, "were unable to come to terms with the (more lenient) minority policies desired by the central government."[187] Krahmer-Möllenberg speculated that concessions on minority issues would have a better chance if the Polish government only felt itself to be stronger; under current conditions, however, none of the leading politicians were in a position to take the lead on this issue without "risking their necks."[188]

Post-Piłsudski leaders were even less willing than their predecessors to rein in chauvinistic organizations like the ZOKZ and ZPS. In the wake of the non-aggression pact, the ZOKZ was required to modify its approach somewhat; it changed its name to Polski Związek Zachodni (PZZ)—members of ZOKZ automatically became PZZ members—and moved its headquarters from Poznań to Warsaw, where the government could presumably exercise closer control over it. The organization's journal was renamed *Polska Zachodnia*, and in keeping with the new climate in German-Polish relations, it agreed to focus less on its admittedly "negative" effort to "liquidate German influence in culture, economy, and politics in Poland" and more on the Polish minority in Germany. Characteristic PZZ projects included summer vacations in Poland for children of this minority and a campaign to get Poles to de-Germanize first names dating from before 1918 (about 13,000 people did so). But the PZZ remained no more satisfied than German nationalists with the current German-Polish frontier; it urged the government to demonstrate the economic vulnerability of East Prussia (and so speed its fall to Poland) by cutting off trade with that province and boycotting the port of Königsberg. At the "Pomeranian Week" that it sponsored in Grudziądz, banners promised "liberation" to countrymen in Ermland and Masuria.[189]

On occasion, government spokesmen also seemed to share this ambitious agenda; a BBWR spokesmen told a rally in Poznań that he welcomed talk of treaty revision, for that would allow Poland to lay claim to "ancestral" lands which were hers by right: Silesia, Pomerania, and East Prussia.[190] The Polish revisionist effort was supported by politically motivated research centers including the Baltic Institute (1925, an offshoot of the ZOKZ, which sponsored such works as Józef Feldman's tract on the eternal enmity of Germans and Poles), and the Silesian Institute (1933).[191]

The PZZ also led the boycott campaign against German businesses and staged most of the anti-German rallies whenever a provocative statement was reported from the Reich. PZZ resolutions denounced German petitions to the Polish government as "outrageously insolent"; Polish Germans already possessed full freedom, which they only abused. The nationalist press warned that the minority's situation would only get worse if it continued to complain, "because Polish patience has limits, and state officials will ultimately be obliged to restrict the exceptional freedoms" allegedly enjoyed by the minority.[192] Other PZZ resolutions called for the nationalization and Polonization of remaining German-owned firms and the "reform" of remaining German estates, the boycott of films from the Reich, and reduced use of German in public schools.[193] A ten-day boycott action in Silesia was aimed at the "numerous advanced positions of an alien economic group, which draws strength from Polish soil to strengthen a foreign national organism. . . . If we want to be sure that no spent penny will be used against us, then we should not put it into foreign hands."[194]

The PZZ's 1938 platform called for still greater restrictions on the minority, including a reduction in the number of German newspapers in Poland, a ban on German-language signs over shops, and the restriction of employment to graduates of Polish schools.[195] *Polska Zachodnia* urged that two-thirds of those Germans still in Silesia be encouraged to emigrate; the PZZ's Silesian section demanded simply the "final removal of the gross manifestations of German life" in that province.[196] The PZZ also kept up a steady agitation in favor of "equalizing" the landed property relationship between Germans and Poles. Though the German share of the population of Poznania and Pomorze had fallen to 10-11 percent by the 1930s, Germans still owned about 25 percent of the land in these provinces, a fact cited as evidence that Germans had more than their share and were "privileged." In the Sejm, Mayor Czesław Michałowski of Grudziądz expressed disappointment that the Versailles Treaty did not permit the dispossession of still more ethnic Germans, and other nationalists called for land to be taken from the minority until it owned no more land per capita than did the Polish majority.[197]

Strictly speaking, the PZZ represented only an extremist minority of the Polish population, yet it often seemed to articulate, if it not actually dominate, majority public opinion in the western provinces. Minority leaders were convinced that this organization held veto power over any concessions the government might otherwise be inclined to make. Moreover, its agitation in favor of tighter restrictions on the minority was shared by some mainstream political forces. Proposals put forward at one time or another in the 1930s by the National Democrats included the expulsion of the remaining residents who had chosen German citizenship, the liquidation of remaining Reich German real estate, the confiscation of remaining ethnic German estates and their division among Polish farmers, the exclusion of Germans from parliamentary or local self-government bodies, tighter controls on minority schools and organizations, additional restrictions on the minority's ties to the Reich, and a boycott of German films and journals.[198] *Kuryer Poznański*, reflecting the views of this party, charged that the German minority was already too much a "state within the state, . . . an exceptional and privileged group [that constitutes] an offense against the national character of the Polish state."[199] A meeting of the ruling OZN likewise called for "the liquidation of the political and economic manifestations of the German minority" and a ban on German-language church services and the public use of German until Germany agreed to treat its Polish minority better.[200]

Anti-German feeling manifested itself on the popular level by the singing of "Rota," a song of anti-German defiance dating from turn-of-the-century Prussian Poland that includes the line "The Germans will not spit in our faces any more"; it was sung so frequently in the 1930s that it acquired for some the status of a second national anthem.[201] Anti-German feeling also continued to find expression in acts of violence against the minority and its property. Official Poland did not condone such violence, but the usually youthful offenders, even when arrested, often received only light sentences, or their actions were rationalized as a natural reaction to the minority's provocative behavior or the mistreatment of Poles in Germany. The quasi-official *Dzien Pomorski*, while regretting violent actions, excused them as a natural expression of popular resentment against the minority's alleged disloyalty and as a useful "first warning" to Germans.[202]

German businesses, meeting halls, churches, and newspaper offices were the favorite targets of such attacks. Most involved only physical destruction (broken windows, damaged cemeteries, and other forms of vandalism), but sometimes they got even uglier. In 1935, for example, one German died and twenty-eight homes were wrecked in the course of an outbreak of mob violence (inspired by a series of articles in *Dzien Pomorski*) at Wejherowo in the Corridor. Officials distanced themselves from this action, and issued a formal apology to the minority. A short time later, however, the same basic scenario was repeated in Ostrów; the local head of the DV was killed by a nationalist mob while the police made little effort to interfere. Officials apologized here, too, but took only pro forma action against the demonstrators, and the national press blamed the minority for having provoked the attack.[203] The following year, a JDP meeting in Silesia was attacked by a group of Insurgents armed with clubs; seventy participants were injured, some seriously.[204] Much of this tension was concentrated in the politically sensitive areas of western Poland, and grew basically in tandem with the Third Reich's assertiveness in European politics. Yet there were almost as many cases of similar violence in Łódź and other areas that lay well beyond the reach of German revisionist appetites. In Bielitz, for example, the home of Senator Wiesner was demolished in 1938, and the main German bookstore went up in flames two days later.[205]

Before long, Polish Germans began to suspect that, far from benefiting from the 1934 non-aggression pact, they had been sacrificed to it. Though few dared to say so publicly, they doubtless missed the more substantial concern for their problems that the Weimar Republic had demonstrated. One year after the non-aggression pact, Krahmer-Möllenberg observed that "discouragement among the Germans was growing day by day"; many felt that there was nothing left to do but leave for the Reich.[206]

Some readily admitted that they had stayed on in Poland not out of any love for that state but only in the hope that Germany would one day "solve" the border problem and reclaim them. They saw the new German-Polish relationship as a resignation to the status quo and thus an inducement to pull out rather than continue to slide into poverty in Poland.[207]

Minority leaders hesitated to express such discontent in public, but others were less constrained. The exile SPD accused Hitler of "selling out" the minority in Poland and abandoning Danzig and the Corridor in order to appease the Poles.[208] The Łódź *Freie Presse* denounced the ban on negative coverage of Polish treatment of the minority in the Reich press as a "National Socialist stab in the back of our minority."[209] There were also some caustic remarks in the minority press about Hermann Goering's hunting vacations with Polish leaders, including rumors (subsequently confirmed by Ambassador Józef Lipski) that he had raised the idea of a formal population transfer; Goering reportedly suggested in August 1938 that it might be better "if German minorities in Poland were to return to Germany and vice versa."[210] Nor did most Polish Germans understand Goering's 1937 declaration that Germany had no territorial claims on Poland as the lie it doubtless was; they assumed that it was an accurate reflection of the Reich's new priorities. Western appeasers were not the only ones who believed Hitler when he declared, following the Munich Conference, that he had no further territorial demands in Europe; Polish Germans too assumed that he meant it.

Adding to their sense of abandonment was the decline in the level of Reich financial support over the course of Hitler's regime. By 1935, because of dwindling reserves of hard currency (in which payments to the minority in Poland had to be made), the government was under growing pressure from Finance Minister Hjalmar Schacht to scale back its foreign support programs. This led finally to a reconsideration of the very rationale for maintaining Germans in Poland at such a stiff price. The German consul in Polish Silesia suggested that it would be better to relocate some 3,500 unemployed Reich citizens and their families living in that province rather than pay about 600,000 marks per year to provide them with Reich-level unemployment benefits. Given political conditions in Grażyński's Silesia, there was no prospect of their finding work in Poland; when the Geneva Convention expired in 1937, they would probably be expelled in any case, so better to let them find work in Germany than maintain them in Poland as a financial burden on the Reich.[211] Others suggested that the Reich's support should be tied more closely to clear German political and strategic objectives, which meant limiting it to areas that Germany hoped to reclaim and so cutting off most of the Germans in Poland.[212]

Krahmer-Möllenberg resisted proposals for the weakening of the programs he administered, citing the 4,000 veterans, 700 pensioned schoolteachers, and 360 employees of minority organizations who were entirely dependent upon the regular flow of funds from the Reich. If these were obstructed, the organizations themselves faced bankruptcy.[213] The German minority in Poland simply could not defend its position without outside help; most Germans in western Poland were "not in a position to conduct the struggle for their nationality independently and with their own resources. . . .[A] complete catastrophe for the whole constructive effort made thus far in the ceded districts" loomed if Germany reduced its level of support.[214] He was satisfied that the German population in western Poland remained reasonably "firm economically," thanks in part to DS, but the combination of popular and governmental pressures, the growing economic gap between Germany and Poland, and the virtual absence of economic opportunities for young Germans in Poland were taking their toll. In light of these conditions, the government should prepare for "considerable loss of national substance" in Poland in the years to come; without a substantial increase in Reich support, there was no longer any alternative but to permit the emigration to Germany of the many Polish Germans whose situation had become "hopeless."[215] He appealed to the "special geopolitical position of these lands" to buttress his view that the Reich had every reason to support the minority "or even to proceed offensively against the aggressive Poles." Given a foreign policy that was supposed to be oriented toward the east, he could not understand the government's apparent willingness to "give up something it already has there."[216]

Krahmer-Möllenberg got some support from Interior Minister Wilhelm Frick, who insisted that "everything would have to be done to keep the German population in Poland . . . even if the shortage of hard currency" remained a problem; one could not just leave one's "fully improvished countrymen over there" to their own resources.[217] Funds did continue to flow to the minority; the DS budget for 1936 included 5 million złoty for the DV, another 1.8 million for minority schools, and 1.1 million for German churches.[218] A *Heimat Grüsst* (Greetings from Home) program was created to employ Polish Germans in domestic work, their production going to the Reich via Danzig. There was also an emergency relief organization, modeled on the Reich's *Winterhilfe*, to which all Polish Germans were asked "voluntarily" to tithe 2 percent of their income.[219] VDA subsidies also continued to play an important role, for example, in support of a *Notgemeinschaft der deutschen Wissenschaft*, which subsidized the scholarly efforts of Kurt Lück and others.[220] Nevertheless, in real terms the level of support for the German minority in Poland clearly declined during the period 1934-38.

For some Polish Germans, the underlying problem was that the Reich did not make clear exactly what it expected of them. Actually, it wanted them to stay put and not move to the Reich, but many continued to do just that. Krahmer-Möllenberg, recognizing how hard it would be to keep Polish Germans from wanting to be part of the "wonderful" things going on in Germany, called on Hitler to issue a personal plea to them to remain in Poland.[221] Addressing minority leaders directly, Krahmer-Möllenberg instructed them, first, to get rid of their "irredenta mentality" and, second, to prepare for an extended stay in Poland.[222] In the margin of a Foreign Office memo containing an almost identical injunction (to "combat the acute irredenta mentality . . . and prepare . . . for a longer existence in the Polish state"), Neurath commented that "this accords also with the view of the *Führer.*"[223] Krahmer-Möllenberg advised minority leaders that improved bilateral relations necessitated different tactics: there should be fewer public protests and more reliance on the "quiet" methods that Prussian Poles had used to such effect before 1918, particularly a greater focus on the family as the key to national resistance. Mothers should be charged with the task of passing along German language and culture and fathers with the task of holding on to German property.[224] If there was any intention at this time to assign the minority a forward role in German foreign policy, it was certainly not communicated to minority leaders. All they learned from Reich officials about Hitler's plans was that they should hold out in Poland with whatever resources were available until, in the words of the German consul in Toruń, "the time for a solution of this question too is ripe."[225]

Thus the Nazi seizure of power in Germany, however welcome to most members of the minority, threw them into what Richard Breyer aptly terms "a two-front struggle: against the measures of the Polish state and against the silence of Reich spokesmen and their controlled press, against the nationalist *raison d'état* of Poland and the foreign policy *raison d'état* of the German Reich."[226] The mood of many Polish Germans fell to its lowest levels during the period of the German-Polish non-aggression pact, in part because Polish pressures intensified during these years but also because many believed that a tough, adversarial Reich was the key to any improvement of their own situation. As their situation became more desperate, the only rationale for trying to stick it out in Poland lay in the hope that the Reich would yet reclaim them. As some of them later testified, faith in the eventual return of German rule was all that kept them going as they gathered around the few radio sets they possessed to listen to Hitler's speeches. (Unfortunately, if Polish nationalists learned the purpose of such a gathering, they brought the enthusiastic participants back to earth by falling upon them as they headed home.)[227]

The fact is, however, that German reacquisition of western Poland seemed more remote than ever until well into 1939; before that time the German minority in Poland seemed to rank quite low on Hitler's list of priorities. Hess refused most requests of minority leaders for meetings with Hitler, and even Steinacher (when he was still running the VR) was often unable to get in. The number and intensity of contacts between Reich officials and minority leaders was certainly lower under Hitler than during the last years of the Weimar Republic.[228] Gotthold Rhode's observation that "much more politics was pursued *with* the [German] minorities than *by* them" summarizes very well the situation of the German minority in Poland in the 1930s.[229]

It was Hermann Rauschning's belated realization that Hitler viewed the minority from which he, Rauschning, was descended only as a forward base for his ambitious foreign policy—not as something worth preserving for its own sake—that helped precipitate their dramatic break in September 1934. Rauschning resigned the presidency of the Danzig senate, sought temporary exile in Poland, and then published a series of books in which he tried to warn the world about Hitler and his real intentions. In his 1940 book of remembered conversations with the *Führer*, Rauschning quoted Hitler to the effect that he would never be satisfied merely to preserve German culture in Poland; nor was he interested in equality of rights among different peoples, only *Herrschaft* (power). He intended to purge minority organizations of their still-too-conservative leaders and make of the minorities themselves blindley obedient "combat troops."[230] As the decade of the 1930s progressed, however, the question for many Germans in Poland was whether they would be able to hold out long enough to fulfill this role—or any other.

7

The Minority in 1939

Hitler cited mistreatment of the German minority as a justification for his attack on Poland in 1939, and so for World War II itself. His limited interest in the minority to that date and its clearly subordinate role in his policies indicate that this was a last-minute and not very credible pretext. But the question remains: was the mistreatment itself just another "big lie," or was it real? Was the situation of the German minority in Poland as bad as German propaganda claimed or, failing that, was it all that bad to begin with? In other words, apart from the credibility of the minority as a pretext for war in 1939, just how real was its plight? Given its overall situation and the evolution of government-minority relations to 1939, what could one have deduced about its long-term prospects for survival in the absence of war?

The Deterioration of the Minority's Economic Foundations

Minority leaders complained of discrimination and official harassment in most areas of public life, but if the question goes to prospects for longer-term survival, some of these are clearly more pertinent than others. Above all, it was the variety of official pressures in the economic sphere that led informed observers to raise the survivability question. The principal economic battlefields included land policy, especially land reform, in predominately agricultural Poznania and Pomorze; the politically inspired denial of employment to Germans in industrial Silesia; and a widespread boycott campaign designed to eliminate the small remaining German middle class in all three provinces.

The land reform program continued to diminish the amount of land owned by Germans, in relative as well as absolute terms. International pressure on Poland to be evenhanded essentially ceased with Germany's withdrawal from the League and Poland's renunciation of the Minorities Protection Treaty. Although the German land reserve in Poznania and Pomorze had fallen to 153,000 hectares by 1936 (versus 258,000 for the

Polish), the 1936 minority guidelines called for two-thirds of the subsequently reformed land in these provinces to come from German owners.[1] Areas of special strategic importance witnessed an even more concerted assault on German land ownership; in the Corridor counties of Sępólno, Tuchola, Świecie, and Tczew, over 90 percent of large German holdings had been taken by 1936.[2] Not even a joint German-Polish agreement specifically pledging an end to national discrimination in land reform in 1937 (see below) brought any real change. The figures for 1939 were as unequal as any before that date: 60 percent of the land to be taken throughout Poland was to come from the three western provinces, and 66 percent of this amount was to come from German landowners. Ethnic Germans remained ineligible, in practice if not in law, for farms created by this program. Officials also regularly turned down requests by Germans to buy or lease farms, invoking a right of first refusal for the state or citing the "inadequate qualifications" of would-be buyers, including the children of farmers.[3]

Overall, Germans owned 38 percent of the original "land supply" in Poznania and Pomorze in 1926, but they contributed 66 percent of the land actually taken by the state. Of the 515,000 hectares they owned at the start of the land reform program, 262,000 went on the land supply list, of which 64 percent (168,000 hectares) was actually taken. Polish owners, by contrast, contributed 417,000 of their 743,000 hectares to the list, of which only 19 percent (79,000 hectares) was actually taken. Germans lost 38.5 percent of their large-estate property in the two provinces to land reform between 1926 and 1939, whereas the Polish estate-owning class was forced to part with only 11.1 percent of its property. Primarily as the result of this politically slanted land reform program, the German share of estate ownership in Pomorze and Poznania fell from 41 percent in 1926 (by which time the great exodus had run its course) to 32 percent in 1939.[4] Other reasons for this decline included the sale of land in anticipation of land reform and the sale of holdings rendered unviable by forced sales under that program. One postwar computation, combining the acreage lost as a result of land reform, the less-than-voluntary sale of other large-estate property, official interference with the property rights of settlers and others, and the 499,000 hectares that Rauschning reckoned were lost before 1926, concludes that Germans lost the startling figure of 685,000 hectares (about 1.7 million acres) during the twenty years of Polish rule.[5]

A new threat to German land ownership in western Poland came with the "border zone decree" of January 22, 1937, which set new guidelines for applying the Border Protection Law of 1927. In effect, it made problematic the right of Germans to inherit or own land in a significant part of western Poland. Under this decree, the ownership of land and of certain businesses in an area comprising close to half the land in the three western provinces became subject to official approval. Within what was called a "large" zone up to thirty kilometers from the western border, any transfer of property, including direct family inheritance, required official approval; within a "small" border zone two to six kilometers from the German frontier, official permission was required to build, own guns, keep homing pigeons, or even reside there to begin with. Noncitizens required special permission to live in either zone; officials could evict people from the smaller zone virtually at will.[6]

Although this decree was in force only for the two years remaining until 1939, its intent was clear enough: officials generally denied Germans the right to purchase land in this area and interfered with the inheritance of land in numerous cases. Of more than a thousand requests by Germans to buy land in the border zone as of early 1939, not one was granted; even direct parent-child inheritance was no longer assured of official approval. In isolated cases the state expelled Germans from the border zone altogether; for example, six hundred fishermen and their families were removed from the Hel Peninsula for "strategic" reasons in 1937-38.[7] In the opinion of the German Foreign Office, the systematic application of the border zone decree would mean "the removal of German landed property in this area within a generation at most." A July 1939 circular from the Finance Office in Grudziądz affirmed that it had "become necessary to reduce the property of the German minority in Poland by all available means"—for example, by raising taxes or denying tax exemptions—and the border zone regulations were further tightened the following month to permit the outright confiscation of German property. These last measures were doubtless occasioned by war fever, but they can also be viewed as a logical outgrowth of previous measures.[9]

To be sure, many German farmers continued to manage fairly well, even under the adverse economic circumstances of the 1930s. And although German land ownership declined, it did so at a slower rate than the German population; as a result, the German share of land ownership in western Poland was more than twice as high as the 10-11 percent German share of the population at large. Most of this land (58 percent) was in the form of farms of a good size—50 hectares (125 acres) or more—and most farmers benefited from membership in well-run cooperatives. The main German cooperative association, headed by Swart, encompassed 608 units and over 30,000 members by 1934; in 1930 another 216 units and 13,000 members belonged to a second co-op association headquartered in Grudziądz.[10] Helped perhaps by a process of "natural selection," surviving German farmers were a generally progressive, middle-class, and (compared with their pre-1918 counterparts) self-reliant group and able to hold their own in the Polish as well as some export markets. Milk production handled by German dairies increased by 59 percent from 1926-36;

butter production grew by 192 percent over the same period, and German co-ops accounted for almost 20 percent of total Polish butter exports in the latter year.[11] Stanisław Mikołajczyk, chief of the Polish agricultural association in Poznania (and future premier), noted with some annoyance that Germans, who comprised only 11 percent of the province's population, controlled 52 percent of its farm co-ops and processed 62 percent of its milk. On the whole, German co-ops did about 60 percent more business than their Polish counterparts in this province.[12]

But the very success of German farmers and agricultural cooperatives attracted the attention of officials and the resentment of Polish nationalists, who frequently saw economic success as some kind of "privilege" or the result mainly of Reich subsidies. In the 1930s, officials moved to weaken minority cooperatives or establish tighter control over them. For example, a 1934 law required that any individual co-op wanting to belong to a German co-op association had to be at least 66 percent German in membership. In 1936 the co-op association's Vereinsbank in Toruń, which helped keep many minority farms and businesses afloat, was the target of tax evasion proceedings, which most Germans believed to be politically inspired. The bank was accused of violating a law that granted tax breaks to cooperatives on ground that it made loans to nonmembers; and it was given thirty days to come up with 745,000 *złoty* in back taxes.[13]

By 1939 a concerted official campaign to cripple or shut down the German cooperative movement was evident. As Mikołajczyk informed Polish co-op leaders, "We have declared war against the significant German economic expansion in our region."[14] Swart's postwar account includes official documents (apparently acquired after the German invasion) which discuss strategies for either creating Polish majorities in individual cooperatives (which would lead to the election of Polish officers, who would take them into the Polish co-op association) or shutting them down altogether. One official urged that "the current period of tension in Polish-German relations be fully exploited for the absolute control of German co-ops by the Polish element."[15]

A directive from Kaysiewicz, Poznanian *wojewode*, to county officials noted that German dairy co-ops "normally have a significant advantage over the Polish in the amount of milk processed, and for this reason one has to devote a lot of attention or effort to them." He included a list of twenty-seven German co-ops with significant Polish membership and urged officials to raise the Polish membership in each one to 34 percent, at which point it would be compelled to assume membership in a Polish co-op association.[16] The *starost* in Września described his procedure as follows: he convened a meeting of most Polish co-op members in his office and had them vote out the German leadership and vote in a new Polish team, which then switched to the Polish association. When the previous leaders refused to recognize this takeover, or declined to turn over their records, the *starost* ordered them jailed for defying state authority.[17]

Kaysiewicz's successor as Wojewode (Woźniak) suggested that one could also force German co-ops to admit more Polish members by threatening to shut them down, and "those German dairies whose control by the Polish element is out of the question should be shut down under various pretexts" (for "sanitary" or other clearly fabricated reasons). If they were in the "border zone," their leaders could simply be expelled.[18] Alternatively, German co-op leaders could be threatened with prison, as they were in Wągrowiec, where the *starost* held local leaders for thirty hours until they agreed to admit 148 Polish farmers to full membership. Or co-op auditors could be forced to retake their qualifying exams; in one such case, all the Poles who took the exam passed, but thirteen of the seventeen Germans who took it failed.[19]

As a result of these efforts, one-third of the German co-ops in western Poland were forced to close during the first eight months of 1939. The German cooperative association itself was dissolved that summer; and when surviving units sought entry into the Polish association they were turned down.[20] In short, the primary economic underpinnings of the German minority in Poznania amd Pomorze—its large-estate properties, numerous medium-sized farms, and its agricultural co-ops—were all under state pressure by 1939 and all restricted in their ability to grow. Though the signs did not yet point to the disappearance of German landed property altogether, they did forecast a steadily diminishing German agricultural population.

In Silesia province the state's use of economic weapons against the minority was even more direct and its impact more devastating. The main thrust of the campaign here was toward control, if not ownership, of most major German-owned enterprises. In August 1934, the much fought-over holdings of the Pless concern, whose twenty factories, six coal mines, and 40,000 hectares of landed property made it the largest single German employer in this industrial region, were placed under state-appointed management because the firm's tax payments were said to be in arrears.[21] The new administrators proceeded to fire German employees and workers in large numbers, and the League of Nations no longer even tried to interfere. Grażyński turned his attention next to the second-largest German enterprise in Silesia, the Henckel von Donnersmarck conglomerate; he pressured its management to Polonize its work force by threatening drastic tax increases and other measures.[22] The state also bought up the IG Bergbau- und Hüttenbetrieb AG (an amalgamation of the former Kattowitzer and Königs- und Laurahütte firms), which accounted for 56 percent of the steel and 12 percent of the coal produced in all of Poland.[23] The Hohenlohe works, another major employer of Germans, were also put under state administration after falling behind in tax payments; one of the first acts of the new administration was to fire forty German salaried employees.[24] Overall, during the fifteen-year life of the Geneva Convention, the German share of capital in Silesia declined from nearly 100 percent to 40 percent.[25]

A greater problem than the loss of German industrial property was the subsequent exclusion of minority members from the Silesian job market. The German consul in Katowice complained in 1937 that "after ten years of Grażyński's official efforts (and three years of the Polish-German non-aggression pact), 75 percent of the Germans in eastern Upper Silesia and their families have been deprived of the basis for their economic existence."[26] German workers were often informed that they were being fired because of "pressure from above" and for no other reason than their nationality. The management of some firms ordered workers, Poles as well as Germans, to remove their children from minority schools if they did not want to lose their jobs. As Hasbach complained before the Senate, "every German [in Silesia] who sends his children to a German school lives in the constant fear that he will lose his job."[27] In some firms, nationalist organizations set up "national committees" to comb personnel records for Germans and then put pressure on management to dismiss them.[28] At a bacon plant in Pomorze, German workers were fired not because of official pressure but as the result of a strike by their Polish peers.[29] German representatives denounced the mass firings in Silesia as a "wave of arbitrariness and injustice," but officials declined even to respond.[30]

The inevitable result of this systematic effort to exclude Germans from the workplace was an astronomical minority unemployment rate, above all in Silesia. In 1934 and again in 1937, the Volksbund reported that forty-five percent of its 33,300 members were currently unemployed. According to other estimates, the unemployment rate among Germans in general in this province ranged between 45 and 60 percent.[31] Membership in the Gewerkschaft Deutscher Arbeiter in Polen, an amalgam of previously socialist, Christian, and liberal labor unions, declined from 35,000 in 1922 to 13,000 by 1936. Moreover, only 3,850 of the latter still had regular employment in the private sector; another 2,500 were in state or make-work employment; the remainder were unemployed. In 1938 this organization reported that 62 percent of its members were without regular work.[32] At roughly the same time, a leader of the ZPS named Doleczyk could boast publicly that almost none of its members was still without work. The German unemployment rate continued to rise long after the slump of the early 1930s had been overcome and overall employment was again on the rise; the official unemployment rate for Silesia as a whole was 16 percent in 1938.[33]

Unemployment was especially high among the young, whose minority-school backgrounds effectively excluded them from jobs and apprenticeships. In 1936-38, 17 percent of the twenty-four-year-old Germans in Silesia, 33 percent of the twenty-one-year-olds, and 50 percent of the nineteen-year-olds had not yet held a job of any kind.[34] A contemporary reported his surprise at the fact that "in most families one would find all the grown children at home, still without any means to support themselves."[35] Superintendent Voss of the Evangelical Church in Silesia concluded simply that, "under present conditions, Protestant German youth do not seem to have any future in this country."[36] There was no reason, of course, to specify "Protestant" youth; by 1939 the labor market in Silesia and elsewhere was closed to a growing proportion of Germans, regardless of confession. Again, the only solution seemed to be emigration: the Foreign Office anticipated that "the situation of these minority members is so desperate that we will not be able to avoid taking them in to Germany."[37] VoMi chief Lorenz raised the possibility of the wholesale "removal of the German minority from Poland to Germany" in light of its "continually growing great distress." (Actual consideration of this idea was postponed indefinitely, however).[38] There were even appeals to foreign states to take in some of those German workers who had no prospect of employment in their native Silesia; the collaborationist DKWB suggested their resettlement in the eastern wojewodships.[39] Surely it is no exaggeration to conclude from these conditions that the bulk of the predominantly industrial German population of Silesia province had no future there, war or no war.

A third threat to the minority's economic survival stemmed from the widespread boycott campaign directed at German businesses. If this campaign was less significant than the attacks on German land ownership and German employment, that was only because there were relatively few German businesses left in Poland. Nonetheless, nationalist groups organized pickets in many towns; sentries and physical intimidation were sometimes employed to keep Polish customers away from German businesses. Even Polish businesses that continued to greet German customers in their own language were affected on occasion by the boycott.[40] Though not officially sanctioned, the boycott campaign did sometimes benefit from official support. Civil servants, for example, were urged (or, according to some accounts, ordered) to shop only at Polish stores, which were to identify themselves clearly with a sign reading *tu polski sklep* (Here is a Polish shop).[41] State-controlled newspapers also played a role; the quasi-official *Dzien Pomorski* published the names of Polish farmers who let German dairies process their milk, implying that they were helping these minority enterprises survive.[42] Another journal close to the government charged a mostly Polish barbers' union in Wąbrzeźno with an absence of "national dignity" because it elected a German as its treasurer.[43]

Adherence to the boycott movement varied from place to place, but many German businesses complained of its effects. The owner of a small construction firm in Śmigiel/Schmiegel (Kościan County), while asking to bid on a school construction project for the DSV, reported that "the granting of construction projects to us by Poles has stopped almost completely. Polish officials and communities have boycotted us for years."[44] The state itself helped diminish the German business class by withholding the licenses needed to engage in various businesses. Most German-owned pharmacies were forced to close, for example; state licenses to sell liquor or tobacco were often denied to Germans; and some German foresters were even denied the gun permits they claimed to need for their work.[45]

One graphic illustration of the minority's precarious economic condition in the late 1930s was its skewed population structure. Young males frustrated by the lack of economic opportunities (or seeking to avoid Polish military service) made up a disproportionate share of those who left for the Reich. In consequence, the minority became disproportionately old and disproportionately female. In the mid-1930s, 16 percent of the Germans in Poznania and Pomorze were over sixty, compared with 11 percent in Germany and only 8 percent in Poland as a whole; only 11 percent of the German minority was under age fifteen, versus 26 percent in Germany. In the twenty-one to fifty age group there were 1.55 females for each male, and three women aged twenty to thirty for every two males aged twenty-five to thirty-five; only 19 percent of German women aged fifteen to thirty in Poznania and Pomorze were married (versus 34 percent in Germany).[46] As a result, young females began to leave for the Reich, simply to improve their chances of marrying. There were, of course, plenty of Polish males, but minority leaders tried to discourage ethnic intermarriage; instead, they turned to a "matchmaking" service to connect local women with available German males from central and eastern Poland, where the gender imbalance was less pronounced.[47]

The minority's distorted population structure depressed its birth rate still further in relation to the Polish. A 1929 survey found that Protestants in Poland (essentially Germans) already had an annual birth rate of only 6.3 per thousand, whereas Catholics (mainly Poles) had a rate of 15.8. During the period 1927-36, the excess of births over deaths among Germans in Pomorze and Poznania was only one per thousand, compared with 5.5 in Germany and 13.5 in Poland as a whole.[48] These demographic trends, which virtually guaranteed the minority's continued numerical decline, were at least partially the direct result of state efforts to limit the minority economically and testimony to their effectiveness.

The Deterioration of German-Polish Relations

The period of the German-Polish non-aggression pact (1934-39) saw several efforts by German officials to exploit superficially improved relations on behalf of the German minority in Poland. In particular, the pending expiration of the Geneva Convention's rules for Silesia in 1937 prompted German suggestions that something be put in its place. When Beck replied that Polish domestic-political considerations probably precluded any such thing, Neurath cautioned him that "the German government cannot possibly distance itself from the fate of the people of German nationality living on Polish territory." To Beck's suggestion that Polish Germans would be better off if their treatment were left to the discretion of Polish officials, Neurath claimed to find "precisely in the current condition of the German minority an irrefutable argument against the Beck theory." A review of official measures since 1934 suggested to him that Poland "was working to shake the economic foundations of the German minority in Poland [and] cause [Germans] to change their attitude toward their nationality." As a result, Germany's "generous policy of reconciliation with Poland . . . was suffering serious damage" in the eyes of the German public.[49]

As part of the search for a bilateral agreement that would benefit the German minority in Poland, Germany signaled its willingness to accept a long-standing Polish demand and put treatment of this minority and the Polish minority in Germany on the same contractual basis. After long negotiations, and over the objections of Grażyński, the PZZ, and the National Democrats, Poland agreed to a watered-down proposal for "a simultaneous and factually identical public declaration concerning the protection of the minorities living in each country." This Joint Declaration on Minorities of November 5, 1937, was not a binding treaty, just a simultaneous declaration of intent by the two governments. President Mościcki read his piece in the presence of Hasbach, Kohnert, and Wiesner, while Hitler received Ambassador Lipski and leaders of the Polish minority in Germany. (Later that same day, however, Hitler convened the meeting immortalized by Colonel Friedrich Hossbach at which he unveiled his plans to solve Germany's "living space" problem by destroying Poland.) Theoretically, this declaration obliged both states to stop pressuring their minority citizens to assimilate; both minorities were promised "just living conditions and peaceful coexistence with the dominant nationality," including the use of their own language in press, assemblies, and religious bodies, their own political organizations and schools, and freedom from discrimination in economic, professional, and land-ownership matters.[50]

Despite having achieved symmetrical treatment of the two minorities,

Poland clearly felt pressured into signing this declaration and began to play down its significance almost from the start. *Polska Zachodnia* denounced it as "superfluous for Poland," and a new round of dismissals of German workers began in Silesia one week after the signing.[51] The PZZ opposed the joint declaration precisely because it did call for equal treatment of the two minorities; its position now was that Polish Germans, because of their remaining areas of economic strength, constituted a danger to Poland, whereas German Poles were economically insignificant and so deserved cultural autonomy and other minority rights. The same rights could not be conceded to the German minority because it was "too strong economically and (too well) organized" and because it served the foreign policy interests of the Reich; indeed, it should enjoy fewer rights even than the other minorities in Poland.[52] Government spokesmen assured the Sejm that, joint declaration or no, they would never again permit minority policies to be affected by foreign powers; minority citizens were subjects of the sovereign Polish state, and attempts to squeeze concessions from the state by political means or by appeals to foreign states were forms of "high treason."[53]

Following the minorities declaration, German Interior Minister Frick issued what sounded like a warning: "What we can never resign ourselves to is that ethnic Germans . . . are persecuted and tormented just because of their German national consciousness. That is no purely domestic political matter. . . . We partake of the fate of our fellow Germans beyond Reich borders. . . . We will never treat the fate of our fellow Germans in foreign countries with indifference."[54] Poland, however, seemed to pay little attention to the increasingly blunt tone of such statements and neither the 1937 declaration nor veiled threats to take a tougher line did anything to improve the minority's situation. The *Kattowitzer Zeitung* celebrated the first anniversary of the minorities declaration under the headline: "A Year That Brought No Turn-around."[55] The German Foreign Office also concluded that its initiative had failed; indeed, "a considerable worsening of the general position of the German population in Poland" was apparent.[56] Germany next suggested that a standing bilateral commission might be set up to deal with minority questions in the two countries; Beck seemed receptive to this idea and thought his government might be interested, but he was mistaken.[57]

Poland's actions in the newly acquired Cieszyn (Teschen/Český Těšín) District (Olsa District) provided an especially striking illustration of indifference to German sensitivities on the minority question. Poland acquired this area, of course, with Hitler's blessing and thanks to the German pressure that led to the partial dismemberment of Czechoslovakia at Munich. Mostly Polish but with a significant German minority, it was incorporated into Grażyński's Silesia province and subjected immediately to an array of anti-German measures. The new regime banned the German language, began firing ethnic Germans, and did other things that made the previous Czech regime seem mild by comparison. As one German resident complained, "Only since we have belonged to Poland do I know what foreign rule means!"[58] Within a few months, most of the German population had been driven away, after being compelled to sign a statement promising not to return.[59] Many German workers were fired as soon as the Poles arrived, and several German firms were put under state-appointed administrators.[60] The local consul predicted that "by autumn [1939] there will not be any more German workers or employees employed in this area at all."[61]

There was also (in the words of the German consul) a "catastrophic decline of the entire German school system" in the area; during the first three months of Polish rule, the number of German schools declined from thirteen with 3,000 students to six with 1,000 students.[62] The Volksheim in Karvina (Karwin) built two years previously at a cost of about 160,000 złoty to serve as the main social center for Cieszyn Germans, was confiscated by the state; the new authorities also took the Schülerheim in Bohumin (Oderberg) valued at 160,000 złoty and the Volksbank in Cieszyn, the last German bank in the region (valued at 400,000 złoty).[63] Officials in Warsaw, conceding that "in the first period of the takeover [in Cieszyn], . . . measures were taken which would not have been taken under conditions of the normal functioning of the administrative apparatus," promised improvements. Several months later, however, the German consul was still of the opinion that "Polish terror considerably overshadows the previous Czech administration."[64]

A final effort to reach a joint understanding on minority questions took place in March 1939, but four days of discussions failed to bring any agreement. Germany reiterated some of the minority's long-standing complaints, including the lack of access to German schools, the denial of passports, restrictions on local border traffic, and the inability to buy property in the "border zone." The proposed remedies (for example, a guarantee of the right of property inheritance for immediate family members in the border area) seemed modest enough, but Polish representatives refused to discuss them and instead presented some far-reaching demands of their own. Having been satisfied in 1937 to achieve equality of status for the two minorities, Poland now wanted to negotiate a formal differentiation between Poles in Germany, weak and in need of special protection, and the Germans in Poland, still too powerful for Poland's own good.

Polish delegates were frank about their desire to see the German minority's economic and "cultural" status reduced to the Polish average. They contended, moreover, that many Germans in western Poland were actually Germanized Poles, a legacy of the years of Prussian rule, and Poland had a legitimate interest in their re-Polonization. They also demanded that the question of "nationality" be struck from the upcoming German census on grounds that it asked for a "subjective" judgment by individuals which was invalid in Polish eyes. Such a question would also result, of course, in a figure for the Polish population in Germany far below the seven-digit figures cited by Polish publicists. When the German side refused to entertain these ideas, the discussions broke up without a joint communiqúe or even an agreement to meet again.[65]

The head of the German delegation to these talks, Ernst Vollert, concluded that "the Poles are not about to change their policies toward the German minority in any way. . . . They are determined to continue their current de-Germanization policies."[66] Ambassador von Moltke also concluded that "it is senseless even to raise minority questions. . . . There are no more prospects of making minority questions the subject of discussions with the Polish government."[67] The usually well-informed Cracow journal Czas seemed to agree: "It is generally assumed that officials, under pressure from public opinion, will intensify the anti-German course" in western Poland.[68] Krahmer-Möllenberg, among others, concluded that the minority's only hope was for Germany to realize the futility of a policy based on overlooking Poland's treatment of the minority as the price of good relations with its government. "A real solution," he argued, "will only be possible when the Reich has full freedom of action versus Poland and is in a position, and willing, to commit its power fully."[69]

Shortly after the collapse of this last effort to exploit the superficially cordial German-Polish relations created by the non-aggression pact and the joint front toward Czechoslovakia, these relations themselves suddenly deteriorated. In quick succession, Germany annexed the remainder of Bohemia and Moravia, demanded (and received) the return of the Memel (Klaipeda) district from Lithuania, made the return of Danzig and a solution to the Corridor problem the next items on its foreign policy agenda, and canceled the non-aggression pact itself as of April 24, 1939.

The Minority under Siege

Minority leaders were basically happy with the Reich's newly aggressive approach toward Poland, though it only made their own position in Poland more difficult. Any restraint displayed by official Poland during the previous five years seemed now to disappear. Minority leaders were subjected to increased surveillance and their homes and offices periodically searched. Kohnert, Ulitz, and others had their passports withdrawn and so could no longer travel legally to the Reich.[70] Numerous local branches of the DV and JDP were dissolved, and many German clubs, meeting halls, hotels, and inns were closed on various pretexts. Within one two-day period in June, the main centers of German public life in four cities were shut down: the Casino in Bydgoszcz, the Deutsches Haus in Tarnowice, the home of the men's chorus in Łódź, and the Evangelical Vereinshaus in Poznań. The Vereinshaus included the only large German assembly hall in Poznań, the only German hotel, and the German theater; valued at several hundred thousand *złoty*, it was seized by the state and its employees released.[71] In Silesia, about twenty-five of the Volksbund's "homes," which functioned mainly as social centers, were closed down, allegedly because they violated building or fire codes.[72]

Acts of popular violence against the minority also increased sharply following the collapse of German-Polish relations. German students at Poznań University were effectively barred from classes by the manifest hostility of Polish fellow students, and their Verein Deutscher Hochschüler was dissolved by officials in June.[73] The windows of the Schiller Gymnasium in Poznań were broken so regularly by mobs made up mostly of Polish students that police decided they could no longer be responsible for protecting it.[74] In Toruń, too, students (primarily) attacked major German buildings over a four-day period and remained essentially unrestrained by police.[75] In Poznań, the main newspaper (*Posener Tageblatt*), the leading confectionery, and other businesses were attacked and shut down (at least for a time) in 1939.[76] In Łódź, 920 German businesses were closed or turned over to Polish management during the first seven months of 1939, mainly as the result of boycotts, physical damage, or official actions of one kind or another.[77]

Polish nationalists also took increasingly violent exception to anyone speaking German in public: the consulate in Katowice reported that "hardly a member of the German minority dares still to speak German on the street. Nonetheless, the attacks on Germans on public streets have not ceased."[78] Father Breitinger stopped holding German-language church services in Poznań in July to avoid attracting any more attention to his parishioners, who by then were "so frightened that they no longer dared to speak one German word aloud."[79] In Silesia, nationalists took to interrupting German-language church services; one priest was sentenced to six weeks in jail for physically resisting such an attack, after which the hierarchy ordered an end to the use of German sermons and hymns.[80] Evangelical churches were the favorite target of nationalist attacks, however; scarcely a single church or parish house in western Poland escaped altogether, and some pastors reported receiving anonymous warnings to leave Poland lest they be killed.[81] The individual and often isolated farms of the minority were also tempting targets. Parents in some areas asked that *Wanderlehrer* stop coming to their homes because of reprisal attacks, and the German consul in Łódź reported that "entire families are sleeping in the fields and forests, because nightly mob attacks on their houses are feared."[82] German children frequently complained also of stone-throwing and other forms of harassment on their way to and from school.[83]

The single most serious such incident occurred not in western Poland but in the central Polish industrial town of Tomaszów, where Germans made up about 7 percent of the population. What organizers billed as their "great anti-German demonstration" of May 13-14, 1939, successfully pressured local factories to dismiss German workers and then, in the words of the German consul, "destroyed virtually all German private property" in the town. Two Germans died in the course of this veritable pogrom, during which police either did nothing or marched with the demonstrators. Sixteen young Poles were arrested but received only two-month suspended sentences.[84]

Minority newspapers risked confiscation if they reported any of the foregoing incidents. The *Kattowitzer Zeitung* was seized almost every day in April 1939 for complaining about the minority's worsening situation; its editor was tried several times and sentenced to jail terms adding up to more than a year. Street sales of German papers ceased in many towns as the result of attacks on those trying to sell them. Out of continued obedience to earlier directives or just out of habit, Reich newspapers continued to give inadequate coverage to the minority's travails; Krahmer-Möllenberg complained (with some exaggeration) that the "Reich has so far basically kept quiet about all these events."[85] By this time, however, most Reich-German newspapers were no longer allowed into Poland in any case.

Only with the termination of the non-aggression pact in April 1939 did Hitler's regime begin to show real interest in the German minority in Poland. Beginning in April the DS provided the Foreign Office with daily lists of official and unofficial acts against the minority, including names, dates, and places. Hardly a day went by during the next five months without numerous things to report, and the total number of incidents soon grew into the thousands: boycott actions, firings, expulsions, political arrests, businesses closed by official edict, minority organizations disbanded, schools dissolved, and (most commonly) acts of vandalism or personal mistreatment.[86]

Of course, compilations made by this particular regime deserve to be treated with skepticism; this material was designed to serve propaganda purposes, and much of it wound up in the controlled press or in post-September "white books." Yet it does not appear that many of these incidents were fabricated; officials insisted on evidence of authenticity before including some items, and the more serious events can be verified from other sources. To be sure, the great majority of incidents were either trivial or the result of general rowdyism rather than any purposeful campaign of national persecution; nevertheless, one cannot peruse these files (deposited in the archives at Koblenz and Bonn) without concluding that this minority was indeed in a precarious situation and under almost daily siege as war approached in 1939.[87]

Even though Polish officials usually condemned major acts of popular violence, they prosecuted the perpetrators without much enthusiasm and rationalized the actions of the accused. In face-to-face meetings with minority leaders, they readily conceded their own inability to provide effective protection from the growing popular violence and usually responded to minority complaints by bringing up the alleged plight of Poles in Germany. In a talk with Senator Hasbach in June 1939, Minister-President Sławoj-Składkowski conceded that he could no longer do much for the German minority, for "the great political tensions overshadow everything," leading necessarily to anti-German feelings among most Poles.[88] Subsequently, Hasbach reported that he could no longer even get an appointment with top officials.[89] When Kohnert complained to the Pomorze *wojewode* about the boycott of German businesses, asking that the state refrain at least from identifying with this campaign, he was met with the (unfounded) claim that the Polish boycott movement was merely a response to the minority's boycott of Poles.[90] According to Ludwig Wolff, head of the main German organization in central Poland, Łódź starost Mosłowski responded to a complaint about popular violence against Germans in that city with the comment: "You have your storm divisions, after all; defend yourselves!"[91]

The *starost* in Bydgoszcz, on the other hand, did denounce an outbreak of anti-German violence in his city as "unacceptable and undignified" and promised to prosecute anyone who attacked German persons or property. At the same time, however, he contended that Polish hostility was aimed only at the "Hitlerites" among the minority; he was willing to intervene in the minority's behalf only if its leaders were prepared to issue a formal denunciation of National Socialism: "The present situation demands from the German minority a clarification of the question whether they want to be Polish citizens or agents of the Third Reich."[92] In fact, though the threat from Nazi Germany clearly contributed to anti-German hostility in Poland in 1939, neither the popular violence nor the official discrimination was limited to National Socialists. The offices of the DSAP, for example, an outspokenly anti-Nazi and unequivocally loyal organization, were also attacked by Polish mobs in 1939.[93]

A most remarkable conversation took place in June 1939 between Kohnert and the number-two official in the Polish Interior Ministry, Wacław Zyborski. According to Kohnert's account of this conversation,

Zyborski could suggest no solution to the minority's grievances; he justified his government's admittedly aggressive policies with reference to unspecified acts of disloyalty by Polish Germans, the end of the non-aggression pact with Germany, and the treatment of Poles in Germany. Polish Germans, he said, "could thank the Reich for all that was happening to them . . . [and] the current measures are just the beginning." He did not expect Polish Germans to "love" Poland, for "one cannot love one's stepmother," but they should abandon the illusion that their adherence to National Socialism could be divorced from politics or made compatible with loyalty to Poland, as Kohnert tried to insist. Yet the choice he articulated went well beyond the question of Nazism: "You must decide today: either citizen of the Polish republic or German patriot. . . . There is war today . . . [and] you cannot serve two masters." It was personally "painful" for him to treat the minority so harshly, he claimed, but "the general situation demands it; we have moved into a phase of struggle, and such struggles claim victims." When Kohnert protested that the minority had no control over Reich policy and challenged Zyborski to support his charge of disloyal acts, the latter countered, "Do not believe, Mr. Kohnert, that we do not know exactly what you are doing; even the dumb Polaks notice such things."[94]

Without any prospect of change from developments within Poland or as the result of Reich diplomatic efforts, and with an actual conflict between Germany and Poland still just a hypothesis, the mood of Polish Germans in the spring and summer of 1939 was understandably bleak. Kohnert expressed this mood in a series of blunt and utterly pessimistic reports to Berlin. He tried to impress the seriousness of the minority's situation and the need for more forceful intervention upon a government that still seemed too aloof. With evident exasperation, he demanded to know just what Hitler's regime had in mind for the minority and warned that "further postponement of a decision by the Reich will leave Polish Germans hopelessly weakened."[95] Two weeks later, he reported that "there is no end to the despair among Polish Germans; . . . our people feel instinctively that the Reich cannot or will not provide any real help for us in our distress." He called again on the government to decide what was "actually going to happen with the Germans in Poland," for things could no longer continue as they were.[96]

Following his revealing talk with Zyborski, Kohnert concluded that the restraining influence of Beck and the Polish Foreign Ministry had virtually disappeared; the army now seemed to be in control, and it regarded the German minority primarily as a security or espionage problem in the event of war. He believed the government was under growing pressure from the army to "decimate, intimidate, or check" the minority and that its efforts to get Germans either to emigrate or to "keep quiet" were close to success. Among Germans still in Poland, the head of the DV saw only "dejection and hopelessness. . . . Almost all German life in Poznania and Pomorze has come to a stop . . . [or] is in the process of dissolution. . . . It is impossible to imagine a revival of regular German activities in Poland in the future."[97]

Kohnert reported also that he could no longer keep most minority youth from leaving for the Reich; indeed, he could no longer even keep track of all the Germans who were moving out, most of them illegally. He estimated that about 25,000 Germans had left Pomorze and Poznania between March and May 1939; Ulitz reported that at least 15,000 mostly younger Germans had left Silesia during the same period and he too was no longer willing to argue against the wisdom of emigration.[98] Those Germans with farms of their own continued to hold out, encouraged no doubt by a June 1939 law that permitted the confiscation of the property of those who left the illegally.[99] The VoMi set up sixteen transient camps along the German-Polish border to receive refugees; the number housed in these camps climbed from about 39,000 in early June 1939 to more than 95,000 in August, of whom 70,000 were from Poland (the rest came from South Tyrol and elsewhere).[100] Clearly, much of the German population of Poland had given up by the summer of 1939 and would doubtless have left had Hitler not launched his war (which merely delayed their departure for five or six years).

Kohnert's pessimistic assessment of the minority's prospects was supported also by other informed observers. It is reflected, for example, in annual assessments of the minority's condition by the consulates in western Poland. The 1937 report from Toruń, warned that "a sense of complete helplessness has taken hold of the minority. . . . They are slipping into complete desperation."[101] The following year's report related that "the Germans here can see with horror their own decline and feel absolutely abandoned."[102] A report filed in November 1938 concluded that emigration to the Reich had become the only solution for many, for "there is no longer a firm place for the Germans here." The minority was greatly weakened, its children without the prospect of being able to earn a living; "what does not fall victim to Polonization must eventually perish."[103] In this official's opinion, Poland's de-Germanization measures "must lead to the destruction and annihilation of the Germans here."[104] Reports from 1939 described the minority as "spiritually and materially destroyed" by the combination of official discrimination, popular hostility, and apparent Reich indifference; the consul himself felt helpless to provide effective assistance any longer.[105]

The consul in Łódź found little sign, in the wake of the Tomaszów "pogrom," that popular "terror" was abating in central Poland; Germans, including a majority of those living in Tomaszów, were "deciding to emigrate . . . for they see their existence in Poland as endangered."[106] He forecast "the most serious damage to if not the complete destruction of" the German minority in central Poland. "The strong feeling of being constantly threatened has greatly strengthened the tendency to emigrate by entire villages in the last weeks. . . . [They are] ready to sell their possessions for ridiculously low prices. . . . In many cases, threatened farmers have just abandoned their possessions. . . . If this campaign is not stopped in the near future, the complete destruction of the German nationality in the Łódź district will be the inevitable result."[107] Wolff gave the German population in central Poland only another half-year, by which time it would have emigrated or agreed to assimilation. Representatives to the "Council of Germans in Poland" from both central Poland and Silesia used the word "collapsing" to describe the condition of the German population in their districts.[108] Even Krahmer-Möllenberg, who had long been charged with sustaining this minority and who followed its situation more closely than anyone else, seemed to give up in 1939. He anticipated another exodus on the scale of the early 1920s, which would largely eradicate the remaining German population of western Poland. "The minority has weakened greatly in its determination to hold out. . . . The continued existence of a German population in Poland [is] seriously in doubt." Not only had the minority suffered serious material setbacks, but there were also clear signs of flagging morale by people who felt left out of German foreign policy successes.[109]

In short, the consensus of both minority leaders and those Reich officials who best understood the minority's situation, expressed in communications *not* meant for the public (and specifically omitted from German "white books" published after the outbreak of war), was that there was no longer much to be done for the Germans in Poland; most of them would soon have to leave and find new homes elsewhere. The August 1939 statement of the British ambassador to Poland, Howard Kennard, that "allegations made by the German press of minority persecutions . . . [are] a gross distortion and exaggeration of the facts" points either to a lack of curiosity or a willingness to shape his opinion to political interests.[110]

Of course, as war became more likely in the summer of 1939, another possible solution to the problem suggested itself: German reconquest. In the short term, however, this prospect led only to increased anxiety in light of the minority's vulnerability and the intensity of popular feeling. In June the Pomorze *wojewode* asked Kohnert for a list of one hundred leading members of the minority as a means of preserving "peace and order"; those on the list were clearly to serve as hostages in case of war and were indeed rounded up during the first days of September.[111] Krahmer-Möllenberg feared that war would mean "open season" on

Polish Germans generally.[112] Kohnert too speculated that in such a case "the worst is to be feared. The Polish people would conceivably become executioners of the German minority."[113] These fears were nourished by the Polish press: the National Democrats' *Kuryer Poznański*, for example, charged Germany with "terror" against its own Polish minority and warned that "the bill for these political methods will be paid by the German element in Poland. . . . There are plenty of German 'big fish' in Poland" who should not expect to get off lightly in the event of war.[114] As war approached, several unnamed minority leaders asked Germany to drop leaflets "at the instant war breaks out" putting Poles on notice that serious reprisals would result if they harmed Polish Germans.[115] Despite concern for their own security, however, most minority leaders remained in Poland; when Ulitz and Wiesner did leave for Germany in August, NSDAP officials criticized their bad example—whereupon Wiesner returned and was promptly jailed.[116]

The Minority as "Fifth Column"

Closely related to the issue of the minority's actual condition in 1939 is the question of whether it behaved in such a way as to warrant such treatment. Were most Germans in western Poland really just defenseless bystanders caught between the fronts of an emerging German-Polish conflict, as they portrayed themselves? Or were they active participants in a Reich-sponsored campaign against the very existence of the state to which they belonged, as they are presented in most Polish accounts? In the latter view, most Germans in Poland were fundamentally disloyal, in thought if not always in action; many of them engaged in espionage for the Reich or plotted sabotage, and some even participated actively in the German offensive in September. According to the Polish "white book" published a short time thereafter, the German minority, though it enjoyed "a position such as hardly any other minority possesse(d), . . . was indirectly controlled by German elements from the Reich [and] drawn into activities aimed against the Polish state," including illegal journeys to the Reich for military training and "diversionist" activities during the September campaign.[117]

More recent assessments by Polish historians vary only insignificantly in the way they present this basic thesis. Marek Drozdowski is representative: "The German minority was widely recruited for intelligence work, defection of conscripts was organized, [and] secret lists of the German population were compiled. . . . Sabotage groups . . . took an active part in the September campaign on the side of the aggressor."[118] The American Edward Wynot is even less equivocal; especially in western

Poland, he writes, Germans "were indeed a revanchist fifth column from the outset. . . . There is no doubt that . . . the politically organized Germans all formed a genuine fifth column, . . . ready, able, and anxious to perform whatever tasks Berlin might request of them. . . . Germans at every level were utilized to transmit information to *Wehrmacht* planners. . . . Wholesale mass migration of Germans to the Reich was promoted immediately before the war."[119] In a later work, Wynot writes that "more and more Germans were surreptitiously developing an elaborate underground conspiratorial program directed against [the Polish state]. Espionage was a major function and Germans at every level were mobilized to gather and transmit vital information to the *Wehrmacht* planners. Nationalist leaders increasingly staged provocations to arouse Polish reaction to the point where it could be used to justify an intervention."[120]

As evidence for these charges, Seweryn Osiński, author of the most thorough Polish study of this problem, cites numerous examples of Polish Germans making pro-Nazi statements, deserting from the Polish army, and being recruited into the Wehrmacht after emigrating to Germany.[121] Such incidents doubtless did take place, but it remains unclear just how representative they were and how directly they support the more serious and specific charges of espionage, sabotage, and active military collaboration. It is alleged that Polish Germans and the German consulates participated in the smuggling of arms into Poland in preparation for the German offensive; shortly before the outbreak of war, suspicion was widespread among Poles that Germans were hiding weapons in their homes with the intent to attack Polish forces.[122] Members of the minority were also said to have radio transmitters with which to relay information about Polish military movements to German forces. The Wehrmacht supposedly arrived in September armed with information that could only have been gathered by means of extensive spying by Polish Germans.[123] One example given is the *Verzeichnis der deutschen Siedlungen in der Weichselniederung* (List of German Settlements in the Vistula Lowlands) with which the German invaders arrived and which they supposedly put to effective use; that list was based, however, on the published research of Albert Breyer and others, who clearly compiled this information without an eye to its eventual military-intelligence usefulness.[124]

Some individuals apparently were active in Reich intelligence; Gerhard Wiestenberg's Pomorze estate is described in more than one account as a major center of Reich intelligence activities.[125] According to other persuasive testimony, at least one JDP leader in Poznania, Paul Peplinski, "distributed arms to the Germans of his district before the outbreak of the war [and] directed the transportation of arms to certain points at the risk of his own life."[126] Other Polish Germans also boasted later of their work for

German intelligence or their subsequent cooperation with the invading German army.[127]

Nevertheless, German historians are basically just as unanimous in their view that, these exceptions aside, the great majority of Polish Germans, whatever their feelings about Polish rule, abstained from acts of disloyalty toward the Polish state in 1939. Richard Breyer and Pawel Korzec, for example, deny that there is "even the slightest supporting evidence . . . [for] claims of disloyal activities dangerous to the state" on the part of Polish Germans.[128] Another German historian asserts bluntly that "the German minority in Poland conducted its struggle for survival with legal means. . . . There was no terror, no sabotage, no conspiracies. And there was also no fifth column."[129]

To be sure, one has to treat the minority's more effusive protestations of loyalty to the Polish state with skepticism, if only because it is difficult to see how anyone could feel real warmth toward a state that had treated them as interwar Poland did; moreover, some Germans did not even pretend to such loyalty. But neither continued resentment of the changes brought about by the Versailles Treaty nor tactlessness in giving vent to them equate with the charge that the minority functioned as an active agent of the Third Reich or directly threatened Poland's security in 1939. The situation reports of Polish officials make clear that although they kept quite close tabs on minority activities, they were unable to uncover evidence of treasonous activity sufficient to satisfy Polish courts. Among numerous Germans charged with disloyal acts of one kind or another before the war, there were no convictions except on technical grounds, and these involved no one prominent in minority affairs.[130] Pastor Kammel's denial of significant minority involvement in spying or sabotage, his insistence that Polish Germans generally did their duty to "their state" (Poland), carries special weight because it was written in 1940, when there was no longer any political reason to deny such things if they were true.[131] Indeed, minority leaders would presumably have earned only official praise if they could have claimed the kind of active role in Poland's defeat that Polish historians usually attribute to them—but they did not do so.

The readiness of so many younger Germans to avoid Polish military service by going to Germany is also cited as evidence of the minority's disloyalty. Polish military service was not likely to be pleasant for Germans, especially at first, when so many could not handle the Polish language. They could usually count on being stationed somewhere in eastern Poland and were often singled out for harassment because of their nationality. Ethnic German recruits were also excluded from high-security positions; according to a 1922 directive by Defense Minister

Sikorski, only soldiers "whose loyalty was beyond question"—that is, ethnic Poles—could be given the more vital positions in the army.[132] Avoiding such service was clearly one reason why so many young males left for the Reich in the 1930s, but there were also plenty of other reasons to leave. Osiński notes a tenfold increase in the annual desertion rate of Germans already in the Polish army between 1927 and 1937, but even in the latter year it reached only a not very considerable 2.5 percent.[133] And even this low figure represented defiance of, rather than obedience to, explicit Reich directives, which called on Polish Germans to accept military service as a normal obligation of Polish citizenship.[134]

More to the point in examining the charge that many or most Polish Germans functioned as a disloyal fifth column is the clear evidence that the Reich did not want them to play such a role. For reasons of their own, German military planners frowned on the use of Polish Germans for intelligence or other military-related purposes. In October 1938 the Foreign Office warned that "the use of ethnic Germans or even organizations in western Poland [was] exceptionally dangerous for the entire existence of the Germans there."[135] The consulate in Toruń assured its government that the DV had not been involved in intelligence activities to date and urged "relevant agencies [not to] turn to ethnic Germans" in the future because of the risk this entailed for the minority as a whole.[136] The German *Abwehr* also issued a blanket prohibition against use of the minority for espionage, which Osiński cites even as he questions whether it applied also to minority "leaders."[137] When it was revealed that a couple of German agents had nevertheless tried to recruit members of the minority for intelligence activities—a radio transmitter had been left with them, but they had been caught and now faced long prison terms—the German consulate was vigorous (and credible) in its condemnation, and Kohnert demanded that "these persons be dealt with most severely."[138]

When NSDAP officials inquired, shortly before the German invasion, whether the minority should be asked to participate, the Foreign Office replied that "the Germans in Poznania and Pomorze are virtually without weapons" and army commanders "do not consider the arming of Polish Germans to be advisable, for they could achieve little against well-armed troops and thus would be sacrificed to no end."[139] Minority leaders themselves were informed that "the *Führer* does not want to solve the Polish question by means of the [German] minority" and that their situation was not comparable to that of the Sudeten Germans, for which reason they should not aspire to any kind of "Henlein role."[140] And Kohnert, even while calling on the Reich to act more forcefully to correct the "injustice of 1919," reminded his own followers in the DV and that they "owed" Poland their loyalty.[141]

The issue of the minority's loyalty and behavior through August

1939—the former dubious but the latter predominantly "correct"—shades over into the question of its role once war began: that is, the question of the German military fifth column in Poland. This issue, too, continues to be viewed in remarkably contrasting terms, even half a century later, by Polish and German scholars. The prevalent view in Poland differs little in its essentials from official statements in 1940, which characterized the German minority as "the nucleus of an army of spies and conspirators who were only awaiting the *Führer's* order to march."[142] According to Karol Grünberg, Polish Germans "not only awaited the entry of the German army in Poland but at the right moment even provided it with active support."[143] Marian Drozdowski suggests that the "very well-armed German diversion troops, [which] came out against the regular troops of the Polish Army . . . in many regions of . . . Pomorze, Poznania, and Upper Silesia," were organized from or by the minority.[144]

The facts of sabotage and diversionary activity in conjunction with the German invasion are not at issue so much as the question whether any of them can be linked to the minority. A 1,200-man volunteer unit, for example, the Freikorps Ebbinghaus, infiltrated into Silesia before the invasion to prevent the destruction of key factories there and engaged in some fighting in the Bielitz region. It included many former members of the minority, especially Silesian JDs, but it was based in (and, of course, arrived from) Germany.[145] Similarly, the "diversionists" cited by Felix-Heinrich Gentzen and others were trained in Germany, entered Poland only in September and do not appear to implicate the minority directly.[146] The same is true of the *Selbstschutz* that was created upon the arrival of German forces; its participation in the fighting involved Reich Germans, or Germans organized by and entering from the Reich, rather than the minority itself.[147]

The most hotly debated allegations of military activity by the minority concern events in Bydgoszcz on the third day of the war. According to some accounts, the German population of the town and surrounding area was ordered to congregate here and supposedly opened fire on Polish forces retreating through the city's streets on September 3. When Polish soldiers and civilians counterattacked, several hundred Germans were killed in the fighting or executed after being captured "weapon in hand." Restytut Staniewicz, who believes this fifth column was an important factor in the quick Polish defeat, cites the testimony of soldiers serving in the Polish army, including some Germans, in support of his claim that they were fired on by civilians (presumably Germans) in Bydgoszcz.[148] German accounts of these events are quite different, however. They deny that the minority, in Bydgoszcz or elsewhere, was assigned any military role, that it was sufficiently armed or organized to fulfill any such charge, or that it participated in any significant way in the war. They present the events of September 3, 1939, in Bydgoszcz as a matter of hundreds of innocent civilians falling victim to mass hysteria in the course of what became known as the *Bromberger Blutsonntag* (Bloody Sunday).[149] According to Peter Aurich, author of the most thorough German account, law and order disappeared in Bydgoszcz after police abandoned the city on September 3; aroused Polish civilians attacked Germans, or charged them with shooting at Polish soldiers, and summarily executed them (along with some Poles who spoke up in their defense). In this view, Polish units may well have come under fire in the confusion of retreat (there were cases of units firing at each other), but the local German population was essentially unarmed and uninvolved in the fighting.[150]

Some historians have fashioned a military rationale for the "diversions" attributed to the minority by speculating that the point was to distract Polish forces from advancing German forces.[151] Bydgoszcz, however, does not seem to have figured significantly in the German invasion plans; the main German offensive passed well to the north. Others deny a military rationale and suggest that the minority wanted to provoke Poles to respond precisely as they did in order to provide Nazi authorities with a pretext for the reprisals they were already contemplating.[152] But this thesis, its convolution aside, presupposes a German willingness to sacrifice the minority itself, and there is no evidence of such a scheme. The principal difficulty facing those who have tried to make the case for an organized minority insurrection in support of the invading Wehrmacht, however, is that during the subsequent German occupation, when local Germans were free (indeed encouraged) to boast of whatever they might have done in this respect, virtually none did so. Furthermore, when Poland later drew up formal charges of anti-state activities in 1939 against 1,159 members of the minority, no one was charged with specific actions in Bydgoszcz on September 3.[153] Of course, this may only reflect the failure of anyone who would have figured on this list to survive "bloody Sunday," and so the debate continues.[154]

Evidence for fifth column military actions by the German minority, in Bydgoszcz and elsewhere in western Poland, consists mainly of Polish "eyewitness" accounts, admittedly quite numerous; Karol Pospieszalski cites multiple witnesses to at least forty-six cases in which German civilians fired on Polish troops.[155] Much of this first-person testimony however, seems a reflection of the one-sided nature of the fighting, especially the frightening display of German air power, and the tendency to rely on fanciful explanations for the rapid defeat. Many Poles were convinced, for example, that "signs of recognition" had been developed to help the Wehrmacht spare German homes or to point out sources of possible aid. Some believed that house lights on German farms, or mirrors, or fires served as "signals" to German aircraft, and two Germans in Poznań were actually shot for "giving light signals" to German aircraft.[156] Reports of shots coming from Protestant church towers were especially common, despite the virtual impossibility of escape from such places (and the claim of German church authorities that such allegations "always proved groundless" upon investigation).[157]

Other evidence cited to support the fifth column thesis includes a German officer's entry in an occupied village's guest book: "We owe our victorious advance also to the loyalty of our Germans in Poland"; no specific military actions are cited, however.[158] In addition, a *Merkblatt* (leaflet) found on the body of a downed German pilot advised that German pilots could expect help from Polish Germans, who could by recognized by special signs and by using the password "echo"; they should also treat ethnic Germans, even those in Polish uniform, differently from other Polish citizens.[159] This document may reflect what Reich authorities hoped or planned or wanted pilots to believe, but Polish Germans clearly failed to get the word (including the alleged password) and evidence for an organized support network in behalf of the invaders is lacking. The same is true of most reports of minority "arms caches," acts of sabotage, and other specific actions designed to facilitate the German advance.[160]

On the other hand, if the fifth column thesis is shifted from questions of active support of the invasion to questions of sentiment, the minority's defenders have a more difficult case to make. Polish Germans were overwhelmingly sympathetic to the Third Reich and made no secret of their elation at being "liberated" by the Wehrmacht. Some had swastika flags prepared by the time German forces arrived. Hasbach denied any pre-September contacts with the German army; he later recalled, however, though still a member of the Polish Senate, that he greeted the first German soldiers he saw with a relieved and enthusiastic *Sieg Heil!*[161] Polish Germans frequently showed their true sympathies by organizing collaborationist militia as soon as Polish forces left. In Rawicz, Czarnków, and elsewhere they did so prematurely, and Polish units reappeared; even then, however, the "militia" chose to flee rather than engage in actual fighting with Polish forces.[162]

In general, if one takes as a guide the six-part definition of "fifth column" fashioned by Louis de Jong, author of the standard account of German fifth columns in Europe, the German minority in Poland seems to qualify in terms of three criteria: it maintained political connections to a hostile power, sympathized with that power, and subsequently cooperated in the occupation regime which that power established. In terms of De Jong's first three criteria, however, which include the more serious and specific kinds of fifth column activity—espionage, sabotage, and active participation in hostile military operations—the case against the minority is much weaker. Individual exceptions aside, the allegation that Polish Germans participated actively or in significant numbers in such actions remains largely unsubstantiated. De Jong divides his material into two basic categories, one entitled "fear" and the other "reality"; he consigns most of his discussion of the alleged German fifth column in Poland to the former rubric. In his opinion, it was "enormously overestimated" by most Poles in 1939 and, by implication, by Polish historians ever since.[163] Other "third party" accounts of this question (such as that of Anthony Komjathy and Rebecca Stockwell) also lean toward the opinion that the German minority, despite its lack of heartfelt loyalty to Poland, did not play an active role in preparing or carrying out the German attack on that country in 1939.[164]

The September Pogrom

While Polish accounts of September 1939 focus on minority misdeeds and collaboration under the fifth column rubric, German accounts present the minority primarily as victim. Prewar concern for the physical security of Polish Germans in the event of war proved only too well founded. Under Poland's official order KO-3031, prominent minority leaders were to be arrested "without warning or delay" as soon as war broke out. Individual arrest decrees had been drawn up months before war began; only the date remained to be inserted at the last minute. Once war was declared, however, the order was extended to apply to all Germans of any social standing to speak of, including thousands who had never been active in politics, Evangelical pastors, and leaders of the collaborationist DKWB.[165] Poland's military situation deteriorated so rapidly, however, that officials were unable to carry out the detention project in an orderly fashion. A first group of detainees was sent eastward in closed boxcars to the concentration camp at Bereza. Eugen Naumann, long since retired from active politics, was killed in the course of his deportation, but most others who were shipped eastward by train came through all right. The trains soon stopped running, however, and so most subsequent groups of arrested Germans were forced to move eastward on foot.[166]

What followed was a human tragedy of major proportions. Several dozen groups of detainees set out from Pomorze and Poznania (Polish Silesia was overrun so quickly that the minority there remained relatively unscathed), and these "treks" often left without adequate food, plans for shelter, or police protection. One group from Bydgoszcz numbered about 4,000 people and was made to travel fifty-eight kilometers, without food or water, in the first day and night. As bad news arrived from the front, crowds gathered to take out their frustration and rage on the trekkers;

guards described them as "German rebels" and "traitors" and did little to keep by-standers from clubbing and stoning the defenseless marchers. Those who failed to keep up were summarily shot; many died along the way, including forty-four in a single day from this particular group. After marching for six days, the survivors reached the vicinity of Łowicz, about 240 kilometers from where they started.[167] A trek from Wąbrzezno also marched at the rate of forty kilometers per day; of the 560 who started out in this group, 188 died along the way, including forty who were shot in a single night.[168] The death toll on the trek from Rogozno/ Rogasen (Oborniki County) was 250 to 300; from Szamotuły and Międzychód, 120 of 300; and on several treks from southern Poznania, a total of 400 of 1,200.[169] Some witnesses claimed that officials gave orders to "liquidate" the marchers, but most of the violence and killing seem to have been the result of general disorder and panic rather than official directions.[170]

Father Breitinger was part of the trek from Poznań and has left a detailed account of his experiences. He was picked up by police on the first day of the war for what was supposed to be a half-hour discussion; instead, he was added to the trek leaving town and spent the next sixteen days walking eastward. When guards informed the agitated crowds along the way that "these are all Germans," there was "an enormous shouting and raging . . . [and] innumerable blows with sticks, shoes, and stones so that we were all full of bruises." Others tossed horse manure or spat: "My face was often completely wet." Polish soldiers, officers, and even priests sometimes participated in the frenzy. The fact that Breitinger was dressed in clerical garb seemed only to make him a target of special abuse, and "that all this was possible in a Catholic county [was] naturally especially bitter for me."

His own Cardinal Hlond passed the marchers, driving eastward; his failure to intervene in behalf of a fellow priest was seized upon by German propaganda at the time, but Breitinger doubts that Hlond actually recognized him, and "justice demands that I report that many Polish priests also used all their influence to calm the people." According to other accounts, however, priests appeared sometimes at the head of violent mobs and instigated some of the anti-German violence; Breitinger reports having seen at least one priest urging on the crowd in Poznań with shouts of "To the wall with these Dogs!" and "Beat them all to death!" Breitinger reports that about thirty-five members of his trek were shot along the way; others had "bound heads, [or] clothes that were covered with blood from top to bottom." A wagon which went along to transport cripples and children was finally left behind one morning; those riding in it had been shot. The group made it as far as Kutno before German units approached; the guards said they had orders to shoot anyone who might fall into

German hands, but in exchange for a small bribe they agreed to abandon the trek instead.[171]

Other members of the minority died at the hands of enraged mobs in their own towns and villages. Sometimes as much as a week passed between the abandonment of a town by Polish forces and the arrival of the first German troops; this interim period proved especially perilous, for the jails were opened and anarchy prevailed. The repeated allegations of disloyalty directed at the minority over the years doubtless fueled popular rage and helped direct it against German civilians. The Bydgoszcz scenario was repeated on a smaller scale in many other places during the first days of the war; eight Germans, for example, were shot for allegedly firing on Polish troops in Leszno.[172] The situation was especially bad along the retreat roads to the east, where most of the violence was perpetrated by soldiers. Many German farmers sought refuge in nearby forests as their farms were looted and burned.[173]

Peter Aurich provides the following figures for the hardest-hit communities: in Tarnowo, three-quarters of the 181 German residents were killed; in Jägerhof, one-third of 200 Germans, including virtually all adult males, were killed on September 3; 145 deaths were recorded in and around Schulitz; 39 died at Jesuitensee; 38 were killed in Eichdorf/Netzheim; and 19 males, ages thirteen to seventy-four, were executed in a single incident in Michałowo.[174] Richard Kammel provides the following death tolls for other places: Gross-Neudorf, 112; Otterau-Langenau, 82; Eigenheim, 26; Wiesenau, 34 of 96 German inhabitants; and Radewitz, 41.[175] Victims included fourteen members of the Evangelical Consistory in Poznań, two deacons, and forty-five pastors, officials, and other employees.[176] The death toll among minority schoolteachers was thirty-six; among employees of the Poznanian co-op association, sixteen.[177]

Another 5,200 Germans who were reported dead or missing had been serving in the Polish army. This was perilous duty, less because of the Wehrmacht than because of the hostility of Polish comrades: German recruits often became scapegoats for defeat and were deprived of weapons and even uniforms. In some cases, new conscripts were simply ordered eastward, only to be seized as spies or deserters and shot. Fear of espionage and treason was rampant; "Germans to the wall!" was a frequent refrain, and many report that their lives were saved only by the rapid German advance or by the intervention of courageous Polish comrades. Ethnic German soldiers had special identification, and so the only salvation for some was to get hold of the ID of a fallen Polish soldier and try to pass as Polish. One such recruit, Johann Kurtziza of Katowice, having successfully passed as Polish, was then ordered to escort a hundred German recruits eastward and to shoot those who failed to keep up.[178]

Kurt Graebe returned to Pomorze in the wake of the German conquest and expressed shock at the results of this pogrom; though having experienced World War I "in all its horror," he claimed "not to have seen anything previously so terrible, a misfortune which in one way or another has affected almost all [German] families" in western Poland.[179] Pastor Karl Berger, coming upon the grave of about one hundred murdered Germans in Turek County, asked the question that others would soon be asking about his fellow Germans: "We stand with horrified incomprehension before such deeds. What must have gone on in the souls of such an entire people which was capable of such mass murder? What kind of forces of predisposition and education, of pride and desperation, must have worked together to produce such a blood-frenzy, bordering on insanity?"[180] Kammel, writing in 1940, felt obliged to point out that not all Poles took part in this violence; some had even risked their own lives to hide German neighbors and had protested the destruction of German churches by authorities.[181] Germans in other districts reported no serious acts of violence by Polish neighbors.[182] But Karol Grünberg's assertion that "Polish society in its mass maintained peace and discipline, never letting itself be provoked into attacks against the German people," is clearly belied by what happened in September 1939.[183]

The overall death toll from this outbreak of communal hysteria continues to be a subject of debate. Many victims, buried in unmarked graves, were never found and remain classified as "missing." A *Zentrale für Gräber ermordeter Volksdeutscher* (Central Office for the Graves of Murdered Ethnic Germans) was set up under Kurt Lück and Karl Berger and charged with compiling a comprehensive list of victims. Their files, deposited today in the Koblenz archives, contain 5,437 names and were the basis for several German propaganda books detailing *polnische Greueltaten* (Polish atrocities).[184] Hitler soon seized upon exaggerated estimates of the number of dead (13,000) and missing (45,000); he combined them and then made everyone adhere to the total of 58,000. The Lück-Berger file was found in Poznań in 1945 and used by Pospieszalski to discredit the 58,000 figure.[185] He reckoned that even 5,437 was an exaggerated count, since it included some who were missing only temporarily as well as about a thousand Polish German soldiers, who were listed whether their deaths were due to Poles or to the Wehrmacht. Pospieszalski argues that most of these, and many of the civilian casualties as well were due to the war itself; still others listed in the file were not ethnic Germans to begin with. He concludes that "only" about 2,000 members of the German minority in western Poland died as a direct result of popular violence during the first weeks of the war.[186]

Peter Aurich, however, studying the same evidence a decade later, found that the deaths of at least 3,841 German civilians as a result of popular violence could be attested to by more than one witness: 2,063 who were killed in or near where they lived, 1,576 who did not survive the treks eastward, and 202 who died later of injuries. Adding these figures to the number of soldiers killed by their Polish comrades, Aurich contends that between 4,000 and 5,000 members of the German minority in western Poland (or about 2 percent of its total number) died as a result of popular violence in September 1939.[187]

It is hard to avoid the conclusion that the Polish state was bent on the elimination of most of the German minority in western Poland—by forced assimilation where possible, but mainly by coerced emigration. Moreover, this goal was well on the way to being achieved in 1939; the Poznanian *wojewode* reportedly assured his supporters that within three years there would no longer be any Germans in Poland.[188] A study of the minority's actual political, cultural, and economic situation merely reinforces the pessimistic assessments of contemporaries cited above. The fact that Hitler took up the minority's case several months before he launched World War II was perhaps the overriding consideration at the time, but it does not make the fact of the minority's plight less compelling.

Of course, any country faced with such an adversary might be justi-fied in relegating consideration for a difficult minority to a back burner; even today, some will respond to this account of the minority's travails with a "So what?" in view of the larger issues at stake in 1939. The point, however, is that only a small proportion of the innumerable measures directed at the German minority in Poland, essentially those dating from after April 1939, can be attributed directly to Poland's anticipation of war with Germany. The bulk of the policies and attitudes that determined the living conditions of the minority in interwar Poland antedated 1939 (and 1933 too) and were unconnected to any immediate external threat. It hardly needs to be added that they did nothing to make Poland more secure when the mortal threat materialized. The fact is that Polish nation-alism, motivated by the irrational but powerful compulsion to create a nationally homogeneous society in its western provinces, created a situa-tion well before 1939 which was bad even by the unenlightened standards of interwar eastern Europe. Moreover, it is hard to see how this situation would have been significantly different had there never been a Hitler.

The "plight" of the German minority in Poland, in other words, was real; it was not merely alleged or fabricated in the interest of Nazi propa-ganda. This is not to suggest any change in the larger perspective in terms of who was right in 1939 or how one approaches the larger issues that were at stake that year. Nor is it an attempt to assign exclusive blame to one side of one of Europe's most intense and mutually destructive national con-flicts. Apart from the macropolitical situation in 1939, however, the evidence cited above makes clear that Germans in Poland had ample justification for their complaints; their prospects for even medium-term survival were bleak; and no German government more principled than Hitler's would have been able to ignore their plight over the long run. Though it was not politic to make these points at the time, there is no reason why they cannot be accepted half a century later.

Conclusion

Strictly speaking, the outbreak of war in 1939 marked the end of the German minority in western Poland. The area ceded to Poland after World War I was reincorporated into Germany, and the surviving German population was once again part of a dominant majority. This meant yet another turning of the tables for the two peoples: Polish Germans happily accepted their installation as part of the new "master race," while their Polish neighbors were subjected to an occupation regime more brutal than any this region had seen previously.[1]

The principal leaders of the interwar minority, already on board ideologically, did not hesitate to embrace the new regime. Some of them found administrative jobs or came into possession of confiscated Polish properties. Kohnert and Wiesner were rewarded with landed estates; Wiesner and Wolff were given seats in the meaningless Reichstag; all three acquired ranks in the SS as well.[2] Otto Ulitz became the head of schools in reunited Upper Silesia before moving into the Interior Ministry; Poles accused him of causing the death or imprisonment of thousands of Polish "insurgents" and other local nationalists by denouncing them to the new rulers.[3] Superintendent Blau, who had remained a Reich citizen, addressed his followers from Berlin after the German invasion and declared that "the miracle has happened"; when Hitler ("by the grace of God") survived as assassination attempt the next month, Blau ordered his pastors to give formal thanks to God in their services.[4] He prefaced Kammel's book on the September pogrom with thanks for the "great deed of the *Führer*," whom Kammel described still more grandiloquently as *"Führer* and savior."[5] Schönbeck, also a Reich citizen, spent the war years working for the new regime in Poznania. Several leading postwar historians of the minority (as their Polish peers have not hesitated to point out) also served the occupation regime. For example, Theodor Bierschenk, a former Young German functionary, worked in the aministration of the *Generalgouvernement,* charged (among other things) with the political "reeducation" of Polish Germans; Otto Heike worked as an archive director and writer for the new *Litzmannstädter Zeitung.*[6] After the war, Ulitz and Kohnert reemerged for a time as heads of their respective *Landsmann-schaften* (expellee organizations) for Upper Silesia and West Prussia in West Germany; Wiesner also moved there but lived under an assumed name until he was exposed, following an arrest for embezzlement.[7]

Despite their presumably valuable knowledge of Poland and its language, however, few members of the interwar minority achieved really important positions in the wartime regime.[8] The administrators of Germany's pre-1939 support system figured somewhat more prominently. Winkler became head of the Haupttreuhandstelle-Ost, which administered confiscated Polish and Jewish property in occupied eastern Europe; Krahmer-Möllenberg was his assistant until his death in a 1942 plane crash.[9] The DV, Volksbund, and DS, having lost their reason for being, were disbanded. Gero von Gersdorff of the SS, substituting for Kohnert (who was already on active duty in the army), formally dissolved the DV at ceremonies in 1940. Simultaneously, he decreed the official end of the DV-JDP rivalry, declaring that there had never been a serious difference in the first place and that both parties had shared a common ideology all along.[10] The property of these organizations became the property of the Reich; indeed, minority leaders were surprised to find that the Reich now cited its pre-1939 financial support as grounds for claiming title to their buildings and other property.[11]

Not all members of the prewar minority adjusted so smoothly to the new conditions. Swart was among those who lost out; he was removed from his position as co-op leader in 1939. Another (anonymous) DV official told of being unceremoniously locked out of his offices by the new rulers.[12] Dietrich Vogt claims that none of the four secondary school principals in western Poland, himself included, was able to get along with the new regime; after failing to get Polish preserved as a subject of instruction in the public schools, and unable to protect his own Polish staff, he entered the army in 1942. Hermann von Tresckow, whose wife was among those who died in the September pogrom, tried nevertheless to enlist the assistance of his sister's friend Hermann Goering to reduce the persecution of Poles and Jews (which only enraged the *Reichsmar-schall*, however).[13] The Lehfeldts expressed some disappointment with the new regime for, among other things, installing an alcoholic party functionary as *Landrat*; they were arrested and held for four days in September after being denounced by a more fervent NS neighbor.[14]

Others among the minority "intelligentsia," such as Kurt Lück and Alfred Lattermann, expressed some discomfort with Nazi occupation policies, though not very loudly; they too wound up on active duty (and gave their lives for the Nazi cause).[15] Kurt Graebe, one of the few minority leaders who never did join the NSDAP, also reentered the army (at age sixty-six) but survived the war.[16] German socialists fled, as did others who had been openly anti-Nazi; some (including Johann Kowoll) moved farther east into Stalin's Soviet Union, where their survival was even more problematic. There was an infusion of new German blood into western Poland from the Baltic states, South Tyrol, and elsewhere; these newcomers, rather than local Germans, usually got the pick of the confiscated properties. Some Polish Germans complained about the "flood of officials, opportunists, and adventurers, [including] many dishonest types," who arrived from the Reich and Danzig.[17]

The exceptionally ruthless character of Nazi occupation policy in Poland, in comparison even with that in other countries of German-occupied Europe, was doubtless conditioned somewhat by the interwar experience of the German minority in that country, especially by the events of September 1939. But Poland's record with respect to the German minority, however unreasonable and counterproductive, quickly paled in comparison with German treatment of occupied Poland during World War II. Indeed, an underlying, often unspoken, theme of much subsequent Polish historical writing on German-Polish relations is that Germany's invasion and subsequent occupation constitute retroactive justification for Poland's efforts to reduce or suppress this minority before 1939.

But even though interwar Polish nationality policy cannot be discussed in terms applicable to Hitler (or to Stalin), the fact remains that it was hardly a model of toleration or reasonableness by the pretotalitarian standards of the day. If it cannot be discussed in terms applicable to the third German Reich, it shows many similarities to the second, to the much-despised Prussian Polish policies of the pre-1918 era. Indeed, a comparison of the two shows that Polish efforts to restrict or diminish the German minority in western Poland were vastly more successful than pre-1918 Prussian efforts to limit the Polish population in the same region. For example, when Prussian Germanizers were finished in 1918, there were considerably more Poles in Prussian Poland than when they began; by contrast, the German population of this same area suffered a dramatic 70 percent decline between 1918 and 1939. On another front, the amount of landed property owned by Poles in Prussian Poland registered a modest net increase from 1871 to 1918 (in spite of the Settlement Commission), whereas Germans lost about 45 percent of their land during the twenty years after 1919.[18]

The victimizer-victim relationship in the German-Polish borderlands was reversed yet again when German occupation of Poland was replaced by Soviet control in 1944. With Stalin's permission, Poland moved to rid itself once and for all of the problem of the German minority; those Germans who did not flee were expelled, and the centuries-old history of Germans in Poland seemed to come to an end. Approximately 18 percent of the German population present in Poland in 1939 perished during the war and the subsequent expulsions; most of the survivors wound up in western Germany.[19] Nazi German treatment of Poland during the war years was doubtless the primary reason why Poland and other eastern European states resorted to such a drastic "final solution" to their German problem. But the long and rancorous history of government-minority relations in the German-Polish borderlands, under the Prussian regime as well as during the interwar period treated here, was doubtless a factor as well.

The same explusion policy was also applied, of course, to all of Germany east of the Oder and Neisse rivers, where Germans were the majority (and often the totality) of the population. Stalin advocated this radical shift of frontiers because, among other things, it would virtually guarantee eternal enmity between Germany and Poland and so serve Soviet interests. Based on the experience of the interwar period, it seemed unlikely that Germany, which had made such an issue of the loss of majority-Polish lands after World War I, could ever resign itself to territorial amputations on the scale of those of 1945. Poland would always have to fear its western neighbor and so remain dependent upon its eastern neighbor. This fact would also serve as a support for an unpopular, Soviet-imposed regime, whose understanding of the connection between eternal German-Polish enmity and its own survival is reflected in the state-controlled Polish historiography of the following decades. The prevailing Polish view of the interwar German minority, a view with which this book takes issue, has doubtless been shaped by this political context. By the same token, however, the political changes that began in Poland in 1989 contain the promise of many such reappraisals from Polish scholars as well.

In this sense, this account of a most unpleasant period of German-Polish relations ends on a happy note, for German-Polish relations in the early 1990s are more genuinely cordial than at any time in the modern era. And as important as it is to understand what happened in the past, it is equally important to know when to put "paid" to unhappy historical experiences. This is especially true when, as in the case of the events described here, it is less a matter of victim and victimizer than of mutual tragedy, where each side paid a huge price for its inability to get along with the other. This reexamination after fifty years should be received in this spirit and not as material for nationalist resentment or incriminations. It is a cliché (but true) that there was right and wrong on both sides of the national divide in interwar Poland; Polish government and society and the German minority alike share responsibility for one of Europe's most destructive national conflicts. How encouraging, therefore, to surmise that this conflict really does belong, figuratively as well as literally, to the past.

Appendix A ——————

Western Polish Place Name
Official Polish Forms and
German Equivalents

In the text, both forms (the one used by the majority listed first) are given at first occurrence; only the majority form is used thereafter.

Polish	German	Polish	German
Bielsko	Bielitz	Nowy Tomyśl	Neutomischel
Brodnica	Strasburg	Opole	Oppeln
Bydgoszcz	Bromberg	Ostrów	
Chełmno	Culm	Wielkopolski	Ostrowo
Chełmża	Kulmsee	Pomorze	Pomerellen
Chodzież	Kolmar	Poznań	Posen
Chojnice	Konitz	Pszczyna	Pless
Cieszyn	Teschen	Rawicz	Rawitsch
Czarnków	Czarnikau	Sępólno	Zempelburg
Działdowo	Soldau	Śmigiel	Schmiegel
Gniezno	Gnesen	Starogard	Preussisch Stargard
Grodzisk		Świecie	Schwetz
Wielkopolski	Graetz	Tczew	Dirschau
Grudziądz	Graudenz	Toruń	Thorn
Inowrocław	Hohensalza	Tuchola	Tuchel
Karwina	Karwin	Wąbrzeźno	Briesen
Katowice	Kattowitz	Wągrowiec	Wongrowitz
Królewska Huta	Königshütte	Wejherowo	Neustadt
Leszno	Lissa	Wolsztyn	Wollstein
Międzychód	Birnbaum	Września	Wreschen
Nakło	Nakel	Żnin	Znin
Notec (River)	Netze		

German Population of Western Poland by Province and County

POMORZE

County (Powiat)	1910[a]		1921		1931	
	Population	(of which German)	Population	(of which German)	Population	(of which German)
Działdowo/Soldau	24,709	9,210 37.3%	23,920	8,187 34.5%	42,716	2,862 6.7%
Lubawa/Löbau	59,037	12,122 20.5	59,765	4,478 7.6	53,621	1,612 3.0
Brodnica/Strasburg	62,142	21,097 34.0	61,180	9,599 15.7	56,287	5,100 9.1
Wąbrzeźno/Briesen	49,506	24,007 48.5	47,100	14,678 31.1	49,852	7,051 14.1
Toruń/Thorn*	105,544	58,266 55.2	79,247	16,175 20.4	114,207	9,574 6.6
Chełmno/Kulm	50,069	23,345 46.6	46,823	12,872 27.5	52,765	7,517 14.2
Świecie/Schwetz	87,712	42,233 47.1	83,138	20,178 24.3	87,998	13,402 15.3
Grudziądz/Graudenz	89,063	62,892 70.1	77,031	21,401 27.8	96,815	11,369 11.7
Tczew/Dirschau	64,321	28,046 43.6	62,905	7,854 12.5	67,399	4,359 6.5
Wejherowo/Neustadt[b]	71,560	24,528 34.3	71,692	7,857 11.0	118,512	5,542 4.7
Kartuzy/Karthaus	66,190	14,170 21.4	64,631	5,037 7.8	68,674	4,445 6.5
Kościerzyna/Berent	52,980	20,804 37.3	49,935	9,290 18.6	51,716	5,978 11.6
Starogard/Preussisch Stargard	65,427	17,165 26.2	62,400	5,946 9.5	71,829	3,433 4.8
Chojnice/Konitz	74,963	30,326 40.5	71,018	13,129 18.5	76,935	7,635 9.9
Tuchola/Tuchel	33,951	11,268 33.2	34,445	5,660 16.4	41,249	3,151 7.6
Sępólno/Zempelburg	30,541	21,554 70.6	27,876	13,430 48.2	29,563	11,942 40.4
TOTAL	989,715	421,029 42.5	935,643	175,771 18.8	1,080,138	104,992 9.6

POZNANIA

County (Powiat)	1910[a]		1921		1931	
	Population	(of which German)	Population	(of which German)	Population	(of which German)
Bydgoszcz/Bromberg*	154,169	105,504 68.4%	140,265	43,798 31.2%	175,339	18,793 10.7%
Szubin/Schubin	48,304	21,035 43.6	46,084	13,431 29.1	47,825	9,638 20.2
Wyrzysk/Wirsitz	67,219	34,235 50.9	62,531	19,599 31.3	68,873	13,736 19.9
Chodzież/Kolmar	47,183	34,004 72.1	41,742	19,223 46.3	44,508	12,493 28.1
Czarnków/Czarnikau	38,897	17,273 44.4	35,586	7,953 22.4	43,256	6,273 14.5
Międzychód/Birnbaum	32,951	16,012 48.6	30,131	8,152 27.1	31,032	2,992 9.6
Szamotuły/Samter	66,856	17,071 25.5	66,056	8,156 12.3	67,742	4,709 7.0
Oborniki/Obornik	55,880	22,450 40.2	55,146	13,987 25.4	50,388	7,960 15.8
Wągrowiec/Wongrowitz	52,574	16,309 31.0	54,373	11,670 21.5	54,259	7,039 13.0
Żnin/Znin	40,910	10,906 27.1	41,063	7,667 18.7	41,521	4,738 11.4

	Population	(of which) German-speaking		Population	(of which) German-speaking		Population	(of which) German-speaking	
Inowrocław/Hohensalza	77,294	28,384	36.7	75,395	12,333	16.4	82,963	8,301	10.0
Strzelno/Strelno[c]	86,873	21,711	25.0	88,811	13,625	15.3	89,196	7,719	8.7
Gniezno/Gnesen[d]	85,344	26,275	30.8	86,736	12,723	14.7	87,931	7,465	8.5
Września/Wreschen	39,878	7,720	19.4	41,104	3,336	8.1	43,698	2,506	5.9
Środa/Schroda	49,176	6,201	12.6	49,812	2,970	6.0	49,902	2,016	4.0
Śrem/Schrem	57,483	10,017	12.4	57,509	4,524	7.9	57,304	2,996	5.2
Poznań/Posen*	248,939	86,807	34.9	266,070	18,493	7.0	337,592	10,983	3.3
Nowy Tomyśl/Neutomischel[e]	87,809	33,244	37.9	86,045	21,003	24.4	87,331	16,289	18.7
Wolsztyn/Wollstein	49,382	22,236	45.0	48,661	13,650	28.1	47,892	9,857	20.6
Leszno/Lissa	54,546	31,033	56.9	54,402	14,170	26.0	61,211	9,814	16.0
Kościan/Kosten[f]	83,257	22,448	27.0	82,709	10,461	12.6	78,899	2,832	3.6
Gostyń	56,250	21,461	38.2	56,488	9,674	17.1	55,929	2,456	4.4
Rawicz/Rawitsch	51,165	21,842	42.7	48,929	9,970	20.4	49,882	4,812	9.6
Krotoszyn/Krotoschin[g]	80,393	21,542	26.7	79,250	9,417	11.9	75,426	5,625	7.5
Jarocin/Jarotschin[h]	88,988	15,435	17.3	92,596	6,291	6.8	87,546	3,744	4.3
Ostrów W./Ostrowo[i]	87,589	17,148	19.6	91,346	9,936	10.9	104,126	3,985	3.8
Kępno/Kempen[j]	91,573	16,531	18.1	92,752	12,695	13.7	86,849	3,273	3.8
TOTAL	1,972,129	679,339	34.4	1,967,865	327,846	16.7	2,106,440	193,044	9.2

POLISH UPPER SILESIA

County (Powiat)	Population	(of which) German-speaking		Votes cast	by German-speaking (of which)		Population	(of which) German-speaking	
Lubliniec/Lublinitz	35,093	5,479	15.6%	19,861	9,969	50.1%	43,877	1,315	3.0%
Tarnowskie Góry/Tarnowowitz	54,440	17,574	32.3	30,970	13,746	44.3	66,162	5,210	7.9
Królewska Huta/Königshütte	72,641	39,276	54.1	46,628	31,864	74.6	80,734	11,929	14.7
Katowice/Kattowitz*	289,475	107,818	38.3	169,311	84,453	49.9	357,534	29,107	8.1
Świętochłowice/Schwientochlau	174,268	52,569	30.1	84,166	36,816	43.6	207,978	11,948	5.7
Rybnik	147,141	24,957	17.0	90,190	29,853	33.0	213,271	4,584	2.1
Pszczyna/Pless	119,694	15,762	13.2	72,357	18,730	25.8	161,987	5,037	3.1
TOTAL	892,752	263,453	29.5	516,938	225,431	44.2	1,131,543	68,755	6.0

*Cities and surrounding counties of same name combined
a. Includes military personnel (1921 and 1931 figures do not)
b. "Maritime County", includes Puck/Putzig in 1919 and 1921
c. Includes Mogilno County in 1910 and 1921
d. Includes Witkowo County in 1910 and 1921
e. Includes Grodzisk Wielkopolski/Grätz County in 1910 and 1921
f. Includes Śmigiel/Schmiegel County in 1910 and 1921
g. Includes Koźmin/Koschmin County in 1910 and 1921
h. Includes Pleszew/Pleschen County in 1910 and 1921
i. Includes Odolanów/Adelnau County in 1910 and 1921
j. Includes Ostrzeszów/Schildberg County in 1910 and 1921

Bibliography

Primary Sources

Archives

Bundesarchiv Koblenz (BA)
    R 43 I, Reichskanzlei
        117-27: Polen
        542-48: Auslandsdeutschtum
        549-52: Deutschtum in den abgetretenen Gebieten
        560-62: Völkische Minderheiten
    R 43 II, Reichskanzlei
        1406-10: Deutschtumsfragen
        1480-84: Polen
    R 57, Deutsches Auslandsinstitut
        1092-1100
    Kleine Erwerbung 619: Swart
    NL ("Nachlass") Graebe
    NL Steinacher
    Ost-Dokumentation 6-8
Politisches Archiv des Auswärtigen Amts Bonn (PA)
    Geheim Abt. IV Politik 11:3 Polen: Grażyński
    Geheim Abt. IV Politik 15A Polen: Lukaschek
    Geheim Abt. IV Politik 25 Polen v. 1-9: Deutschtum im Ausland
    Geheim Abt. IV Politik 25 Polen/Oberschlesien v. 1-8: Deutschtum im Ausland
    Geheim Abt. IV Politik 25L Polen: Deutscher Unterstützungsverband in Polen
    Geheim Abt. IV Politik 25M Polen: Verband Deutscher Katholiken in Polen
    Geheim Abt. IVa Politik 25H Polen v. 1-5: Polnische Aktionen gegen Deutschtumsorganisationen
    Geheim Abt. IVa Politik 28A Polen v. 1-2: Deutscher Kultur- und Wirtschaftsbund in Polen
    Abt. IV Politik 25 Polen v. 1-37: Deutschtum im Ausland
    Abt. V Politik 25 Polen v. 1-11: Deutschtum in Ausland
    Abt. V Politik 25C Polen v. 1-3: Volksdeutsche in Polen
    Abt. V Politik 25E Polen v. 1-7: Ausschreitungen gegen Reichs- u. Volksdeutsche

Institut für Zeitgeschichte Munich (IfZ)
  MA 128: NSDAP/AO, Abt. Ost
  MA 195/2-5: Deutsche Stiftung
  MA 197: Deutscher Ostmarkenverein
  Fb 110: Varia
Wojewódzkie Archiwum Państwowe w Poznaniu (WAPP)
  Urząd Wojewódzki Poznański (UWP)
      1211-15: Niemieckie organizacje polityczne
      1218: Sprawy stowarzyszeń i związków niemieckie mniejszości
        narodowej
      1240-41: Niemieckie Towarzystwo Szkolne w Poznaniu
      1244-45: Deutsche Bücherei
      1258-59: Verein Deutscher Bauern
      1260-61: Zachodnio-polskie Towarzystwo Rolnicze
      1262-64: Rozwiązanie niemieckiej organizacji "Deutschtumsbundu"
  Organizacji niemieckie (Org. niem.)
      4-7: Jungdeutsche Partei
      524-27: Deutscher Schulverein Leszno
      541: Wspomnienia niemieckie z czasów polskich
  Konsistórz Ewangelicki (EK)
      262: Verhalten der Behörden
      291-97: Rundschreiben, Rundverfügungen
      471: Wahlen zum Sejm
      503: Regierungserklärungen
      514-18: Minderheitenangelegenheiten
      526: Deutsche Vereinigung
      528: Deutschland-Polen
      529: Verhandlungen mit Polen
      536-37: Die Zukunft der Kirche
      538-40: Ausführung des Friedensvertrages
      543: Liquidationen
Hoover Institution (HI), Stanford, Ca.
  Germany, Gestapo, Aussendienststelle Beuthen
  Poland, Ambasada (USA), #60
  Hugh Gibson Papers
Piłsudski Institute (PI), New York
  Ambasada RP w Londynie
  Prezydium Rady Ministrów; protokoły posiedzeń
  Władysław Studnicki
League of Nations, 1919-1946. Council Documents, Category 1B (Minorities).
  Microfilm, 25 reels. Research Publications, Woodbridge, Conn.

Published Works

Akten zur deutschen auswärtigen Politik, 1918-45. Göttingen: Vandenhoeck & Ru-
  precht, 1967-, series B (1925-33); series C (1933-39).
Beck, Józef. *Beiträge zur europäischen Politik.* Essen: Essener Verlagsanstalt, 1939.
Breyer, Richard, and Paweł Korzec. "Polnische Nationalitätenpolitik und die

deutsche Volksgruppe in Lageberichten des polnischen Innenministeriums aus den Jahren 1935 und 1937." *Zeitschrift für Ostforschung* 29 (1980): 260-366.

British Foreign Ministry. *British War Blue Book.* New York: Farrar & Birchart, n.d.

"Der deutsch-polnisches Abkommen über Oberschlesien vom 15. Mai 1922." *Reichsgesetzblatt* (1922): 237-540.

Deutscher Volksbund für Polnisch-Schlesien. *Geschäftsbericht für das Jahr 1936* (n.p., 1937); *Jahr 1937* (n.p., 1938).

Diplomat in Berlin 1933-39: Lipski Papers. Ed. W. Jędrzejewicz. New York: Columbia Univ. Press, 1968.

Documents concerning German-Polish relations and the Outbreak of Hostilities between Great Britain and Germany on Sept. 3, 1939. London: H.M. Stationery Office, 1939.

Dokumente der deutschen Politik. Vol. 3. Ed. Hans Volz. Berlin, 1942.

Dokumente zur Vorgeschichte des Krieges. Auswärtiges Amt (AA). Berlin: Reichsdruckerei, 1939.

Dziennik Polskiego Sejmu Dzelnicowego w Poznaniu w grudniu 1918. Poznań: Sw. Wojciech, 1918.

Eingabe des Deutschen Volksbundes für Polnisch-Schlesien an den Völkerbundsrat. Katowice, 1931.

Eingabensammlung der deutschen Volksgruppe in Westpolen. Deutsche Vereinigung. Bromberg, 1936.

Eingaben und Denkschriften zur Agrarreformfrage, Deutsche Vereinigung. Bromberg: Dittmann, 1938.

Die Frage des Besitzes und Erwerbs von Grundstücken durch Angehörige der deutschen Volksgruppe in Westpolen. Deutsche Vereinigung. Bromberg, 1938.

The German White Paper [text of the Polish documents]. New York: Howell, Soskin, 1940.

Grenztrup, Theodor. *Die kirchliche Rechtslage der deutschen Minderheiten in Europa.* Berlin: Deutsche Rundschau, 1928.

Hans Steinacher, Bundesleiter des VDA, 1933-7. Ed. H.A. Jacobsen. Schriften des Bundesarchivs. Boppard: Harald Boldt, 1970.

Hubatsch, Walther, ed. *Die evangelischen General-Visitationen in den von Ost- und Westpreussen sowie Posen 1920 abgetretenen Kirchenkreisen.* Göttingen: Vandenhoeck & Ruprecht, 1971.

Jahrbuch deutscher Lehrer in Polen 1928. Ed. W. Damaschke. Bromberg: Johne, 1928.

Jungdeutsche Partei. *Rettung oder Untergang.* Bielitz: JDP, 1935.

———. *Unsere Leitsätze.* Bielitz: JDP, 1933.

———. *Wir schmieden die Zukunft.* Bromberg: JDP, 1935.

Kirche, Volk, und Staat in Polen. Ed. A.v. Hoogenguyze. Amsterdam: Ev. Maatschoppij, 1937.

Kraus, Herbert, ed. *Das Recht der Minderheiten.* Stilke's Rechtsbibliothek 57. Berlin: Georg Stilke, 1927.

Madajczyk, Czesław. "Dokumenty w sprawie politiyki narodowościowej władz polskich po przewrocie majowym." *Dzieje Najnowsze* 4 (1972): 137-69.

Ministerstwo Spraw Wewnętrznych. *Sprawozdanie z życia mniejszości narodowych za 1. kwart 1937 r.* Warsaw: Wydział Narodowościowy, 1937.

Oberschlesien im Genfer Vertrag. Breslau: Schlesische Zeitung, 1922.

Permanent Court of International Justice. *Publications de la Cour Permanente de Justice Internationale.* Series A/B. Leyden-Sijthoff, 1931—. #58, 60.

Piłsudski, Józef. *Erinnerungen und Dokumente.* 4 vols. Essen: Essener Verlagsanstalt, 1936.

———. *Pisma zbiorowa.* 10 vols. Warsaw, 1937-38.

Polish Acts of Atrocity against the German Minority in Poland. New York: German Library of Information, 1940.

The Polish and Non-Polish Populations of Poland: 1931 Census. Warsaw: Institute for the Study of Minority Problems, 1931.

Polish Foreign Ministry. *Official Documents concerning Polish-German and Polish-Soviet Relations.* London: Hutchinson, 1939.

Stresemann, Gustav. *Vermächtnis.* 3 vols. Ed. H. Bernhard. Berlin: Ullstein, 1932.

Wiesner, Rudolf. *Für Recht und Freiheit.* Berlin, 1941.

Winkler, Wilhelm. *Statistisches Handbuch der europäischen Nationalitäten.* Vienna: Wilh. Braumuller, 1931.

———. *Statistisches Handbuch des gesamten Deutschtums.* Berlin: Deutsche Rundschau, 1927.

Wybór źródeł do historii Polski, 1918-1944. Ed. J. Grzywna & M. Markowski. Kielce, 1977.

Memoirs

Auf den Strassen des Todes. Ed. F. Menn. Leipzig: Hase & Koehler, 1940.

Basedow, E., and P. Correns, eds. *Schicksalstunden—Unvergessliches aus schweren Tagen in Posen und Westpreussen.* Berlin: Decker's, 1924.

Beck, Józef. *Final Report.* New York: Robt. Speller, 1957.

Bickerich, Wilhelm. *Evangelisches Leben unter dem weissen Adler.* Poznań: Lutherverlag, 1925.

Breitinger, Hilarius. *Als Deutschenseelsorger in Posen und im Warthegua, 1934-45.* Mainz: Grunewald, 1984.

Curtius, Julius. *Sechs Jahre Minister der deutschen Republik.* Heidelberg: Carl Winter, 1948.

Dennoch: Erinnerungsheft für die deutschen Lehrer in Polen, 1919-1939. Ed. O. Schönbeck. Bromberg: DSV, 1940.

Eichler, Adolf. *Deutschtum im Schatten des Ostens.* Dresden: Meinhold, 1942.

Gerlach, Helmut von. *Der Zusammenbruch der deutschen Polenpolitik.* Berlin: Neues Vaterland, 1919.

Goerdeler, Oda. *Leben auf Grenzgut T.* Lüneburger Ostdeutsche Dokumentationen 1. Lüneburg: Nordostdeutsches Kulturwerk, 1983.

Hassell, Ulrich von. *Vom anderen Deutschland.* Zürich: Atlantikverlag, 1946.

Heda, Karl. "Die Diözese Kattowitz und die deutschen Katholiken in den Jahren 1925 bis 1939." *Archiv für schlesische Kirchengeschichte* 42 (1984): 51-58.

Heike, Otto. *Leben im deutsch-polnischen Spannungsfeld.* (Memoirs) Essen: Reimar Hobbing, 1989.

Hein, Gottfried. *Unser letzte Weg in Polen.* Posen: Lutherverlag, 1940.

Heyking, Ernst von. *Rechtfertigungsschrift des Landeshauptmannes der Provinz Posen.* Meseritz: Landeshauptverwaltung, 1919.

Kammel, Richard, ed. *Er hilft uns frei aus aller Not. Erlebnisberichte aus den Sep-tembertagen 1939.* Posen, 1940.

Kesik, Władysław. *Podziemny ogień: Walk o Górny Śląsk.* Warsaw, 1938.

Kessler, Harry. *Tagebücher, 1918-37.* Ed. W. Pfeiffer-Belli. Frankfurt: Insel, 1961.

Knospe, Franz. *Selbst-Schütz Ober-Schlesien.* Berlin, 1933.

Kolicz, Josef [J. Kołodziejczyk]. *Czas grozy.* Wspomnienie o tzw. "krwawy niedzieli bydgoskiej." Gdynia: Wyd.Morskie, 1959.

Lehfeldt, Walburg. *Gut Lehfelde.* Eine deutsche Geschichte, 1932-50. Wiesbaden: Limes, 1986.

Modrow, Hans Joachim. *Heimat an der Weichsel in Westpreussen 1920-1939 im "Korri-dorgebiet."* Reinhausen, 1967.

Müller, Ludolf. *Meine Ausweisung aus Polen.* Leipzig: Sächsische Verlagsanstalt, n.d.

Naczelna Rada Ludowa. *Beitrag zur Entstehung und Bethätigung des "Heimat-schützes" in den preussisch-polnischen Grenzgebieten.* Posen: Winiewicz, 1919.

Paetzold, Paul. *Wie Neutomischel polnisch wurde.* Berlin, 1928.

Piotrowski, A. *50 dni rządów Rady Robotników i Żółnierzy w Poznaniu.* Poznań: Kapel, 1919.

Ręgorowicz, Ludwik. *Wspomnienia śląskie i poznańskie z lat 1919-1934.* Opole: Inst. Śląski, 1976.

Reinhold, "Pfarrer." In *Aus polnisch-Oberschlesien.* Leipzig: Sächsische Verlags-gemeinschaft, n.d.

Rybka, Stanisław. *Zerwane pęta.* Berlin, n.d.

Rzepecki, Karol. *Oswobodzenie Poznania.* Poznań, 1923.

Schneider, Rudolf. *Gedenkbuch der evangelischen Kirche in Polnisch-Schlesien.* Posen: Lutherverlag, 1937.

Seeckt, Hans von. *Aus meinem Leben.* Ed. F. v. Rabenau. Leipzig: Hase & Koehler 1941.

Skiba, Mikolaj. *Szamotuły w powstaniu wielkopolskiem.* Szamotuły: Gazeta Szamo-tułska, 1923.

Sonnenberg, A.S. *Die Polenknute über Posen.* Berlin: Gersbach, 1920.

Tokarski, L., and J. Ziolek, eds. *Wspomnienia powstanców wielkopolskich.* Poznań: Wyd. Poznańskie, 1970.

Vogt, Dietrich. *Das Schiller-Gymnasium in Posen.* Lüneburg: Posener Stimmen, 1964.

Voss, Hermann. *Die unierte ev. Kirche in Polnisch-Schlesien.* Katowice, 1937.

Wittek, Erhard. *Der Marsch nach Lowitsch.* Erlebter Krieg 2. Berlin: Zentralverlag, 1942.

Wohlgemuth, Thea. *Das deutsche Gymnasium in Thorn zwischen den beiden Welt-kriegen.* Berlin: Berliner Buchdruckerei, 1963.

Zehn Jahre "Elternhilfe" in Posen-Pomerellen (1926-1936). Deutsche Vereinigung. Bromberg: Dittmann, 1936.

Zerener, Max. *Unter der weissen Adler–wie Posen polnisch wurde.* Berlin: Wilh, Greve, n.d.

Secondary Sources

Ahlers, Johannes. *Polen.* Berlin: Zentralverlag, 1935.

Albee, Parker. "American and Allied Policies at the Paris Peace Conference: The Drawing of the Polish-German Frontier." Ph.D. diss., Duke University, 1968.

Ammende, Ewald, ed. *Die Nationalitäten in den Staaten Europas*. Im Auftrage des Europäischen Nationalitäten-Kongresses. Vienna: Wilh. Braumuller, 1931.

Andrzejewski, Czesław. *Das Deutschtum in Westpolen*. Poznań: Pilczek, 1919.

Andrzejewski, Marek. "Polnische Literatur über den deutsch-polnischen Propagandakampf in den Jahren 1918-38." *Acta Poloniae Historica* 51 (1985): 83-100.

Aurich, Peter [Peter Nasarski]. *Der deutsch-polnische September 1939*. Munich: Günter Olzog, 1969.

Das Auslandsdeutschtum des Ostens. Ed. H. Rothfels. Auslandsstudien v. 7. Königsberg: Gräfe & Unzer, 1932.

Azcarate, Pedro de. *The League of Nations and National Minorities*. Washington, D.C.: Carnegie Endowment for International Peace, 1945.

Bahr, Richard. *Volk jenseits der Grenzen*. Hamburg: Hanseatische Verlagsanstalt, 1933.

Ballerstedt, K. *Gegenwartsfragen der ländlichen Siedlung in Posen und Pomerellen*. Königsberg: Institut für osteuropäische Wirtschaft, 1938.

Balogh, Arthur von. *Der internationale Schutz der Minderheiten*. Munich: Südost-Verlag, 1928.

Der befreite Osten. Ed. M.H. Boehm and K.v. Loesch. Berlin: Kurt Hofmann, 1940.

Benes, Vaclav, and Norman Pounds. *Poland*. London: Ernest Benn, 1970.

Biały, Franciszek. *Górnośląski Związek Przemysłowców Górniczo-Hutniczych 1914-1932*. Wrocław: Ossoliński, 1967.

———. *Niemieckie ochotnicze formacje zbrojne na Śląsku, 1918-23*. Katowice: Śląski Inst. Naukowy, 1975.

Bierschenk, Theodor. "Die deutschen politischen Organisationen in Polen, 1919-39." *Jahrbuch Weichsel-Warthe* 32 (1986): 22-29.

———. *Die deutsche Volksgruppe in Polen, 1934-9*. Beiheft zum Jahrbuch der Albertus-Universität Königsberg X. Würzburg: Hölzner, 1954.

———. "Die polnischen Richtlinien zur Behandlung der deutschen Volksgruppe vom 9.7.1936." *Zeitschrift für Ostforschung* 17 (1968): 534-38.

———. "Die Vereine deutscher Hochschüler in Polen, 1922-39." *Jahrbuch Weichsel-Warthe* 27 (1981): 89-99.

Blanke, Richard. "The German Minority in Inter-War Poland and German Foreign Policy: Some Reconsiderations." *Journal of Contemporary History* 25 (1990): 87-102.

———. *Prussian Poland in the German Empire, 1870-1900*. Boulder, Co.: East European Quarterly, 1981.

———. "Upper Silesia 1921: The Case for Subjective Nationality." *Canadian Review of Studies in Nationalism* 2 (1975): 241-60.

Bloch, Walter. *Die deutschen Genossenschaften in Westpolen*. Poznań, 1938.

Boehm, Max-Hildebert. *Das eigenständige Volk*. Berlin, 1930.

———. *Europa Irredenta*. Berlin: Reimar Hobbing, 1923.

———. "Die Reorganisation der Deutschtumsarbeit nach dem 1. Weltkrieg." *Ostdeutsche Wissenschaft* 5 (1958): 9-34.

Boelitz, Otto. *Das Grenz- und Auslanddeutschtum*. Munich: R. Oldenbourg, 1926.

Böhm, Hermann. "Die Nationalitäten- und Minderheitenpolitik der Republik Polen (1918-1939) in der polnischen Geschichtswissenschaft seit 1945." Manuscript, 1974.

Bohmann, Alfred. *Menschen und Grenzen*. Strukturwandel der deutschen Bevölkerung im polnischen Staats- und Verwaltungsbereich 1. Cologne: Wissenschaft und Politik, 1969.

Bostick, Darwin. "Diplomacy in Defeat: Germany and the Polish Boundary Dispute in 1919." *Historical Reflections* 4 (1977): 171-89.

Breyer, Richard. *Das Deutsche Reich und Polen, 1932-7.* Marburger Ostforschungen 3. Würzburg: Hölzner, 1955.

———. "Deutsche und polnische Förderung des Auslandsvolkstums, 1919-1939." *Jahrbuch Weichsel-Warthe* 31 (1985): 34-42.

———. "Die deutsche Volksgruppe in Polen und der Kriegsausbruch 1939." *Westpreussen-Jahrbuch* 19 (1969): 5-13.

———. Polnischer Parlamentarismus und Nationalitätenfrage." In *Die Krise des Parlamentarismus in Ostmitteleuropa zwischen den beiden Weltkriegen,* ed.H.-E. Volkmann, pp. 64-78. Marburg: Herder Institut, 1967.

———. "Die Septemberereignisse 1939 in polnischer Sicht." *Jahrbuch Weichsel-Warthe* 15 (1969): 28-35.

Broszat, Martin. "Aussen- und innenpolitische Aspekte der preussisch-deutschen Minderheitenpolitik in der Ära Stresemann." In *Politische Ideologien und Nationalstaatliche Ordnung,* ed. K. Kluxen and W. Mommsen, pp. 393-445. Munich: R. Oldenbourg, 1968.

———. "JDP und DV in Posen-Pomerellen." *Gutachten des Instituts für Zeitgeschichte* 1 (1958): 404-7.

Brown, MacAlister. "The Third Reich's Mobilization of the German 5th Column in Eastern Europe." *Journal of Central European Affairs* 19 (1959): 128-48.

Bruns, Carl Georg. *Gesammelte Schriften zur Minderheitenfrage.* Ed. M.H. Boehm. Berlin: Carl Heymanns, 1933.

———. *Staatsangehörigkeitswechsel und Option im Friedensvertrag von Versailles.* Berlin: De Gruyter, 1921.

Budding, Carl. *Der polnische Korridor als europäisches Problem.* 2d ed. Danzig: Deutscher Verlagsges., 1933.

Buell, Raymond. *Poland: Key to Europe.* New York: Knopf, 1939.

Burleigh, Michael. *Germany Turns eastwards: A Study of "Ostforschung" in the Third Reich.* Cambridge: Cambridge Univ. Press, 1988.

Cambridge History of Poland. Vol. 2. Ed. W. Reddaway et al. Cambridge: Cambridge Univ. Press, 1951.

Carsten, Francis. *Britain and the Weimar Republic.* New York: Schocken, 1984.

Chałasiński, Józef. *Antagonizm polsko-niemiecki w osadzie fabrycznej "Kopalnia" na Górnym Śląsku.* Warsaw: Dom Książki Polskiej, 1935.

Chodera, Jan. *Literatura niemiecka o Polsce w latach 1918-39.* Katowice: Śląsk, 1969.

Chojnowski, Andrzej. *Koncepcje polityki narodowościowej rządów polskich w latach 1921-1939.* Polska myśl polityczna XIX i XX wieku 3. Wrocław: Ossolineum/ PAN, 1979.

Cienciala, Anna. "German Propaganda for the Revision of the Polish-German Frontier in Danzig and the Corridor." *Antemurale* 20 (1976): 77-129.

———. "The Significance of the Declaration of Non-Aggression of 1/26/34 in Polish-German and International Relations." *East European Quarterly* 1 (1967): 1-30.

Cienciala, Anna, and Titus Komarnicki. *From Versailles to Locarno: Keys to Polish Foreign Policy, 1919-25.* Lawrence: University Press of Kansas, 1984.

Cleinow, Georg. *Der Verlust der Ostmark.* Berlin: Volk & Reich, 1934.

Coester, Robert. *Die Loslösung Posens.* Berlin: Stilke, 1921.

Conze, Werner. *Polnische Nation und deutsche Politik im 1. Weltkrieg.* Cologne: Bohlau, 1958.

Cygański, Mirosław. *Hitlerowskie organizacje dywersyne w województwie śląskim 1931-36.* Katowice: Śląsk, 1971.

———. *Volksbund w służbie III. Rzeszy, 1933-38.* Opole: Inst. Śląski, 1968.

———. "Wpływ rewizjonistycznej polityki rządów Republiki Weimarskiej na mniejszość niemiecką w Polsce (1919-32)." *Najnowsze Dzieje Polski* 10 (1966): 157-67.

———. *Zawsze przeciwko Polsce.* Kariera Otto Ulitza. Warsaw: Zach. Agencja Prasowa, 1966.

———. *Z dziejów Volksbundu (1921-1932).* Opole: Inst. Śląski, 1966.

Czech, Joseph. *Die Bevölkerung Polens.* Breslau: Marcus, 1932.

Czubiński, Antoni. "Das Deutschlandbild der Polen 1918-39—zu einem Buch von Frank Golczewski." *Studia Historica Slavo-Germanica* 7 (1978): 135-49.

———. *Polska odrodzona.* Poznań: Wyd. Poznańskie, 1982.

Dąbrowski, Roman. *Mniejszość niemiecka w Polsce i jej działalność społeczno-kulturalna w latach 1918-39.* Szczecin: Wyższa Szkoła Pedagogiczna, 1982.

Datner, Szymon. "Z Dziejów dywersji niemieckiej w czasie kampanii wrześniowej." *Wojskowy Przegląd Historyczny* 4 (1959): 148-80.

Debicki, Roman. *The Foreign Policy of Poland, 1919-39.* New York: Praeger, 1962.

De Jong, Louis. *Die deutsche 5. Kolonne im 2. Weltkrieg.* (translated from English) Quellen und Darstellungen zur Zeitgeschichte, v. 4. Stuttgart: DVA, 1959.

Denne, Ludwig. *Das Danzig-Problem in der deutschen Aussenpolitik.* Bonn: Ludwig Rohlscheid, 1959.

Der deutsche Imperialismus in Polen 1918 bis 1939. Studien zur Geschichte der deutsch-polnischen Beziehungen 2. Rostock: Pieck Univ., 1978.

Deutschland und Polen. Ed. A. Brackmann. Munich: R. Oldenbourg, 1933.

Deutschland und Polen von der national-sozialistischen Machtergreifung bis zum Ende des zweiten Weltkrieges. Ed. W. Jacobmeyer. Schriftenreihe des Eckart-Instituts für Internationale Schulbuchforschung, v. 22/IX. Braunschweig, 1986.

Die deutsch-polnischen Beziehungen 1919-32. Ed. W. Jacobmeyer. Schriftenreihe des Eckart-Instituts für Internationale Schulbuchforschung, Braunschweig, 1985.

Dibelius, Otto. *Wie erfüllen die Polen ihre feierlich übernommene Pflicht, die evangelischen Minderheiten zu schützen?* Berlin: Ev. Presseverband, 1921.

Długajczyk, Edward. *Sanacja śląska 1926-39.* Katowice: Śląsk, 1983.

Dobbermann, Paul. *Die deutsche Schule im ehemals preussischen Teilgebiet Polens.* Posen: Hist. Ges. für Posen, 1925.

Doose, Günther. *Die separatische Bewegung in Oberschlesien nach dem 1. Weltkrieg.* Wiesbaden: Harrassowitz, 1987.

Doss, Kurt. *Zwischen Weimar und Warschau: Ulrich Rauscher, Deutscher Gesandter in Polen, 1922-30.* Düsseldorf: Droste, 1984.

Drozdowski, Marian. "The National Minorities in Poland, 1918-39." *Acta Poloniae Historica* 22 (1970): 226-51.

———. *Polityka gospodarcza rządu polskiego, 1936-9.* Warsaw: PWN, 1963.

Dworecki, Zbigniew. *Problem niemiecki w świadomości narodowo-politycznej spo-*

łeczeństwa polskiego województw zachodnich rzeczpospolitej 1922-39. Poznań: Univ. Mickiewicza, 1981.

Dyboski, Roman. *Poland.* New York: Scribner, 1933.

Dziewanowski, Marian. *Poland in the 20th Century.* New York: Columbia University Press, 1977.

Eichstadt, Kurt. "Selbsthilfe der deutschen Minderheit in Polen—Erinnerungen." *Westpreussen-Jahrbuch* 14 (1964): 51-55.

Falęcki, Tomasz. *Niemieckie szkolnictwo mniejszościowe na Górnym Śląsku w latach 1922-39.* Katowice: Śląski Instytut Naukowy, 1970.

Fasbinder, Horst. "Das Weichselkorridorgebiet im Versailler Vertrag." Diss., Univ. of Würzburg, 1931.

Fechner, Helmut. *Deutschland und Polen.* Ostdeutsche Beiträge 27. Würzburg: Hölzner, 1964.

Feldman, Józef. *Problem polsko-niemiecki w dziejach.* Rev. ed. *Antagonizm,* 1934. Katowice: Instytut Śląski, 1946.

Fiedor, Karol, Janusz Sobczak, and Wojciech Wrzesiński. "Obraz Polaka w Niemczech i Niemca w Polsce w latach międzywojennych." *Sobotka* 2 (1978): 163-89.

Fink, Carole. "Defender of Minorities: Germany in the League of Nations, 1926-33." *Central European History* 5 (1972): 330-57.

———. "Stresemann's Minority Policies, 1924-9." *Journal of Contemporary History* 14 (1979): 403-22.

Firnhaber, W. *Die Wahrheit über die Klagen Polens.* Bromberg: Dittmann, 1919.

Flascha, Leo. "Der Schutz der erworbenen Rechte im deutsch polnischen Abkommen über Oberschlesien vom 15. Mai 1922." Diss., Univ. of Breslau, 1937.

Fuchs, Werner. *Der neue Polenspiegel.* Selbstzeugnisse polnischer Eroberungswillens. Berlin: Deutscher Ostmarkenverein, 1930.

Fuks, Rafał. *Na przykład Kohnert.* Gdynia: Wyd. Morskie, 1962.

Gąsiorowski, Zygmunt. "Did Piłsudski Attempt to Initiate a Preventive War in 1933?" *Journal of Modern History* 27 (1955): 135-51.

———. "Stresemann and Poland after Locarno." *Journal of Central European Affairs* 18 (1958): 292-317.

———. "Stresemann and Poland before Locarno." *Journal of Central European Affairs* 18 (1958): 25-47.

Gentzen, Felix-Heinrich. "Deutsche Stiftung—Tajna instytucja rządu niemieckiego do organizowania 5. kolumny." *Przegąd Zachodni* 17, no. 2 (1961): 295-303.

———. "Die Legende vom 'Bromberger Blutsonntag' und die deutsche 5. Kolonne in Polen." In *September 1939.* Ed. B. Spiru, pp. 41-82. East Berlin: Rütten & Loening, 1959.

———. "Rola rządu niemieckiego w dziele budowy niemieckich organizacji mniejszościowych na terenach zwroconych Polsce (1919-1922)." *Najnowsze Dzieje Polski* 10 (1966): 127-46.

———. "Die Rolle des DOV bei der Bildung einer 5. Kolonne in Polen." In *Der deutsche Imperialismus und der 2. Weltkrieg,* 2:199-215. East Berlin: Rütten & Loening, 1961.

Gersdorff, Gero von. *20 Jahre Front gegen Polenterror.* Berlin: Grenze und Ausland, 1940.

Gerson, Louis. *Woodrow Wilson and the Rebirth of Poland, 1914-20.* New Haven: Yale Univ. Press, 1953.

Golczewski, Frank. *Das Deutschlandbild der Polen, 1918-39.* Düsseldorf: Droste, 1974.

———. *Polnisch-jüdische Beziehungen, 1881-1922.* Wiesbaden: Steiner, 1981.

Goodhart, Arthur. *Poland and the Minority Peoples.* New York: Brentano, 1920.

Gostyński, Karol. "Przewrót hitlerowski w Niemczech i Niemcy w Polsce." *Sprawy Narodowościowe* 10 (1936): 22-39, 197-222.

Grabski, Stanisław. *Państwo Narodowe.* Lwów, 1929.

Grot, Zdisław. "Powstanie wielkopolskie." *Studia i Materiały do Dziejów Wielkopolski i Pomorza* 5 (1960): 77-121.

Grünberg, Karol. *Nazi-Front Schlesien.* Katowice: Śląsk, 1963.

———. *Niemcy i ich organizacji polityczne w Polsce międzywojennej.* Warsaw: Wiedza Powszechna, 1970.

Grześ, Bolesław, Jerzy Kozłowski, and Aleksander Kramski. *Niemcy w Poznańskiem wobec polityki germanizacyjnej 1815-1920.* Ed. L. Treciakowski. Poznań: Inst. Zachodni, 1976.

Grzyb, Mieczysław. *Narodowościowo-polityczne aspekty przemian stosunków własnościowych i kadrowych w górnośląskim przemyśle, 1922-39.* Katowice: Univ. Śląski, 1978.

Günther, O.E. *Die Minderheitenerklärungen vom 5.11.1937 im Urteil der polnischen Presse.* Breslau: Osteuropa-Institut, 1937.

Gütermann, Christoph. *Das Minderheitenschutzverfahren des Völkerbundes.* Berlin: Düncker & Humblot, 1979.

Haase, Berthold. *Der deutsch-polnische Staatsvertrag uber Staatsangehörigkeits- und Optionsfragen.* Berlin: Carl Heymann, 1925.

Hahn, A. *Polnische Kampfverbände.* Berlin: Bund Deutscher Osten, 1938.

Hahn, Gunther. "Die deutsche Publizistik im Kampf um Oberschlesien." Diss., Berlin Univ., 1940.

Hahn, Wichard. "Die Arbeitslosigkeit der deutschen Volksgruppe in Ost-Oberschlesien." *Deutsches Archiv für Landes- und Volksforschung* 2 (1938): 555-74.

Halecki, Oscar. *A History of Poland.* 2d ed. New York: Roy, 1956.

Hansen, Ernest. *Polens Drang nach dem Westen.* Berlin: Koehler, 1927.

Harrier, Alexander von. "Beitrag zur Geschichte des deutschen Grossgrundbesitzes im Lande der Netze und Warthe." Manuscript, 1971.

Harrington, Joseph. "The League of Nations and the Upper Silesia Boundary Dispute." *Polish Review* 23 (1978): 86-101.

———. "Upper Silesia and the Paris Peace Conference." *Polish Review* 19 (1974): 25-45.

Hauser, Przemysław. *Mniejszość niemiecka w województwie pomorskim w latach 1920-39.* Wrocław: Ossolinski, 1981.

———. *Niemcy wobec sprawy polskiej, 1918-9.* Poznań: Univ. Mickiewicza, 1984.

Heidelck, Friedrich. *Die deutschen Ansiedlungen in Westpreussen und Posen in den ersten zwölf Jahren der polnischen Herrschaft.* Breslau: Priebatsch, 1934.

———. "Das Deutschtum in Pomerellen und Posen." *Deutsche Blätter in Polen* 4 (1927): 221-58.

———. *Das Deutschtum in Westpreussen und Posen.* 2d ed. Berlin: Deutscher Schutzbund, 1935.

————. "Die Stellung des Deutschtums in Polen." *Deutsche Blätter in Polen,* 6 no. 2 (1929): 49-104.

Heike, Otto. "Die deutsche Arbeiterbewegung in Polen." In *Ostdeutschlands Arbeiterbewegung,* ed. W. Matull, pp. 507-45. Würzburg: Hölzner, 1973.

————. *Die deutsche Minderheit in Polen bis 1939.* Leverkusen, 1985.

————. "Die Deutsche Sozialistische Arbeitspartei Polens." *Zeitschrift für Ostforschung* 29 (1980): 224-49.

————. *Das Deutschtum in Polen 1918-1939.* Bonn, 1955.

Heit, Siegfried. "National Minorities and their Effect on Polish Foreign Relations." *Nationalities Papers* 8 (1980): 9-19.

Hemmerling, Zygmunt. *Ruch ludowy w Wielkopolsce, 1919-39.* Warsaw: Ludowa Spółdzielnia Wydawnicza, 1971.

Hesse, J.C. "National Minorities in Europe VII: The Germans in Poland." *Slavonic and East European Review* 16 (1937): 93-101.

Hiden, John. "The Weimar Republic and the Problem of the *Auslanddeutschen.*" *Journal of Contemporary History* 12 (1977): 273-89.

Höltje, Christian. *Die Weimarer Republik und das Ostlocarno-Problem, 1919-34.* Würzburg: Hölzner, 1958.

Horak, Stephen. *Poland and Her National Minorities, 1919-39.* New York: Vantage, 1961.

Irredentism and Provocation: A Contribution to the History of the German Minority in Poland. Ed. A. Leśniewski. Poznań: Wyd. Zachodni, 1960.

Iwanicki, Mieczysław. *Polityka oświatowa w szkolnictwie niemieckim w Polsce w latach 1918-39.* Warsaw: PWN, 1978.

Jablonowski, Horst. "Probleme der deutsch-polnischen Beziehungen zwischen den beiden Weltkriegen." *Jahrbuch der Albertus-Universität zu Königsberg* 19 (1969): 27-61.

Jacobsen, Hans-Adolf. *National-sozialistische Aussenpolitik, 1933-8.* Frankfurt: Alfred Metzner, 1968.

Jaeckel, Maria. "Die kultur- und vokspolitische Wirksamkeit der deutschen Presse in Ostoberschlesien 1919-1932." Diss., Univ. of Cologne, 1933.

Janowsky, Oscar. *Nationalities and National Minorities.* New York: Macmillan, 1945.

Jastrzębski, Włodziemierz. "Czy Selbstschütz to V kolumna?" *Wojskowy Przegląd Historyczny* 10, no. 4 (1965): 435-37.

————. *Der Bromberger Blutsonntag: Legende und Wirklichkeit.* Poznań: Instytut Zachodni. 1990.

Jaworski, Rudolf. "Deutsch-polnische Feindbilder 1919-32." *Internationale Schulbuchforschung* 6 (1984): 140-56.

Jędrzejewicz, Wacław. "The Polish Plan for a 'Preventive War' against Germany in 1933." *Polish Review* 11 (1966): 62-91.

Jeżowa, Kazimiera. *Die Bevölkerungs- und Wirtschaftsverhältnisse im westlichen Polen.* Danzig: Towarzystwo Przymysłów Nauk i Sztuki, 1933.

Junckerstorff, Kurt. *Das Schulrecht der deutschen Minderheit in Polnisch-Oberschlesien nach dem Genfer Abkommen.* Berlin: Reimar Hobbing, 1939.

————. *Die Völkerbundsgarantie des Minderheitenrechts.* The Hague: Nijhoff, 1930.

Junghann, Otto. *Das Minderheitenschützverfahren vor dem Völkerbund.* Tübingen: Mohr, 1934.

Kaczmarek, Zygmunt. "Endecja wielkopolska wobec problemu niemieckiego i kwestii mniejszościowej w latach 1926-34." *Przegląd Zachodni* (1976): 228-38.

Kaeckenbeeck, Georges. *The International Experiment of Upper Silesia*. Oxford, 1942.

Kaltenbach, Frederick. *Self-Determination 1919*. London: Jarolds, 1938.

Kammel, Richard. *Kriegsschicksale der deutschen evangelischen Gemeinden in Posen und Westpreussen*. Berlin: Ev. Bund, 1940.

Karzel, Karl. *Die deutsche Landwirtschaft in Posen in der Zeit zwischen den beiden Weltkriegen*. Wissenschaftliche Beiträge zur Geschichte und Landeskunde Ost-Mitteleuropas 51. Marburg: Herder-Institut, 1961.

Katelbach, Tadeusz. *Niemcy współczesne wobec zagadnień narodowościowych*. Warsaw: Instytut Badań Spraw Narodowościowych, 1932.

Kauder, Viktor, ed. *Das Deutschtum in Polen*. 5 vols. Plauen: Günther Wolff, 1932.

Kaufmann, Erich. *Die Rechtsverhältnisse der an Polen abgetretene Ostmark*. Berlin: Grenzboten, 1919.

Keitsch, Frank. *Das Schicksal der deutschen Volksgruppe in Ostoberschlesien in den Jahren 1922-1939*. Dülmen: Laumann, 1982.

―――. *Die sprachlichen Verhältnisse im oberschlesischen Teil der Wojewodschaft Schlesien und das deutsche Minderheitenschulwesen in der Zwischenkriegszeit*. Ratingen: Haus Oberschlesien, 1977.

Kellermann, Volkmar. *Schwarzer Adler, weisser Adler: Die Polenpolitik der Weimarer Republik*. Cologne: Markus, 1970.

Keyser, Erich. "Der Deutschtumsverlust in Westpreussen 1918 bis 1939." *Ostdeutsche Wissenschaft* 8 (1961): 63-79.

―――. *Geschichte des deutschen Weichsellandes*. Leipzig: S. Hirzel, 1939.

―――. *Der Kampf um die Weichsel*. Stuttgart: DVA, 1926.

―――. *Westpreussen*. 2d ed. Aus der deutschen Geschichte des Weichsellandes. Würzburg: Holzner, 1967.

Kierski, Kazimierz. *Ochrona praw mniejszości w Polsce*. Poznań, 1933.

―――. *Prawa mniejszości niemieckiej w Polsce*. Poznań: ZOKZ, 1923.

Kimmich, Christoph. *Germany and the League of Nations*. Chicago: Univ. of Chicago Press, 1976.

Kleindienst, Alfred, & Oskar Wagner. *Der Protestantismus in der Republik Polen, 1918-39*. Marburg: Herder Institut, 1985.

Klessmann, Christoph. "Osteuropaforschung und Lebensraumpolitk im 3. Reich." *Aus Politik und Zeitgeschehen*, Feb. 18, 1984, pp. 33-45.

Klusak, Gustav. "Die Welage in Posen." *Jahrbuch Weichsel-Warthe* 32 (1986): 62-71; 33 (1987): 37ff.

Koehl, Robert. *RKFDV: German Resettlement and Population Policy, 1939-45*. Cambridge, Mass.: Harvard Univ. Press, 1957.

Koenigsfeld, Ernst. *Der Versailler Vertrag und Oberschlesien*. Koethen, 1928.

Kohnert, Hans. "Agrarreformstatistik aus Polen." *Nation und Staat* 12 (1939): 617-22.

―――. "Die Betriebsverhältnisse der deutschen Bauernwirtschaften in der ehemaligen Provinz Westpreussen." Diss., Techniscke Hochschule Danzig, 1932.

Kohte, Wolfgang. "Deutsche landesgeschichtliche Forschung im Posener Land." *Ostdeutsche Wissenschaft* 8 (1961): 96ff.

258   Bibliography

Komar, Stanisław. *Górnośląska konwencja genewska pomiędzy Polską i Niemcami, 1922-1937*. Polski i Śląsk 32. Katowice: Inst. Śląski, 1937.

Komjathy, Anthony, and Rebecca Stockwell. *German Minorities and the Third Reich*. New York: Holmes & Meier, 1980.

Korbel, Josef. *Poland between East and West*. Princeton, N.J.: Princeton Univ. Press, 1963.

Korowicz, Marek. *Górnośląska ochrona mniejszości, 1922-1937*. Katowice, 1937.

Korzec, Paweł. "Der Block der Nationalen Minderheiten im Parlamentarismus Polens des Jahres 1922." *Zeitschrift für Ostforschung* 24 (1975): 193-220.

———. "Polen und der Minderheitenschutzvertrag (1919-1934)." *Jahrbücher für Geschichte Osteuropas* 22 (1974): 515-55.

———. "Der zweite Block der nationalen im Parlamentarismus Polens 1927-1928." *Zeitschrift für Ostforschung* 26 (1977): 76-116.

Kotowski, Wojciech. "Die Lage der deutschen Katholiken in Polen, 1919-33." *Zeitschrift für Ostforschung* 39 (1990): 39-67.

Kowalak, Tadeusz. *Prasa niemiecka w Polsce, 1918-39*. Warsaw: Książka i Wiedza, 1971.

———. *Spółdzielczość niemiecka na Pomorzu, 1920-38*. Warsaw: Książka i Wiedza, 1965.

———. *Zagraniczne kredyty dla Niemców w Polsce, 1919-39*. Warsaw: Książka i Wiedza, 1972.

Koza, August. "Das Minderheitenschutz in der polnischen Verfassung und Verwaltung." Diss., Univ. of Breslau, 1934.

Kozicki, Stanisław. *Sprawa granic Polski na konferencji pokojowey w Paryżu*. Warsaw: Perzynski/Niklewicz, 1921.

Krasuski, Jerzy. *Stosunki polsko-niemieckie, 1919-1925*. Studium Niemcoznawsze Instytutu Zachodniego 2. Poznań: Instytut Zachodni, 1962.

———. *Stosunki polsko-niemieckie, 1926-1932*. Poznań: Instytut Zachodni, 1964.

Krekeler, Norbert. "Die deutsche Politik in Polen und die Revisionspolitik des deutschen Reiches, 1919-33." In *Die Vertreibung der Deutschen aus dem Osten*, ed. W. Benz, pp. 16-28. Frankfurt: Fischer, 1985.

———. *Revisionsanspruch und geheime Ostpolitik der Weimarer Republik*. Stuttgart: DVA, 1973.

Kroll, Vincent. "Die Genfer Konvention betreffend Oberschlesien vom 15.5.1922." Diss., Univ. of Cologne, 1956.

Krysiński, Alfons. "Tendencje rozwojowe ludności Polski pod względem narodowościowym i wyznań w dobie powojennej." *Sprawy Narodowościowe* 5 (1931): 16-45.

Kubiak, Stanisław. *Niemcy i Wielkopolska, 1918-1919*. Dzieje polskiej granicy zachodniej 4. Poznań: Instytut Zachodni, 1969.

———. "Rady robotniczo-żołnierskie a powstanie wielkopolskie 1918-19." *Studia i Materiały do Dziejów Wielkopolski i Pomorza* 5 (1960): 53-75.

Kucner, Alfred. "Kilka uwag o polityce mniejszości niemieckiej w Polsce." *Przegląd Zachodni* 13, no. 6 (1957): 350-55.

———. "Mniejszość niemiecka w Polsce i dążenie rządu niemieckiego do utrzymania jej stanu osiadania w b. zaborze pruskim." *Przegląd Zachodni* 14, no. 4 (1958): 272-305.

Kuhn, Walter. "Die Berufsgliederung der Deutschen in Polen nach der Zählung von 1921." *Deutsche Monatshefte in Polen* 1 (1935): 435-63.

------. "Das Deutschtum in Polen und sein Schicksal in Kriegs- und Nach-kriegszeit." In *Osteuropa-Handbuch Polen*, ed. W. Markert, pp. 138-64. Cologne: Bohlau, 1959.

------. "Zahl und Siedlungsweise der Deutschen in Polen 1931." *Deutsche Monatshefte in Polen* 4 (1937): 143-60.

Kulski, W.W. *Germany and Poland*. Syracuse, N.Y.: Syracuse Univ. Press, 1976.

Kutrzeba, Stanisław. *Kongres, Traktat, i Polska*. Warsaw: Gebethner & Wolff, 1919.

Łączewski, Jan. "Eduard Pant—sylwetka śląskiego niemca-antyfaszysty." *Studia Śląskie* 43 (1984): 229-43.

Laeuen, Harald. *Polnisches Zwischenspiel*. Berlin: Hans von Hugo, 1940.

Lamla, Joseph. *Der Aufstand in Posen*. 2d ed. Berlin: Carl Heymanns, 1919.

Landau, Zbigniew, and Jerzy Tomaszewski. *Wirtschaftsgeschichte Polens im 19. und 20. Jahrhundert*. East Berlin: Akademie, 1986.

Lapter, Karol. *Pakt Piłsudski-Hitler*. Warsaw: Książka i Wiedza, 1962.

Laubert, Manfred. *Deutsch oder slawisch—Kämpfe und Leiden des Ostdeutschtums*. Berlin: Deutscher Ostbund, 1928.

------. *Nationalität und Volkswille im preussischen Osten*. Breslau: Ferd. Hirt, 1925.

Lemberg, Eugen. "Zur Geschichte der deutschen Volksgruppen in Ost-Mittel-europa." *Zeitschrift für Ostforschung* 1 (1952): 321-45.

Lemberg, Hans. "Polnische Konzeptionen für ein neues Polen in der Zeit vor 1918." In *Staatsgründungen und Nationalitätsprinzip*, ed. T. Schieder. Munich, 1974.

Lippelt, Helmut. "Politische Sanierung—zur deutschen Politik gegenüber Polen, 1925-6." *Vierteljahrshefte für Zeitgeschichte* 19 (1971): 323-73.

Loesch, Karl von. *Die Verlustliste des Deutschtums in Polen*. Berlin: Juncker & Dünnhaupt, 1940.

Loessner, Adolf. *Der Abfall Posens 1918/9 im polnischen Schrifttum*. Ostland-Schriften 6. Danzig: Deutsche Verlagsges., 1933.

Lossowski, Piotr. *Zbrojny czyn ludu Wielkopolski (1918-19)*. Warsaw: PZWZ, 1970.

Lück, Kurt, ed. *Marsch der Deutschen in Polen*. Der Deutsche Osten 2. Berlin: Grenze und Ausland, 1940.

------, ed. *Volksdeutsche Soldaten under Polens Fahnen*. Der Deutsche Osten 3. Berlin: Grenze und Ausland, 1940.

Lukas, Richard. *The Forgotten Holocaust: Poles under German Occupation*. Lexington: Univ. Press of Kentucky, 1986.

Łukasiewicz, Witold. "Rady robotnicze, żółnierskie, i chłopskie w Wielkopolsce i na Pomorzu gdańskim w latach 1918-20." *Rocznik Gdański* 17-18 (1958-59): 5-56.

Lundgreen-Nielsen, Kay. *The Polish Problem at the Paris Peace Conference*. Odense: Odense Univ. Press, 1979.

Lutman, Roman. "Oblicze Śląska." *Strażnica Zachodnia* 13 (1937): 17-34.

Macartney, C.A. *National States and National Minorities*. Oxford: Oxford Univ. Press, 1934.

Macartney, C.A., and A.W. Palmer. *Independent Eastern Europe*. London: Macmillan, 1962.

Machray, Robert. *The Poland of Piłsudski*. London: Allen & Unwin, 1936.

————. *The Problem of Upper Silesia*. London: George Unwin, 1945.

McKale, Donald. *The Swastika outside Germany*. Kent, Ohio: Kent State Univ. Press, 1977.

Madajczyk, Czesław. *Burżuazyno-obszarnicza reforma rolna w Polsce (1918-1939)*. Warsaw: Książka i Wiedza, 1956.

Majchrowski, Jacek. "Problem mniejszości narodowych w myśli polityczney Obozu Zjednoczenia Narodowego." *Studia Historyczne* 24 (1981): 423-40.

Makowski, Edmund. *Kształtowanie się stosunków społeczno-politycznych w Wielkopolsce, 1926-39*. Poznań: PWN, 1979.

Mann, Fritz, ed. *Auf den Strassen des Todes*. Leipzig, 1940.

Martin, Gottfried [Richard Kammel]. *Brennende Wunden*. 2d ed. Tatsachenberichte über die Notlage der evangelischen Deutschen in Polen. Berlin: Eckhart, 1939.

Mauersberg, Stanisław. *Szkolnictwo powszechne dla mniejszości narodowych w Polsce w latach 1918-1939*. Wrocław: Ossoliński, 1968.

Meissner, Lucjan. *Niemieckie organizacje antyfaszystowskie w Polsce, 1933-9*. Warsaw: Książka i Wiedza, 1973.

Mendelssohn, Ezra. *The Jews of East-Central Europe between the Wars*. Bloomington, Ind.: Indiana Univ. Press, 1983.

Mense, Traugott. "Die nationale Aufgabe der deutschen politischen Tagespresse in Westpreussen." Diss., Berlin Univ., 1940.

Meyer, Arnold Oskar. "Eindrücke von der schlesisch-polnischen Grenze." In *Auslanddeutschtum und evangelische Kirche*, pp. 170-88. Munich: Chr. Kaiser, 1933.

Meyer, Heinz. *Das Recht der religiösen Minderheiten in Polen*. Berlin: Walter Rothschild, 1933.

Micewski, Andrzej. *Z geografii politycznej II Rzeczypolspolitej*. Warsaw: Znak, 1966.

Michejda, Władysław. *Stosunki w ewangelickim kościele unijnym na polskim Górnym Śląsku*. Katowice: Tow. Polaków Ewang., 1935.

Michowicz, Waldemar. *Walka dyplomacji polskiej przeciwko traktatowi mniejszościowemu w Lidze Narodów w 1934 r.* Łódź: Tow. Naukowe, 1963.

Moczulski, Leszek. "Aspekty politycznej i tło operacyjne dywersji niemieckiej w Bydgoszczy." *Przegląd Zachodni* 17, no. 3 (1963): 61-91.

Modrow, Hans Joachim. "Die deutsche Landwirtschaft in Pomerellen, 1920-39 und ihr Landbund Weichselgau innerhalb der deutschen Volksgruppe." Manuscript, 1969.

Mornik, Stanislaus [Erich Jaensch]. *Polens Kampf gegen seine nichtpolnischen Volksgruppen*. Berlin: Walter de Gruyter, 1931.

Morrow, Ian. *The Peace Settlement in the German-Polish Borderlands*. Oxford: Condon, 1936.

Mroczko, Marian. *Polska myśl zachodnia, 1918-1939*. Poznań: Inst. Zachodni, 1986.

————. *Związek Obrony Kresów Zachodnich 1921-1934*. Gdańsk: Wyd. Morskie, 1977.

Müller, Ludolf. *Die unierte evangelische Kirche in Posen-Westpreussen under der polnischen Gewaltherrschaft*. Leipzig: Gustav-Adolf-Stiftung, 1925.

Nachbarn seit tausend Jahren. Ed. R. Breyer, P. Nasarski, and J. Piekalkiewicz. Mainz: Hase u. Koehler, 1976.

Nasarski, Peter. *Deutsche Jugendbewegung und Jugendarbeit in Polen, 1919-39*. Ostdeutsche Beiträge 6. Würzburg: Hölzner, 1957.

Newman, Karl. *European Democracy between the Wars.* South Bend, Ind.: Notre Dame Univ. Press, 1971.

Niemcy i Polska. Lwów: Pol. Tow. Hist., 1934.

Nordblom, Pia. "Dr Eduard Pant." *Oberschlesisches Jahrbuch* 3 (1987): 112-45.

Noszczyński, Eustachy. *Szkolnictwo mniejszości niemieckiej na Górnym Śląsku w świetle polskiego prawa traktatowego.* Katowice: Inst. Śląski, 1939.

Oberländer, Theodor. *Die Landwirtschaft Posen-Pomerellens vor und nach der Abtrennung vom Deutschen Reich.* Berlin: Volk & Reich, 1937.

Oertel, Maria. "Beiträge zur Geschichte der deutsch-polnischen Beziehungen in den Jahren 1925-30." Diss., Berlin Univ., 1968.

Oertzen, F.W.v. *Das ist Polen.* 2d ed. Munich: Langen/Müller, 1939.

Ohlhoff, Gerhard. *Das Jahr 1919 in Bromberg.* Wilhelmshaven: Bidegast-Vereinigung, 1969.

Orski, Marek. "Organizacja okręgu pomorskiego Związku Obrony Kresów Zachodnich w latach 1921-37." *Zapiski Historyczne* 51 (1986): 479-529.

Olszewski, Marian. *Powstanie Wielkopolski 1918-1919.* Poznań: Wyd. Poznańskie, 1978.

Orzechowski, Marian. "O mniejszości niemieckiej i Volksbundzie—uwagi polemiczne," *Zaranie Śląskie* 30 (1967): 735-45.

———. *Wojciech Korfanty.* Wrocław: Ossoliński, 1975.

Osiński, Seweryn. "Hitlerowska dywersja na Pomorzu gdańskim w latach 1933-1939." *Wojskowy Przegląd Historyczny* 9, no. 4 (1964): 83-125.

———. *V kolumna na Pomorzu gdańskim.* Warsaw: Książka i Wiedza, 1965.

Osmańczyk, Edmund, ed. *Dowody prowokacji.* Warsaw, 1952.

Osteuropa-Institut Breslau. *Oberschlesien und der Genfer Schiedspruch.* Berlin: Hermann Sack, 1925.

Pabisz, Jerzy. *Walka klasy robotniczej województwa śląskiego w okresie wielkiego kryzysu gospodarczego.* Katowice: Śląski Inst. Naukowy, 1972.

Pajewski, Janusz, ed. *Problem polsko-niemiecki w traktacie wersalskim.* Poznań: Inst. Zachodni, 1963.

Palmer, Alan. *The Lands Between.* New York: Macmillan, 1970.

Paprocki, Stanisław. *La Pologne et le problème des minorités.* Warsaw: Institut pour l'Étude des Questions Minoritaires, 1935.

Pearson, Raymond. *National Minorities in Eastern Europe, 1848-1945.* New York: St. Martin's, 1983.

Pease, Neal. *Poland, the United States, and the Stabilization of Europe, 1919-33.* New York: Oxford Univ. Press, 1986.

Pieper, Helmut. *Die Minderheitenfrage und das Deutsche Reich, 1919-33/4.* Hamburg: Alfred Metzner, 1974.

Piotrowski, Bernard. "Die Westidee an der Poznaner Universität (1919-39)." *Polnische Weststudien* 4 (1985): 117-45.

Plat, Wolfgang. *Deutsche und Polen.* Cologne: Pohl-Rügenstein, 1980.

Polacy i Niemcy: 10 wieków sąsiedztwa. Ed. A. Czubiński. Warsaw: PWN, 1987.

Polish and German Minorities in their Relation to the League of Nations. Polish Library of Facts 3. New York: Polish Information Service, 1932.

Polish Ministry of Information. *The German Fifth Column in Poland.* London: Hutchinson, 1940.

Polnische Ansichten über die rechtliche Bedeutung des Genfer Abkommens über Oberschlesien für Ostoberschlesien. Breslau: Osteuropa-Institut, 1937.

Pologne, 1919-1939. Vol. 1. Neuchatel: De la Baconnière, n.d.

Polonicus. *Die Deutschen unter der polnischen Herrschaft.* Berlin: Zentralverlag, 1927.

Polonius, Edgar [J. Golla], *Ost-Oberschlesien als Polens Kolonie.* Breslau: Wahlstatt, 1933.

Pomeranus. *Das Deutschtum in Westpreussen und Posen.* Berlin: Deutscher Schutzbund, [1927].

Pośpieszalski, Karol. *The Case of the 58,000 Volksdeutscher.* Poznań: Inst. Zachodni, 1959.

Potocki, Stanisław. *Położenie mniejszości niemieckiej w Polsce 1918-38.* Wydawnictwa Instytutu Bałtyckiego 4. Gdańsk: Wyd. Morskie, 1969.

Powstania śląskie i plebiscyt z perspektywy 60-lecia. Opole: Inst. Śląski, 1981.

Prause, Fritz. *Die polnische Presse im Kampf gegen die deutsche Volksgruppe in Posen und Westpreussen.* Zeitung und Leben 89. Würzburg: Konrad Triltsch, 1940.

Problem niemiecki na ziemiach zachodnich. Poznań: *Strażnica Zachodnia,* 1933.

Próchnik, Adam. *Pierwsze piętnostolecie Polski niepodległy.* Warsaw: Książka i Wiedza, 1957.

──────. "Rada robotniczo-żółnierska w Poznaniu w okresie przełomie 1918-9 r." *Niepodległość* 5 (1931): 83-108, 258-81, 428-39.

Przewłocki, Jan. *Międzysojusznicza Komisja Rządząca i Plebiscytowa na Górnym Śląsku, 1920-2.* Wrocław, 1970.

──────. *Stosunek mocarstw zachodnioeuropejskich do problemów Górnego Śląska, 1918-39.* Warsaw: PWN, 1978.

Raina, Peter. *Stosunki polsko-niemieckie 1937-9.* London: OpiM, 1975.

Rasmus, Hugo. *Jugend im Aufbruch.* Zur Geschichte der Jugendbewegung in Westpreussen. Bonn: Deutsche Jugend des Ostens, 1956.

Ratynska, Barbara. *Stosunki polsko-niemieckie w okresie wojny gospodarczej (1919-30).* Warsaw: Książka i Wiedza, 1968.

Rauschning, Hermann. "Bedeutung und Entwicklung der abgetretenen Gebiete Westpreussens." In F. Heiss and A. Hillen, eds., *Deutschland und der Korridor.* Berlin: Volk and Reich, 1933.

──────. *Deutsche und Polen.* Danzig: Gesellschaft zum Stadium Polens, 1934.

──────. *Die Entdeutschung Westpreussens und Posens.* Berlin: Reimar Hobbing, 1930.

──────. *Gespräche mit Hitler.* Zürich: Europa, 1940.

Rechowicz, Henryk. *Sejm Śląski 1922-39.* 2d ed. Katowice: Śląsk, 1971.

Recke, Walter. *Die historisch-politischen Grundlagen der Genfer Konvention vom 15. Mai 1922,* Marburg, 1969.

Ręgorowicz, Ludwik. "Otto Ulitz i jego działalność w latach obowiązywania Konwencji Genewskiej, 1922-1937." *Zaranie Śląskie* 25 (1961): 845-50.

──────. "Stosunki narodowościowe na Śląsku . . ." *Strażnica Zachodnia* 11 (1932): 414-27.

──────. *Wykonanie polsko-niemieckiej górnośląskiej konwencji zawartej w Genewie 15 maja 1922 r. w zakresie szkolnictwa.* Katowice: Śląsk, 1961.

Rhode, Gotthold. "Das Deutschtum in Posen and Pomerellen in der Zeit der Weimarer Republik." In *Die deutschen Ostgebiete zur Zeit der Weimarer Republik,* pp. 88-132. Studien zum Deutschtum in Osten 3. Cologne: Bohlau, 1966.

──────. *Geschichte Polens.* Darmstadt: Wissenschaftliche Gesellschaft, 1980.

————. Review of De Jong, *The German Fifth Column*. In *Jahrbücher für die Geschichte Osteuropas* 8 (1960): 108ff.

————. "Völker und Staaten in Ost-Mittleuropa zwischen den beiden Weltkriegen." In *Volk und Staat*, Festschrift Karl Massmann, pp. 176-200. Kiel: Verein Deutscher Studenten, 1954.

Riekhoff, Harold von. *German-Polish Relations, 1918-1933*, Baltimore, Md.: Johns Hopkins Univ. Press, 1971.

Ritter, Ernst. *Das Deutsche Ausland-Institut in Stuttgart, 1917-45*. Wiesbaden: Franz Steiner, 1976.

Rogala, Władysław. "Niemiecka mniejszość narodowa w Polsce w okresie rokowań gospodarczych (1927-1932)." *Przegląd Zachodni* 17, no. 3 (1961): 103-20.

————. "Polityka niemieckiej mniejszości narodowej w Wielkopolsce w latach 1919-1923." *Przegląd Zachodni* 13, no. 2 (1957): 173-87.

————. "Wzrost nastrojów rewizjonistycznych wśród niemieckiej mniejszości narodowej w Polsce w latach 1924-6." *Przegląd Zachodni* 15, no. 6 (1959): 298-317.

Rogowski, Stanisław. *Komisja Mieszana dla Górnego Śląska 1922-37*. Opole: Inst. Śląski, 1977.

Rohrbach, Paul. *Deutschtum in Not!* Die Schicksale der Deutschen in Europa ausserhalb des Reiches. Berlin: Wilh. Andermann, 1926.

Rola mniejszości niemieckiej w rozwoju stosunków politycznych w Europie 1918-1945. Ed. A. Czubiński. Poznań: Univ. Mickiewicza, 1984.

Rola Wielkopolski w dziejach narodu polskiego. Ed. S. Kubiak and L. Trzeciakowski. Poznań: Mieckiewicz Univ., 1979.

Roos, Hans. [Hans-Otto Meissner]. *A History of Modern Poland*. New York: Knopf, 1966.

————. *Polen und Europa*. Studien zur polnischen Aussenpolitik, 1931-39. Tübingen: J.C.B. Mohr, 1957.

Rose, William. *The Drama of Upper Silesia*. Brattleboro, Vt.: Stephen Daye, 1935.

————. *The Rise of Polish Democracy*. London: G. Bell, 1944.

Rosenthal, Harry. *German and Pole: National Conflict and Modern Myth*. Gainesville: University Presses of Florida, 1976.

Ross, Friedrich. *Polnische Kampfverbände und Propaganda-Institute*. Königsberg: Gräfe & Unzer, 1935.

Roth, Paul. *Die Entstehung des polnischen Staates*. Berlin: Otto Liebmann, 1926.

Rothschild, Joseph. *East-Central Europe between the Two World Wars*. History of East-Central Europe 9. Seattle: Univ. of Washington Press, 1974.

Roucek, Joseph. "Minorities." In *Poland*, ed. B. Schmidt, pp. 148-66. Berkeley: Univ. of California Press, 1945.

Rukser, U. *Die Rechtsstellung der Deutschen in Polen*, Berlin: Walter de Gruyter, 1921.

————. *Staatsangehörigkeit und Minoritätenschutz in Oberschlesien*. Berlin: Politik und Wirtschaft, 1922.

Rzymowski, W. *Oberschlesien und Polen*. Bibliothek des oberschlesischen Arbeiters. n.p., 1921.

Santoro, Cesare. *Through Poland during the Elections of 1930*. Geneva: Albert Kundig, 1931.

Sawicki, Jakub. *Kościol Ewangelicki a państwo na polskim Górnym Śląsku*. Katowice, 1938.

Schmitz, Hans-Jakob. *Die Posener Grenzschutzkämpfe 1918/9*. Schneidemühl: Comenius, 1938.

Schot, Bastiaan. *Stresemann, der deutsche Osten, und der Völkerbund*. Wiesbaden: Franz Steiner, 1984.

Schrader, H. *The Treatment of National Minorities in the Republic of Poland*. Berlin, 1920.

Schubert, Albrecht. *Die Entwicklung der Posen Landwirtschaft seit 1919 im Rahmen der gesamten Staatswirtschaft*. Posen: Historische Gesellschaft für Posen, 1929.

————. "Strukturwandlungen in der wirtschaftlichen Entwicklung des Deutschtums der abgetretenen Gebiete Posens-Westpreussens." *Der Auslanddeutsche* 13 (1930): 377-81.

Schubert, Ernst. *Die deutsche evangelische Kirche in Polen, 1920-1939*. Berlin: Verlag des Evangelischen Bundes, 1939.

Schulz, Gerhard. "Deutschland und Polen vom ersten zum zweiten Weltkrieg." *Geschichte in Wissenschaft und Unterricht* 33 (1982): 154-172.

Schulze, Hagen. *Freikorps und Republik, 1918-20*. Boppard: Boldt, 1969.

————. "Der Oststaat-Plan 1919." *Vierteljahrshefte für Zeitgeschichte* 18 (1970): 123-63.

Schwabe, Klaus. *Woodrow Wilson, Revolutionary Germany, and Peacemaking, 1918-9*. Chapel Hill: Univ. of North Carolina Press, 1985.

Septimus, *Irredenta niemiecka. Z tajników Volksbundu i Deutschtumsbundu*. Poznań: ZOKZ, 1927.

Seraphim, Peter-Heinz. "Die Kapitalverflechtung zwischen Deutschland und Polen." *Osteuropa* 7 (1931): 197-207.

Seton-Watson, Hugh. *Eastern Europe between the Wars, 1918-1941*. 3d ed. Hambden, Conn.: Archon, 1962.

Sharp, Alan. "Britain and the Protection of Minorities at the Paris Peace Conference, 1919." In *Minorities in History*, ed. A. Hepburn, pp. 170-88. London: Edward Arnold, 1978.

Six, Franz. *Die Presse in Polen*. Berlin: Deutscher Verlag für Politik und Wirtschaft, 1938.

Skorzyński, Józef. "Selbstschütz—V kolumna." *Biuletyn Głównej Komisji Badania Zbrodni Hitlerowskich w Polsce* 10 (1958): 5-56.

Smelser, Ronald. *The Sudeten Problem 1933-8: Volkstumspolitik and the Formulation of Nazi Foreign Policy*. Middletown, Conn.: Wesleyan Univ. Press, 1975.

Sobczak, Janusz. *Propaganda zagraniczna Niemiec Weimarskiej wobec Polski*. Poznań: Inst. Zachodni, 1973.

Sontag, Ernst. *Die Franzosenherrschaft in Oberschlesien*. Berlin: Spaeth & Linde, 1921.

Sprawy polskie na konferencji pokojowej w Paryżu w 1919 r. 3 vols. Polski Instytut Spraw Międzynarodowych. Warsaw: PWN, 1965-68.

Staniewicz, Restytut. "Legendy i rzeczywistość V kolumny niemieckiej." *Przegląd Zachodni* 12, no. 6 (1957): 356-79.

————. "Mniejszość niemiecka w Polsce—V kolumna Hitlera?" *Przegląd Zachodni* 15, no. 2. (1959): 395-438.

————. *Mniejszość niemiecka w województwie śląskim w latach 1922-1933*. Katowice: Śląsk Inst. Nauk., 1965.

————. "Niemiecki ruch młodzieżowy w Polsce w swietle dokumentów." *Przegląd Zachodni* 3 (1958): 180-93.

———. "Szersze tło historyczne i rzeczywiste cele dywersji niemieckiej w Bydgoszczy 3.9.39 r." *Wojskowy Przegląd Historyczny* 7, no. 4 (1962): 360-406.

Stan Posiadania ziemi na Pomorzu. Toruń: Instytut Bałtycki, 1933.

Stephan, Karl. *Der Todeskampf der Ostmark, 1918/9.* 3d ed. Schneidemühl: Comenius, 1933.

Steyer, Donald. *Organizacji robotnicze na terenie województwa pomorskiego w latach 1920-1939.* Toruń: Univ. Kopernika, 1961.

Stoliński, Zygmunt. *Die deutsche Minderheit in Polen.* Warsaw: Institut für Erforschung der Minderheitsfragen, 1928.

Stone, Julius. *Regional Guarantees of Minority Rights.* New York: Macmillan, 1933.

Stosunki narodowościowe w rolnictwie pomorskim. Ed. A. Wrzosk and S. Zwierz. Gdynia Instytut Bałtycki, 1937.

Stroynowski, Juliusz. *Polen und Deutsche.* Stuttgart: Seewald, 1973.

Studia z najnowszej historii Niemiec i stosunków polsko-niemieckich. Ed. S. Sierpowski. Poznań: Univ. Mickiewicza, 1986.

Studnicki, Władysław. *Irrwege in Polen.* Göttingen: Göttinger Arbeitskreis, 1951.

———. *Polen im politischen System Europas.* Berlin: Mittler, 1936.

Swart, Friedrich, *Diesseits und jenseits der Grenze.* Das deutsche Genossenschaftswesen im Posener Land und das deutsch-polnische Verhältnis bis zum Ende des 2. Weltkrieges. Leer: Rautenberg & Mockel, 1954.

Swart, Friedrich, and Richard Breyer. "Die deutsche Volksgruppe im polnischen Staat." In *Das östliche Deutschland,* ed. Göttinger Arbeitskreis, pp. 477-526. Würzburg: Hölzner, 1959.

Szefer, Andrzej. *Mniejszość niemiecka w Polsce i w Czechosłowacji w latach 1933-8.* Katowice: Śląski Inst. Naukowy, 1967.

———. "Secesja z Partii Młodoniemieckiej w 1937 r." *Zaranie Śląskie* 27 (1964): 531-37

Szturm de Sztrem, Edward. "Prawdziwa Statystyka." *Kwartalnik Historyczny* (1973): 664-67.

Szymański, Zbigniew. *Niemieckie korpusy ochotnicze na Górnym Śląsku (1918-22).* Opole: Inst. Śląski, 1969.

Taylor, J. *The Economic Development of Poland, 1919-50.* Ithaca, N.Y.: Cornell Univ. Press, 1952.

Thalheim, Karl. *Das Grenzlanddeutschtum.* Leipzig: Walter de Gruyter, 1931.

Thalheim, Karl, and H. Ziegfeld. *Der deutsche Osten.* Berlin: Propyläen, 1936.

Tomaszewski, Jerzy. "Konsekwencji wielonarodowościowej struktury ludności Polski 1918-1939 dla procesów integracyjnych społeczeństwa." In *Drogi integracji społeczeństwa w Polsce XIX-XX w.,* ed. H. Zieliński, pp. 109-38. Wrocław: Ossoliński, 1976.

———. *Rzeczpospolita wielu narodów.* Warsaw, 1985.

Tooley, T. Hunt. "German Political Violence and the Border Plebiscite in Upper Silesia, 1919-21." *Central European History* 21 (1988): 56-98.

Trampler, Kurt. *Die Krise des Nationalstaates.* Munich: Knorr & Hirth, 1932.

———. *Staaten und nationale Gemeinschaften.* Eine Lösung des europäischen Minderheiten-Problems. Munich: R. Oldenbourg, 1929.

Truhart, Herbert von. *Völkerbund und Minderheiten-Petitionen.* Vienna: Wilh. Braumuller, 1931.

Türcke, Kurt Egon von. *Das Schulrecht der deutschen Volksgruppen in Ost- und Südosteuropa*. Berlin: Carl Heymanns, 1938.

Ulitz, Otto. *Oberschlesien—Aus seiner Geschichte*. Bonn: Landsmannschaft der Oberschlesier, 1971.

Um die Ostmark Posen. Deutscher Heimatbund Posener Flüchtlinge. Frankfurt, 1919.

Urban, Laszlo. "German Property Interests in Poland during the 1920s." *East European Quarterly* 10: 181-221.

Urbański, Zygmunt. *Mniejszość narodowe w Polsce*. Warsaw, 1932.

Viefhaus, Erwin. *Die Minderheitenfrage und die Entstehung der Minderheitenschutzverträge auf der Pariser Friedenskonferenz 1919*. Würzburg: Hölzner, 1960.

Vogt, Dietrich. *Der grosspolnische Aufstand 1918-1919*. Marburg: Herder-Institut, 1980.

Volksdeutsche Soldaten under Polens Fahnen. Ed. K. Lück. Deutscher Osten 3. Berlin: Grenze und Ausland, 1940.

Von Unserer Art. Ed. F. Weigelt. Vom Leben und Wirken deutscher Menschen im Raum von Weichsel und Warthe. Wuppertal: Landsmannschaft Weichsel-Warthe, 1963.

Vosberg, Fritz. *Der polnische Aufstand in seiner Entstehung*. Berlin: Preuss. Verlagsanstalt, 1919.

Wagner, Gerhard. *Deutschland und der polnisch-sowjetischer Krieg 1920*. Wiesbaden: Franz Steiner, 1979.

Waite, Robert. *Vanguard of Nazism*. Cambridge, Mass.: Harvard Univ. Press, 1952.

Walczak, Jan. *Polska i niemiecka socjaldemokracja na Górnym Śląsku i w Cieszyńskiem po przewrocie majowym 1926-39*. Katowice: Śląski Inst. Naukowy, 1980.

Wambaugh, Sarah. *Plebiscites since the World War*. 2 vols. Washington, D.C., 1933.

Wandycz, Piotr. *France and her Eastern Allies, 1919-25*. Minneapolis: Univ. of Minnesota Press, 1962.

Wapiński, Roman. "Disputes over the Social and National Shape of Reborn Poland," *Polish Western Affairs* 20 (1979): 291-306.

———. *Endecja na Pomorzu 1920-1939*. Gdańsk: Gdańskie Towarzystwo Naukowe, 1966.

———. "Endecja wobec problemów polskich ziem zachodnich w latach 1919-1939." *Zapiski Historyczne* 31 (1966): 61-81.

———. *Narodowa Demokracja, 1893-1939*. Wrocław: Ossolineum, 1980.

———. "Z dziejów kultury politycznej Wielkopolski i Pomorza w dwudziestoleciu międzywojennym." *Przegląd Zachodni* 4 (1978): 1-16.

———. "Z dziejów tendencji nacjonalistycznych; o stanowisku Narodowej Demokracji wobec kwestii narodowej w latach 1873-1939." *Kwartalnik Historyczny* 80 (1973): 817-43.

———. *Życie polityczne Pomorza w latach 1920-39*. Toruń: PWN, 1983.

Warderholt, J. [Paul v. Husen]. *Das Minderheitenrecht in Oberschlesien*. Berlin: Brückenverlag, 1930.

Wartel, Zenon. "Dążenie mniejszości niemieckiej do rozszerzenia swych uprawnień w Polsce po przewrocie majowym." *Dzieje Najnowsze* 9 (1977): 123-35.

———. "Sprawa parcelacji majątków niemieckich w Polsce w latach 1920-39." *Kwartalnik Historyczny* 83 (1976): 548-61.

Wasilewski, Leon. *Sprawy narodowościowe w teorii i w życie*. Cracow: Mortkowicz, 1929.

Watt, Richard. *Bitter Glory: Poland and Its Fate, 1918-1939*. New York: Simon & Shuster, 1979.

Weber, Friedrich. *Der deutsch-polnische Staatsvertrag vom 30. August 1924*. Munich, 1930.

Webersinn, Gerhard. *Otto Ulitz*. Augsburg: Oberschles. Heimatverlag, 1974.

Wedel, Hasso von. "Die Agrarreform in Polen." *Osteuropa* 3 (1928): 361ff.

———. "Die Landwirtschaft in Polen." *Osteuropa* 2 (1926): 422-33.

Wehler, Hans-Ulrich, "Deutsch-polnische Beziehungen im 19. und 20. Jahrhundert." In *Krisenherde des Kaiserreiches 1871-1918*, pp. 201-17. Göttingen: Vandenhoeck & Ruprecht, 1970.

Weinberg, Gerhard. *The Foreign Policy of Hitler's Germany*. 2 vols. Chicago: Univ. of Chicago Press, 1970.

Weiss, Moritz. *Die Stellung des Deutschtums in Posen und Westpreussen*. 2d ed. Berlin: Wilh. Greve, 1919.

Wengersdorf, Rolf. *Die Vernichtung der deutschen Presse in Polen*. Danzig: Brückenverlag, 1921.

Wereszycki, Henryk. "Poland, 1918-1939." In *History of Poland*, ed. A. Gieysztor et al. Warsaw: PWN, 1968.

Wertheimer, Fritz. *Deutschland, die Minderheiten, und der Völkerbund*. Berlin: Carl Heymanns, 1926.

———. *Von deutschen Parteien und Parteiführern im Ausland*. Berlin: Zentralverlag, 1927.

Wieliczka, Zygmunt. *Wielkopolska a Prusy w dobie powstania 1918-19*. Poznań: Związek Weteranów, 1932.

Wierzbicki, Andrzej. *Le Problème de la Haute-Silesie*. Warsaw: Sejm, 1921.

Wiese, Hans. *Uns rief Polen! Deutsches Schicksal an Weichsel und Warthe*. Leipzig: Voigtlander, 1937.

Winiewicz, Jozef. *Mobilizacja sił niemieckich w Polsce*. Warsaw: Polityka, 1939.

Wintgens, Hugo. *Der völkerrechtliche Schutz der nationalen, sprachlichen, und religiösen Minderheiten*. Stuttgart: W. Kohlhammer, 1930.

Wojan, Ryszard [R. Staniewicz]. *Bydgoszcz, niedziela 3 września 1939 r.* Poznań: Wyd. Poznańskie, 1959.

Wojciechowski, Marian. "Geneza dywersji hitlerowskiej w Bydgoszczy w świetle historiografii i publicystyki polskiej." In Bydgoski Tow. Naukowa, *Prace komisji historii* 4 (1967): 135-48.

———. "Mniejszość niemiecka w województwie pomorskim a III Rzesza w latach 1936-9." *Zapiski Historyczne* 26, no. 2 (1961): 45-57.

———. *Polsko-niemiecka declaracja o nieagresji z 26.1.1934*. Katowice: Śląski Inst. Naukowy, 1963.

———. *Die polnisch-deutschen Beziehungen, 1933-38*. Leiden: Brill, 1971.

———. *Rewizjonizm w historiografii niemieckiej lat 1920-1957*. Bydgoszcz: Univ. Kopernika w Toruniu, 1957.

Wojciechowski, Mieczysław. *Powrót Pomorza do Polski, 1918-20*. Poznań: PWN, 1981.

Wolff, Anna. "Pomorze gdańskie w programie i działalnosci ZOKZ." *Przegląd Zachodni* (1969): 363-73.

Wynot, Edward. "The Case of German Schools in Polish Upper Silesia, 1922-1939." *Polish Review* 19, no. 2 (1974): 47-69.

———. "Poland's Christian Minorities." *Nationalities Papers* 13 (1985): 209-46.

———. "The Polish Germans, 1919-1989: National Minority in a Multinational State." *Polish Review* 17 (1972): 23-64.

———. *Polish Politics in Transition: The Camp of National Unity and the Struggle for Power, 1935-39*. Athens: Univ. of Georgia Press, 1974.

———. "World of Delusions and Disillusions: The National Minorities of Poland during World War II." *Nationalities Papers* 7 (1979): 177-96.

Wysocka, Barbara. *Regionalizm wielkopolski w II Rzeczypospolitej, 1919-1939*. Poznań: Univ. Mickiewicza, 1981.

Zaleski, Władysław. *Międzynarodowa ochrona mniejszości*. Warsaw, 1932.

Zarys historii ruchu robotniczego w Wielkopolsce. Ed. A. Czubiński. Poznań: Wyd. Poznańskie, 1978.

Zehn Jahre Versailles. 3 vols. Ed. K.v. Loesch & M.H. Boehm. Berlin: Brückenverlag, 1930.

Zieliński, Henryk. "The Economy." In *Poland*, ed. B. Schmidt, pp. 175-78. Berkeley: Univ. of California Press, 1945.

———. "The Social and Political Background of the Silesian Uprisings." *Acta Poloniae Historica* 26 (1972): 73-108.

Zieliński, Ryszard. *Powstanie Wielkopolskie 1918-19*. Warsaw: Min. Obrony Narodowy, 1968.

Zieliński, Władysław. *Polska i niemiecka propaganda plebiscytowa na Górnym Śląsku*. Wrocław: Ossoliński, 1972.

Z czarnego kraju: Górny Śląsk w reportażu międzywojennym. Katowice: Śląsk, 1981.

Żmidziński, Franciszek. *Realizacja reformy rolnej na Pomorzu 1920-1938*. Poznań: PWN, 1978.

Z problemów integracji społeczno-politycznej na Górnym Śląsku przed II wojną swiatową. Ed. W. Zieliński. Katowice: Śląski Inst. Naukowy, 1980.

Zorn, Gerda. *Nach Ostland geht unser Ritt*. Bonn: Dietz, 1980.

Zweig, Ferdynand. *Poland between Two Wars*. London: Secker & Warburg, 1944.

Notes

Abbreviations

AA	Auswärtiges Amt
ADAP	*Akten zur Deutschen Auswärtigen Politik, 1918-45.*
BA	Bundesarchiv Koblenz
EK	Konsistórz Ewangelicki (WAPP)
HI	Hoover Institution
IfZ	Institut für Zeitgeschichte Munich
League	League of Nations, (Minorities) Council documents Section 1B
Org. niem.	Organizacji niemieckie (WAPP)
Ost-Dok.	Ost-Dokumentation (BA)
PA	Politisches Archiv des Auswärtigen Amts Bonn
PI	Piłsudski Institute
RK	Reichskanzlei (BA)
UWP	Urząd Wojewódzki Poznański (WAPP)
VB	Deutscher Volksbund für Polnisch- Schlesien
WAPP	Wojewódzkie Archiwum Pánstwowe w Poznaniu

Introduction

1. Joseph Czech, *Die Bevölkerung Polens*, p. 35; Stanislaus Mornik [Erich Jaensch], *Polens Kampf gegen seine nichtpolnischen Volksgruppen*, p. 12.

2. Richard Breyer, *Das Deutsche Reich und Polen*, pp. 48ff.; Theodor Bierschenk, *Die deutsche Volksgruppe in Polen*, pp. 31-32.

3. Moritz Weiss, *Die Stellung des Deutschtums in Posen und Westpreussen*, pp. 4ff.

4. Stanisław Potocki, *Położenie mniejszości niemieckiej w Polsce*, p. 288.

5. Marian Drozdowski, "The National Minorities in Poland, p. 232. This and all subsequent translations are mine.

6. Premysław Hauser, *Mniejszość niemiecka w województwie pomorskim w latach 1920-1939*, pp. 33, 39-40.

7. Cf. Marian Mroczko, *Związek Obrony Kresów Zachodnich, 1921-1934*, and *Polska myśl zachodnia, 1918-1939, passim.*

8. Jerzy Krasuski, *Stosunki polsko-niemieckie*, pp. 262-63; also Potocki, p. 433.

9. Drozdowski, "National Minorities," p. 245. The same point is made by Restytut Staniewicz, *Mniejszość niemiecka w województwie śląskim w latach 1922-1933*,

p. 101, and Karol Grünberg, *Niemcy i ich organizacje polityczne w Polsce międzywojenney,* pp. 22-23.

10. Jerzy Tomaszewski, *Rzeczpospolita wielu narodów* pp. 10-11, 17, and "Konsekwencje wielonarodowościowej struktury ludności Polski 1918-1939 dla procesów integracyjnych społeczeństwa," p. 123.

11. Andrzej Chojnowski, *Koncepje polityki narodowościowej rządów polskich w latach 1921-1939,* pp. 5, 68.

12. Tomaszewski, "Konsekwencje," p. 117.

13. Roman Wapiński, *Endecja na Pomorzu,* p. 46.

14. Alfred Kucner, "Mniejszość niemiecka w Polsce i dążenie rządu niemieckiego do utrzymania jej stanu posidania w b. zaborze pruskim," p. 279.

15. Tadeusz Kowalak, *Prasa niemiecka w Polsce,* pp. 232ff.

16. Tomaszewdki, "Konsekwencje," pp. 124, 137 and *Rzeczpospolita,* pp. 17-18.

1. Establishment of the German Minority

1. Dietrich Vogt, *Der Grosspolnische Aufstand,* pp. 9ff., 20, 32ff.; Zygmunt Wieliczka, *Wielkopolska a Prusy w dobie powstania;* Adam Próchnik, "Rada robotniczo-żółnierska w Poznaniu w okresie przełomie 1918-1918 r.," pp. 83-108, 258-81, 428-39; Fritz Vosberg, *Der polnische Aufstand in seiner Entstehung,* pp. 33ff.; Robert Coester, *Die Loslösung Posens,* p. 17; Przemysław Hauser, *Niemcy wobec sprawy polskiej.*

2. Vogt, *Aufstand,* p. 19ff.

3. Próchnik, "Rada," p. 279.

4. Ibid., pp. 431ff.

5. Ibid., p. 260; Coester, p. 13.

6. Gerhard Ohlhoff, *Das Jahr 1919 in Bromberg,* pp. 7ff.

7. Vogt, *Aufstand,* pp. 41f.

8. Próchnik, "Rada," p. 279; Vogt, *Aufstand,* p. 21.

9. Karl Stephan, *Der Todeskampf der Ostmark,* p. 16; Wieliczka, p. 24; Vosberg, pp. 43ff.; Georg Cleinow, *Der Verlust der Ostmark,* p. 86; Vogt, *Aufstand,* p. 26.

10. Vosberg, pp. 50ff.; Wieliczka, p. 34; Hauser, *Niemcy* p. 63; Stephan, p. 18.

11. Wieliczka, p. 21; Vogt, *Aufstand,* pp. 28ff.; Vosberg, p. 49; Stephan, p. 18.

12. Vogt, *Aufstand,* pp. 22ff.; Vosberg, pp. 41, 76; Hauser, *Niemcy,* p. 69.

13. Hauser, *Niemcy,* p. 65; Vosberg, p. 76; Ohlhoff, p. 14; Cleinow, pp. 163ff.

14. Cleinow, pp. 69ff., 82-83, 179-80; Max Hildebert Boehm, "Die Reorganisation der Deutschtumsarbeit nach dem 1. Weltkrieg," p. 15; Ohlhoff, p. 24; Stanisław Kubiak, *Niemcy a Wielkopolska,* p. 84; Hagen Schulze, "Der Oststaat-Plan 1919," p. 132.

15. Hans Roos, *A History of Modern Poland,* pp. 14ff.

16. Ibid., pp. 39ff.; Kay Lundgreen-Nielsen, *The Polish Problem at the Paris Peace Conference,* p. 92; Gotthold Rhode, *Geschichte Polens,* p. 458.

17. Vogt, an eyewitness to these events and an officer in the German unit allegedly involved, takes the latter position, *Aufstand,* pp. 43ff.; Vosberg, pp. 84ff.

18. Vogt, *Aufstand,* pp. 54ff.; Vosberg p. 100.

19. Kubiak, p. 63; Wieliczka, pp. 37ff; Marian Olszewski, *Powstanie Wielkopolskie.*

20. Lundgreen-Nielsen, p. 139; Vogt, *Aufstand*, p. 2

21. Roos, *History*, p. 50.

22. Vogt, *Aufstand*, pp. 66ff.; Ohlhoff, p. 23; Hauser, *Niemcy*, p. 109. See also the first-hand accounts: Paul Paetzold, *Wie Neutomischel polnisch wurde*, pp. 20ff.; *Um die Ostmark Posen*, p. 11; A.S. Sonnenburg, *Die Polenknute über Posen*, p. 3.

23. According to Coester (an official in Poznania at the time of the insurrection), p. 47.

24. Vogt, *Aufstand*, p. 69; Ohlhoff, p. 21.

25. Hauser, *Niemcy*, p. 106; Vogt, *Aufstand*, p. 68; Coester, p. 33; Schulze, p. 127; *Dokumente der deutschen Politik*, p. 742.

26. Lundgreen-Nielsen, p. 165.

27. Karl Stephan, contemptuous of the "council soldiers" in the regular army, was a veteran of the Great War and a future SA leader; he was probably representative of Germans who volunteered for this campaign. He recounts (pp. 10, 33) the story of "Grenzschutz Battalion III," which suffered 270 deaths in fighting in this sector. Cf. Ohlhoff, p. 20.

28. Vogt, *Aufstand*, pp. 68ff.; Ohlhoff, pp. 30ff.; Schulze, pp. 148f.; Gero von Gersdorff, *20 Jahre Front gegen Polenterror*, p. 7.

29. Vogt, *Aufstand*, p. 91; Friedrich Swart, *Diesseits und jenseits der Grenze*, p. 67; Blau to NRL, June 27, 1919, and NRL to Blau, April 7 and July 13, 1919, EK 529, 536; Brockdorff-Rantzau to British government, Jan. 17, 1919, *Dokumente* (Volz), pp. 744ff.

30. Vogt, *Aufstand*, p. 85.

31. Lundgreen-Nielsen, pp. 140ff.

32. Gotthold Rhode, "Das Deutschtum in Posen und Pomerellen in der Zeit der Weimarer Republik," p. 92; Erich Keyser, ed. p. 92; *Der Kampf um die Weichsel*, pp. 157ff.; Lundgreen-Nielsen, pp. 38ff.

33. Cited in Lundgreen-Nielsen, p. 75.

34. Ibid., pp. 42, 82ff.; Frank Golczewski, *Polnisch-jüdische Beziehungen*, pp. 286ff.

35. Cited in Lundgreen-Nielsen, p. 64; cf. pp. 59, 155.

36. Harald von Riekhoff, *German-Polish Relations*, p. 18; Lundgreen-Nielsen, pp. 197ff.

37. Lundgreen-Nielsen, pp. 234-44.

38. Ibid., p. 243.

39. Ibid., pp. 267ff., 312.

40. Erwin Viefhaus, *Die Minderheitenfrage und die Entstehung der Minderheitenschutzverträge auf der Pariser Friedenskonferenz 1919*, p. 69.

41. Lundgreen-Nielsen, pp. 360ff.

42. Paweł Korzec, "Polen und der Minderheitenschutzvertrag," p. 521; Lundgreen-Nielsen, p. 302.

43. Golczewski, *Beziehungen* p. 290.

44. Pedro de Azcarate, *The League of Nations and National Minorities*, p. 92; Viefhaus, pp. 193ff.

45. English text of treaty in C.A. Macartney, *National States and National Minorities*, pp. 502ff.

46. Korzec, "Polen," p. 526.

47. Paderewski-Clemenceau correspondence in Oscar Janowsky, *Nation-*

alities and National Minorities; Hermann Rauschning, *Die Entdeutschung West-preussens und Posens,* p. 23; Stanisław Paprocki, *La Pologne et le problème des minorités,* pp. 10ff; Korzec, "Polen," pp. 522.

48. Korzec, "Polen," p. 528.

49. Rhode, *Geschichte,* p. 463; Rhode, "Deutschtum," p. 94; Norbert Krekeler, "Die deutsche Politik in Polen and die Revisionspolitik des deutschen Reiches," p. 16; Weiss, p. 3.

50. Erich Kaufmann, *Die Rechtsverhältnisse der an Polen abgetretenen Ostmark,* pp. 13-14; Carl Georg Burns, *Staatsangehörigkeitswechsel und Option im Friedens-vertrag von Versailles,* p. 11; Rauschning, *Entdeutschung,* p. 97.

51. Cleinow, p. 244; Ohlhoff, pp. 46, 55.

52. *Deutsche Tageszeitung,* Dec. 28, 1918, cited in Hauser, *Niemcy,* p. 79.

53. Cited in Schulze, p. 141.

54. Grünberg, *Niemcy,* p. 10.

55. Another who attended this meeting was future anti-Nazi resistance leader Carl Goerdeler, who concluded that Cleinow was a "political fool" and the meeting a "complete fiasco" for his idea. See Schulze, pp. 133ff.; Cleinow, pp. 223, 306.

56. Letter from Cleinow to DOV founder, Heinrich von Tiedemann; see Schulze, p. 140; Cleinow, pp. 353.

57. Proclamation of July 3, 1919, cited in Cleinow, pp. 335ff.; Schulze, p. 163.

58. Quotations taken from NRL proclamations dated March 14, June 30, and July 30, 1919, *Posener Tageblatt,* March 16 and Aug. 5, 1919; Vogt, *Aufstand,* p. 104; Ohlhoff, p. 59.

59. E. Basedow and P. Correns, eds., *Schicksalstunden—Unvergessliches aus schweren Tagen in Posen und West preussen,* provides fifty-three firsthand accounts of the Polish takeover in various Poznanian and West Prussian towns. See Ohlhoff, p. 69; Felix-Heinrich Gentzen, "Die Legende vom 'Bromberger Blutsonntag' und die deutsche 5. Kolonne in Polen," p. 46; Rauschning, *Entdeutschung,* p. 47.

60. Basedow and Correns, pp. 49ff.; Ohlhoff, p. 66.

61. Rhode, "Deutschtum," p. 93; Anna Cienciala, "German Propaganda for the Revision of the Polish-German Frontier in Danzig and the Corridor," p. 86.

62. See Richard Blanke, "Upper Silesia 1921: The Case for Subjective Nation-ality"; Jan Przewłocki, *Międzysojusznicza Komisja Rządząca i Plebiscytowa na Górnym Śląsku, 1920-2* (Wrocław, 1970); Sarah Wambaugh, *Plebiscites since the World War* (Washington, D.C., 1933), 1:223, 242; Walther Recke, *Die historisch-politischen Grundlagen der Genfer Konvention vom 15. Mai 1922* (Marburg, 1969), p. 62; Ernst Sontag, *Die Franzosenherrschaft in Oberschlesien,* pp. 15ff.; Ernst Koenigsfeld, *Der Versailler Vertrag und Oberschlesien* (Koethen, 1928), p. 10.

63. Anna Cienciala and Titus Komarnicki, *From Versailles to Locarno,* p. 53; Sontag, pp. 22ff.; Przewłocki, *Komisja,* p. 62.

64. Francis Carsten, quoting Colonel Percival, in *Britain and the Weimar Repub-lic* (New York, 1984), p. 67.

65. *Kuryer Poranny,* Feb. 25, 1921; Sontag, p. 34.

66. Cf. Blanke, "Upper Silesia," pp. 243-44.

67. Józef Chałasiński, *Antagonizm polsko-niemiecki w osadzie fabrycznej "Kopalnia" na Górnym Śląsku,* pp. 17, 22, 42.

68. Cienciala and Komarnicki, pp. 62ff.; Sontag, p. 45.

69. Cienciala and Komarnicki, pp. 66ff.; Sontag, p. 54; U.S. Ambassador Hugh Gibson, report of May 3, 1921, in HI, Gibson Papers; Zusammenstellung von Protokollen und Berichte uber den 3. polnischen Aufstand im oberschlesischen Abstimmungsgebiet, BA, R 43 II 1483b, pp. 167ff.

70. Joseph Harrington, "The League of Nations and the Upper Silesia Boundary Dispute," pp. 88ff; Krasuski, *Stosunki*, p. 154; Otto Heike, *Die deutsche Minderheit in Polen bis 1939*, p. 162.

71. Harrington, "League," pp. 90ff.; Vincent Kroll, "Die Genfer Konvention betreffend Oberschlesien," pp. 45ff; Georges Kaeckenbeeck, *The International Experiment of Upper Silesia* (Oxford, 1942).

72. Frank Keitsch, *Das Schicksal der deutschen Volksgruppe in Ostoberschlesien*, pp. 56-57; Viktor Kauder, ed., *Das Deutschtum in Polen* 1:7. For similar estimates, see Breyer, *Deutsches Reich*, p. 42; Heike, *Minderheit*, p. 162; and Joseph Roucek, "Minorities," p. 162—but Krasuski (*Stosunki*, p. 154) puts the figure at 260,000.

2. The Great Exodus

1. Rauschning, *Entdeutschung*, p. 342. Others cite even higher figures: e.g., Chojnowski, p. 13; Drozdowski, "Minorities," p. 227; Grünberg, *Niemcy*, p. 17.

2. Rauschning, *Entdeutschung*, p. 338; Czech, p. 36; Mornik, p. 12; Heike, *Minderheit*, p. 162; Drozdowski, "Minorities," p. 244; Roucek, p. 162.

3. Johannes Ahlers, *Polen*, p. 59; Czech, p. 44; Mornik, p. 25.

4. Rauschning, *Entdeutschung*, pp. 360-61; Walter Kuhn, "Zahl und Siedlungsweise der Deutschen in Polen 1931," p. 148; Kroll, p. 56; Kauder, p. 7; Edmund Makowski, "Mniejszość niemiecka w Polsce w polityce niemieckiej," in *Rola mniejszości niemieckiej w rozwoju stosunków politycznych w Europie*, p. 317.

5. Kuhn, "Zahl," p. 157; Breyer, *Reich*, p. 43.

6. Rhode, "Deutschtum," p. 99; Alfons Krysiński, "Tendencje rozwojowe ludności Polski pod względem narodowościowym i wyznań w dobie powojennej," pp. 26ff.; Paprocki, p. 112; Chojnowski, p. 13.

7. Albrecht Schubert, "Strukturwandlungen in der wirtschaftlichen Entwicklung des Deutschtums der abgetretenen Gebiete Posen-Westpreussens," pp. 377ff.; Swart, *Diesseits*, p. 77.

8. Ezra Mendelssohn, *The Jews of East-Central Europe between the World Wars* (Bloomington, Ind., 1983), pp. 18, 29-30; Tomaszewski, *Rzeczpospolita*, p. 148; Ahlers, p. 56; Swart, p. 77; Rauschning, *Entdeutschung*, p. 156.

9. Cleinow, p. 379.

10. Ludolf Müller, *Die unierte evangelische Kirche in Posen-Westpreussen unter der polnischen Gewaltherrschaft*, p. 11; "Übergabe der westpreussischen Schulen an den polnischen Staat, 1919-1920," Ost-Dok. 6 C1 #6; Dudek to Prussian School Ministry, Oct. 27, 1921, and Prussian School Ministry, Aug. 6 and Oct. 27, 1921, IfZ MA 195 2-5 1066, pp. 50, 73, and 1067, p. 510.

11. Polonicus, *Die Deutschen unter der polnischen Herrschaft*, p. 36; Wojewode Celichowski, July 6, 1921, WAPP, EK 529; Budding to AA, Sept. 7, 1923, and German Consul Poznań to AA, March 4, 1924, PA Abt. IV Pol. 25 Polen, v. 14, p. 51, and v. 15.

12. Karl Karzel, *Die deutsche Landwirtschaft in Posen in der Zeit zwischen den beiden Weltkriegen*, p. 28; H. Schrader, *The Treatment of National Minorities in the Republic of Poland*, p. 6.

13. German intelligence report, Sept. 4, 1920, PA, Abt. IV Pol. 25 Polen, v. 2; Riekhoff, p. 29; Volkmar Kellermann, *Schwarzer Adler, weisser Adler*, pp. 58ff.

14. Hannuschek to Kessler (AA), Nov. 5, 1920, PA, Abt. IV Pol. 25 Polen, v. 3, pp. 3ff; Ota Goerdeler, *Leben auf Grenzgut T.*, p. 14; Krasuski, *Stosunki 1919-25*, p. 86; Friedrich Heidelck, "Die Stellung des Deutschtums in Polen," p. 57.

15. July 10, 1920, PA, Abt. IV Pol. 25 Polen, v. 1; Friedrich Heidelck, "Das Deutschtum in Pomerellen und Posen," p. 247; Polonicus, p. 49.

16. Report from Chełmno, July 23, 1920, PA, Abt. IV Pol. 25 Polen, v. 1.

17. Landesgrenzpolizei-Ost to AA, Oct. 11, 1920, PA, Abt. IV Pol. 25 Polen, v. 2, pp. 137ff.; German representative in Warsaw to AA, Nov. 20, 1920 (citing declaration by *starost* in Puck), *Dokumente* (Volz), p. 7; Heidelck, "Deutschtum," p. 249.

18. The idea was dropped primarily because their were so many more Germans in Poland than Poles in Germany, and also because it would further undermine the position of remaining Polish Germans. See East Prussian *Oberpräsident* to AA, Sept. 29, 1920, PA, Abt. IV Pol. 25 Polen, v. 2. Stories of the mistreatment of Germans in the wake of the Russian retreat also reached the United States, where a Lutheran pastor in Wisconsin set up an "American Relief Committee for Poles of German Extraction." See Rev. Otto Engel, Randolph, Wis., to AA, Nov. 6, 1920, Ibid., v. 3 p. 74; Ludolf Müller, *Meine Ausweisung aus Polen*, p. 7; Goerdeler, p. 14.

19. Zbigniew Landau and Jerzy Tomaszewski, *Wirtschaftsgeschichte Polens im 19. und 20. Jahrhundert*, pp. 131ff.; Karzel, p. 63.

20. Roman Wapiński, "Z dziejów kultury politycznej Wielkopolski i Pomorza w dwudziestoleciu międzywojennym," p. 7; Mornik, p. 43; Hermann Rauschning, "Bedeutung und Entwicklung der abgetretenen Gebiete Westpreussens," in F. Heiss and A. Hillen, eds., *Deutschland und der Korridor*, p. 118; Walter Kuhn, "Das Deutschtum in Polen und sein Schicksal in Kriegs- und Nachkriegszeit," p. 141.

21. Landau and Tomaszewski, pp. 126-27; Roos, *History*, p. 108; Rauschning, *Entdeutschung*, p. 132; Basedow and Correns, p. 52; Czech, p. 142.

22. Wapiński, *Endecja*, p. 48; Ahlers, pp. 96-97.

23. Chałasiński, p. 92; Joseph Rothschild, *East-Central Europe between the Two World Wars*, p. 30; German Consul Poznań, to AA, June 15, 1921, PA, Abt. IV Pol. 25 Polen, v. 5, p. 4.

24. AA to German Embassy Warsaw, Nov. 16, 1920, PA Abt. IV Pol. 25 Polen, v. 2, p. 12; AA to Polish Ambassador, July 18, 1923, *Dokumente* (Volz), p. 8.

25. Rauschning, *Entdeutschung*, p. 15; Riekhoff, pp. 205-6.

26. Hannuschek to Kessler, Nov. 3, 1920, PA Abt. IV Pol. 25, v. 3; Rauschning, *Entdeutschung*, p. 60.

27. Berend to AA, Feb. 22, 1921, PA Abt. IV Pol. 25, v. 5; Chałasiński, pp. 44ff.

28. Otto Dibelius, *Wie erfüllen die Polen ihre feierlich übernommene Pflicht, die evangelische Minderheit zu schützen*, p. 12. German Consul Poznań, June 4, 10, and 11, 1921, and Ziemke to AA, June 7, 1921, PA, Abt. IV Pol. 25 Polen, v. 4, pp. 146ff., 301; "Verein Heimattreuer Ostrower," Breslau, June 6, 1921, v. 4, pp. 263ff.; unsigned report on rally of June 8, 1921, ibid., v. 4 p. 274. Mornik, p. 86.

29. Kiernik in Sejm, Aug. 24, 1923; Evangelical Consistorium to Poznanian *wojewode*, Sept. 1, 1923; and Minister for Religion and Enlightment to Evangelical Consistorium, Sept. 27, 1923, all in WAPP, EK 539. Education Ministry to RK, BA R 43 I 119, p. 37; Ziemke to AA, June 7, 1921, PA Abt. IV Pol. 25 Polen, v. 4.

30. Stresemann, Feb. 14, 1924, BA R 43 I 120, pp. 203-4. This view was reiterated the following year when Bavaria proposed to expel some additional Polish citizens: Schubert, Aug. 23, 1925, BA R 43 I 120, p. 166; Krahmer-Möllenberg to AA, Oct. 19, 1920, PA, Abt. IV Pol. 25 Polen, v. 1, pp. 146ff.

31. Ziemke to AA, June 9, 1921, PA, Abt. IV Pol. 25 Polen, v. 4, p. 276.

32. *Dziennik Urzędowy*, June 23, 1921; German Consul Poznań to AA, June 22, 23, and 30, 1921, PA, Abt. IV Pol. 25 Polen, v. 5, pp. 74ff., 120ff., 134ff.; AA to German Embassy Warsaw, Nov. 16, 1920, PA, Abt. IV Pol. 25 Polen, v. 2, p. 12; Polish flier, dated June 1921, p. 120.

33. Quote from Riekhoff, p. 195; German Consul Poznań to AA, May 24, 1921, PA Abt. IV Pol. 25 Polen, v. 4, pp. 135ff., and v. 10, pp. 34ff., 50ff.; Rauschning, *Entdeutschung*, pp. 109, 141, 151; Polonicus, p. 38; Heidelck, "Deutschtum," p. 251; Potocki, p. 89.

34. Potocki, pp. 24-25; Drozdowski, "Minorities," p. 227; Krasuski, *Stosunki, 1919-25*, p. 260.

35. Roman Lutman, "Emigracja Niemców z Pomorza w okresie powojennym," in *Stan posiadania ziemi na Pomorzu*, pp. 172ff.; Krysiński, p. 16.

36. Rauschning, *Entdeutschung*, p. 64; Heike, *Minderheit*, p. 171; Riekhoff, p. 57; Mornik, p. 87.

37. Czesław Andrzejewski ["Liber"], *Das Deutschtum in Westpolen* (Poznań, 1919), pp. 17ff.

38. Kazimiera Jeżowa, *Die Bevölkerungs- und Wirtschaftsverhältnisse im westlichen Polen* (reply to Rauschning), pp. 14ff., 36, 64, 150; Zygmunt Stoliński, *Die deutsche Minderheit in Polen*, p. 9.

39. Friedrich Swart and Richard Breyer, "Die deutsche Volksgruppe im polnischen Staat," p. 478; Czech, p. 117.

40. W.W. Kulski, *Germany and Poland*, p. 24; Tomaszewski, *Rzeczpospolita*, p. 214; Grünberg, *Niemcy*, p. 17; Stoliński, p. 10.

41. Mornik, p. 84; Rauschning, *Entdeutschung*, p. 10; Friedrich Heidelck, "Stellung" p. 62.

42. This incident is related by a pastor and school committee member who was subsequently arrested and fined before removing himself to the Reich. See Basedow and Correns, pp. 18ff.; Krasuski, *Stosunki 1919-25*, p. 263.

43. Hauser, *Niemcy*, pp. 19ff.; Makowski (in *Rola*, pp. 312-13) focuses more on the "worsening of their political and material condition" as the "main cause for the voluntary departure of about 50 percent of the German population of western Poland."

44. Hannuschek to AA, PA Abt. IV Pol. 25 Polen, v. 3.

45. Budding to AA, Sept. 7, 1923, ibid., v. 15; Otto Heike, *Das Deutschtum in Polen*, p. 17.

46. Franz Lüdtke, Aug. and Oct. 1919, in Jeżowa, p. 149.

47. H. Schütz, in ibid., p. 173.

48. Ibid., p. 180; Stresemann to RK, Dec. 11, 1925, BA R 43 I 121, pp. 323ff.

49. Müller, *Kirche*, p. 11.

50. Heike, *Deutschtum*, p. 20, and *Minderheit*, p. 169.

51. Rhode, "Deutschtum," p. 100.

52. German Consul Toruń, Feb. 23, 1927, PA Abt. IV Pol. 25 Polen, v. 22, pp. 43ff., and Budding to Mixed Commission, Sept. 7, 1923, v. 11; minutes of conference in AA, April 6, 1921, PA Geh. Abt. IV Pol. 25 Polen, v. 1; WAPP, UWP 1262, p. 330; Kellermann, p. 107.

53. On teachers: PA Abt. IV Pol. 25 Polen, v. 1; v. 13, p. 252. On pastors: Oberkirchenrat Berlin (Moeller), Feb. 28, 1921, WAPP, EK 538.

54. Stoliński, p. 74.

55. Jan. 18, 1921, BA R 43 I 549, p. 204; Graebe memo, Dec. 19, 1928, BA R 43I 123, pp. 150-51; Krekeler, "Politik," p. 53.

56. Breyer, *Reich*, pp. 40ff.; Hauser, *Niemcy*, p. 27; Stoliński, pp. 84, 97; Paprocki, p. 116.

57. Walter Kuhn, "Berufsgliederung der Deutschen in Polen nach der Zählung von 1921," pp. 438, 443, 459; Rhode, "Deutschtum," p. 100; Rauschning, p. 9; Mornik, p. 42.

58. Kuhn, "Berufsgliederung," pp. 438ff.; Heidelck, "Deutschtum," p. 221; Beirschenk, *Volksgruppe*, p. 12; Kowalak, *Prasa*, p. 16; Drozdowski, "Minorities," p. 228.

59. Karzel, pp. 41ff.; Rhode, "Deutschtum," pp. 118-19; Potocki, p. 91; Stoliński, p. 73; Bierschenk, *Volksgruppe*, p. 12.

60. Rauschning, *Entdeutschung*, p. 372; Heidelck, "Deutschtum," p. 221; Drozdowski, "Minorities," p. 244; Mornik, p. 42; Stoliński, p. 73; Paprocki, p. 116; Potocki, pp. 89ff.; Krekeler, "Politik," p. 119.

61. See Richard Blanke, *Prussian Poland in the German Empire, 1871-1900*, p. 192; Karzel, p. 57; Heike, *Deutschtum*, p. 20; Polonicus, p. 71.

62. Swart and Bryer, pp. 480ff.; Landau and Tomaszewski, p. 117; Drozdowski, "Minorities," p. 244; Paprocki, p. 116; Stoliński, p. 97; Władysław Rogala, "Niemiecka mniejszość narodowa w Polsce w okresie rokowań gospodarczych," p. 110; Mieczysław Grzyb, *Narodowościowo polityczne aspekty przemian stosunków własnościowych i kadrowych w górnośląskim przemyśle*, p. 209.

3. Coming to Terms

1. Fleischer to Albert, Oct. 15, 1919; AA to RK, April 20, 1920, both in BA R 43 I 549, pp. 13ff., 60. IfZ MA 195/2-5 1064, p. 546. On Nauman, see *Von Unserer Art*, and Fritz Wertheimer, *Von Deutschen Parteien und Parteiführern im Ausland*, p. 94. Hauser, *Mniejszość*, pp. 48ff.; Heike, *Deutschtum*, pp. 47-48.

2. Norbert Krekeler, *Revisionsanspruch und geheime Ostpolitik der Weimarer Republik*, p. 25; German Consul Poznań to AA, Dec. 5, 1920, PA Geh. Abt. IV Pol. 25 Polen, v. 1; Heike, *Minderheit*, p. 172; Bierschenk, *Volksgruppe*, p. 25; Hauser, *Mniejszość*, pp. 54-55.

3. Report on negotiations leading to the Deutschtumsbund, *cum* charter, in IfZ MA 195/2-5 1064, p. 270; Potocki, pp. 115ff.; Kraususki, *Stosunki 1919-25*, p. 320; Consul Łódź to AA, Nov. 12, 1921, PA Abt. IVa Pol. 25 Polen, v. 7, pp. 844ff., and v. 8, p. 17; UWP 1262 (Deutschtumsbund), pp. 440ff., 545.

4. German Consul Poznań to AA, May 28 and June 11, 1921, PA Abt. IVa Pol. 25 Polen, v. 4, pp. 143ff.; Wertheimer, *Parteien*, p. 96; Potocki, p. 114.

5. Cf. Pia Nordblom, "Dr Eduard Pant," pp. 112ff.; Jan Łaczewski, "Eduard Pant," pp. 229ff.; Wojciech Kotowski, "Die Lage der deutschen Katholiken in Polen," pp. 39ff.

6. Otto Heike, "Die deutsche Arbeiterbewegung in Polen," pp. 508-9, 522; Ohlhoff, p. 65; Potocki, p. 132.

7. Stolinski, p. 80.

8. Heike, *Minderheit*, p. 51; Breyer, *Deutsches Reich* p. 57; Wertheimer, *Parteien*, p. 108; Potocki, p. 132.

9. Wertheimer, *Partheien*, p. 108; Gerhard Webersinn, *Otto Ulitz;* Kauder, p. 280.

10. Figures from Rothschild, p. 49; Heike, *Deutschtum*, pp. 70ff.

11. Paweł Korzec, "Der Block der nationalen Minderheiten im Parlamentarismus Polens," pp. 202ff.; Richard Breyer, "Polnischer Parlamentarismus und Nationalitätenfrage," pp. 69ff.; Krasuski, *Stosunki 1919-25*, 322; Polonicus, p. 47.

12. Stanisław Grabski, *Państwo Narodowe*, esp. conclusion.

13. *Kuryer Poznański*, March 15, 1921; August 21, 1924; April 19, 1925.

14. *Der Auslanddeutsche* 7 (1924): 74; Heike, *Deutschtum*, pp. 91-92; Dirksen to AA, July 13, 1921, PA Abt. IV Pol. 25 Polen, v. 5, p. 112.

15. Józef Piłsudski, *Pisma zbiorowe*, 5:154ff.

16. Rauschning, *Entdeutschung*, pp. 83f.

17. *Wybór źródeł do historii Polski, 1918-1944*, ed J. Grzywna and M. Markowski (Kielce, 1977), 1:219ff.; Rhode, "Deutschtum," p. 96; Rothschild, pp. 47ff.; Swart and Breyer, p. 488.

18. Mendelssohn, p. 37.

19. Quoted in Richard Breyer and Paweł Korzec, "Polnische Nationalitätenpolitik und die deutsche Volksgruppe," p. 275.

20. Tomaszewski, *Rzeczpospolita*, p. 221.

21. *Deutsche Zeitung*, Nov. 2, 1919.

22. German Consul Poznań to AA, April 12, 1923, *Dokumente zur Vorgeschichte des Krieges*, (AA) pp. 10-11; *Posener Neueste Nachrichten*, April 10, 1923; German Embassy Warsaw to AA, PA Abt. IV Pol. 25 Polen, v. 14, p. 20; EK 552; Rauschning, *Entdeutschung*, p. 67; Müller, p. 24.

23. *Dziennik Poznański*, Feb. 20, 1923; Kazimierz Kierski, *Prawa mniejszości niemieckiej w Polsce* (Poznań, 1923), p. 87, and "Podstawy prawne osadnictwa polskiego na Pomorzu," in *Stan Posiadania ziemi na Pomorzu*, pp. 185ff.; Mroczko, *Związek*, p. 211.

24. *Nasz Przegląd*, Nov. 26, 1924; Rauschning, *Entdeutschung*, p. 53; Czech, p. 141.

25. A. Schubert, "Strukturwandlungen," p. 380; also Kellermann, p. 107; Swart and Breyer, p. 494.

26. Pomorze Wojewode Stanisław Wachowiak, quoted in Wapiński, *Endecja na Pomorzu*, p. 47.

27. *Posener Tageblatt*, Sept. 10, 1929; Rauschning, *Entdeutschung*, pp. 50, 103, 116ff.; Rhode, "Deutschtum," p. 103.

28. Friedrich Weber, *Der deutsch-polnische Staatsvertrag vom 30. August, 1924*

(Munich, 1930); Krasuski, *Stosunki 1919-25*, pp. 246, 258; Riekhoff, pp. 60ff.; Polonicus, pp. 35-36.

29. Riekhoff, pp. 68-69; Krasuski, *Stosunki, 1919-25*, p. 515.

30. Graebe/Naumann petition to Polish government, Feb. 25, 1929, and Stresemann statement, League C. 264.1919.I.

31. Celichowski to EK, Nov. 20, 1919; Exin Church Council to EK, July 15, 1920, both in EK 529. Celichowski circular, July 6, 1920, BA R 43 I 117, p. 164. German Embassy Warsaw to AA, Sept. 5, 1921; German Consul Poznań to AA, April 10, 1923, PA Abt. IV Pol. 25 Polen, v. 7, p. 16, and v. 14, p. 27. *Der Auslanddeutsche* 7 (1924): 205; Müller, *Kirche*, p. 42; Basedow and Correns, pp. 52ff.

32. *Deutsche Rundschau*, December 6, 1929; Rhode, "Deutschtum," p. 107; Rauschning, *Entdeutschung*, p. 50.

33. *Der Auslanddeutsche* 8 (1925): 282.

34. Rauschning, *Entdeutschung*, pp. 185, 194ff., 200; Polonicus, p. 26; Gottfried Martin [Richard Kammel], *Brennende Wunden*, p. 28; Czech, p. 145; unsigned reports, Oct. 1926 and April 6, 1927, BA R 43 I 122, pp. 135ff., 267ff.; Reikhoff, p. 140.

35. Nachlass Rutzen, Ost-Dok. 6 D1 #6; Dyck letter, BA R 43 I 117, pp. 145ff.; Rauschning, *Entdeutschung*, pp. 171ff.; Rhode, "Deutschtum," p. 106.

36. Edmund Makowski, "Tajne zabiegi Niemiec o utrzymanie kolonistów w zachodniej Polsce, 1919-1929," in *Polacy i Niemcy*, pp. 305ff.; Riekhoff, p. 138; Martin, p. 27.

37. Narutowicz to League, July 3, 1922; Poland to League, July 5, 1922; Askenazy to Secretary-General, August 30, 1922; Da Gama report, Sept. 30, 1922; Graebe complaint, Nov. 13, 1922; Narutowicz reply, Dec. 7, 1922, all in League, C.461, 590, 612, 789.1922.I. Helmut Lippelt, "Politische Sanierung," p. 327; Rauschning, *Entdeutschung*, p. 70; Makowski, in *Polacy i Niemcy*, pp. 313ff.; Riekhoff, p. 139.

38. Rauschning, *Entdeutschung*, pp. 91ff.; Riekhoff, pp. 139f.; leaseholders appeal, League, May 26, 1921, C94.1920.I.

39. Werner Pünder to Reichskanzlei, Nov. 27, 1926, BA R 43 I 122, pp. 170ff.; Rhode, "Deutschtum," p. 107; Bierschenk, *Volksgruppe*, pp. 112-13.

40. Quote from Schubert, "Strukturwandlungen," p. 380; Rauschning, *Entdeutschung*, pp. 222, 242; Mornik, p. 92; Bierschenk, *Volksgruppe*, pp. 116ff.

41. NL Graebe 1, BA, pp. 52ff.

42. NL Graebe, BA; German Consul Poznań to AA, Jan. 23, 1923, and Graebe memo, Feb. 13, 1923, PA Abt. IV Pol. 25 Polen, v. 13, pp. 112, 129.

43. Krahmer-Möllenberg, June 29, 1921, PA Abt. IVa Pol. 25 Polen, v. 5, p. 227, and v. 10; Abt. IV Pol. 25 Polen, v. 11; Krekeler, *Revisionsanspruch*, p. 28.

44. Pomorze Wojewode to Supreme Administrative Court Warsaw, March 17, 1925, PA Geh. Abt. IV Pol. 25 Polen, v. 1; *Zehn Jahre Versailles*, ed. K. v. Loesch and M.H. Boehm 3:277; Heidelck, "Deutschtum," p. 247; Mornik, p. 109; suit filed by Germans following dissolution, Aug. 10, 1023, UWP 1264, pp. 10ff.; other material in PA Abt. IV Pol. 25 Polen, v. 15-6 and v. 20, p. 40. An article on the "history and goals" of the DB, based on files seized during the crackdown, is in *Strażnica Zachodnia* 2 (1927): 9ff.

45. Stoliński, pp. 46ff.; Bierschenk, *Volksgruppe*, p. 26; German Consul Poznań to AA, Sept. 11, 1925, PA Abt. IV Pol. 25 Polen, v. 20, p. 71; Bydgoszcz City

President to Wojewode, June 27, 1924, UWP 1263, p. 13; DViSuS memo, Jan. 18, 1927, EK 471.

46. Hieke, "Arbeiterbewegung," pp. 511, 520; Jan Walczak, *Polska i niemiecka socjaldemokracja na Górnym Śląsku*, p. 31; UWP 1212, p. 22.

47. Swart, p. 83; Karzel, p. 121; Breyer and Korzec, pp. 321, 353.

48. Swart, pp. 92ff.; Heike, *Minderheit*, pp. 410-11.

49. Rhode, "Deutschtum," pp. 127f.; Wolfgang Kohte, "Deutsche landesgeschichtliche Forschung im Posener Land," p. 102; Heike, *Deutschtum*, p. 202; Peter Nasarski, *Deutsche Jugendbewegung und Jugendarbeit in Polen*, p. 52.

50. Kowalak, *Prasa*; Heike, *Deutschtum*, pp. 163-64; Hauser, *Mniejszość*, p. 160; Stoliński, p. 67; Drozdowski, "Minorities," p. 245; Rolf Wengersdorf, *Die Vernichtung der deutschen Presse in Polen*, p. 39; Lucjan Meissner, *Niemieckie organizacje antyfazystowskie w Polsce*, p. 49.

51. Budding to AA, Sept. 7, 1923, PA Abt. IV Pol. 25 Polen, v. 15; Heike, *Deutschtum*, p. 166; Breyer, *Deutsches Reich*, p. 55; Wengersdorf, pp. 38-39; Edward Wynot, "The Polish Germans, 1919-1939," p. 38.

52. Stoliński, p. 29; Polish Education Minister to League, Jan. 23, 1923, League, L.56.1923.I. See Kurt Egon von Türcke, *Das Schulrecht der deutschen Volksgruppen in Ost- und Südosteuropa*, pp. 168, 193ff., for most key treaties and laws pertaining to German schools in Poland.

53. Drozdowski, "Minorities," p. 230; Breyer and Korzec, p. 264; Hauser, *Mniejszość*, p. 142.

54. *Deutsche Rundschau*, May 19, 1924; Paul Dobbermann, *Die deutsche Schule im ehemals preussischen Teilgebiet Polens* p. 153; Rhode, "Deutschtum," p. 114; Martin, p. 45; Bierschenk, *Volksgruppe*, p. 164; Potocki, p. 232; Stoliński, p. 131.

55. *Das Deutschtum in Polnisch-Schlesien*, p. 298; *Dennoch*, pp. 6ff.; Bierschenk, *Volksgruppe*, pp. 162ff.

56. Dobbermann, pp. 143ff., 156ff., Rhode, "Deutschtum," p. 114; Bierschenk, *Volksgruppe*, p. 159; official reply to S., Aug. 22, 1925, in German protest, League, C.493.1925.I

57. Polish Education Minister to Secretary-General, Jan. 23, 1923, League, C.56.1923.I; Rhode, "Deutschtum," p. 114.

58. Müller, *Kirche*, p. 25; Theodor Grenztrup, *Die kirchliche Rechtslage der deutschen Minderheiten in Europa*, p. 221; Heike, *Minderheit*, p. 229.

59. Wojewode to EK, June 24, 1920; Chrzanowski to EK, June 1 and 30, 1920, EK 529; Rhode, "Deutschtum," p. 122.

60. Superintendent Blau to "Weltbund für Freundschaftsarbeit der Kirchen," Aug. 27, 1920, EK 529; Blau petition, Aug. 4, 1920, League, M.6.1920.I; German Consul Poznań to AA, Nov. 9, 1923, PA Abt. IV Pol. 25 Polen, v. 16, p. 45; Müller, *Kirche*, p. 62.

61. Heike, *Minderheit*, p. 276; Graebe to EK, Sept. 15, 1922, EK 471; Blau to Wojewode, Nov. 30, 1923, EK 291; Blau memo, Jan. 12, 1924, EK 539.

62. Blau circulars, March 5, 1923, and Dec. 19, 1927, EK 291, 471; Staemmler to Leibrandt, Dec. 15, 1927, EK 471.

63. Staemmler to Leibrandt, EK 262; Blau circular, Nov. 5, 1928, EK 293. His fifteenth anniversary homily was less positive: "For many . . . this is a day of painful memories, . . . [but] the fate of peoples lies in God's hands" (Blau circular, Nov. 11, 1933, EK 294).

64. Blau circular, Sept. 28, 1933, EK 294, 646.

65. Rhode, "Deutschtum," p. 123; Müller, *Kirche*, p. 60; Bierschenk, *Volksgruppe*, p. 190; Czech, p. 141; Polonicus, p. 63. German Consul in Poznań to AA, April 16, 1924; National Lutheran Council (US), Nov. 18, 1920, and German response, March 26, 1921; Dibelius to AA, April 14, 1921, all in PA Abt. IV Pol. 25 Polen, v. 17, p. 176, and v. 4, pp. 58ff. Heike, *Minderheit*, p. 270; *Kirche, Volk, und Staat in Polen*. See also the most recent study of this problem by Alfred Kleindienst and Oskar Wagner. *Der Protestantismus in der Republik Polen*.

66. Władysław Michejda, *Stosunki w ewangelickim kościele unijnym na polskim Górnym Śląsku*, pp. 9, 23; Hermann Voss, *Die unierte evangelische Kirche in Polnisch-Schlesien*, p. 22; Keitsch, *Schicksal*, p. 125; Heike, *Minderheit*, p. 281.

67. Eduard Pant, "Das Katholische Organisationswesen," in Kauder, ed., *Das Deutschtum in Polen*, vol. 4, pp. 337ff.; BA R 43 I 121, p. 340; Heike, *Deutschtum*, p. 139; *Der Auslanddeutsche* 6 (1923): 508; Nordblom, pp. 49ff.

68. Quoted from speech in Silesian Sejm, in Kotowski, p. 49.

69. Hilarius Breitinger, *Als Deutschenseelsorger in Posen und im Warthegau*, esp. p. 10; Wertheimer, *Parteien*, p. 95; Polonicus, p. 66; German Consul Poznań to AA, Jan. 5, 1928, PA Geh. Abt. IV Pol. 25 Polen, v. 4; Kotowski, p. 40ff.

70. *Domkapitular* Paech to Wenz, Jan. 26, 1934, in Breitinger, p. 165.

71. Breitinger, pp. 8, 18, 171 (Breitinger report, May 17, 1934).

72. Birschel to EK, March 22, 1928, EK 471; Potocki, pp. 185ff.; Basedow and Correns, p. 69; Swart and Breyer, p. 109; Heike, *Deutschtum*, p. 89.

73. Goerdeler, pp. 10-11, 21ff., 65, 160, 168.

74. Walburg Lehfeldt, *Gut Lehfelde*.

75. Rauschning, *Entdeutschung*, p. 47; Czech, pp. 140ff.; Hannuschek to AA, Nov. 1920, PA Abt. IVA Pol. 25 Polen, *v*. 3, p. 6.

76. Postwar accounts by Pieper, Weiss, Jonanne, Hans von Rosen, and Erich Spitzer, Ost-Dok. 6 A3, D1-14.

77. PA Abt. IV Pol. 25 Polen, v. 19 pp. 159ff.; Rhode, "Deutschtum," p. 112.

78. Nordblom, p. 118.

79. German Consul Poznań to AA, Sept. 18, 1926, PA Abt. IV Pol. 25 Polen, v. 21 p. 95; Heidelck, Aug. 1, 1929, PA Geh. Abt. IV Pol. 25 Polen, v. 5; on Lattermann and Lück, see *Von Unserer Art*, pp. 90-95; Kohte, p. 108.

80. See Kurt Trampler, *Staaten und nationale Gemeinschaften*, and Trampler, *Die Krise des Nationalstaats*, focusing especially on the problem of Germans in Poland.

81. Max-Hildebert Boehm, a prominent advocate of this approach, distinguished between "minorities of fate," or *Auslanddeutsche* (those more or less voluntary emigrant German populations far from the Reich) and "coincidental minorities," or *Grenzdeutsche* (such as the Germans in western Poland, who lived just across the Reich's borders, were involuntarily separated, and were much more likely to harbor revanchist thoughts). See Boehm, "Reorganisation," esp. p. 26; *Das eigenständige Volk* (Berlin, 1930) and Boehm, *Europa Irredenta* (Berlin, 1923.)

82. Maria Rothbarth, "Imperialistyczne Niemcy a utworzenie Europejskiego Kongresu Mniejszości Narodowych," in *Rola Mniejszości*, pp. 74-75; Drozdowski, "Minorities," p. 234; Boehm, "Reorganisation," p. 30; Gotthold Rhode, "Völker und Staaten in Ost-Mittleuropa," p. 197; Hans-Adolf Jacobsen, *National-*

sozialistische Aussenpolitik, p. 166; Erik von Witzleben, quoted in *Posener Tageblatt*, May 26, 1934.

83. *Posener Tageblatt*, March 30, 1927. The large store of clippings and other material on international minorities congresses preserved in EK 514 testifies to the importance of such efforts in the eyes of at least some minority leaders.

84. Lütgens to AA, Dec. 23, 1929, Jan. 21 and June 5, 1930, PA Geh. Abt. IV Pol. 25 Polen, v. 6.

85. Potocki, p. 221.

86. Paweł Korzec, "Der zweite Block der nationalen Minderheiten im Parlamentarismus Polens," p. 113.

4. The Piłsudski Era and the Economic Struggle

1. See, e.g., Rothschild, p. 58; Roos, *History,* pp. 110ff.; Rhode, *Geschichte,* pp. 485ff.; Marian Dziewanowski, *Poland in the 20th Century,* pp. 84ff.

2. Quoted in Rhode, "Deutschtum," p. 97.

3. *Posener Tageblatt*, Nov. 7, 1926.

4. Czesław Madajczyk, "Dokumenty w sprawie polityki narodowościowej władz polskich po przewrocie majowym," pp. 140ff.

5. Ibid.; Breyer and Korzec, p. 268.

6. *Sprawy Narodowościowe* 1 (1927): 1; cf. also Daczko to Blau, Sept. 24, 1926, WAPP, EK 514, for example of optimistic German expectations.

7. Korzec, "Zweite Block," pp. 90ff.; Edward Wynot, "Poland's Christian Minorities," p. 243.

8. Deutsche Stiftung (DS) to AA, July 25, 1935, PA Abt. IV Pol. 25 Polen, v. 35.

9. From Senate speech, March 5, 1931, PA Abt. IV Pol. 25 Polen, v. 29, p. 91.

10. German Consul Katowice to AA, Oct. 1, 1930, PA Geh. Abt. IV Pol. 28A Polen, pp. 8845, 4034; *Polonia,* Sept. 22, 1930.

11. Meissner, pp. 267ff.; Hauser, *Mniejszość,* pp. 83f.; Heike, *Minderheit,* p. 218; Breyer and Korzec, pp. 319, 348.

12. E.g., Polish Ambassador to Berlin Kazimierz Olszowski in 1926; cf. Krasuski, *Stosunki 1919-25,* p. 502; Jerzy Krasuski, *Stosunki Polsko-Niemieckie 1926-1932,* p. 48.

13. Mroczko, *Związek,* pp. 56ff.; *Kuryer Poznański,* Jan. 23, 1929; German Consul Poznań to AA, Feb. 28, 1929, PA Abt. IV Pol. 25 Polen, v. 26; Friedrich Ross, *Polnische Kampfverbände und Propaganda-Institute,* pp. 17ff.

14. German Consul Poznań to AA, Oct. 26, 1926, PA Abt. IV Pol. 25 Polen, v. 21 p. 128.

15. Volksbund petition, June 1, 1928, League, C.404.1928.I; German Consul Poznań to AA, Oct. 15, 1923, PA Abt. IV Pol. 25 Polen, v. 15, p. 261; German Consul Poznań to AA, Feb. 28, 1929, PA Geh. Abt. IVa Pol. 25H Polen, v. 26, pp. 50ff.; *Der Auslanddeutsche* 14 (1931): 408; Edward Wynot, "The Case of German Schools in Polish Upper Silesia," p. 53.

16. Breyer, *Deutsches Reich* p. 30; Kellerman, p. 133.

17. Kuhn, "1931," table 1; Hans Kohnert, "Die deutsche Volksgruppe in Zahlen," BA Kleine Erwerbungen 619, pp. 35ff.

18. Edward Szturm de Sztrem, "Prawdziwa Statystyka," *Kwartalnik Historyczny* (1973): 664-67. Census figures were "an instrument of the political struggle" and "consciously falsified" (Chojnowski, p. 6).

19. Kuhn, "1931," p. 156; Czech, p. 157; Heidelck "Stellung"; Mornik, pp. 23ff.; Kohnert, *Volksgruppe* in BA, p. 35; Kauder, 1:7.

20. Stoliński, p. 40; Hauser, *Mniejszość*, p. 66.

21. AA memo, Dec. 1930, PA Abt. IV Pol. 25 Polen, v. 28, p. 10; *Der Auslanddeutsche* 13 (1930): 818; Roos, p. 136; Heike, *Deutschtum*, p. 163.

22. Report of May 15, 1927, BA R 43 I 122, p. 287; Henryk Rechowicz, *Sejm Śląski*, app. Wertheimer, p. 107; Kauder, I:281; Heike, "Arbeiterbewegung," p. 515, and *Minderheit*, p. 181; Potocki, p. 132; Hauser, *Mniejszość*, p. 70; Czech, p. 157.

23. *Posener Tageblatt*, June 27, 1928.

24. Otto Ulitz, *Oberschlesien—Aus seiner Geschichte*, p. 87; F.W.v. Oertzen, *Das ist Polen*, pp. 165ff.; Volksbund to Secretary-General, Feb. 13, 1929, and Polish reply, March 4, 1929, League, C.95.1929.I; Adatci report, March 7, 1929, League, C.125.1929.I; articles by Cesare Santoro, *Abendpost* (Berlin), June 2 and July 29, 1930.

25. Rechowicz, app.; Ulitz, pp. 81ff.

26. German petitions, League C.665, 681, 699.1930, and C.58.1931 (two of these, Nov. 27 and Dec. 9, dealt with Silesia, where the violence seems to have been worst, while a third, Dec. 17, dealt with Poznania and Pomorze); Christoph Kimmich, *Germany and the League of Nations*, p. 148.

27. Cesare Santoro, *Through Poland during the Elections of 1930*, pp. 27ff.; Ulitz, pp. 83ff.; Heike, *Deutschtum*, pp. 80ff.; Kauder, I:28. Korfanty, after three months' imprisonment, went into exile; in 1936, he was indicted *in absentia* for tax evasion and for taking bribes. Returning to Poland in 1939 he was again jailed briefly and died two weeks before the German invasion.

28. Santoro, pp. 26ff.

29. *Eingabensammlung der deutschen Volksgruppe in Westpolen*, p. 17; Stephen Horak, *Poland and Her National Minorities*, pp. 104ff.; Rothschild, p. 65; Zygmunt Kaczmarek, "Endecja wielkopolska wobec problemu niemieckiego," p. 232; Breyer, *Deutsches Reich*, p. 257; Roos, p. 120; Rhode, *Geschichte*, p. 488.

30. German Consul Poznań to AA, Oct. 15, 1929, and Feb. 10, 1930; PA Geh. Abt. IVa Pol. 25H Polen, v. 1; AA memo, May 2, 1930, ibid., v. 2; German Consul Poznań to AA, Nov. 15, 1934, ibid., v. 5.

31. Nasarski, esp. pp. 10ff.; Hauser, *Mniejszość*, p. 76; Hugo Rasmus, *Jugend im Aufbruch*, pp. 36-37.

32. German Consul Poznań to AA, Oct. 11, 1929, PA Geh. Abt. IVa Pol. 25H Polen, v. 1; Geh.IV Pol. 25 Polen v. 5; Heike, *Deutschtum*, p. 48; *Der Auslanddeutsche* 12 (1929): 752.

33. Position of German government, March 27, 1930, PA Geh. Abt. IVa Pol. 25H Polen, v. 1; Heike, *Minderheit*, pp. 426ff.; *Der Auslanddeutsche* 13 (1930): 819.

34. Krahmer-Möllenberg to AA, Sept. 30, 1932; German Embassy in Warsaw to AA, Jan. 2, 1933, both in PA Geh. IV Pol. 25 Polen, v. 7.

35. German Consul Poznań to AA, Feb. 28, 1929, PA Abt. IV Pol. 25 Polen, v. 26, pp. 50ff.

36. Bierschenk, *Volksgruppe*, p. 166; Breyer, *Deutsches Reich*, p. 53; Heike, *Deutschtum*, pp. 143ff.

37. Krahmer-Möllenberg to AA, Nov. 12, 1930, *ADAP*, [Ser. B, v. 16] pp. 131ff.; also his article "Das deutsche Schulwesen in Polen," *Der Auslanddeutsche* 14 (1931), pp. 574ff.

38. Breyer *Deutsches Reich*, p. 54; Bierschenk, *Volksgruppe*, p. 165; Martin, p. 45.

39. Poland to League, Dec. 16, 1927, League C.229.1927.I; Ludwik Ręgorowicz, "Stosunki narodowościowe na Śląsku," pp. 414-27; Potocki, p. 236.

40. Prussian Interior Ministry, Sept. 22, 1926, PA Geh. Abt. Pol. 25 Polen/ Oberschlesien, v. 1, KO 64234ff.; German Consul Katowice to AA, Feb. 7, 1928, ibid., v. 2, KO 64745.

41. Calonder to Secretary-General, Oct. 1923, League, C.67.1923.I; Wynot, "German Schools," p. 50; Keitsch, *Schicksal*, pp. 144f.; Tomasz Falęcki, *Niemieckie szkolnictwo mniejszościowe na Górnym Śląsku*.

42. *German Embassy Warsaw to AA, Oct. 23, 1924*, BA R 43 I 560, p. 25; League C.404.1928; Kroll, p. 112.

43. Ulitz to League, League, C.218.1928.I; petitions by Silesian parents, June-Aug. 1928, League, C.275, 398, 404-1928.I. Wynot, "Schools," p. 56.

44. Falęcki, App. 1; Oberpres. Wagner to Lammers, Dec. 11, 1938, PA Abt. V Pol. 25 Polen, v. 4; Wynot, "Schools," p. 58; Chałasiński, p. 84.

45. Bierschenk, *Volksgruppe*, p. 170; Stanisław Mauersberg, *Szkolnictwo powszechne dla mniejszości narodowych w Polsce*, p. 140.

46. Bierschenk, *Volksgruppe*, pp. 54, 63; Hauser, *Mniejszość*, p. 147; *Dennoch*, p. 22.

47. WAPP, Org. niem. 524, p. 152, and 525, p. 69; *Dennoch*, p. 21; *Von unserer Art*, pp. 128-35; Swart and Breyer, p. 504; Sewern Osiński, *V kolumna na Pomorzu gdańskim*, p. 149.

48. *Głos Leszczyński*, July 8, 1930.

49. Graebe to Secretary-General, League, C.333, 603, 710.1922.I; *Dennoch*, p. 10; Heidelck, "Deutschtum," p. 252; Polonicus, p. 54; Heike, *Minderheit*, pp. 324-25; *Deutsche Rundschau*, March 8, 1929.

50. Krahmer-Möllenberg (to AA), Nov. 12, 1930, *ADAP*, [ser. B, v. 16] pp. 131ff; Rhode, "Deutschtum," p. 115; Bierschenk, *Volksgruppe*, pp. 54ff., 174-75; Mornik, pp. 80-81.

51. Thea Wohlgemuth, *Das deutsche Gymnasium in Thorn zwischen den beiden Weltkriegen*.

52. Dietrich Vogt, *Das Schiller-Gymnasium in Posen*.

53. In 1937 it dropped to only 33 percent when, Vogt (ibid.) alleges, officials used his school's graduates to show their displeasure with the treatment of Polish secondary schools in Germany. See also WAPP, Org. niem. 524, p. 66.

54. Vogt.

55. WAPP, Org. niem. 524, p. 8; 525, p. 8; Smend to Roehr, p. 178; Roehr to Smend, March 28 and May 2, 1934, pp. 185ff.; Saenger to Kurator Pollak, April 18, 1934, p. 182; Wojewode to DSV Leszno, June 11, 1934, p. 200; Roehr to DSV, p. 216.

56. DSV Leszno to DSV, April 29, 1933, WAPP, Org. niem p. 199; DSV to DSV Leszno, April 9, 1936, 525, p. 289; report of Polish school inspector, p. 167; Schönbeck to Bickerich, Aug. 14, 1931, p. 69; Bickerich to Schönbeck, p. 94; 527 pp. 99, 229.

57. Nasarski, p. 37; Heike, *Deutschtum*, p. 147; Bierschenk, *Volksgruppe*, p. 56; *Dennoch*, p. 16.

58. Blau, April 16 and Nov. 18, 1932, WAPP, EK 294.

59. Hasso von Wedel, "Die Agrarreform in Polen," *Osteuropa* 3 (1928): 361; *Eingaben und Denkschriften zur Agrarreformfrage*, p. 4; Landau and Tomaszewski, p. 132; Karzel, p. 34.

60. *Eingaben*, p. 4; Landau and Tomaszewski, p. 134; Karzel, p. 35.

61. Petition of Aug. 16, 1927, and Polish reply, Nov. 6, 1927, League, C.563.1927.I, C.386.1928.I; Trautmann memo, Feb. 6, 1930, with figures for first three years, *ADAP*, ser. B, v. 14, p. 185; *Eingaben*, pp. 9ff.; Zenon Wartel, "Sprawa parcelacji majątków niemieckich w Polsce," p. 549; K. Ballerstedt, *Gegenwartsfragen der ländlichen Siedlung in Posen und Pomerellen.*

62. Memo Dec. 22, 1929, BA R 43 I 124, pp. 215ff.; German Consul Toruń to AA, March 14, 1929, PA Abt. IV Pol. 25 Polen, v. 26, p. 82.

63. *Eingaben*, p. 28; Wartel, "Sprawa," pp. 550ff.; Günther von Pflug, "Meine Erfahrungen mit der Agrarreform in Polen," BA Ost-Dok. D1 #2.

64. Landau and Tomaszewski, pp. 115, 128-29; Dziewanowski, p. 86; Henryk Wereszycki, "Poland, 1918-1939,"p. 687; Kellermann, p. 112.

65. Landau and Tomaszewski, pp. 139, 144ff., 161, 168, 194; Karzel, p. 110.

66. Hasso von Wedel, "Die Landwirtschaft in Polen," *Osteuropa* 2 (1926): 422-33; Theodor Oberländer, *Die Landwirtschaft Posen-Pomerellens vor und nach der Abtrennung vom Deutschen Reich*, pp. 45ff.; Hans Kohnert, "*Die Betriebsverhältnisse der deutschen Bauernwirtschaften in der ehemaligen Provinz Westpreussen;* Karzel, p. 77; Landau and Tomaszewski, p. 135.

67. German Consul Toruń to AA, June 2, 1933, PA Abt. IV Pol. 25 Polen, v. 27, p. 109, and v. 31 p. 68; *Eingabensammlung*, pp. 11-12; Bierschenk, *Volksgruppe*, pp. 104ff.

68. Dowództwo Okręgu Korpusu #7, July 7, 1933, WAPP, UWP 1218, p. 10; *Eingabensammlung*, p. 10.

69. German Consul Poznań to AA, March 6, 1931, PA Abt. IV Pol. 25 Polen, v. 29, p. 70, and v. 25, pp. 87, 111; *Eingabensammlung*, p. 13; Bierschenk, *Volksgruppe*, p. 106.

70. *Polska Zachodnia*, Sept. 14, 1931; Chojnowski, pp. 110ff.; Breyer, *Deutsches Reich* p. 302.

71. Chojnowski, pp. 107ff.; Krasuski, *Stosunki 1926-32*, p. 228.

72. Katowice Labor Office to DVG, July 1, 1929, and Oct. 23, 1934, PA Geh. Abt. Pol. 25 Polen/Oberschlesien, v. 3, K064942, and v. 5; German Consul Katowice to AA, July 9, 1930, on layoffs at the Königs- und Laurahütte and the Kattowitzer Aktiengesellschaft, *ADAP*, ser. B, v. 15, p. 315; Swart and Breyer, p. 500; Heike, *Deutschtum*, pp. 24-25.

73. Neal Pease, *Poland, the United States, and the Stablization of Europe* pp. 71, 121ff.

74. Norbert Lubos petition, Nov. 8, 1928, League, C.40.1929.I; *Polska Zachodnia*, Oct. 3, 1928.

75. Adatci report, March 6, 1929, League, C.110.1929.I.

76. Volksbund petition, Sept. 25, 1929, and Calonder opinion, June 30, 1929, League, C.6.1930.I, C.350.1930.I.

77. Pless to Polish Interior Ministry, March 6, 1929, and Pless petition to

League, Jan. 7, 1931, League, C.72.1931.I; Polish reply, May 19, 1931, League, C.373.1931.I.

78. "Union of German Employees in Polish Upper Silesia," June 6, 1935, PA Geh. Abt. Pol. 25 Polen, v. 6, p. 204; "De-Germanization Actions among Employees of the Hohenlohe Works in Polish Upper Silesia, Jan. 1, 1933-June 30, 1934," PA Geh. Abt. Pol. 25 Polen/Oberschlesien, v. 5; Wichard Hahn, "Die Arbeitslosigkeit der deutschen Volksgruppe in Ost-Oberschlesien," p. 564; Bierschenk, *Volksgruppe*, p. 140.

5. The Minority in the International Arena

1. Landau and Tomaszewski, pp 119, 171; German cabinet meeting, Nov. 9, 1920, BA R 43 I 117, p. 76.

2. Interior Ministry, Sept. 17, 1920, BA R 43 I 117, pp. 11-12; Agriculture Ministry, Oct. 26, 1920, 117, pp. 40-41, and Oct. 29, 1920, p. 158; cabinet meeting, Oct. 1, 1920, 118, p. 39; AA to RK, Oct. 11, 1920, 118, pp. 40-41.

3. Economics Ministry, Oct. 11, 1920; cabinet meetings, Nov. 8, 1920, and March 26, 1921, BA R 43 I 118, pp. 57ff., 106, 119.

4. Hans von Seeckt, *Aus meinem Leben*, ed. F. v. Rabenau (Leipzig, 1941), p. 136.

5. Horst Jablonowski, "Probleme der deutsch-polnischen Beziehungen zwischen den beiden Weltkriegen," p. 42.

6. Ibid., p. 43.

7. Cabinet meeting, April 11, 1921, IntMin, May 3, 1921, BA R 43 I 119, pp. 39, 47; Kellermann, p. 47; Korzec, "Polen," pp. 528-29.

8. Puttlitz to AA [1926], PA Abt. IV Pol. 25 Polen, v. 20, p. 207. See also remarks by Stresemann and Schacht, cabinet meeting, May 11, 1927, BA R 43 I 122, p. 277; Riekhoff, pp. 186ff., Henryk Zieliński, "The Economy," pp. 175-76.

9. Stresemann to RK, Dec. 11, 1925, BA R 43 I 121, pp. 323ff.; cabinet agreement, Dec. 22, 1925, p. 336.

10. Meeting of Nov. 24, 1927, BA R 43 I 122, pp. 364ff.; meeting in AA, Dec. 19, 1927, *ADAP*, ser. B, v. 7, p. 570.

11. Rauscher to Schubert and AA, Oct. 23, 1927, *ADAP*, ser. B, v. 7, pp. 114ff.

12. Rauscher to AA, Nov. 11, 1929, BA R 43 I 123, pp. 395ff.; text of the agreement, pp. 416ff.

13. Riekhoff, p. 150; Julius Curtius, *Sechs Jahre Minister der deutschen Republik*, p. 99; lower figures in Rhode, "Deutschtum," p. 106.

14. Krysiński, pp. 16ff.; *IKC*, Oct. 26, 1929.

15. Curtius to Rauscher, Feb. 18, 1930, *ADAP*, ser. B, v. 14, p. 254; Curtius, p. 99; Józef Feldman, *Problem polsko-niemiecki w dziejach*, p. 142.

16. Schubert to German Embassy Warsaw, April 5, 1930, PA Geh. Abt. IVa Pol. 25H Polen, v. 2.

17. State Secretary (AA) von Bülow to German Embassy Warsaw, Nov. 6, 1930, PA Geh. Abt. IV Pol. 25 Polen, v. 28, p. 41.

18. A German-Polish trade agreement of March 17, 1930, designed to end the tariff war, was unable to win Reichstag approval; see Mroczko, p. 160.

19. Kellermann, p. 115; Zieliński, "Economy," p. 175; Peter-Heinz Seraphim,

"Die Kapitalverflechtung zwischen Deutschland und Polen," *Osteuropa* 7 (1931): 197-207.

20. Polish Embassy Washington, Dec. 12, 1932, HI #60.

21. Cienciala, "German Propaganda," pp. 86, 106; Pease, p. 148.

22. Breyer, *Deutsches Reich*, p. 34; Kellermann, p. 151; Polish Embassy Washington, HI #60.

23. Rauscher to Bülow, Nov. 8, 1930; Bülow to Rauscher, Nov. 18, 1930; Rauscher to Bülow, Nov. 22, 1930; cabinet meeting, Nov. 26, 1930, all in BA R 43 I 125, pp. 51ff.; Noebel memo, Dec. 17, 1930, 561 p. 28.

24. Curtius, p. 98.

25. Secretary-General Drummond, League, C.82.1920.I and C.171.1921.I; Kimmich, p. 136; Janowsky, p. 117; Otto Junghann, *Das Minderheitenschutzverfahren vor dem Völkerbund*, pp. 70ff. For the text of most of the pertinent treaties and League declarations, see Julius Stone, *Regional Guarantees of Minority Rights;* and Macartney.

26. Azcarate, p. 29; Herbert von Truhart, *Völkerbund und Minderheiten-Petitionen*, p. 8; Drozdowski, "Minorities," p. 235; Horak, p. 65; Roucek, p. 153.

27. Stresemann to the ex-Crown Prince, Sept. 7, 1925, in Gustav Stresemann, *Vermächtnis*, 2:554.

28. Stresemann memo and appendix, Jan. 13, 1925, BA R 43 I 560, pp. 3ff.

29. Reichstag speech, July 24, 1929, in Bastiaan Schot, *Stresemann, der deutsche Osten, und der Völkerbund*, p. 52.

30. Stresemann to Polish Ambassador Oszowski, Dec. 3, 1926, Polish Embassy Washington, HI #60; Stresemann, 2:548; Dirksen memo, March 2, 1926, *ADAP*, ser. B, V. I,1, pp. 318ff. Cf. Carole Fink, "Stresemann's Minority Policies," pp. 402ff.; Kimmich, p. 133; Krasuski, *Stosunki 1926-32*, pp. 219ff.

31. Schot, p. 51; Kimmich, p. 142.

32. Rhode, "Völker," p. 197; Janowsky, p. 125; Truhart, pp. 121-22.

33. Polish statements, Jan. 16 and April 12, 1923, League, C.65.1923.I, C.364.1923.I.

34. Sokol, Sept. 21, 1928, League, C.510.1928.I and Annex 1077a.1928.I

35. Stresemann, 3:413; Kimmich, pp. 139-40; Naumann speech, Jan. 22, 1929, WAPP, EK 514.

36. Azcarate, p. 147.

37. Wynot, "German Schools," pp. 55f.; Fink, "Stresemann," p. 341; Schubert to SG, Nov. 14, 1927, League, C.567.1927.I.

38. E.g., officials refused to permit a minority school in Koszecin after the denial of admission to many bilingual children left its enrollment below forty; five parents received jail terms for refusing to send their children to the local Polish school instead. For other examples, see *Volksbund* peititons of Jan. 13 and 18, 1927, League, C.67-69.1927.I; Jan. 30, 1928, C.47.1928.I; Urrutia report, C.273.1928.I.

39. Sock petition, Sept. 5, 1930, League, C.674.1930.I.

40. Calonder opinion, Feb. 10, 1930, and *Volksbund* petition, June 5, 1930, League, C.468.1930.I.

41. Report of May 23, 1931, League, C.405.1931.I.

42. Graebe *et al.*, Sept. 1 and Sept. 15, 1931, League, C.6 and C.306.1931.I.

43. Report of Dec. 1, 1932, League, C.818.1932.I.

44. *Publications de la Cour Permanente de Justice Internationale*, pp. 175ff; *Eingaben*, p. 20.

45. German petitions, League, C.665, 681, 699.1930.I/and C.58.1931; Polish reply, C.68.1931.

46. Adatci report, Jan. 24, 1931, League, C.138.1931; Kimmich, pp. 148-49.

47. Cabinet meeting, Jan. 25, 1931, BA R 43 I 561, p. 127.

48. Polish replies, March 20 and May 14, 1931, League, C.308.1931.

49. *Volksbund* to SG, Aug. 14, 1931, League, C.582.1931.

50. All of BA R 43 I 127 deals with League treatment of German-Polish questions in 1930-31 and the recommended German strategies.

51. Petitions of April 26 and 28, and May 19, 1928, League, C.219, C.221, and C.240.1928.I; League report, June 8, 1928, C.313.1928.I.

52. Helmuth Fechner, *Deutschland und Polen*, p. 166; Fink, "Stresemann," p. 337. Martin Broszat, "Aussen- und innenpolitische Aspekte der preussisch-deutschen Minderheitenpolitik in der Ära Stresemann," p. 401, estimates the number of Polish speakers in the Weimar Republic at about one million, including 150,000 in the Rhineland, 500,000 in Upper Silesia, and most of the rest in other eastern border regions.

53. *Polonia* (Katowice). July 27, 1932; Theodor Bierschenk, "Die polnischen Richtlinien zur Behandlung der deutschen Volksgruppe," pp. 537-38; Fechner, p. 166.

54. Quoted in Broszat, "Aspekte," pp. 398ff.

55. State Secretary Loehrs (Int.Min.) to DOV, Sept. 16, 1920, BA R 43 I 118, p. 16.

56. Note of Jan. 13, 1925, BA R 43 I 560, pp. 3ff.

57. Appendix to Stresemann memo, Jan. 13, 1925, ibid., pp. 7ff.

58. Broszat, "Aspekte," pp. 407-8, 425ff.; Schot, pp. 32ff.

59. Naumann meeting with Luther, April 1, 1925, BA R 43 I 560, pp. 71ff.; Naumann to *Hauptwahlausschuss* (Bydgoszcz), Jan. 17, 1927, WAPP, EK 471; Broszat, "Aspekte," p. 424.

60. Feb. 16, 1926, *ADAP*, ser. B, v. I, 1 p. 244ff.

61. Ibid., Schot, pp. 32-33.

62. BA R 43 I 545, p. 321; Kellermann, p. 124.

63. Broszat, "Aspekte," p. 439.

64. Stresemann on Lasisk incident, Jan. 7, 1929, and circular dated Dec. 13, 1928, League, C.106-8.1928.I; Polish complaint and Schubert reply, Aug. 7, 1929, C.335.1929.I.

65. Cabinet meeting, Oct. 17, 1919, BA R 43 I 542; Konkordia charter, Feb. 20, 1920, and minutes of Kondordia meeting, April 13, 1920, IfZ MA 195 1064, pp. 572, 589; Tadeusz Kowalak, *Zagraniczne Kredyty dla Niemców w Polsce*, p. 36; Krekeler, *Revisionsanspruch*, p. 15; Makowski, p. 315.

66. Meeting in RK, Jan. 26, 1920, BA R 43 I 549, pp. 9ff., 58; IfZ MA 195 1064, p. 523.

67. Cabinet meeting, Nov. 19, 1920, PA Abt. IVA Pol. 25 Polen, v. 3; DS charter, IfZ MA 195 1064, p. 119; Krekeler, *Revisionsanspruch*, pp. 15ff., 47; Felix-Heinrich Gentzen, "'Deutsche Stiftung'—Tajna instytucja rządu niemieckiego do organizowania 5. kolumny," p. 295; Stanisław Potocki, "DS: Tajna agenda rządu

niemieckiego do spraw mniejszości niemieckich w okresie międzywojennym," in *Rola Mniejszości*, pp. 268ff.

68. Krekeler, *Revisionsanspruch*, pp. 16ff., 51; app., Jan. 30, 1928, PA Geh. Abt. IV Pol. 25 Polen, v. 5; Pol. 25 Polen/Oberschlesien, v. 1, 64501.

69. See also the contract between DS and Graebe, including a life insurance policy should Graebe die in the service of the German cause in Poland: IfZ MA 195 1069, p. 599; Kellermann, p. 107.

70. Gentzen, "Legende," p. 49; Osiński, *V kolumna*, p. 156.

71. Dec. 12, 1925, PA Abt. IV Pol. 25 Polen, v. 20, p. 182; German Consul Łódź to AA, Dec. 8 and 17, 1927, ibid., v. 4.

72. In return for a full subsidy, Rauschning even offered to let Krahmer-Möllenberg "censor" the book prior to publication, but the offer was refused. Rauschning to K-M, March 27, 1928; reply, March 29, 1928, IfZ MA 195 1124, pp. 6ff.

73. German Consul Katowice to DS, March 3 and Oct. 28, 1927, April 19, 1929, April 14 and Sept. 28, 1930, PA Geh. Abt. Pol. 25 Polen/Oberschlesien, v. 2, 64643; v. 3, p. 997; v. 4, 65086. Roman Dąbrowski, "Pomoc finansowa Niemiec dla mniejszości niemieckiej w Polsce," in *Rola Mniejszości*, p. 352.

74. Kotowski, p. 57.

75. Gentzen, "Deutsche Stiftung," p. 300.

76. *Dennoch*, p. 20.

77. Silesian delegation to Chancellor Luther, July 8, 1925; cabinet meeting, July 31, 1925, BA R 43 I 121, pp. 118, 133; PA Geh. Abt. Pol. 25 Polen, v. 1, KO 64234.

78. Cabinet meeting, July 15, 1927, BA R 43 I 121, pp. 332-33.

79. Krekeler, *Revisionsanspurch*, pp. 54, 104; Kowalak, *Kredyty*, p. 210; Steger-wald to AA, April 28, 1932, BA R 43 I 126.

80. Meyer memo, Aug. 16, 1932, *ADAP*, ser. B, v. 21 pp. 3ff.

81. German Consul Katowice to AA, April 1, 1931, *ADAP*, ser. B, v. 17, p. 156.

82. Meeting of June 9, 1932; cabinet meeting, July 21, 1932, *ADAP*, ser. B, v. 20 pp. 277, 481ff., 526ff.

83. Meyer memo, Feb. 19, 1935, *ADAP*, ser. C, v. III, 2, pp. 918-19.

84. Cf. BA R 43 I 547, pp. 71ff.

85. Krekeler, *Revisionsanspruch*, pp. 80ff.; BA R 43 I 545, p. 279.

86. Stresemann memo, "Förderung des bodenständigen Deutschtums im europáischen Ausland," *ADAP*, ser. B, v. I, 1, pp. 430ff.; BA R 43 I 546, pp. 51ff.; Krekeler, *Revisionsanspruch*, pp. 90ff.; Schot, pp. 39-40.

87. Krahmer-Möllenberg to AA, Dec. 18, 1926; cabinet meeting, Oct. 4, 1927, PA Geh. Abt. IV Pol. 25 Polen, v. 2-4.

88. Cabinet meeting, July 23, 1928, BA R 43 I 547, pp. 71ff., and 549, pp. 337ff.; PA Abt. IV Pol. 25 Polen, p. 66.

89. Meeting of Jan. 29, 1931, BA R 43 I 550, pp. 254ff.; Hey memo, Oct. 15, 1932, *ADAP*, ser. B, v. 21, p. 235.

90. Seiler memo, March 1, 1930; *Ressort* meeting, April 8, 1930; Finance Minister, May 30, 1930, all in *ADAP*, ser. B, v. 14, pp. 305ff, 467; v. 15, 123. Krekeler, *Revisionsanspruch*, pp. 120ff.; cabinet meeting, April 8, 1930, BA R 43 I 547, p. 274.

91. Summary of support efforts, BA R 43 I 548 pp. 287-88; and meeting of Jan. 29, 1932, ibid., 550, pp. 254ff.; Krekeler, *Revisionsanspruch*, p. 138.

92. German Consul Katowice, Sept. 24, 1930, PA Geh. Abt. IV Pol. 25

Polen/Oberschlesien, v. 4, 65087; Ross, pp. 37ff.; Richard Breyer, "Deutsche und polnische Förderung des Auslandsvolkstums," pp. 41-42.

93. *Gazeta Olsztyńska*, quoted in *Posener Tageblatt*, April 12, 1928.

94. Krekeler, *Revisionsanspruch*, p. 22. Nor does he provide evidence for his (counter-factual) assertion (p. 27) that many Polish Germans remained unaware of the source of the support they received and of the close ties between their leaders and Reich agencies.

95. German Consul Poznań to AA, Sept. 15, 1927, PA Geh. Abt. IV Pol. 25 Polen, v. 3.

96. Krahmer-Möllenberg to AA, Jan. 30, 1928, PA Geh. Abt. IV Pol. 25 Polen, v. 4.

97. Graebe to RK, Oct. 19, 1929, BA R 43 I 123, p. 301.

98. AA (Zechlin) to consulates, Nov. 15, 1927, and German Consul Poznań to AA, Nov. 17, 1927, PA Geh. Abt. IV Pol. 25 Polen, v. 4; Krekeler, *Revisionsanspruch*, p. 19; *Kuryer Poznański*, Feb. 13, 1928.

99. Pochhammer to AA, Nov. 14, 1931, PA Geh. Abt. IV Pol. 25 Polen, v. 7; Kowalak, p. 205-6.

100. Meeting of Feb. 11, 1920, BA R 43 I 543, p. 6; cf. Carl Severing's survey of the main *Deutschtum* organizations, their chief characteristics and sources of funding, in "Verzeichnis der mit Deutschtumspflege befassten Verbände," BA R 43 I 547, pp. 196ff.

101. Löbe letter, Aug. 18, 1922, and Interior Ministry, Aug. 15, 1922, BA R 43 I 544 pp. 335ff.; Wirth/Rathenau note, Oct. 17, 1922, 545, p. 116.

102. "Verzeichnis," BA R 43 I 547, pp. 196ff.; Ernst Ritter, *Das Deutsche Ausland-Institut in Stuttgart*.

103. Boehm, "Reorganisation" pp. 17-18; Krasuski, *Stosunki 1926-32* pp. 214ff.; Krekeler, *Revisionsanspruch*, p. 30.

104. Letter from Fleischer (DS advisory council) to Chancellor, Jan. 1921, urging that the DOV and its affiliates (e.g., the *Ostwacht*) be shunned as reactionary and revanchist: BA R 43 I 543, pp. 200ff.

105. Report of Jan. 5, 1923, BA R 43 I 545, pp. 54ff; AA memo, Aug. 8, 1923, ibid., 120, p. 152.

106. BA R 43 I 547: figures for 1929, meetings of Reich and Prussian representatives, March 25 and May 8, 1929, pp. 97ff.; Severing, p. 128; Prussian Minister-President, June 14, 1929, p. 150; meeting in AA, April 12, 1930, p. 277.

107. Interior Minister, July 23, 1927, BA R 43 I 546, p. 263; meeting of May 10, 1929, 547, p. 125; *Berliner Tageblatt*, Aug. 15, 1926.

108. Meeting, June 18, 1931, BA R 43 I 547; 548, pp. 174ff.

109. See IfZ MA 195/4 1129.

110. Meeting in Reichskanzlei, Jan. 8, 1926, BA R 43 I 121, p. 337; Pünder to RK, Nov. 27, 1926, 122, pp. 170ff.

111. Dirksen to German Embassy Warsaw, June 17, 1926, urging support for Naumann/Graebe vs. Reineke; German Embassy Warsaw to AA, June 6 and Aug. 21, 1926, PA Geh. Abt. IV Pol. 25 Polen, v. 1.

112. This faction soon faded following the 1931 suicide of its leader, Kopp; cf. German Consul Toruń to AA, Oct. 21, 1930; Prussian Culture Minister, Nov. 12, 1931, PA Geh. Abt. IV Pol. 25 Polen, v. 7; WAPP, UWP 1212, p. 25; Hauser, *Mniejszość*, p. 82.

113. Vassel to AA, Oct. 19, 1927; AA, Feb. 24, 1928; Lütgens to AA, July 10, 1930, PA Geh. Abt. IV Pol. 25L Polen.

114. Vassel to Zechlin (AA), March 3, 1927, PA Geh. Abt. IV Pol. 25 Polen, v. 3.

115. Vassel to AA, Sept. 15, 1927, PA Geh. Abt. IV Pol. 25 Polen, v. 3; and Graebe to Dirksen (AA), March 17 and Dec. 31, 1927, v. 4.

116. Lütgens, Vassel's replacement as German Consul in Poznań, also sided with minority leaders against Reich aid agencies: too much of the money meant for minority programs was absorbed by complicated administrative procedures; it took too long to reach those in need; and minority organizations in Poland needed to have more control over its distribution. See Lütgens to AA, Dec. 23, 1929, PA Geh. Abt. IV Pol. 25 Polen, v. 6.

117. Meeting of Nov. 24, 1927, BA R 43 I 122, pp. 364ff.; meeting in AA, Dec. 19, 1927, *ADAP*, ser. B, v. 7, p. 570.

118. Graebe to Müller, Sept. 14, 1928, BA R 43 I 123, p. 298; Finance Minister to AA, April 9, 1929, PA Geh. Abt. IV Pol. 25 Polen, v. 5.

119. Krahmer-Möllenberg to AA, July 25, 1928, PA Geh. Abt. IV Pol. 25 Polen, v. 5; State Secretary (RK), May 14, 1929, BA R 43 I 124, p. 222; Seiler, April 12, 1930, *ADAP*, ser. B, v. 14. pp. 490ff.

120. DVA petition, Nov. 28, 1930, BA R 43 I 548, p. 153; WAPP, UWP 1212, pp. 1ff.

121. State Secretary (RK), May 18, 1929, BA R 43 I 123, p. 298; AA, Nov. 30, 1930, ibid., 550, pp. 150ff.

122. Conference on "refinancing debt in Pomorze," Nov. 4, 1930, *ADAP*, (ser. B., v. 16, pp. 92ff.; Seiler report of meeting in Imperial Chancellery, Nov. 26-27, 1930, *ADAP*, ser. B, v. 16 pp. 207ff.

123. Büllow to RK, Jan. 20, 1930, BA R 43 I 548, pp. 205ff.

124. Ossa to RK, Nov. 11, 1930, BA R 43 I 550, p. 148; meeting in Imperial Chancellery, Dec. 9, 1930, ibid., pp. 158ff.

125. "Ideas," Jan. 6, 1931, BA R 43 I 550, pp. 188ff.

126. Graebe to Brüning, Jan. 7, 1931, BA R 43 I 550; Graebe/Brüning meeting, Jan. 10, 1931, ibid., 561, pp. 335.

127. Cabinet meeting, Jan. 21, 1931, BA R 43 I 550, p. 238; Curtius to Deitrich, March 7, 1931, *ADAP*, ser. B, v. 17, p. 21.

128. Curtius to Dietrich, March 7, 1931, *ADAP*, ser. B, p. 21; Seiler, March 18, 1931, *ADAP*, ser. B, v. 17, p. 138; ministerial conference, June 8, 1931, *ADAP*, ser. B, v. 17, pp. 426ff.

129. Bülow (AA) to RK, Jan. 20, 1931, BA R 43 I 561, pp. 205ff.; Jan. 24, 1931, *ADAP*, ser. B, v. 16, p. 478.

130. Meeting of Dec. 1, 1931, BA R 43 I 561, pp. 665-66; Heribert von Plupart to Brüning, Dec. 19, 1931, BA R 43 I 550, pp. 190ff.

131. Graebe memo, BA R 43 I 126, pp. 209-10.

132. Bülow to RK, Jan. 28, 1932, BA R 43 I 551, pp. 36ff.

133. Graebe memo, Jan. 12, 1933, BA R 43 I 126, pp. 223ff.

134. Moltke to AA, Jan. 25, 1933, *ADAP*, ser. B, v. 21, p. 591.

135. Bülow to RK, Jan. 11, 1933, *ADAP*, ser. B, v. 21, p. 525.

136. Kimmich, p. 138.

137. Krekeler, *Revisionsanspruch*, p. 29.

138. Krekeler, *Revisionsanspruch*, p. 73.

139. Krekeler, "Deutsche Politik," p. 28; other critical comments in John Hiden, "The Weimar Republic and the Problem of the *Auslanddeutsche*," pp. 273-89.

140. Cabinet meeting, July 23, 1926, BA R 43 I 547, p. 76.

141. Krahmer-Möllenberg to AA, Jan. 30, 1928, PA Geh. Abt. IV Pol. 25 Polen, v. 4.

142. Meyer to RK, Nov. 15, 1932, BA R 43 I 548, pp. 278ff.

143. Bülow memo, Jan. 25, 1934, in Gerhard Weinberg, *The Foreign Policy of Hitler's Germany*, 1:187.

144. Jacobsen, p. 162.

145. Consul Hertz, quoted in Krekeler, *Revisionsanspruch*, p. 62.

146. Kowalak, *Kredyty*, p. 10.

6. The Impact of National Socialism

1. *Posener Tageblatt*, July 9, 1933.

2. Cf. J.C. Hesse, "National Minorities in Europe VII: The Germans in Poland," p. 95; Krahmer-Möllenberg, Oct. 26, 1933, IfZ MA 128 #6; Breyer, *Deutsches Reich* p. 226, Bierschenk, *Volksgruppe*, p. 32, and Nasarski, p. 71 share this assessment.

3. Blau "guidelines," Oct. 24, 1933, WAPP, EK 294.

4. Jacobsen, pp. 177ff., 198; Krekeler, "Deutsche Politik," p. 19; BA R 43 II 1406, p. 22f.

5. *Hans Steinacher: Bundesleiter des VDA*, pp. 98ff.; RK to DAI, Feb. 18, 1933, and Wertheimer appeal, March 30, 1933, BA R 43 II 1410, p. 5, 15.

6. BA R 43 II: VDA executive committee, April 1, 1933, 1406, p. 79; DSb and BdA, 1406, pp. 124, 195; jurisdictional matters, Jan. 23, 1934, and Aug. 27, 1936, 1406, p. 235, and 1408.

7. Jacobsen, pp. 186ff.

8. See his 22-page policy statement, simultaneously pro-NS and pro-Poland but rather confused overall, PA Abt. IV Pol. 25 Polen, v. 34, pp. 12ff.; Breyer, *Deutsches Riech*, p. 222; Swart, p. 133; Heike, *Minderheit*, p. 203.

9. Quoted in Heike, *Minderheit*, p. 206.

10. BA NL Graebe; German Consul Toruń, May 24, 1933, PA Geh. Abt. IV Pol. 25 Polen, v. 7.

11. Krahmer-Möllenberg, May 6, 1935, IfZ MA 195/3 1071, p. 123.

12. Mirosław Cygański, *Zawsze przeciwko Polscę*, p. 143.

13. Ulitz, in Deutscher Volksbund für Polnisch-Schlesien, *Geschäftsbericht für das Jahr 1937*, pp. 40-41; BA R57 1094, #4.

14. Heike, "Arbeiterbewegung," pp. 524ff.

15. Report of Feb. 7, 1935, PA Abt. IV Pol. 25 Polen, v. 34, p. 225.

16. Heike, "Arbeiterbewegung," p. 513; Breyer and Korzec, pp. 295, 319, 349; Hesse, pp. 94-95.

17. Pant contributed the piece on German Catholics for v. I ("Polnisch-Schlesien") of the 1932 work *Das Deutschtum in Polen*, edited by Viktor Kauder (see esp. the chapters by Pant, Willner, and Kowoll,) interesting also because German socialists and Jews were still treated as full-fledged members of the *Volksgruppe*; the German patriotism of each group was affirmed, as was the harmony of class

and confessional interests with this patriotism and everyone's desire to get along with the Poles.

18. March 5, 1933, quoted in Meissner, p. 228; Kotowski, p. 57.

19. *Polska Zachodnia*, Jan. 10, 1936; German Embassy Warsaw to AA, March 2, 1934, PA Abt. IV Pol. 25 Polen, v. 32; *Hans Steinacher*, p. 527; Łaczewski, p. 238.

20. German Consul Toruń to AA, Aug. 30, 1934, PA Geh. Abt. IV Pol. 25M Polen, #3509.

21. PA Geh. Abt. IV Pol. 25M Polen: Krahmer-Möllenberg memo, Jan. 12, 1934; German Consul Poznań to AA, Feb. 15 and 23, 1934; German Consul Katowice to AA, and DS to AA, May 30, 1934. Also Meissner, p. 235; Kotowski, p. 58.

22. German Consul Poznań to AA, Feb. 5 and Aug. 23, 1934, PA Geh. Abt. Pol. 25M Polen.

23. *Reichspost*, Jan. 22, 1934.

24. Krahmer-Möllenberg, May 14 and June 6, 1934, PA Geh. Abt. IV Pol. 25M Polen, #3509; Meissner, p. 229.

25. German Consul Katowice to AA, Oct. 24 and Dec. 12, 1934, PA Geh. Abt. Pol. 25M Polen: Breitinger, p. 13; *Oberschlesischer Kurier*, Dec. 17, 1934; Heike, *Deutschtum*, p. 63, and *Minderheit*, p. 432; Breyer, *Deutches Reich*, p. 224; Kotowski, p. 59.

26. Breyer and Korzec, p. 349.

27. Blau circulars, July 28, 1934, and December 1936, WAPP, EK 295-96.

28. Blau circular, July 29, 1939, WAPP, EK 297.

29. Hein circular, July 31, 1936, WAPP, EK 296; Blau circular, Nov. 15, 1938, and agenda for the 7th provincial synod, Feb. 1939, WAPP, EK 297.

30. Breyer, *Deutsches Reich*, pp. 239ff.

31. Osiński, *V. kolumna*, p. 121; Potocki, p. 160.

32. Krahmer-Möllenberg to AA, Jan. 9, 1934, PA Abt. IV Pol. 25 Polen, v. 32 p. 112; German Embassy Warsaw to AA, March 31, 1936, and Krahmer-Möllenberg, May 2, 1936, ibid., 647656; German Consul Katowice to AA, Jan. 27, 1936, ibid., 647592.

33. Neurath, Feb. 20, 1936, PA Geh. Abt. Pol. 25 Polen/Oberschlesien, v. 7, 647604.

34. German Consul Toruń to AA, May 4, 1933, PA Abt. IV Pol. 25 Polen, v. 30.

35. Gestapo Aussendienststelle Beuthen, June 16 and 24, 1935, Jan. 9, 1936, HI; Gestapo Berlin to AA, Nov. 8, 1935, PA Geh. Abt. Pol. 25 Polen/Oberschlesien, v. 5 p. 307.

36. Jungdeutsche Partei, *Unsere Leitsätze*, and *Rettung oder Untergang;* Wiesner, April 9, 1935, WAPP, Org. niem. 4, p. 16.

37. Wiesner circular, Oct. 5, 1935, WAPP, Org. niem. 4, p. 45.

38. Lemke, Aug. 3, 1936, WAPP, Org. niem. 4, p. 124.

39. AA directive on uniforms and insignia, Dec. 1935, PA Abt. IV Pol. 25 Polen, v. 36.

40. *Hans Steinacher*, p. 527.

41. Jungdeutsche Partei, *Wir schmieden die Zukunft*, pp. 7ff.; Uhle circular, Nov. 22, 1935, WAPP, Org. niem. 4, p. 58. The best brief account of this schism is Martin Broszat, "JDP und DV in Posen-Pomerellen," pp. 404-7. See also Breyer,

Deutsches Reich, p. 247; Osiński, pp. 133ff.; and cf. postwar account by Erich Spitzer, JDP chief in Pomorze, omitting all references to the party's NS orientation (BA Ost-Dok. 8, #14).

42. Steinacher to Naumann, Aug. 14, 1931, BA, NL Steinacher, #41; *Hans Steinacher*, p. 527.

43. *Hans Steinacher*, pp. 527ff.; Jacobsen, p. 587.

44. Krahmer-Möllenberg to AA, March 22, 1934, PA Abt. IV Pol. 25 Polen, v. 34, p. 343; RK to Propaganda Ministry, May 29, 1934, BA RD 43 I 551, p. 113; *Hans Steinacher*, p. 530.

45. German Consul Poznań to AA, June 5, 1934, PA Geh. Abt. IV Pol. 25 Polen, v. 9.

46. "Grundsätze des Deutschen Jungblocks in Polen," and Koerber memo (n.d.), BA R 43 I 551, pp. 102ff.

47. German Consul Poznań to AA, April 26, 1934, PA Geh. Abt. IV Pol. 25 Polen, v. 9.

48. Agreement signed July 17, 1934, ibid., *Deutsche Rundschau*, Sept. 15, 1934; Hauser, *Mniejszość*, p. 179; Paprocki, p. 350.

49. Rafał Fuks, *Na przykład Kohnert*.

50. *Posener Tageblatt*, July 8, 1935.

51. German Consul Toruń to AA, Sept. 13, 1934, PA Abt. IV Pol. 25 Polen, v. 33, pp. 216ff.; German Consul Toruń, Feb. 16, 1935, ibid., v. 34, p. 209.

52. Boeck to Steinacher, Feb. 22, 1935, PA Abt. IV Pol. 25 Polen, v. 34, p. 219; Breyer and Korzec, pp. 306ff.

53. Volksbund convention, July 28, 1934, PA Geh. Abt. Pol. 25 Polen, v. 8.

54. Tucher memoranda, April 26 and May 9, 1934, PA Geh. Abt. IV Pol. 25 Polen, v. 9.

55. Boeck to Steinacher, Feb. 22, 1935, PA Abt. IV Pol. 25 Polen, v. 34, p. 219.

56. Jacobsen, pp. 198, 590-91.

57. Krahmer-Möllenberg, Sept. 8, 1933, IfZ MA 195/3 1083, p. 136.

58. *Völkischer Beobachter*, June 6, 1934, and Gestapo Berlin to AA, April 27, 1934, PA Abt. IV Pol. 25 Polen, v. 32, p. 442; Kohnert to Oberländer, Dec. 17, 1935, IfZ Fb 110.

59. Steinacher to Haushofer, Feb. 2, 1935, in *Hans Steinacher*, p. 268.

60. *Hans Steinacher*, p. 531.

61. German Consul Poznań to AA, June 18, 1937, PA Abt. V Pol. 25 Polen, v. 2, pp. 285, 363.

62. Gestapo Berlin in AA, Sept. 16, 1935, PA Abt. IV Pol. 25 Polen, v. 35, p. 148.

63. Quoted in Gersdorff, p. 10.

64. Rival submissions to DAI, July 1935, and JD circular, Feb. 8, 1935, BA R 57 1094; JDP, *Zukunft*, pp. 34ff.; German Consul Poznań to AA, Feb. 25, 1936, PA Abt. IV Pol. 25 Polen, v. 37, p. 119. See also JDP, *Zukunft*, pp. 7ff.; Uhle circular, Nov. 22, 1935, WAPP, Niem. org. 4, p. 58; Broszat, "JDP und DV," pp. 404ff.; Osiński, *V. kolumna*, pp. 133ff; *Deutsche Nachrichten*, Jan. 4, 1935.

65. Jacobsen, p. 167; *Hans Steinacher*, p. 529. Cf. Krahmer-Möllenberg, Nov. 28, 1936, IfZ MA 195/4 1100, p. 268; May 3, 1935, IfZ MA 195/3 1071, p. 124.

66. Wiesner circulars, June 18, 1935, and Sept. 11, 1936; Uhle circular, Nov. 22, 1935, WAPP, Org. niem. 4, pp. 27, 58, 136.

67. German Consul Poznań to AA, May 9, 1934, PA Geh. Abt. IV Pol. 25 Polen, v. 9; Breyer and Korzec, p. 314.

68. BA R 43 I 551, pp. 102ff.; Deutsche Passtelle Bydgoszcz to AA, May 24, 1934, PA Geh. Abt. IV Pol. 25 Polen, v. 9; JDP, *Zukunft*, p. 15; Wiesner circular, May 3, 1935, WAPP, Org. niem. 4, p. 20.

69. Gestapo Berlin to AA, April 6, 1935, PA Abt. IV Pol. 25 Polen, v. 35. ·

70. JDP, *Zukunft*, p. 24; Breyer and Korzec, p. 314.

71. DSV Leszno to Schönbeck, Sept. 14, 1934, WAPP, Org. niem. 525, p. 230.

72. Blau speeches, April 24, May 15, and Oct. 1, 1934, WAPP, EK 295.

73. Wiesner to Blau, Nov. 23, 1934, and Blau reply, Dec. 15, 1934, ibid.

74. PA Geh. Abt. IV Pol. 25 Polen, v. 8; Hauser, *Mniejszość*, p. 84; Breyer and Korzec, p. 354.

75. German Consul Poznań to AA, April 26, 1934, PA Abt. IV Pol. 25 Polen, v. 32; Breyer and Korzec, pp. 284, 301, 322, WAPP, UWP 1218, p. 26.

76. *Hans Steinacher*, p. 530.

77. Gestapo to AA, April 6, 1935, PA Abt. IV Pol. 25 Polen, v. 34, p. 343; Krahmer-Möllengerg to AA, Sept. 10, 1935, PA Geh. Abt. IV Pol. 25 Polen, v. 9; Swart, pp. 137ff.; Osiński, *V. kolumna*, p. 140.

78. Breyer and Korzec, pp. 284, 310-11, 314; German Consul Poznań to AA, June 25, 1935, PA Geh. Abt. IV Pol. 25 Polen, v. 9.

79. *Völkischer Beobachter*, Nov. 29, 1934.

80. Gestapo Berlin to AA, April 6, 1935, PA Abt. IV Pol. 25 Polen, v. 34, p. 343.

81. German Consul Poznań to AA, June 5, 1934, PA Geh. Abt. IV Pol. 25 Polen, v. 9.

82. Hermann Rauschning, *Gespräche mit Hitler*, p. 137.

83. Krahmer-Möllenberg to AA, April 25, 1935, PA Abt. IV Pol. 25 Polen, v. 35; Krahmer-Möllenberg, Nov. 1936, IfZ MA 195/3 1100, pp. 375ff

84. Jacobsen, p. 588.

85. Jacobsen, pp. 164-65, 182-83, 204, 246ff.; decree on terminology, Jan. 25, 1938, BA R 43 II 1408a, p. 42.

86. Jacobsen, pp. 186ff., 240; BA NL Steinacher.

87. Jacobsen, p. 593.

88. Ronald Smelser, *The Sudeten Problem*, pp. 251-52; Heike, *Minderheit*, p. 213; Jacobsen, pp. 234ff.; RK, Oct. 28, 1937, BA R 43 II 1408c, p. 45.

89. Louis de Jong, *Die deutsche 5. Kolonne im 2. Weltkriege*, p. 147; Jacobsen, p. 241; Heike, *Minderheit*, pp. 214-15.

90. Behrends to AA, May 19, 1937, quoted in Osiński, *V. kolumna*, p. 305; Germany Embassy Warsaw to AA, May 9, 1939, PA Abt. IV Pol. 25 Polen, v. 7, p. 15.

91. *Deutsche Rundschau*, June 4, 1936; *Hans Steinacher*, p. 532. See also Swart, p. 136; Breyer, *Deutches Reich*, p. 253.

92. The complete records of the Jaztrzębzko branch of the party show that attendance at its monthly meetings fell from an average of about 130 in 1935 to 80 by 1938: WAPP, Niem. org. 6; Stapo Elbing to Gestapo Berlin, Jan. 20, 1936, PA Abt. IV Pol. 25 Polen, v. 37, p. 82.

93. Andrzej Szefer, "Secesja z Partii Młodoniemieckiej w 1937 r.," pp. 531ff.; Wiesner circular, June 3, 1937, WAPP, Niem. org. 4, p. 180; Heike, *Minderheit*, p. 212.

94. *Osteuropa* 13 (1938): 117; German Consul Poznań to AA, Nov. 28, 1938, and DS to AA, Dec. 30, 1938, PA Abt. V Pol. 25 Polen, v. 4, p. 174, and v. 5, p. 12; Heike, *Minderheit*, p. 212.

95. Cf. the similar observation about the analogous Sudeten-German problem in Smelser, pp. 251ff.

96. Some question the existence of a preventive war scenario; the purported discussions with the French took place outside official channels, and little documentary evidence remains; see Zygmunt Gąsiorowski, "Did Piłsudski Attempt to Initiate a Preventive War in 1933?" pp. 135-51. But most believe that Piłsudski was stopped only by French disapproval. See Wacław Jędrzejewicz, "The Polish Plan for a 'Preventive War' against Germany in 1933," pp. 62-91; Roos, *History*, p. 130; Weinberg, 1:51.

97. Breyer, *Deutches Reich*, pp. 71ff.; Jędrzejewicz, p. 82.

98. *Deutsche Rundschau*, March 14, 1933.

99. *Eingabensammlung*, p. 4.

100. *Freie Presse*, April 10, 1933; German consul Łódź to AA, May 30, 1933, PA Abt. IV Pol. 25 Polen, v. 31, p. 59; Breyer, *Deutsches Reich*, p. 250.

101. German Consul Toruń to AA, April 18, 1933, PA Abt. IV Pol. 25 Polen, v. 30, p. 388; *Deutsche Rundschau*, May 31, 1933.

102. Quoted in Kellermann, p. 159.

103. Breyer, *Deutsches Reich*, pp. 87ff.; Sławomir Łozowski, "Hermann Rauschning a próba normalizacji stosunków polsko-gdańskich," in *Rola Mniejszości*, pp. 260ff.

104. *Eingabensammlung*. p. 5.

105. German Consul Toruń to AA, Nov. 5, 1933, and German Embassy Warsaw, Nov. 29, 1933, PA Abt. IV Pol. 25 Polen, v. 32, pp. 17ff., 41; Breyer, *Deutsches Reich*, p. 100.

106. Published as Hermann Rauschning, *Deutsche und Polen*.

107. Korzec, "Minderheitenschutzvertrag," pp. 533ff.; *Deutsche Rundschau*, Sept. 8, 1934.

108. *Posener Tageblatt*, Nov. 8, 1933.

109. *Deutsche Rundschau*, Sept. 27, 1933.

110. Breyer, *Deutsches Reich*, pp. 131-32, 144, 163.

111. Breyer and Korzec, p. 351. The best treatment of post-Piłsudski politics is Edward Wynot, *Polish Politics in Transition*. See also Roos, *History*, p. 145; Dziewanowski, p. 92; Rhode, *Geschichte*, p. 494.

112. Gestapo report, Feb. 1, 1934, BA R 43 II 1480a, p. 487; Feldman, p. 158.

113. Graebe to Lieres, Feb. 8, 1935, PA Abt. IV Pol. 25 Polen, v. 34, p. 194.

114. *Deutsche Rundschau*, March 11, 1936.

115. Speech at DV annual meeting 1935, quoted in *Posener Tageblatt*, July 8, 1935.

116. Saenger speech to Sejm, Feb. 6, 1935, transcribed in PA Abt. IV Pol. 25 Polen, v. 34; Breyer and Korzec, p. 353.

117. Hauser, *Mniejszość*, p. 193.

118. Wiesner circular, Feb. 26, 1936, WAPP, Niem. org. 4, p. 79.

119. Circulars of May 12 and June 22, 1936, and June 5, 1937, ibid., pp. 113ff., 181.

120. "Circular #23," 1936, ibid., p. 98.

121. Breyer and Korzec, p. 346.

122. Cited in Breyer and Korzec, pp. 280, 305.

123. Nehring, May 15, 1936, WAPP, EK 295.

124. *Deutsche Rundschau*, May 8, 1934.

125. Breyer and Korzec, p. 331.

126. Ibid., p. 277.

127. *Deutsche Nachrichten*, Aug. 27, 1937; Breyer and Korzec, p. 321.

128. Memo, November 1936, IfZ MA 195/4 1100, pp. 275.

129. The same position is taken by Edmund Makowski, "Wpływ zwycięstwa Hitlerizmu w Niemczech na mniejszość niemiecka w Wielkopolsce," in *Rola Wielkopolski w dziejach narodu polskiego*, p. 348.

130. German Consul Toruń to AA, June 16, 1934, PA Geh. Abt. IV Pol. 25 Polen, v. 9.

131. Breyer and Korzec, p. 344.

132. *Posener Tageblatt*, Sept. 10, 1936; *Słowo Pomorski*, March 17, 1935; Breyer and Korzec, p. 344.

133. Uhle memo, May 8, 1935, WAPP, Org. niem. 4, p. 22.

134. Krahmer-Möllenberg to AA, May 8, 1934, PA Geh. Abt. IV Pol. 25 Polen, v. 9.

135. Deutsche Bücherei, Dec. 18, 1937, WAPP, UWP 1244, pp. 37, 49.

136. Kohnert to Blau, April 22, 1938, WAPP, EK 526.

137. Breyer and Korzec, pp. 281ff., 308.

138. Heike, *Deutschtum*, p. 221; *Osteuropa* 14 (1938-39): 567.

139. *Posener Tageblatt*, Sept. 10, 1936.

140. *Osteuropa* 11 (1936): 587.

141. Antoni Czubiński, "Das Deutschlandbild der Polen," 141.

142. Oct. 13, 1938, *ADAP*, ser. D, v. 5, p. 118; Breyer, *Deutsches Reich*, p. 214.

143. April 8, 1936, BA R 43 II 1482, p. 29.

144. Minutes of Foreign Office meeting, May 27, 1937, *ADAP*, ser. D, v. VI, 2, p. 844.

145. Heike, *Minderheit*, p. 205.

146. German Consul Toruń to AA, May 7, 1935, PA Abt. IV Pol. 25 Polen, v. 35, p. 214; also Abt. V Pol. 25, Polen, v. 1, p. 44.

147. German Consul Katowice to AA, Nov. 5, 1934, PA Geh. Abt. Pol. 25 Polen/Oberschlesien, v. 5.

148. July 31, 1934, BA R 43 II 1407, p. 49.

149. Neurath, March 12, 1935, in *Dokumente* (AA), p. 48.

150. Quoted in *Deutsche Rundschau*, February 1936.

151. Jan. 24, 1938, quoted in *Posener Tageblatt*, Jan. 26, 1938.

152. *Deutsche Rundschau*, Aug. 5, 1937.

153. Władysław Studnicki, *O metodę zarządzania Śląskiem* (1933), in *Irrwege in Polen*, p. 25; Studnicki, *Polen im politischen System Europas*; *Deutsche Rundschau*, Dec. 29, 1928; *Oberschlesischer Kurier*, Oct. 11, 1932.

154. Bierschenk, "Richtlinien"; Breyer and Korzec, p. 275.

155. Quoted in Mauersberg, p. 158.

156. German Consul Toruń to AA, May 10, 1935, PA Abt. IV Pol. 25 Polen, v. 35, p. 192.

157. *Gazeta Polska,* May 3, 1935; Breyer and Korzec, p. 321; Potocki, p. 183; German Consul Toruń, May 10, 1935, PA Abt. IV Pol. 25 Polen, v. 35, p. 192.

158. Quoted in *Deutsche Rundschau,* April 1934; Breyer and Korzec, p. 356.

159. *Dziennik Poznański,* Dec. 24, 1936.

160. *Deutsche Rundschau,* Nov. 22, 1936.

161. Küchler to AA, May 18, 1936, PA Abt. V Pol. 25 Polen, v. 1, p. 3; Marian Drozdowski's suggestion ("Minorities," p. 232) that Polish Germans took advantage of the relaxation of tensions, 1934-38, "to improve their living conditions and means of cultural expansion" hardly accords with objective evidence of their situation during these years.

162. Quoted in Edward Wynot, "The Polish Germans," p. 49, and in Mauersberg, p. 158.

163. Schönbeck circular, June 28, 1933, WAPP, Niem. org. 524, p. 218; Bierschenk, "Richtlinien," p. 534; Hesse, p. 98.

164. Silesian *Oberpräsident* Wagner to RK, Dec. 11, 1938, PA Abt. V Pol. 25 Polen, v. 4; German Consul Katowice to AA, Jan. 26, 1939, *Dokumente* (AA), p. 94; Wynot, "German Schools," pp. 60-61; Türcke, p. 168.

165. WAPP, UWP 1240, pp. 4, 17. Officials kept records of the public and recorded private statements and activities of minority leaders and issued more or less formal "grades" on their attitude toward Poland. Swart, e.g., was classified as an "enemy of Polish nationality"; Pastor Richard Kammel was entered three times in the "File of Those Hostile to Poland"; Welage chief Waldemar Kraft was "not favorably inclined toward the Polish state," etc. ibid.; see also 1245, p. 64, and 1260, p. 128.

166. Silesian Wojewode to DSV Katowice, Sept. 30, 1935, WAPP, Org. niem, 525, p. 248.

167. May 25, 1934, WAPP, Org. niem. 525, p. 194.

168. *Von Unserer Art,* pp. 49ff.

169. Kühn, "Deutschtum," p. 148; Swart and Breyer, p. 490; Heike, *Deutschtum,* p. 143; German Consul Toruń to AA, Feb. 13, 1939, PA Abt. V Pol. 25 Polen, v. 6.

170. WAPP, Org. niem. 541, pp. 159ff.

171. Moltke to AA, May 22, 1939, *Dokumente* (AA), p. 374; Mielke, in *Deutsche Rundschau,* March 1, 1938.

172. Ernst Schubert, *Die deutsche evangelische Kirche in Polen,* pp. 16-17; Bierschenk, *Volksgruppe,* p. 146; *Osteuropa* 11 (1936-37): 729.

173. Voss, pp. 13ff.; *Osteuropa* 12 (1937-38): 129; Heike, *Deutschtum,* pp. 135-36.

174. Blau agenda for 7th provincial synod, Feb. 1939, WAPP, EK 297; Bierschenk, "Richtlinien," p. 534; Breyer and Korzec, p. 361.

175. Blau agenda for 7th provincial synod, Feb. 1939, WAPP, EK 297; Heike, *Minderheit,* p. 276.

176. E. Schubert, p. 10; Martin, p. 33; Heike, *Minderheit,* p. 274.

177. According to edict of mayor of Czarnków, July 8, 1938, PA Abt. V Pol. 25 Polen, v. 4, p. 51.

178. Blau circular, Nov. 7, 1938, WAPP, EK 297.

179. German Consul Poznań to AA, Aug. 2, 1935, PA Abt. IV Pol. 25 Polen, v. 36, p. 45.

180. *Osteuropa* 10 (1934-35): 474; cf. *Eingabensammlung*, pp. 168, 176.

181. Lieselotte von Koerber, 1956-57, BA Ost-dok. 6, B1-2.

182. German Consul Toruń to AA, May 18, 1936, PA Abt. V Pol. 25 Polen, v. 1, p. 3.

183. Nasarski, pp. 43, 84f.; German Consul Toruń to AA, Jan. 11, 1937, PA Abt. V Pol. 25 Polen, v. 2, p. 42; BA R 43 II 1428b, pp. 16, 651.

184. Theodor Bierschenk, "Die Vereine Deutscher Hochschüler in Polen," p. 89.

185. Urząd Wojewódzki to *starosts*, April 13, 1932, WAPP, UWP 1218, p. 5; Heidelck, "Deutschtum," p. 251; Bierschenk, *Volksgruppe*, p. 108.

186. DS to AA, April 14, 1936, PA Geh. Abt. IV Pol. 25 Polen, v. 7.

187. Moltke to AA, July 30, 1937, *ADAP*, ser. C, v. VII, 2, p. 1041.

188. DS to AA, Nov. 3, 1938, PA Abt. V Pol. 25 Polen, v. 3, p. 96.

189. *Kattowitzer Zeitung*, Nov. 19, 1934; Ross, pp. 26-27; *Osteuropa* 12 (1936-37): 519; Mrozcko, *Myśl*, p. 264; Czubiński, "Deutschlandbild," p. 142.

190. *Deutsche Rundschau*, May 31, 1933.

191. Fritz Morre, "Das Baltische Institut in Polen," *Osteuropa* 12 (1936-37): 204ff.; Ross, pp. 17ff.; Fritz Prause, *Die polnische Presse im Kampf gegen die deutsche Volksgruppe in Posen and Westpreussen* p. 19; Mroczko, *Myśl*, pp. 184ff.; Feldman.

192. *Dziennik Poznański*, Dec. 24, 1936.

193. *Polska Zachodnia*, Dec. 14, 1936.

194. *Osteuropa* 12 (1936-37): 519.

195. *Deutsche Rundschau*, Jan. 31, 1939.

196. Ibid.

197. *Posener Tageblatt*, Feb. 17, 1938; *Dzien Pomorski*, Feb. 19, 1938; *Dziennik Poznański*, Dec. 12, 1936.

198. Kaczmarek, pp. 322ff.

199. *Kuryer Poznański*, June 19, 1937.

200. *Posener Tageblatt*, June 21, 1939.

201. Prause, p. 9.

202. *Dzien Pomorski*, April 16, 1935.

203. *Posener Tageblatt*, April 21, 1935; German Consul Danzig to AA, April 14 and 16, 1935, PA Abt. IV Pol. 25 Polen, v. 34, p. 439, and v. 35, p. 151; German Consul Poznań to AA, May 20, 1935, v. 35, p. 225; *Dokumente* (AA) #58-60; Bierschenk, *Volksgruppe*, p. 225.

204. Heike, *Deutschtum*, p. 97.

205. *Osteuropa* 14 (1938-39): 45.

206. Krahmer-Möllenberg to AA, July 26, 1935, PA Abt. IV Pol. 25 Polen, v. 35, p. 473.

207. German Consul Toruń to AA, March 4, 1937, PA Abt. V Pol. 25 Polen, v. 2.

208. Łozowski, in *Rola mniejszości*, p. 264; Kellermann, p. 170; Goerdeler, p. 38.

209. Quoted in *Der Deutsche in Polen*, Feb. 27, 1935.

210. *Diplomat in Berlin*, ed. W. Jędrzejewicz, p. 386; cf. Weinberg, 2:404.

211. German Consul Katowice, Dec. 3, 1935, PA Geh. Abt. IV Pol. 25 Polen/Oberschlesien, v. 5.

212. Interior Ministry memo, Nov. 7, 1936, IfZ MA 195/4 1100, p. 352.

213. Krahmer-Möllenberg, March 2, 1936, IfZ MA 195/3 1099, p. 236. In 1937 the *Volksbund* was obliged to lay off twenty-five employees; see Breyer and Korzec, p. 339.

214. Krahmer-Möllenberg to AA, Jan. 21, 1936, and memo ("very secret"), Nov. 1936, IfZ MA 195/3 1099, pp. 122ff.; 310, and 1100, pp. 275ff.

215. Memo of Nov. 1936, IfZ MA 195/3 1100, pp. 275ff.

216. Krahmer-Möllenberg to AA, July 26, 1935, PA Abt. IV Pol. 25 Polen, v. 35, p. 473; Krahmer-Möllenberg, IfZ MA 195/3 1100, p. 268.

217. Ministers' meeting of Jan. 9, 1937, *ADAP*, ser. C, v. VI, 1, p. 384.

218. Krahmer-Möllenberg to AA, IfZ MA 195/3 1100, p. 268; German Consul Poznań to AA, July 26, 1935, PA Geh. Abt. IVa Pol. 25H Polen.

219. Kurt Eichstädt, "Selbsthilfe der deutschen Minderheit in Polen," pp. 51ff.

220. Kauder to Steinacher, Sept. 22, 1933, BA NL Steinacher, #50. Other minority scholarship was subsidized by the Reich-based Nordostdeutsche Forschungsgemeinschaft; see Gentzen, "Deutsche Stiftung," p. 59.

221. Krahmer-Möllenberg to RK, Oct. 3 and Dec. 15, 1933, BA R 43 I 557, pp. 83, 98.

222. Memo of November 1936, IfZ MA 195/3 1100, p. 387.

223. Twardowski memo, quoted in Jacobsen, p. 595.

224. March 16, 1937, PA Abt. V Pol. 25 Polen, v. 2, p. 135; Heike, *Deutschtum*, p. 96.

225. Küchler to AA, Oct. 3, 1938, PA Abt. V Pol. 25 Polen, v. 4, p. 5; and DS to AA, Nov. 5, 1938, v. 6.

226. Breyer, *Deutsches Reich*, p. 277.

227. Fitzke memoir, WAPP, Org. niem. 541, pp. 33ff.

228. RK, May 22, 1933, Jan. 26 and April 8, 1934, BA R 43 II 1406, pp. 116, 212, 248.

229. Rhode, "Völker," p. 199.

230. Rauschning, *Gespräche*, pp. 136ff.; Eugen Lemberg, "Zur Geschichte der Deutschen Volksgruppen in Ost-Mitteleuropa," p. 337.

7. The Plight of the Minority in 1939

1. Wartel, "Sprawa," p. 556; *Eingaben*, pp. 29ff.; *Deutsche Rundschau*, March 13, 1936.

2. *Stosunki narodowościowe w rolnictwie pomorskim*, p. 18; Hans Kohnert, "Agrarreformstatistik aus Polen," p. 622.

3. *Eingabensammlung*, pp. 6f.; several hundred individual cases in *Die Frage des Besitzes und Erwerbs von Grundstücken durch Angehörige der deutschen Volksgruppe in Westpolen*; *Osteuropa* 14 (1938-39): 464.

4. Karzel, p. 33; *Eingaben*, p. 38; Kohnert, "Agrarreformstatistik," pp. 621f.; VoMi, Jan. 21, 1939, BA R 43 II 1483, p. 29.

5. Bierschenk, *Volksgruppe*, p. 132.

6. "Das polnische Grenzzonengesetz," *Osteuropa* 14 (1938): 383ff.; Kauder, 1:10; *Posener Tageblatt*, Jan. 1, 1925 (analyzing the original Border Zone Law); Swart and Breyer, p. 499.

7. VoMi, Jan. 21, 1939, BA R 43 II 1483, pp. 27ff.; Moltke to AA, Dec. 11, 1937, *Dokumente* (AA), p. 75; German Consul Toruń to AA, and Wiesner to Sławoj-Składkowski, Aug. 6, 1938, PA Abt. V Pol. 25 Polen, v. 6, p. 9, and v. 4, p. 77.

8. Schleip memo, June 8, 1938, *ADAP*, ser. D, v. 5, p. 52.

9. *Dokumente* (AA) p. 263; Kammel, *Kriegsschicksale*, p. 10.

10. Heike, *Minderheit*, pp. 413f.

11. Walter Bloch, *Die deutschen Genossenschaften in Westpolen*, (Poznań, 1938), pp. 150ff.; Schubert, *Entwicklung*, pp. 377ff.

12. Karzel, p. 177.

13. PA Abt. V Pol. 25 Polen, v. 2, p. 4.

14. Quoted in Karzel, p. 178.

15. Bociański in Swart, p. 222; cf. p. 145.

16. Kaysiewicz to *starosts*, June 17, 1939, in Swart, pp. 213ff.

17. Swart, pp. 224f.

18. Woźniak, Aug. 10, 1939, in Swart, p. 218; Behrends (VoMi) to Lammers (RK), Aug. 21, 1939, BA R 43 II 1408d, p. 48.

19. Besson report, May 6, 1939, BA R 43 II 1483, p. 17.

20. Swart, p. 148.

21. *Osteuropa* 10 (1934-35): 166.

22. Meyer, Feb. 19, 1935, *ADAP*, ser. C, v. III, 2, p. 918.

23. Landau and Tomaszewski, p. 151.

24. *Osteuropa* 14 (1938-39): 681.

25. *Gazeta Polska*, cited in *Osteuropa* 12 (1937-38): 128.

26. Nöldecke, Nov. 22, 1937, *Dokumente* (AA), p. 74; cf. German representative in Upper Silesian Labor Office to AA, March 24, 1934, PA Geh. Abt. IV Pol. 25 Polen/Oberschlesien, v. 5.

27. Quoted in *Deutsche Rundschau*, March 11, 1936; Moltke to AA, March 11, 1938, *Dokumente* (AA), pp. 77f.

28. German Consul Katowice to AA, June 26, 1939, *Dokumente* (AA), p. 256.

29. Report of July 10, 1939, BA R 43 II 1408d, pp. 55f.

30. Saenger speech in Sejm, Feb. 6, 1935, transcribed in PA Abt. IV Pol. 25 Polen, v. 34.

31. PA Geh. Abt. IV Pol. 25 Polen, v. 8, p. 10; Heike, *Deutschtum*, p. 103; Kauder, 1:8; Swart and Breyer, p. 500.

32. German Consul Katowice to AA, Nov. 24, 1938, *Dokumente* (AA), pp. 90-91; Wichard Hahn, "Die Arbeitslosigkeit der deutschen Volksgruppe in Ost-Oberschlesien," pp. 561-62.

33. *Kattowitzer Zeitung*, Dec. 7, 1937; German Consul Katowice to AA, March 29, 1935, PA Geh. Abt. IV Pol. 25 Polen, v. 6, p. 136; Moltke to AA, May 30, 1938, *Dokumente* (AA) p. 106.

34. Wagner to Lammers, Dec. 11, 1938, PA Abt. V Pol. 25 Polen, v. 4, p. 10.

35. Herrnbitz Fitzke, WAPP, Org. niem. 541, pp. 33ff.

36. Voss, p. 13.

37. May 28, 1937, *ADAP*, ser. C, v. 6, 2, p. 846.

38. Ibid.

39. "Schlesische Auswandererberatung" to German Consul Katowice, March 5, 1935, PA Geh. Abt. IV Pol. 25 Polen/Oberschlesien, v. 6; Meissner, p. 271.

40. German Consul Toruń to AA, May 22, 1939, PA Abt. V Pol. 25 Polen, v. 7;

BA R 43 II 1483, p. 80; German Consul Toruń to AA, Jan. 19 and March 4, 1939, *Dokumente* (AA), pp. 94, 98.

41. German Consul Toruń to AA, May 17, 1935, PA Abt. IV Pol. 25 Polen, v. 35, p. 214; *Eingabensammlung*, p. 10.

42. German Consul Toruń to AA, 1929-30, PA Abt. IV Pol. 25 Polen, v. 27, p. 109.

43. *Słowo Pomorskie*, Feb. 19, 1938.

44. Paul Gemming to DSV Leszno, Sept. 6, 1934, WAPP, Org. niem. 525, p. 224.

45. German Consul Toruń to AA, Jan. 23, 1939, PA Abt. V Pol. 25 Polen, v. 5, p. 65. Pomorze Wojewode Władysław Raczkiewicz refused also to renew the hunting licenses of some Germans who opposed the government slate in local elections in 1938; see *Eingabensammlung*, p. 16.

46. Wildemann report, PA Abt. V Pol. 25 Polen, v. 2, p. 255; Kauder, 3:8; Hauser, *Mniejszość*, p. 168.

47. Hans Kohnert, "Die deutsche Volksgruppe in Westpolen in Zahlen" (1938), BA Kleine Erwerbung 619, pp. 35ff.; German Consul Toruń to AA, June 3, 1930, PA Abt. IV Pol. 25 Polen, v. 27, pp. 197ff.

48. Kohnert, "Volksgruppe," in BA; Czech, p. 190f.

49. Minutes of meeting in German Foreign Office, May 27, 1937, in *ADAP*, ser. C, v. VI, 2, p. 844; Neurath to Moltke, May 28, 1937, *ADAP*, ser. C, v. VI, 2, pp. 847-48.

50. Text in Swart and Breyer, p. 521, and in *Nachbarn seit tausend Jahren*, p. 249; Weinberg, 2:195ff.

51. *Osteuropa* 12 (1937-38): 197; cf. *Deutsche Rundschau*, May 31, 1933.

52. *Kattowitzer Zeitung*, Nov. 5, 1938.

53. Wojciechowski quoted in *Freie Presse*, Feb. 4, 1938.

54. *Deutsche Rundschau*, Nov. 18, 1937.

55. *Kattowitzer Zeitung*, Nov. 5, 1938; Potocki provides no support for his contention ("DS," in *Rola*, p. 273) that "the German minority drew major advantages" from the 1937 declaration.

56. Schliep, June 8, 1938, *ADAP*, ser. D, v. 5, p. 52.

57. Moltke to AA, July 9, 1938, *ADAP*, ser. D, v. 1, p. 54.

58. BA Ost-dok. 6 D1-12, p. 17; R 43 II 1482b, pp. 33ff.

59. Vollert to AA, Nov. 5, 1938, *Dokumente* (AA), pp. 117f.

60. Woermann (AA) to German Embassy Warsaw, Nov. 26, 1938, *Dokumente* (AA), p. 83.

61. German Consul Cieszyn to AA, July 28, 1939, *Dokumente*, (AA), p. 261.

62. Ibid.; AA to German Embassy Warsaw, Feb. 1, 1939, *Dokumente* (AA), p. 86.

63. German Consul Cieszyn to AA, June 2 and June 6, 1939, *Dokumente* (AA), p. 250.

64. German Consul Cieszyn to AA, May 12, 1939, *Dokumente* (AA), p. 87; Moltke to AA, Dec. 20, 1938, *Dokumente* (AA), p. 85; *Osteuropa* 14 (1938-39): 566.

65. Report on negotiations, March 29, 1939, BA R 43 II 1408c, pp. 18ff.

66. Quoted by Frick, in ibid.

67. Moltke to AA, June 11, 1939, condemning Grażyński in particular as "the gravedigger of German-Polish understanding": *Dokumente* (AA), p. 259.

68. *Czas,* July 17, 1939.

69. January 1939 presentation to the Akademie für Deutsches Recht, IfZ MA 195/4 1133, pp. 74ff.; Küchler to AA, Feb. 13, 1939, PA Abt. V Pol. 25 Polen, v. 6, p. 9.

70. DS to AA, March 4, 1939, PA Abt. V Pol. 25C Polen, v. 2, p. 137; Heike, *Deutschtum,* p. 220.

71. German Consul Poznań to AA, June 16, 1939, *Dokumente* (AA), p. 253; Kohnert to AA, June 19, 1939, PA Abt. V Pol. 25 Polen, v. 8; *Osteuropa* 14 (1938-39): 680-81.

72. *Eingabensammlung,* pp. 17, 24.

73. German Consul Poznań to AA, May 25, 1939, *Dokumente* (AA), p. 249; Bierschenk, *Volksgruppe,* p. 340, and "Vereine," p. 98.

74. According to the school principal, Vogt, *Gymnasium,* p. 30.

75. German Consul Toruń to AA, Feb. 28, 1939, *Dokumente* (AA), p. 97. This consul also claimed to have seen one sign reading "Germans, Jews, and Dogs: No Entrance": German Consul Toruń to AA, May 22, 1939, PA Abt. V Pol. 25 Polen, v. 7.

76. Besson report, May 6, 1939, BA R 43 II 1483, p. 17.

77. VoMi to RK, Sept. 2, 1939, BA R 43 II 1409, p. 27; German Consul Toruń to AA, July 3, 1939, PA Abt. V Pol. 25 Polen, v. 9, p. 59; Bierschenk, *Volksgruppe,* p. 332.

78. German Consul Katowice to AA, May 30, 1939, *Dokumente* (AA), p. 249.

79. Breitinger, p. 28.

80. Karl Heda, "Die Diözese Kattowitz und die deutschen Katholiken," p. 56.

81. VoMi, BA R 43 II 1408d, pp. 53-54, and 1409, p. 27; Martin, pp. 69ff.; Heike, *Deutschtum,* p. 223.

82. German Consul Łódź to AA, July 7, 1939, *Dokumente* (AA), pp. 251-52.

83. Hans von Rosen (1968), BA Ost-dok. 6; PA Abt. V Pol. 25 Polen, v. 7; p. 61.

84. German Consul Łódź to AA, May 15, 1939, *Dokumente* (AA), p. 247; *Osteuropa* 14 (1938-39): 680.

85. DS to AA, July 31, 1939, and Kohnert to AA, June 19, 1939, PA Abt. V Pol. 25 Polen, v. 9, p. 190, and v. 8; Bierschenk, *Volksgruppe,* pp. 344-45.

86. The report of Aug. 23, 1939, PA Abt. V Pol. 25E Polen, v. 6, contains more than 1,500 entries. Cf. PA Abt. V Pol. 25 Polen, v. 7; v. 8, p. 271; v. 9, pp. 149ff. Also BA R 43 II 1483, pp. 27ff.; 1483a, pp. 99ff.; 1480d, pp. 47ff.; 1409, pp. 20ff.

87. It is difficult to square this documentary record with the contention of Edward Wynot that "Warsaw seemed determined to avoid giving either the minority or its patrons in Berlin any pretext for hostile moves. . . . Polish authorities went to remarkable lengths to avoid harassing the Germans, despite repeated provocations." See Wynot, "Polish Germans," pp. 63-64, and "Christian Minorities," p. 243.

88. Hasbach report, June 15, 1939, PA Abt. V Pol. 25 Polen, v. 7, p. 150.

89. Kohnert to AA, July 28, 1939, ibid., v. 9.

90. Kohnert to AA, June 5, 1939, ibid., v. 7.

91. Wolff (1970), BA Ost-dok. 6 A4-7.

92. Kohnert to AA, May 20, 1939, PA Abt. V Pol. 25 Polen, v. 7; *Deutsche Rundschau,* April 2, 1939.

93. Heike, "Arbeiterbewegung," p. 532.

94. Kohnert to AA, BA R 43 II 1843a, pp. 58ff.; PA Abt. V Pol. 25 Polen, v. 9, pp. 174ff.

95. Kohnert to AA, June 5, 1939, PA Abt. V Pol. 25 Polen, v. 8, p. 55.

96. Kohnert to AA, June 19, 1939, ibid., v. 8, p. 55.

97. Kohnert to AA, June 26, 1939, BA R 43 II 1483a, p. 65.

98. Kohnert to AA, July 28, 1939, PA Abt. V Pol. 25 Polen, v. 9.

99. Kammel, *Kriegsschicksale*, p. 10.

100. BA R 43 II 1409, pp. 7ff.; Bierschenk, *Volksgruppe*, p. 351.

101. German Consul Toruń to AA, March 4, 1937, PA Abt. V Pol. 25 Polen, v. 2, p. 135.

102. German Consul Toruń to AA, Feb. 25, 1938, PA Abt. V Pol. 25 Polen, v. 3, p. 139.

103. German Consul Toruń to AA, Oct. 5, 1938, *Dokumente* (AA), p. 88.

104. German Consul Toruń (Küchler) to AA, Dec. 20, 1938, *Dokumente* (AA), p. 92. Cf. German Consul Toruń to AA, Jan. 19, 1939, *Dokumente* (AA), p. 39.

105. German Consul Toruń to AA, Feb. 25 and June 22, 1939, PA Abt. V Pol. 25 Polen, v. 3, p. 139; v. 8, p. 217.

106. German Consul Łódź to AA, May 15, 1939, *Dokumente* (AA), pp. 247-48.

107. German Consul Łódź to AA, June 7 and July 7, 1939, PA Abt. V Pol. 25 Polen, v. 8, p. 102.

108. Ibid.

109. DS to AA, July 31, 1939, PA Abt. V Pol. 25 Polen, v. 9, p. 190.

110. Kennard to Halifax, Aug. 24, 1939, British Foreign Ministry, *British War Blue Book*, p. 121.

111. Kohnert to AA, June 5, 1939, PA Abt. V Pol. 25 Polen, v. 7.

112. DS to AA, June 10, 1939, ibid., v. 8, p. 63.

113. Kohnert to AA, May 20, 1939, ibid., v. 7.

114. *Kuryer Poznański*, June 16, 1939.

115. German Embassy Warsaw to AA, Aug. 15, 1939, PA Abt. V Pol. 25 Polen, v. 9, p. 251.

116. Bohle to AA, Aug. 24, 1939, PA Abt. V Pol. 25 Polen, v. 9, p. 264, leaves no doubt that he still preferred the Young German leader to Ulitz et al. Cf. PA Abt. V Pol. 25E Polen, v. 3, p. 166; German Consul Katowice to AA, Aug. 19, 1939, and Pol. 25C Polen. By contrast, Bohle *ordered* the 13,000 Reich citizens still living in Poland (including several thousand NSDAP members) to leave the country a week before the war began.

117. Polish Foreign Ministry, *Official Documents concerning Polish-German and Polish-Soviet Relations*, p. 5.

118. Drozdowski, "Minorities," p. 235.

119. Wynot, "Polish Germans," pp. 58, 60, 63.

120. Wynot, "Christian Minorities," p. 244.

121. Osiński, *V kolumna*, p. 189.

122. Gentzen, "Legende," p. 67; Staniewicz, "The German Fifth Column in Poland," in *Irredentism and Provocation*, p. 23. Behrends (VoMi) reports these suspicions but dismisses them as fantasy: note to RK, Aug. 21, 1939, BA R 43 II 1408d, p. 51.

123. Karol Pospieszalski, *"The Case of the 58,000 Volksdeutsche,"* p. 46, suspects the "reading societies" run by the "German Library."

124. VoMi to RK, Aug. 17, 1939, BA R 43 II 1408d, pp. 1ff.
125. Restytut Staniewicz, "Fifth Column," p. 27.
126. Grünberg, *Niemcy,* p. 147, citing SS-Gruppenführer Wilhelm Koppe.
127. E.g., Gisbert von Romberg-Klitzing, cited in Pospieszalski, pp. 83ff.
128. Breyer and Korzec, p. 277.
129. Ohlhoff, p. 74.
130. Bierschenk, *Volksgruppe,* p. 364. This does not impress Pospieszalski, who suggests (p. 50) that Polish courts were restrained by concern for Polish-German relations and so declined to look with sufficient vigor for evidence that was surely there.
131. Kammel, *Kriegsschicksale,* p. 44.
132. Cf. reminiscenses of Hernbitz Fitzke, "Twenty Years of Polish Rule in Poznania," WAPP, Org. niem. 541, pp. 33ff.; Heike, *Minderheit,* p. 424; Osiński, *V. kolumna,* p. 189; Kammel, *Kriegsschicksale,* p. 44.
133. Osiński, *V kolumna,* p. 189.
134. Krahmer-Möllenberg speech to Akademie für deutsches Recht, January 1939, IfZ MA 195/4 1133, pp. 74ff.
135. Schwager memo, Oct. 27, 1938, *ADAP,* ser. D, v. 5, p. 94.
136. German Consul Toruń to AA, Dec. 7, 1939, PA Abt. V Pol. 25C Polen, v. 2, p. 33; Breyer, *Deutsches Reich,* p. 263.
137. Osiński, *V kolumna,* p. 188.
138. Kohnert to DS, PA Abt. V Pol. 25C Polen, v. 1, p. 54; German Consul Toruń to AA, April 19, 1939, PA Abt. V Pol. 25 Polen, v. 7, p. 122.
139. Veesenmayer querry, Aug. 23, 1939, and Woermann response, Aug. 24, 1939, PA Abt. V Pol. 25 Polen, v. 10, pp. 2ff. Cf. Restytut Staniewicz, "Szersze tło historyczne i rzeczywiste cele dywersji niemieckiej w Bydgoszcz," p. 372. The weapons and even the cars of well-to-do Germans were confiscated in the weeks before the war and soldiers quartered on some of their estates. See Claus von Jonanne-Malince, BA Ost-dok. 6; Goerdeler, p. 180. When Lehfeldt (p. 81) tried to turn in her family's firearms, the *starost* declined them and asked for the family car instead.
140. Schliep, quoting Lorenz (VoMi), Aug. 23, 1939, PA Abt. V Pol. 25 Polen, v. 9, p. 300. Konrad Henlein was the Sudeten German leader who cooperated closely with Hitler to destroy Czechoslovakia in 1938.
141. Kohnert memo, Feb. 13, 1939, ibid., v. 5; Hauser, *Mniejszość,* p. 203.
142. Polish Ministry of Information, *The German Fifth Column in Poland,* p. 12.
143. Grünberg, *Niemcy,* p. 150.
144. Drozdowski, "Minorities," p. 246.
145. Peter Aurich (= Peter Nasarski), *Der deutsche-polnische September 1939,* p. 112; Gentzen, "Legende," p. 70; Staniewicz, "Fifth Column," p. 27.
146. Gentzen, "Legende," p. 73.
147. Seweryn Osiński, "Hitlerowska dywersja na Pomorzu gdańskim w latach 1933-1939," *Wojskowy Przegląd Historyczny* 9, no. 4 (1964): 83-125; reply by Włodzimierz Jastrzębski, "Czy Selbstschutz to V. kolumna?" pp. 435-37; Staniewicz, "Fifth Column," in *Irredentism,* p. 31.
148. Staniewicz, "Szersze," p. 396.
149. Heike, *Minderheit,* p. 455. Staniewicz, ("Fifth Column," p. 28,) concedes that many innocent civilians were doubtless among those killed.

150. Aurich, pp. 74ff.

151. Szymon Datner, "Z dziejów dywersji niemieckiej w czasie kampanii wrześniowej," pp. 148-80; critical replies in Staniewicz, "Szersze," pp. 360-406, and Marian Wojciechowski, "Geneza dywersji hitlerowskiej w Bydgoszczy w świetle historiografii i publicystyki polskiej," pp. 135-48.

152. Ryszard Wojan [R. Staniewicz], *Bydgoszcz, niedziela, 3 września 1939 r.*

153. Aurich, pp. 15, 74.

154. The most recent summary of the Polish point of view is Włodzimierz Jaztrzębski, *Der Bromberger Blutsonntag; Legende und Wirklichkeit* (Poznań, 1990), esp. chap. 6.

155. Pospieszalski, pp. 85ff.

156. Aurich, pp. 118ff.

157. Kammel, *Kriegsschicksale*, p. 41.

158. Kokocko near Chełmno; see Kammel, *Kriegsschicksale*, p. 22.

159. Pospieszalski, pp. 78ff.

160. Aurich, p. 112.

161. BA Ost-dok. 6 A1-8; Kammel, *Kriegsschicksale*, p. 67. The other German senator, Wambeck, joined the *Selbstschutz* after the invasion and later participated in SS punitive expenditions in western Poland: Grünberg, *Niemcy*, pp. 141ff.

162. Kammel, *Kriegsschicksale*, pp. 19ff.

163. See De Jong; and review by Gotthold Rhode, *Jahrbücher für die Geschichte Osteuropas* 8 (1960): 108ff.

164. Anthony Komjathy and Rebecca Stockwell, *German Minorities and the Third Reich*, p. 97.

165. Kammel, *Kriegsschicksale*, pp. 23ff.; Heike, *Minderheit*, p. 218; Vogt, *Gymnasium*, p. 40; Aurich, pp. 49ff.

166. Kammel, *Kriegsschicksale*, p. 27; Aurich, p. 66.

167. Anonymous account (probably by Gottfried Starke), Sept. 12, 1939, BA R 43 II 1409, pp. 53ff.; Aurich, pp. 49ff.; Kammel, *Kriegsschicksale*, p. 28. Wilhelm Pieper, age sixty-eight at the time, provides another first-hand account of a six-day trek to Łowicz that covered 300 km.: BA Ost-dok. 6 D1-12.

168. Kammel, *Kriegsschicksale*, pp. 30ff.

169. Aurich, p. 59; ed. Kurt Lück, *Marsch der Deutschen in Polen*, p. 10.

170. Richard Breyer, "Die Septemberereignisse 1939 in polnischer Sicht," p. 30.

171. Account dated Oct. 9, 1939, in Breitinger, app. (pp. 176ff.), and pp. 28ff.; Aurich, pp. 57, 75.

172. Aurich, p. 118.

173. Ibid., pp. 96-97; BA Ost-dok. 6 D1-12.

174. Aurich, pp. 62, 88ff.

175. Kammel, *Kriegsschicksale*, p. 46.

176. Kammel, *Kriegsschicksale*, pp. 100ff.; WAPP, EK 543.

177. *Dennoch*, pp. 42ff.; Swart, p. 152.

178. Johann Kurtziza and Eugen Jeschke, BA Ost-dok. 6 A4-3; ed, Kurt Lück *Volksdeutsche Soldaten unter Polens Fahnen*, pp. 23ff.; Aurich, pp. 103ff.; Kammel, *Kriegsschicksale*, pp. 57ff.; Breyer p. 262.

179. Graebe to RK, Sept. 21, 1939, BA R 43 II 1409 p. 48.

180. Quoted in Kammel, *Kriegsschicksale*, p. 93.

181. Kammel, *Kriegsschicksale*, pp. 43, 60.

182. E.g., Lehfeldt, pp. 72, 89.

183. Grünberg, *Niemcy*, p. 150.

184. *Polish Acts of Atrocity against the German Minority in Poland*; Kammel, *Kriegsschicksale*, p. 90.

185. Pospieszalski, p. 60; Aurich, p. 8.

186. Pospieszalski, pp. 68ff., 76.

187. Aurich, p. 11; Heike *Minderheit*, p. 445, puts the number at 4,332.

188. According to Wilhelm Pieper (1951), BA Ost-dok. 6 D1-12.

Conclusion

1. Cf. Richard Lukas, *The Forgotten Holocaust: Poles under German Occupation* (Lexington, Ky., 1986).

2. Ludwig Wolff, BA Ost-dok. 6 A4-7; Grünberg, *Niemcy*, p. 145.

3. Cygański, *Zawsze*, p. 220.

4. Blau, Sept. 8 and Nov. 10, 1939, WAPP, EK 297.

5. Kammel, *Kriegsschicksale*, pref.

6. Grünberg, *Niemcy*, p. 146.

7. Ibid., p. 142.

8. Ibid., p. 141 (who describes their role in the new regime as "negligible"); Kühn, "Deutschtum," p. 152; *Von Unserer Art*, p. 20.

9. Krekeler, *Revisionsanspruch*, p. 16.

10. Gersdorff, p. 10.

11. Krahmer-Möllenberg to AA, Oct. 12, 1939, IfZ MA 128/6 Fb 110; Heike, *Minderheit*, p. 447.

12. Graebe to RK, Sept. 21, 1939, BA R 43 II 1409, p. 50.

13. Tresckow, BA Ost-dok. 6; confirmed by Hassell, *Vom anderen Deutschland*, p. 112. Wolff (BA Ost-dok. 6 A4-7) also claimed after the war to have intervened in Berlin to stop the killing of Polish intellectuals; if true (and his membership in the SS permits doubts on this score), this was clearly without effect.

14. Lehfeldt, p. 91; Heike, *Deutschtum*, p. 533.

15. Vogt, *Gymnasium*, p. 32; *Von Unserer Art*, pp. 60ff., 90ff.

16. BA NL Graebe.

17. Pieper in BA Ost-dok. 6 D1-12; Graebe to RK, Sept. 21, 1939, BA R 43 II 1409, p. 48; Edward Wynot, "World of Delusions and Disillusions," p. 179.

18. Cf. Blanke, *Prussian Poland*, p. 192.

19. *Von Unserer Art*, p. 23; Kühn, "Deutschtum," p. 161.

Index

Abwehr (German), and Polish Germans, 228
Adatci, Baron, 134-36
Algeria, French exodus from, 47
Allenstein, theatre in, 141
Ammende, Ewald, 88
Andrzejewski, Czesław, 44-45
Annulment Law (1920), 68-69
Anti-German feeling, popular, 94, 212
anti-semitism, German. *See* National Socialism
anti-semitism, Polish, 18, 20, 193-94; international investigations, 20
army (Polish), Germans in, 227-28, 234-35
atrocities (Polish), German publications on, 235
Aufbruch, Der (Bielitz), 176
Augsburg Lutheran Church, 81, 196-97; Polonization of, 197
Aurich, Peter, 230, 234, 235
Auslandsorganisation (AO/NSDAP), 164, 175-76, 181
Austrian Poland (former), 3-4, 56

Ballestrem Corporation, 145
Baltic Institute, 200
Bartel, Kazimierz, 90-91
Batocki, Adolf v. (West Prussian Oberpräsident), 24
Beck, Józef (Polish foreign minister), 185, 187, 193, 199, 215-16, 222
Becker, Carl (Prussian culture minister), 140
Behrends, Hermann (SS and VoMi), 181-82, 303 n 122
Below, Gen. Otto v., 24
Bereza Kartuska (concentration camp), 96, 99, 232
Berger, Karl, 235
Bernhardt, Johannes (German consul), 176
Bethesda Hospital (Gniezno), 69
Bezpartyiny Blok Współpracy z Rządem (BBWR), 91, 100, 183, 187, 200

Bielitz (Bialsko), Germans in, 3, 170; popular violence in, 202
Bierschenk, Theodor, 238
birth rates. *See* Germans in Poland: demography
Bismarck- u. Baildenhütte (firm), 145
Blau, Paul (superintendent), 17, 80-81, 111; and Polish state, 81, 197-98, 279 (n 63); and National Socialism, 164, 169; and DV/JDP schism, 178; during WWII, 238
"Bloody Sunday." *See* Bydgoszcz
Bock und Polach, Gen. Friedrich v., 15
Boehm, Max-Hildebert, 13, 280 n 81
Bohle, Ernst (AO/NSDAP), 164, 175, 181, 303 n 116
boycotts, of Germans in Poland, 159, 200-201, 213-14, 221
Borah, William (U.S. senator), 127
Border Protection Law (1927), 208-09, 211, 217
Braun, Otto (Prussian minister-president), 95, 138
Breitinger, Hilarius, 83, 219, 233-34
Breyer, Albert, 196, 226
Breyer, Richard, 205, 227
Briand, Aristide (French foreign minister), 132
Brüning, Heinrich (German chancellor), 128, 141, 157-58
Bruns, Carl-Georg, 13, 49, 56, 88, 139-40
Bülow, Bernhard v. (state secretary, German Foreign Office), 128, 155, 157-58
Bülow, Fritz v. (Regierungspräsident Bromberg), 16
Bund der Auslanddeutschen (BdA), 151-52, 165
Bund der Deutschen in Polen, 56
Bursche, Juliusz (bishop), 81-82, 193, 197-98
Bydgoszcz (Bromberg), in 1918, 11; popular violence in, 41, 183; "Bloody Sunday" (1939), 229-30; trek from, 232-33

Calonder, Felix (president, Mixed Commission); 30, 103-4, 119, 133-34
Camp of National Unity (OZN), 187-88, 201
capital (German), in Poland, 52
Cashubians, 190, 194
Catholic Church in Poland, 83
Catholic Peoples Party (German) (DKVP), 56-57, 87, 97-98
Catholics (German), in Poland, 52, 56, 82, 145, 168-69, 194
Celichowski, Witold (Poznanian Wojewode), 67, 80
census figures. *See* Germans in Poland: demography
Center Party (German), 54, 56, 126
Central Mines Administration (Silesia), 118
Central Poland, Germans in, 3-4, 102-3. *See also* consulates (German): Łódź; *Deutscher Volksverband*; Łódź; Tomaszów
Chałasiński, Józef, 28, 41
Chamberlain, Austen (British foreign secretary), 131
children (German), in Polish schools, 196-97
Chojnice (Konitz), political trials in, 199
Chojnowski, Andrzej, 7, 117
Chorzów Nitrogen Works, 69
Christian Democrats (Polish), 59, 61
Christian Peoples Party (German) (DCVP), and National Socialism, 167-69
Chrzanowski, Bernard (Polish minister for the Formerly Prussian Partition), 80
church-state relations, Poland, 79-80
Ciechanowski, Jan, 21
Cieszyn, Germans in, 216-17
citizenship (Polish), right to, 23, 65-67; opting for, 37, 44
civil servants (Polish), and Germans, 45, 116
Cleinow, Georg, 13, 23-24, 35, 55
Clemenceau, Georges (French premier), 21
Committee for Nationality Questions (Polish), 194
Committee of Five/Nine. *See Deutsche Vereinigung in Sejm und Senat*
"co-nationalism." *See* "cultural autonomy"
Concordia Publishing Co. (Poznań), 96
constitution (Polish), and Germans, 58; 1935 changes, 187
consulates (German), and situation of Germans in 1930s: Cieszyn, 217; Łódź, 220, 223-24; Katowice, 203, 211, 219; Toruń, 195, 205, 223, 228, 302 n 75
cooperatives (German), in Poland, 74-75, 148, 177, 209-11, 234; official intimidation of, 210-11. *See also* Swart, Friedrich
cooperatives (Polish), 210

Corridor (Polish), Germans in, 102, 113, 157, 208
Council of Germans in Poland, 224
councils movement (Poznania), 10
credits for Germans in Poland. *See* financial aid
"cultural autonomy" (German), in Poland, 87-88, 163, 180
cultural institutions (German), in Poland, 75
Curtius, Julius (German foreign minister), 126-28, 135, 156-57
Curzon, Lord (British foreign secretary), 29
Czas (Cracow), 193-94, 218
Czerwiński, Sławomir (Polish education minister), 92

Danilewski, Johannes, 93
Danzig (Gdańsk): and peace settlement, 18-19; Free City of, 37, 183-84
De Jong, Louis. 231-32
Democratic Party (German) (DDP), 54
deportation of Germans, 1939, 232-36
Deutsche Blätter in Polen, 75
Deutsche Bücherei. See German Library
Deutsche Bürgerpartei (Bydgoszcz), 153
Deutsche in Polen, Der, 168
Deutsche Jungenschaft in Polen (DJiP), 100
Deutsche Nachrichten, 177
Deutsche Partei (Silesia). *See* German Party
Deutsche Rundschau (Bydgoszcz), 56, 75, 176, 183, 191, 195
Deutsche Stiftung (DS), 143-49, 155, 164, 204, 239. *See also* Krahmer-Möllenberg, Erich
Deutsche Vereinigung (1918-1919), 13
Deutsche Vereinigung für Westpolen (DV), 173-74, 178, 180, 182, 228, 239; and Polish state, 192-93, 198; attacks on, 218. *See also* Kohnert, Hans; schism
Deutsche Vereinigung in Sejm und Senat (DViSuS), 74, 88-89, 100-101, 144, 149, 153-54; and National Socialism, 165-66, 172-73, 183, 188. *See also* Graebe, Kurt; Heidelck, Friedrich; Naumann, Eugen
Deutsche Wissenschaftliche Zeitschrift für Polen, 75
Deutsche Zentrale für Heimatdienst, 142
Deutscher Jungblock in Polen, 173
Deutscher Kultur- u. Wirtschaftsbund (DKWB), 93, 213, 232
Deutscher Ostbund, 151-52
Deutscher Ostmarkenverein (DOV), 13, 138, 151
Deutscher Schulverein (DSV). *See* German School Association
Deutscher Schutzbund (DSb), 150-52, 165
Deutscher Unterstutzungsverband, 153-54

Deutscher Volksblock für Schlesien, 173
Deutscher Volksbund für Schlesien. See
Volksbund, Deutscher, für Schlesien
Deutscher Volksverband (DVV), 181
Deutsches Wohlfahrtsbund, 101, 150, 154
Deutsches Auslands-Institut (DAI), 150-52, 165
Deutschnationale Volkspartei (DNVP), 55, 174-75
Deutschtumsbund (DB), 55, 73-74;
suppression of, 73-74; trial, 101, 126
Dibelius, Otto, 82
Dittmann, Klara, 66
Dmowski, Roman: and peace conference, 14, 18; and anti-semitism, 18, 188; and fascism, 188
Dollfuss, Engelbert (Austrian chancellor), 168, 175
Drozdowski, Marek, 6, 44, 77, 225, 229, 297 n 161
Działdowo (Soldau): Soviet occupation of, 37; Polish reprisals, 38, 41
Dzień Pomorski, 202, 213

economic conditions, in West Poland, 38, 114-15; of Germans in Poland, 6, 204; decline of, 72, 115, 275 n 43; German-Polish disparities, 6; Polish regional disparities, 7, 38, 97, 115
economic discrimination, against Germans, 43, 46, 116-20, 137, 207-14
Eichdorf, in September 1939, 234
Eigenheim, in September 1939, 234
Eisenhart-Rothe, Johann v. (Poznanian Oberpräsident), 15
elections (Polish), 55, 56, 58-59, 96;
campaign violence, 96, 98-99, 126, 135, 185
emigration (German), from Poland, 32-34, 44-47, 95, 223-24; and German middle class, 34, 46, 49; Polish encouragement of, 40-41; and German, 40, 48-49, 142-43, 161; demographic consequences, 49
emigrés (German), in Germany: organizations, 49; support for, 48-49
Entente powers, and Poland, 14-16, 18-19.
See also individual powers
Ernst, Eugen (Prussian interior minister), 12, 16
Ernst, Robert, 164-65
estates (German), in Poland. *See* land ownership (German)
European Nationalities Congress, 88, 186, 281 n 83
Evangelical Church (United), in Poland: and Poznanian insurrection, 17; and Polish state, 17, 48, 79-82, 189, 197; and National Socialism, 169, 191; and

minority politics, 80, 178; attacks on, 219, 234; in Silesia, 82, 197. *See also* Blau, Paul
Everling, Otto, 143
exodus (of Germans). *See* emigration (German)
expulsions, of German citizens from Poland, 42-44, 66-67
Expropriation Law (Prussian), 23

"fallen" peoples, nationalism of, 5
farmers (German), in Poland, 50-51, 146, 209; import quotas for, 157-58. *See also* financial aid
Feldman, Józef, 200
Fifth Column (German), in Poland, 225-32;
espionage, 226; military activities, 226, 229, 231
financial aid (German), for Germans in Poland, 73, 104, 106, 108, 142, 162, 203, 239; secrecy of, 148-50; and revisionism, 160-61, 203-4; and *Gleichschaltung* of minority, 164, 168
financial crises (Polish), 39, 90, 124
Fleischer, Paul, 143
food deliveries, Poznania to Reich, 11-12
Foreign Office (German), and Germans in Poland, 123, 155, 159-60, 170, 192, 213, 216, 228; and minority politics, 55, 73, 89, 153-54, 168, 172-74, 176, 182; and *Deutsche Stiftung* (DS), 143-45, 147; and international protection for minorities, 88
Fourteen Points (Woodrow Wilson's), and Poland, 18
France: and German-Polish relations, 18; and Upper Silesia, 26, 29, 183
Frederick II (king), 196
Free Corps: in Poznania, 16; in Silesia, 29; *Freikorps* Ebbinghaus (1939), 229
Freie Presse (Łódź), 183, 203
Frick, Wilhelm (interior minister), 204, 216
Furohjelm (Poznanian police chief), 65

Gebauer, Bruno, 93
Gebrüder Koerting AG, 123
Geneva Convention (Upper Silesia), 30, 66, 68, 117; and schools, 103-4, 133; expiration of, 195, 197, 203, 215
Gentzen, Felix-Heinrich, 229
Gerlach, Helmut v., 11-12
German Catholics in Poland (Association of) (VdK). *See* Catholics (German)
German Library (Poland), 75, 176, 190-91
germanophilia (Polish), in western Poland, 39-40, 97, 104, 193-94
German Party (Silesia), 56-57, 168
German-Polish Press Service, 76
German-Polish relations: during WW I, 13;

economic relations, 122-24, 127, 191; and frontier revisions, 127-28; and Germans in Poland, 121, 138, 192; and public opinion, 126-27; rapprochement, 184-87, 190-92, 202-3; joint declaration on minorities (1937), 208, 215; deterioration, 218, 220

German School Association (DSV), 106-11, 143, 178, 190, 196

Germans in Poland: origins, 45; numbers, 95-96, 240, 244-45, 282 n 18; geographic distribution, 22; demography, 214; occupational structure, 49-52; attitudes toward peace settlement, 24-25, 45, 54, 68, 84-86; signs of resignation, 87-89; and Polish state, 44-45, 179, 188, 225-32; and National Socialism, 222-24; professions of loyalty, 188-90; and Third Reich, 191-92, 204-5, 222-28; in 1939, 218-25; expulsion of, 240

German Welfare League, 101, 150, 154

Gersdorff, Gero v., 239

Gestapo (German), and Germans in Poland, 171, 180

Goebbels, Joseph, 191-92

Goehre, Paul (German state secretary, Defense), 11

Goerdeler, Carl, 272 n 55

Goerdeler, Oda, 84-85

Goering, Hermann, 203, 239

Grabski, Stanisław (Polish education minister), 60, 63, 77-78

Graebe, Kurt, 13, 37, 55, 73, 88-89, 149, 173; and German government, 152-59, 186, 188; trials of, 73, 100-101; and National Socialism, 165-66; during WW II, 235, 239. *See also Deutsche Vereinigung in Sejm und Senat; Deutschtumsbund*

Grażyński, Michał (Silesian Wojewode), 96-99, 105, 116-17, 119, 133-36, 193, 195, 197, 199, 211, 215, 301 n 67

Grenzschutz-Ost, 12, 15-16

Grimm, Hans, 191

Gross-Neudorf, in September 1939, 234

Grudziądz (Graudenz), anti-German violence in, 183, 185

Grunbaum, Izaak, 88, 92

Grünberg, Karol, 45, 229, 235

Haller Army (in Poland), 20

Harriman, W. Averill, & Co., 117-18

Hasbach, Erwin, 55, 113, 156, 173, 181-82; as Polish senator, 187-88, 212, 215, 221, 231

Haupttreuhandstelle-Ost, 239

Hauptwahlausschuss. See Deutsche Vereinigung in Sejm und Senat

Hauser, Przemysław, 6, 45

Haushofer, Karl, 164, 175

Heidelck, Friedrich, 13, 55, 101, 150, 153

Heike, Otto, 47, 238

"Heimat Grüsst" (program), 204

Heimatschutz-Ost, 11-12

Hel Peninsula, expulsion of Germans from, 209

Henckel von Donnersmarck (firm), 211

Herrmann, Alfred, 13

Herzfeld & Victorius (firm), 43

Hess, Rudolf, 164, 175, 206

Hirsch, Paul (Prussian minister-president), 12

historians (German), and Germans in Poland, 3-5, 229

historians (Polish), and Germans in Poland, 6-8, 43-44, 227-29, 241

Historical Society (Poznania), 75

Hitler, Adolf, 163, 191; and Germans in Poland, 180-81, 191-92, 205-7, 215, 222, 235-36; and Poland, 183, 203, 215, 239-40

Hitler Youth, and Germans in Poland, 192, 194

Hlond, Cardinal August, 83, 233

Hoetzsch, Otto, 143

Hohenlohe Works (firm), 211-12

Hollandse Buitenland Bank (HBB), 146-47

Hossbach, Colonel, 215

House, Col. Edward, 18

IG Bergbau u. Hüttenbetrieb AG (firm), 146, 211

illiteracy, in Poland, 38

Illustrowany Kuryer Codzienny (Cracow), 126, 195

immigration (German), to Poland, 4

import quotas, for Polish-Germans. *See* financial aid

Independent Socialists (USDP), 11, 16

innkeepers (German), in Poland, 43, 116

Institute for the Study of Nationality Questions (Polish), 92

"insurgents" (Silesia), 94, 99, 116, 135-36, 185, 202, 212, 238

Jacob, Dr. (German teacher), 106

Jacobsen, Hans-Adolf, 161

Jaensch, Erich, 178

Jägerhof, in September 1939, 234

Jägerhof Circle, 173-74

Janta-Półczyński, Leon (Polish minister), 41

Jesuitensee, in September 1939, 234

Jews, in Poland, 34-35, 183, 291 n 17

Jeżora, Kazimiera, 45

Jonanne, Claus v., 86

Jungdeutsche Partei (JDP). *See* Young German Party

Kaeckenbeeck, Georges, 30
Kammel, Richard, 227, 234-35, 238, 297 n
    165
Kant Association, 106
Katowice German Gymnasium, 196
Kattowitz, IG (firm), 146, 211
Kattowitzer Zeitung (Katowice), 76, 216, 220
Kaysiewicz (Poznanian Wojewode), 210
Kempf, Venantius, 83
Kennard, Howard (British ambassador to
    Poland), 224
Kiernik, Władysław (Polish interior
    minister), 42
Kierski, Kazimierz, 64, 68
Kimmich, Christoph, 159
Klinke, Josef, 83
Koc, Col. Adam, 187
Koch-Weser, Erich, 23
Koerber, Nordewin v., 113, 156
Koester, Adolf (German interior minister),
    151
Kohnert, Hans, 173-74, 176, 178, 181-82,
    188, 191, 215, 218; and Polish
    government, 221-24, 225, 228; during
    WW II, 238-39. *See also Deutsche
    Vereinigung*
Koło County, schools in, 103
Komjathy, Anthony, 232
Konkordia GmbH, 142
Korfanty, Wojciech, 9, 16, 27, 96, 99, 116,
    282 n 27
Korzec, Paweł, 89, 227
Kowalak, Tadeusz, 7, 161
Kowoll, Johann, 240
Kraft, Waldemar, 297 n 165
Krahmer-Möllenberg, Erich, 143, 147, 149,
    154-55, 160, 165; and condition of
    Germans in Poland, 199-200, 202, 204-5,
    218, 220, 224; and minority politics, 168,
    175, 180; and National Socialism, 189-90;
    during WW II, 239. *See also Deutsche
    Stiftung*; financial aid
Krasuski, Jerzy, 6, 44-45, 47
Krekeler, Norbert, 143, 149, 160
Krysiński, Alfons, 34, 225
Kucner, Alfred, 7
Kuhn, Walter, 95
Kulski, Władysław, 45
Kursell, Otto v., 181
Kurtziza, Johann, 234
Kuryer Poranny, 27
Kuryer Poznański (Poznań), 60, 201, 225

Labor Front (Reich), and Germans in
    Poland, 192
labor unions (German), in Poland, 57, 212
Lamot, Wiktor (Pomorze Wojewode), 113

Lamprecht, Arthur, 192
Lanckorona Pact, 62
Landbund Weichselgau, 74, 101
*Landesvereinigung des deutschen Volkstums in
    Polen*, 55
land ownership (German), in Poland, 51,
    69-70, 72, 111-14, 208-9, 240; restrictions
    on, 72, 208-9
land reform (Polish), and Germans, 111-14,
    126, 134-35, 207-8
Landwirtschaftlicher Bank (Danzig), 147
language (official): Polish policies, 36,
    67-68, 107-8, 195-98; German attitudes
    toward, 84-85, 198
Lansing, Robert (U.S. secretary of state),
    18
Lattermann, Alfred, 87, 239
Laura/Kattowitzer AG. *See* IG
    Bergbau
law code (Polish), and Germans, 101
League of Germans in Poland, 56
League of Nations: and Germany, 29-30,
    135-36; and Germans in Poland, 129-32,
    136-37, 186, 192; and Poland, 183; and
    citizenship disputes, 66; and "settlers,"
    70-71; and job discrimination, 118-19; and
    minority schools, 133-34; and land
    reform, 134-35
League of Poles in Germany, 141
leaseholders (German), in Poland, 71
Lehfeldt, Walburg, 85-86, 239, 304 n 139
Leszno (Lissa): and peace settlement, 21;
    German Gymnasium, 109-10, 178; in
    September 1939, 234
Liegnitz-Rawitsch Railway, 43
Lipski, Józef (Polish ambassador to
    Germany), 203, 215
liquidation of German property, 23, 68,
    122, 124-25; Liquidation Treaty (1929),
    125-26
Lloyd George, David (British prime
    minister), 19, 29
Löbe, Paul, 150
local government, Germans in, 100
Łódź: Germans in, 3, 102; popular violence
    in, 183, 202, 219, 224
Loehrs, Edgar, 138
Lord, Robert, 18
Lorenz, Werner (VoMi and SS), 181, 213
Lück, Kurt, 87, 176, 204, 235, 239
Ludendorff, Gen. Erich, and Polish
    border, 14
Lütgens, Hans (German consul), 95, 140
Lutherans (U.S.), and Polish Germans, 82,
    274 n 139
Lutman, Roman, 44
Lutosławski, Kazimierz, 59

Mackiewicz, Stanisław, 193
Main Elections Committee. *See Deutsche Vereinigung in Sejm und Senat*
Makus, Fritz, 177
Manchester Guardian, and Polish Germans, 101
Manjura, Paul, 170-71
Marienwerder district, 19, 26
Marx, Wilhelm (German chancellor), 125, 152
Massenbach, Georg v., 150, 173
Masuria/Masurians, 19, 140-41, 156
Mauer, Wilhelm, 133-34
Meister, Friedrich (state secretary, Prussian Interior Ministry), 140
Mendelssohn, Ezra, 62
Michałowski, Czesław, 201
Międzychód county: and peace settlement, 21; in 1939, 233
Mikołajczyk, Stanisław, 210
Miłachowo, in 1939, 234
military strength (German), erosion of in 1918, 11-12, 15-16
Minorities Bloc, 59, 92, 97
minorities in Poland: in general, 7-8, 32-33, 58; and German government, 59
Minorities Protection Treaty, 20-21: Polish views of, 21, 32; and minority schools, 76, 79, 101-2; renunciation of, 186
Mixed Commission (Silesia), 30, 98, 134. *See also* Calonder, Felix
Młodzianowski, Kazimierz (Pomorze Wojewode), 39, 91-92
Modrow, Gunther, 173
Moltke, Helmut v. (German ambassador to Poland), 159, 197, 218
Mościcki, Ignacy (Polish president), 98, 187, 215
Mosłowski (Łódź Starost), 221
Mroczko, Marian, 6
Müller, Hermann (German chancellor), 152, 154

Naczelna Rada Ludowa (NRL). *See* Supreme National Council
Namier, Lewis, 18
Narutowicz, Gabriel (Polish president), 59-60
National Assembly (German), elections to, 17; and Germans in Poland, 24
national councils (German), 12-13, 23, 25, 54-55, 142
National Democrats (Polish): in Poznania, 11-12, 14-15; in Polish government, 59-60, 90, 187; and Germans, 60-61, 201, 215, 225
nationalism (Polish): and minorities, 60-62;

and Germans, 63, 93, 190-91, 194, 216, 236-37
National Peoples Party, German (DNVP), 55, 174-75
National Radical Camp (ONR), 188
National Socialism (German): and Germans in Poland, 163-64, 175, 189, 191, 205, 221, 225; organizations in Poland, 170; and Poles, 170; in 1939, 231
National Socialist German Workers League (NSDAB), 170-71
National Socialist German Workers Party (NSDAP). *See* National Socialism
Naumann, Eugen, 37, 55, 84, 88-89, 133, 150, 156, 159; and National Socialism, 165-66; death, 232
Netze district, fighting in, in 1919, 16
Neurath, Konstantin v. (German foreign minister), 136, 146, 182, 184, 186, 192, 205, 215
Non-Aggression Pact (German-Polish): and Germans in Poland, 195, 202-3, 205, 215-18, 220, 222. *See also* German-Polish relations

Oberschlesischer Kurier (Królewska Huta), 56, 76, 98, 168
occupation of Poland (WW II), 238-40
Oder-Neisse line, 241
officials (local), and Germans, 65
Olsa district. *See* Cieszyn
organizations (minority), in general, 218-19. *See also under individual names*
Osiński, Seweryn, 226, 228
Ossa GmbH, 147. *See also* Deutsche Stiftung; financial aid
"Osthilfe," 141, 158
Ostrów (Ostrowo), popular violence in, 41, 43, 202
"Oststaat" plan, 23
Otterau-Langenau, in September 1939, 234

Paderewski, Ignacy (Polish premier): and Poznanian insurrection, 14-15; and peace settlement, 18-21
Pankratz, Arthur, 167
Pant, Edward, 56, 83, 98; and National Socialism, 167-69
Papen, Franz v. (German chancellor), 167, 169, 176, 183
Paprocki, Stanisław, 194
pastors (Evangelical), in Poland, 48, 70, 191, 197; education of, 81-82; shortage of, 198
Peoples Party (German) (DVP), 55
Peplinski, Paul, 226
Permanent Court of International Justice, The Hague (PCIJ), 66, 70, 132; and

"settlers," 71; and land reform, 135; and minority schools, 133-34

personal security (German), in Poland. *See* popular violence

physicians (German), in Poland, 43, 116, 118-19

"Piast" (party), 59, 61

Pieper, Wilhelm, 86

Pieracki, Bronisław (Polish interior minister), 193

Piłsudski, Józef: in WWI, 13-16; as Polish head of state, 19, 58, 187; and *coup d'état*, 90; and Germans in Poland, 61, 91, 96, 184; and German-Polish relations, 128, 183-84, 187; death, 188-89

place-names, German and Polish, 242

plebiscites, post-WW I, 19-20, 63. *See also* Upper Silesia

Pless, Johann v. ("Prince"), 119-20, 174-75

Pless conglomerate, 119-20, 146-47, 161, 211

Poland, and German minority: post-Piłsudski, 187-88, 194, 200; 1936 guidelines, 194-97. *See also* National Democrats; nationalism (Polish); Piłsudski, Józef

Poles in Germany, 42, 137, 141, 194, 202, 215-18, 221-22, 287 n 52; and League of Nations, 141-42; Polish support of, 148-49

Polish Frontier Commission, 19

Polish-German Institute (Berlin), 191

Polish-German Society (Warsaw), 191

Polish National Council (KNP), and peace settlement, 14, 17-18

Polish Socialist Party (PPS), and Germans in Poland, 57, 59, 61, 74

Polish-Soviet war. *See* Russo-Polish War

Polish-speaking Germans, 28-29, 95, 103-5, 116, 133, 137, 141, 170-71, 190, 194, 218. *See also* Masuria; Upper Silesia

Polska Organizacja Wojskowa (POW), 9-10

Polska Zachodnia, 200-201, 216

Polski Związek Zachodni (PZZ), 200-201, 215-16. *See also* Związek Obrony Kresów Zachodnich

"Pomeranian Week," 200

Pomerellen. *See* Pomorze

Pomereller Tageblatt, 76

Pomorze: and peace settlement, 17-26; national balance in, 18, 25-26, 32

popular violence and Germans in Poland, 36, 41, 43, 183, 202, 217, 219-21; 223-24; official attitudes toward, 41, 199, 202, 221; compilations of, 220-21; in September 1939, 232-36

Posener Tageblatt (Poznań), 56, 76, 96, 176, 191, 219

Pospieszalski, Karol, 230, 235, 304 n 130

Potocki, Stanisław, 6, 43, 301 n 55

Poznań, in September 1939, 233

Poznania (1918/19): Germans in, 4, 32; Polish national movement in, 9; Polonization of local government in, 10-12; German government and, 11, 13, 16; Polish insurrection in, 15-17; and Paris peace conference, 16

"Poznań Program" (1919), 63. *See also* National Democrats

press (German), in Poland, 75-76, 96-97, 220; and Non-Aggression Pact, 167, 192, 220

priests (German), in Poland, 82, 145, 219

priests (Polish), and Germans, 83, 233

property (German), sale of, 36. *See also* land ownership; liquidation

Proske, Alfons (Upper Silesian Oberpräsident), 141

Protestant church. *See* Evangelical Church

Protestants (Polish), 82, 194

Prussia (state), and Poles, 139-41

Prussian Polish policies (pre-1918), 65, 68, 240

Raczkiewicz, Władysław (Pomorze Wojewode), 301 n 45

Radewitz, in September 1939, 234

Raschdau, Ludwig, 25

Ratajski, Cyryl (Poznań mayor), 64-65

Rat der Deutschen in Polen, 224

Räte, in Poznania. *See* councils movement

Rathenau, Walter (German foreign minister), 150

Rauscher, Ulrich (German ambassador to Poland), 62, 125, 128, 136

Rauschning, Hermann: and exodus of Germans, 33, 40, 45, 69, 125, 144, 177, 288 n 72; and Historical Society, 75, 154; as Danzig Senate president, 184-86, 206; and Hitler, 206

refugee camps (German) in 1939, 223

regional disparities (Polish). *See* economic conditions

Reineke, Heinrich, 153, 178-79

repurchase, right of, and German property, 71

resurrected Poland, competing views of, 14

revisionism: German, 63, 95, 121, 127, 159-61, 182; Polish, 141, 200

Rhode, Gotthold, 33, 47, 206

Roehr, Ludwik, 110

Rogoźno, in September 1939, 233

Rosen, Hans v., 173

Rosenberg, Alfred, 191

Rossbach Corps, 16

"Rota" (song), 202

Russian Poland. *See* Central Poland
Russian Revolution, and German-Polish
  relations, 14
Russo-Polish War: and Germans in
  Poland, 36-37, 122; reprisals, 38
Rydz-Smigły, Marshall Edward, 187-88

Sackett, Frederic (US ambassador to
  Germany), 127-28
Saenger, Bernd v., 84, 173, 188
Schacht, Hjalmar, 203
Schiller-Gymnasium (Poznań), 108-9, 196,
  219
schism (DV/JDP), 172-75, 196; and German
  government, 172, 175, 179, 181-82, 239;
  and Polish government, 179
Schneider, Wilhelm, 182
Scholz, Ernst (German economics
  minister), 123
Scholz, Johannes, 76
Schönbeck, Otto, 106, 110, 145, 196, 238
schools (public minority), 76-79, 102;
  private, 105-7, 109, 143, 196; official
  policies toward, 77-78, 107-10, 195-97, 283
  n 53; in Silesia: 103-6, 133, 136, 195; in
  Cieszyn, 217
Schubert, Carl v. (state secretary, German
  Foreign Office), 142, 160
Schulitz, in September 1939, 234
Schutzstaffel (SS), 181
Scouts, Polish, 9; German, 100, 198
Seeckt, Gen. Hans v., 24, 123
Sejm (Polish National), 21, 58, 100;
  Germans in, 62, 100, 187-88
Sejm (Poznanian), 12
Sejm (Silesian), 97-99
Selbstschutz, Silesian, 29; in 1939, 229
Senate (Polish), 58
Sępólno County, 21
Settlement Commission (Prussian), 51,
  70-71, 240
"settlers," 43, 70-71, 125, 153
Siehr, Ernst (East Prussian Oberpräsident),
  140-41
Sierakowski, Stanisław, 88
Sikorski, Władysław (Polish premier),
  63-64, 73, 228
Silesia (Polish), Germans in, 52
Silesian-American Corporation, 117-18
Silesian Institute, 200
Skrzyński, Aleksander (Polish foreign
  minister), 61-62, 67
Sławek, Walery (Polish minister-
  president), 187
Sławoj-Składkowski, Felicjan (Polish
  minister-president), 91, 193, 221
Słowo (Vilnius), 193-94

Sobolewski (Polish senator), 189
Social-Democratic Labor Party (German)
  (DSAP), 57, 74, 99; and National
  Socialism, 167, 221
Social Democratic Party of Germany
  (SPD), 54, 157, 203
Social Democrats (German): in Poznania,
  10-11, 291 n 17; German Social
  Democratic Party (DSP), 56-57, 74; and
  National Socialism, 167, 176
social legislation (Polish), 39
Sokół societies, 9
South Tyrol, Germans in, 181
Spółka Bracka, 118-19
Sprawy Narodowościowe, 92
Stalin, Josef, 240-41
Staniewicz, Restytut, 229, 304 n 149
Staniewicz, Witold (Polish minister), 114
Starke, Gotthold, 76, 173, 176
Steinacher, Hans, 164-66, 206; and DV/JDP
  schism, 172, 175, 177, 180; and German
  minorities in Europe, 180-82. *See also*
  Verein für das Deutschtum im Auslande
Stephan, Karl, 271 n 27
Stimson, Henry (U.S. secretary of state),
  127
Stockwell, Rebecca, 232
Straż Ludowa, 10
Stresemann, Gustav (German foreign
  minister): and exodus of Germans, 42,
  47; and Poles in Germany, 42, 138-41,
  275 n 30; and League of Nations, 130,
  133, 136; and German minorities in
  Europe, 130-31; and minority politics, 55;
  and Poland, 67, 123, 131; and financial
  aid for Polish Germans, 147
Stroelin, Georg, 165
students (German), in Poland, 219-20
Studnicki, Władysław, 193
Stürmer, Der (Nuremberg), 166, 171
"subjective" nationality. *See* Polish-
  speaking Germans
Supreme National Council (NRL), 9-10, 12,
  15, 17, 25
surveillance, official, of minority
  organizations, 227
Swart, Friedrich, 75, 154, 172-73, 175,
  177-78, 209-10, 239, 297 n 165
Święcie County, schools, 102
Szamotuły, in September 1939, 233
Szczeponik, Thomas, 56
Szczypiorno (detention camp), 17
Szturm de Sztrem, Edward, 95

tariff war (German-Polish), 87, 124, 127,
  153, 191. *See also* German-Polish
  relations

teachers (German), in Poland, 35, 43, 48,
77-78; in September 1939, 234
Thorner Zeitung (Toruń), 76
Tomaszewski, Jerzy, 7-8, 45, 63
Tomaszów "pogrom," 220, 223
Tarnowice, political trials in, 198-99
Tarnowo, in September 1939, 234
Toruń, German Gymnasium, 107-8;
popular violence in, 219
Trąmpczyński, Wojciech, 12
Tresckow, Hermann v., 239
Treviranus, Gottfried (German minister),
95, 128, 156-59
trials, political, 100-101, 198-99
Trier Armistice (1919), 16
Tucher (German Consul), 175
Twachtmann, August, 10, 16

Uhle, Ulrich, 179
Ukrainians, in Poland, 59, 97, 186
Ulitz, Otto, 57, 98, 132, 145, 158, 218, 223,
225; and National Socialism, 166; schism
of DV/JDP, 172-74, 177, 181; in WW II,
238-39. *See also* Volksbund
unemployment (German), in Poland. *See*
workers
unions, 57, 212
United States, and German-Polish frontier,
18, 26-27
universities (Polish), and Germans, 219-20
Upper Silesia: and peace settlement, 19;
national balance in, 20, 30-31; plebiscite,
26-29; Polish uprisings, 26-29; Inter-
Allied Commission, 26-27; partition of,
29-30. *See also* Geneva Convention
Utta, August, 92, 144

Verband deutscher Ansiedler, 178-79
Verband deutscher Bauern (VdB), 178-79
Verband deutscher Volksgruppen in Europa,
88, 172
Verein deutscher Katholiken (VdK). *See*
Catholics (German)
Verein für das Deutschtum im Auslande
(VdA), 150-52, 155, 165, 177, 180, 204
Vereinigte Finanzkontore, 147
Versailles Treaty: debates on, 18-19; terms,
21, 23, 80; German reaction to, 23-24;
Polish reassurances, 25; defiance of,
186-87; implementation of, 25, 68
Verzeichnis der deutschen Siedlungen, 226
Vienna agreement on citizenship rights
(1924), 66-67
visa policy (Polish), 199
Vogt, Dietrich, 108-9, 239, 270 n 17
Volhynia, Germans in, 3
Volksbund, Deutscher, für Schlesien, 57, 75,

98, 105, 132-34, 136, 145, 166, 172, 174,
178, 192, 212, 239; attacks on, 185, 219
Volksdeutsche Arbeitsstelle (VA). *See*
Volksdeutscher Rat
Volksdeutsche Mittelstelle (VoMi), 181-82,
223
Volksdeutscher Rat (VR), 164, 172-73, 180-81
Volkszietung (Łódź), 95, 167
Vollert, Ernst, 218
Voss, Hermann, 82, 197, 213

Wąbrzeźno, in September 1939, 233
Wągrowiec, Starost in, 211
Wambeck, Max, 179, 182, 305 n 13
Wanderlehrer, 111, 219
Wanner, Theodor, 165
Wapiński, Roman, 7
Warsaw, University of, and Protestant
theology, 81-82
Weber, Rolf, 93
Wegener, Leo, 75
Wehrmacht, and Germans in Poland. *See*
Fifth Column
Weimar Coalition, and Germans in
Poland, 54-55
Weiss, Axel, 86
Wejherovo (Neustadt), popular violence
in, 202
Wende, Richard, 143
Wertheimer, Fritz, 165
Westerplatte, in 1933, 183
West Polish Agricultural Society (Welage),
74, 175
West Prussia. *See* Pomorze
Wiese, Hans, 173-74, 178
Wiesenau, in September 1939, 234
Wiesner, Rudolf, 170-74, 177-78, 180-82,
188-89, 202, 225; as senator, 187, 215; in
WW II, 238-39
Wiestenberg, Gerhard, 226
Willesen, Maj. Friedrich, 12
Wilson, Woodrow, and German-Polish
frontier, 18-20
Winkler, Max, 142-43, 147, 239
Winnig, August, 24
Wirth, Joseph (German chancellor), 123,
150
Witos, Wincenty (Polish premier), 62, 65,
96
Witzleben, Erik v., 55, 150, 173-75
Wohlgemuth, Thea, 107-8
Wojciechowski, Stanisław, 60
Wolff, Ludwig, 181, 221, 224; in WW II,
238, 306 n 13
Wolsztyn, national conditions in, 85-86
workers (German), in Poland, 52, 117, 193,
201, 203, 212-13, 217

Workers and Soldiers Council (Poznań),
10-11
World Court. *See* Permanent Court of
International Justice
Woźniak (Poznanian Wojewode), 211
Września, Starost, 210-11
Wynot, Edward, 225-26, 302 n 87

Young German Party (JDP), 170-71;
DV/JDP schism, 171-72, 174-79, 181-82;
and Polish state, 179, 189-90
youth organizations (German), in Poland,
100, 198-99

Zaleski, August (Polish foreign minister),
91, 98, 126, 132
*Zentralarbeitsgemeinschaft der politischen
Parteien*, 54-55
*Zentrale für Gräber ermordeter
Volksdeutschen*, 235
złoty, introduction of, 39
Związek Obrony Kresów Zachodnich (ZOKZ),
81, 94, 98-99, 135, 159, 183, 200. *See also
Polski Związek Zachodni*
Związek Powstańców Śląskich (ZPS). *See*
"insurgents"
Zyborski, Wacław, 221-22